D1000224

white-collar trade unions

white-collar trade unions

CONTEMPORARY DEVELOPMENTS IN INDUSTRIALIZED SOCIETIES

EDITED BY ADOLF STURMTHAL

UNIVERSITY OF ILLINOIS PRESS, URBANA AND LONDON, 1966

331.881
S936

© 1966 BY THE BOARD OF TRUSTEES
OF THE UNIVERSITY OF ILLINOIS.
MANUFACTURED IN THE
UNITED STATES OF AMERICA.
LIBRARY OF CONGRESS CATALOG
CARD NO. 66-10059.

PREFACE

The great manpower revolution of the post–World War II period has focused attention upon a change in the structure of the American labor force that has been underway for a long time: the shift from blue-collar to white-collar. For the first time in history, the Census shows that this heterogeneous group is larger than manual labor. Statistically, the "typical" American worker wears street clothes rather than overalls and works at a desk rather than in a factory. A similar process, though perhaps not as far advanced, seems to be occurring in other industrial nations.

The rise of the white-collar worker is only one aspect of the process of change in the occupational structure which industrialization brings with it. Other facets—such as the relative decline of the agricultural population in the industrialized nations—are at least equally important. Indeed, changes in the occupational structure accompany the evolution of industrial societies from the moment they emerge from their pre-industrial state.

The structure of the labor force seems to be one of the most important indexes of the stage of industrial development of a nation or a region. We are just beginning to be aware, however, of the manifold social, cultural, and political implications of these changes. What do they mean in terms of occupational choice, educational policy, class structure, social adjustment, political system, etc.?

The present volume deals with only one aspect of this wider problem, namely, the implications of the rise of the white-collar worker for the industrial relations systems in the advanced industrial nations. In particular, how will the trade-union movements be affected? Can we continue to think of the labor movements in traditional terms even though they were devised at a time when the occupational structure was quite different than it is today? Marx foresaw a society with a labor force increasingly consisting of manual workers, perhaps (or even probably) more and more deprived of their skills. Evolution seems to have led in a different direction. How does this affect that movement which in the Marxian vision was to be the main instrument of the social change he predicted?

The essays in the present volume attempt to provide material for thought about these questions and, to some extent, they suggest an-

5/11/67 Univ of Illinois Press 2.15

swers. In so doing, they lead the reader to question some facile assumptions about the nature of white-collar organizations. Are they necessarily of the same kind as traditional unionism? In looking for signs of conventional unionism among some of the white-collar categories, we may be overlooking significant organizations of a different kind that have arisen among them. White-collar unionism, in other words, may exist to a greater extent than we assume, but we may not identify it as such because, thinking in traditional terms, we may not recognize white-collar unionism in some of its current expressions. Similarly, it is by no means certain, in the light of some of the overseas experiences reported in this volume, that white-collar unionism is bound to lead to an increase in the strength of organized labor. On the contrary, one of the motivations for white-collar organization seems to be sometimes the wish to assert the separate identity of the white-collar worker in the face of the unions of manual workers as well as of management and employers.

The drive toward what the French call the "économie concertée" —a society based upon consensus among the main social forces—may contribute to the need for organization of groups which in the past were reluctant to organize. For, in practice, consensus is agreement among organizations rather than individuals and the "économie concertée" rests upon consultation and compromises among spokesmen of organized groups. Power relationships thus underlie consensus and concert. To some extent, the relationship between white- and blue-collar organizations may depend upon the degree of insight that both sides have into the special situation and the needs of the other. The essays that follow may make some contribution to such mutual understanding.

The material presented in the pages that follow is limited to modern and predominantly industrialized societies. The role of white-collar unions in countries entering upon their industrial career is quite different from the function which they perform in industrially advanced societies. A comparison between the two would have been interesting and would have illuminated many problems. However, this is not what we set out to do. The issues which the present volume is intended to illustrate are large and intricate. Their understanding is difficult enough, and it seemed wise to limit the scope of our study.

Circumstances beyond our control have unduly delayed the publication of this volume. Wherever possible, data have been brought up to date.

Milton Derber and Melvin Rothbaum made valuable comments on various parts of the manuscript. Barbara Dennis, Anice Duncan, and Suzanne Appelbaum assisted in editorial work and the preparation of the manuscript. The Institute of Labor and Industrial Relations at the University of Illinois provided financial support. My thanks go to all of them as well as to the long-suffering contributors.

ADOLF STURMTHAL

Institute of Labor and Industrial Relations
University of Illinois
December 1965

THE CONTRIBUTORS

Michel Crozier, Director of the Groupe de Sociologie des Organisations at the Centre de Sociologie Européenne and Maitre de Recherches at the Centre National de la Recherche Scientifique, Paris, holds a Docteur es Lettres degree. In 1959-60 he was a fellow at the Center for Advanced Study in the Behavioral Sciences in Stanford. Since 1955 he has conducted a number of empirical studies at French banks, insurance companies, and industrial organizations. He is coeditor of two sociological journals, *Sociologie du Travail* and *Archives Européennes de Sociologie,* and is author of *Petits Fonctionnaires au Travail* (Paris, 1965), *Le Phenomène Bureaucratique* (Paris, 1964), American edition, *The Bureaucratic Phenomenon* (Chicago, 1964).

Günter Hartfiel, Doctor rerum politicarum 1960, has been Assistant at the Institute of Sociology of the Free University in Berlin since that time. Among his publications are: with Dieter Claessens and others, *Angestellte und Arbeiter in der Betriebspyramide* (White Collar Employees and Workers in the Plant Hierarchy), Berlin, 1959; *Angestellte und Angestelltengewerkschaften in Deutschland* (White Collar Workers and Their Unions in Germany), Berlin, 1961; with D. Claessens and L. Sedatis, *Beamte und Angestellte in der Verwaltungspyramide* (Civil Servants and White Collar Workers in the Administrative Hierarchy), Berlin, 1964.

Ernst Lakenbacher, one of the leaders of the white-collar unions in Austria, was a member of the executive committee of the union of insurance employees. Later he was secretary of the white-collar section of the Chamber of Labor in Vienna. During the Nazi occupation of Austria, he was in exile in England and Argentina. Upon his return to Austria in 1948 he became editor of the monthly review of the Chamber of Labor, *Arbeit und Wirtschaft* (Labor and the Economy) and of several other periodicals. In 1955 he was appointed one of the three directors of the Chamber of Labor and put in charge of social insurance, education, and the library and publications of the Chamber of Labor. He has been retired since 1958.

Everett M. Kassalow, Professor of Economics and Director of the International Labor Studies Section at the University of Wisconsin, came to his present position in 1964 after seven years as Director of

Research, Industrial Union Department, AFL-CIO. Previously he was in national and international union positions and on government assignments in the labor field here and abroad. His essays and articles on labor relations, wage determination, and automation have appeared in a number of books and journals. He was editor of *National Labor Movements in the Post-War World* (Northwestern University Press, 1963) and is working on a new volume, *Labor Movements in the World Today.*

Solomon B. Levine, Professor of Labor and Industrial Relations at the University of Illinois, has been Director of the University's Asian Studies Center since 1963. His interest in Asia and in Japan, in particular, dates from his Navy service there following World War II. He has traveled extensively in the Far East to lecture and to study the postwar development of labor movements and industrial relations systems. He is the author of *Industrial Relations in Postwar Japan* (Illinois, 1958) and numerous articles for both English- and Japanese-language journals. He holds degrees from Harvard and Massachusetts Institute of Technology and has been on the Illinois faculty since 1949.

Arne H. Nilstein, Ph.D. and Master of Political Sciences, is General Secretary and Head of the Research Department of the Central Organization of Salaried Employees (Tjänstemännens Centralorganisation). Before joining TCO in 1948, he was an actuary in the Statistical Office of the City of Stockholm. His publications include *Sweden, Scandinavia and Western Europe* (Sverige, Norden och Vasteuropa), as well as articles in various journals.

Guy Routh, Lecturer in Economics at the University of Sussex, received his B. Com. from the University of the Witwatersrand and his Ph.D. from the University of London (London School of Economics). He served as General Secretary of the Industrial Council for the Clothing Industry in Transvaal, Research Officer of the Post Office Engineering Union in the United Kingdom, and Senior Research Officer of the National Institute of Economic and Social Research. He is the author of *Occupation and Pay in Great Britain, 1906 to 1960,* forthcoming.

Adolf Sturmthal, Doctor rerum politicarum from the University of Vienna, has been Professor of Labor and Industrial Relations at the University of Illinois since 1960. He also has been a visiting professor at Columbia, Yale, and other universities. He is the author of *The Tragedy of European Labor* (New York, 1951), *Unity and Diversity in European Labor* (Glencoe, 1953), *Contemporary Collective Bargaining* (Ithaca, 1957), *Workers Councils* (Cambridge, Massachusetts, 1964), and many other books and articles.

Kenneth F. Walker, Professor and Head of the Department of Psychology at the University of Western Australia since 1952, studied psychology, anthropology, and economics at Sydney and Harvard Universities. After four years of teaching social psychology and social economics at the University of Sydney, he spent ten years with the Australian Department of Labor, working on personnel and industrial relations problems. Among his publications are *Industrial Relations in Australia* (Harvard, 1956), *Research Needs in Industrial Relations* (University of Western Australia, 1960), and various papers on industrial psychology and industrial relations including the chapter on Australia in Walter Galenson's *Comparative Labor Movements* (1952).

CONTENTS

Tables

I

WHITE-COLLAR UNIONISM IN AUSTRALIA

BY K.F. WALKER

White-collar unionism in Australia is of particular interest to the student of industrial relations because of two special features of Australian industrial relations. The first special feature is the unusually thoroughgoing attempt to regulate industrial relations by legislation and governmentally administered compulsory conciliation and arbitration. Australia and New Zealand led the world in their attempts to establish this "new province for law and order," [1] and despite the controversy surrounding the Australian arbitration systems from their earliest days, they must be regarded as an important experiment in social regulation deserving searching study.

The second feature of industrial relations in Australia which deserves particular attention is that the Australian strike pattern does not conform to the expectations engendered by the comparative study of strike patterns in other countries. Ross and Hartman [2] point out that the high degree of organization of the labor movement, the importance of the political labor movement, the general existence of multi-employer agreements, and the existence of compulsory arbitration would all suggest a strike pattern like that of Great Britain, Hol-

[1] H. B. Higgins, *A New Province for Law and Order* (Sydney: Workers' Educational Association of New South Wales, 1922).
[2] A. M. Ross and P. T. Hartman, *Changing Patterns of Industrial Conflict* (New York: Wiley, 1960).

land, or Denmark. In fact, however, the Australian strike pattern of frequent short strikes conforms more closely to that of France, Italy, and Japan.

A study of the strength and character of the Australian white-collar unions and their achievements in an industrial relations environment dominated by compulsory arbitration should thus throw considerable light on the forces shaping the development of white-collar unionism.

GROWTH AND ORGANIZATION OF WHITE-COLLAR UNIONS

Unionism was an early growth in Australia. At least 15 to 20 years before any other country, Australian trade unions had established themselves firmly in the community and in the organization of industry. By 1929, 56 per cent of Australian wage and salary earners were organized in trade unions compared with 32 per cent in Sweden, which was then the next most strongly organized country. Membership of trade unions fell off during the 1930's, but it had recovered by 1948 and since 1955 it has remained at 58 or 59 per cent of the workforce. (See Table 1.)

Table 1. Australian Trade Unions and Membership, 1891-1963

Year	*Number of Unions*	*Total Members*	*Members as Per Cent of Employees*	*Number of Unions of 10,000 or More Members*	*Per Cent of Total Members in These Unions*
1891	124	54,888	4.1	n.a.	n.a.
1902	621	433,224	38.5	7	30.5
1920	388	684,450	53.3	14	45.9
1930	362	855,757	52.7	28	63.5
1940	381	955,862	47.9	28	61.7
1950	360	1,605,344	58.0	38	73.4
1960	363	1,912,392	58.0	46	77.4
1963	347	2,003,450	57.0	48	79.4

Source: *Commonwealth Labour Reports.*

It is not possible to give any precise figures on the number of white-collar unions in Australia. Official statistics [3] report that 347

[3] See *Commonwealth Labour Reports.*

unions were in existence in Australia in 1963, but it seems certain that some unions are not included in these figures. In 1961 the Australian Council of Salaried and Professional Associations, the major inter-union white-collar organization, listed approximately 195 white-collar unions known to it. Sixty-three of the unions which are registered with the federal arbitration tribunal may be classified as white-collar unions (including musicians and shop assistants). Of these 63 unions, 29 cover employees in private industry, the others being unions of employees of federal or state governments and their instrumentalities.

Some of the white-collar unions are quite large by Australian standards. The Australian Teachers' Federation, for example, numbers approximately 55,000 members, the Administrative and Clerical Officers' Association of the Commonwealth Public Service has 20,600 members, the Australian Bank Officials' Association has 12,500, the Municipal Officers' Association of Australia 16,500 members, the Association of Professional Engineers of Australia 8,300 members, the Australasian Transport Officers' Association 8,200 members, the Federal Public Servants Assistants' Association 8,700 members, the Australian Journalists' Association 5,000 members. Some white-collar unions, however, are quite small. For example, the Australian Theatre Managers' Association has about 500 members, the Commonwealth Medical Officers' Association has 95 members, and probably the smallest of the unions is the Australian Industrial Arbitration Registrars' Association, which has only 5 members.

The total membership of white-collar unions in Australia can only be roughly estimated. In 1957 the Australian Council of Salaried and Professional Associations (ACSPA) stated that it represented 320,000 white-collar employees and adopted a membership target of one million. In 1958 it said that 200,000 members of white-collar organizations would be affected by a decision of the federal arbitration tribunal. In 1965, the research officer of ACSPA estimated the membership of affiliated organizations at approximately 220,000. Working from the only published figures available, which are for the state of New South Wales and do not include all unions, Hughes and Rawson [4] found that in 1957 19 per cent of the membership of the trade unions registered in New South Wales were in white-collar unions. Applying this percentage to the total union membership in Australia of approximately 1,950,000 in 1962, we arrive at a figure of approxi-

[4] H. Hughes and D. W. Rawson, "Collective Bargaining and the White Collar Pay Structure," *The Journal of Industrial Relations,* II (1960), 75-89.

mately 390,000 if we allow for some expansion in the membership of white-collar unions since 1957. It seems likely, therefore, that the total number of members of white-collar unions in Australia is around 400,000 members at the present time.

The white-collar unions are much stronger in government than in private employment. The New South Wales figures suggested that about two-thirds of the members of white-collar unions are employed in government departments and instrumentalities. Of nearly 200 white-collar unions listed by the ACSPA in 1961, only 65 covered employees in private industry.

Growth of white-collar unions in the private sector of the economy has been relatively recent. Table 2 shows that of the white-collar

***Table* 2.** Dates of Registration of White-Collar Unions with Federal Arbitration Tribunal

Period	*Number of Unions of Government Employees*	*Number of Unions of Employees in Private Industry*
Pre–1922	19	9
1922–45	8	9
Post–1945	6	11
Total	33	29

unions registered with the Commonwealth industrial tribunal, those covering employees in private industry have been registered later than the government unions. In passing it may be noted that only two new unions of manual workers have been registered since 1945, and these were formed from a larger union which had lost its registration with a tribunal. Another indication of the relatively recent growth of white-collar unions in private industry is the extent of awards of the federal arbitration tribunal covering white-collar employees in private industry. Before World War II such awards covered only white-collar employees in banks, insurance companies, and trustee companies, but since World War II awards have extended to shipping, oil, airways, wool, aluminum, sugar, and building supplies, etc.

There are six important interunion bodies among the white-collar unions. Of these, the largest and probably the most important is the Australian Council of Salaried and Professional Associations (ACSPA) which was founded in 1956, following a national conference of 61 white-collar associations called to try to achieve cooperation between these associations in a claim for improved salaries from the federal arbitration tribunal. In 1963 40 white-collar associations were affiliated with the ACSPA and, as indicated earlier, this council aims at covering approximately one million members in 200 or more white-collar unions.

The ACSPA is a consultative body and the affiliated organizations retain their autonomy in every way. Organizations which have members employed as salaried officers in professional, commercial, technical, or like occupations are eligible to affiliate. The Council has constitutional powers to act on behalf of any affiliated organization which desires it to do so, to assist in or conduct publicity campaigns, and to appear before industrial tribunals. The Council is not itself registered with an industrial tribunal but by naming the affiliated organizations for which it is appearing, it may appear before such tribunals. In 1958, the Council made its first appearance before the Commonwealth arbitration tribunal. In 1959 it cooperated with the Australian Council of Trade Unions (ACTU, the main central organization of unions in Australia) in a claim for increased margins for skill before the federal industrial tribunal. As part of its campaign in this case, the Council in cooperation with the Federal Council of University Staff Associations of Australia (referred to below) organized an ambitious seminar on the distribution of the Australian national income. In 1961, the Council organized a white-collar festival week which aimed at getting wide publicity for the problems and interests of the white-collar unions and their members. This was a major organizing effort which received considerable publicity involving not only serious discussions but various entertainment activities appropriate to a festival. The Council launched a major campaign for improved margins in 1962 and was involved in the case for an increase in the basic wage in 1963.

The Council has engaged in a great deal of general publicity in the newspapers and also by the production of leaflets of a high quality. It has encouraged the adaptation of American union folk songs to Australian themes and has arranged for the production of records of these for sale to its members at reduced rates.

Friendly relations have existed between the ACSPA and the ACTU since the formation of the former. A most important step, however, was taken in 1962 when a standing joint committee was established between the ACSPA, the ACTU, and the High Council of Commonwealth Public Service Organizations (referred to below). This committee represents the greatest degree of coordination yet achieved between the various branches of the Australian union movement.

The ACSPA has one paid officer, a research officer. Its other officials are fully employed in their occupations and give their time voluntarily.

The High Council of Commonwealth Public Service Organizations covers 29 organizations and was formed in 1920 to coordinate their activities in the presentation of claims to the Commonwealth Public Service Arbitrator. Not all Commonwealth public service organizations belong to the High Council, the most important exception being the Australian Postal Workers' Union which has a large membership; nevertheless, this union collaborates informally with the High Council. It should be noted that the High Council includes a number of Commonwealth government manual workers' unions. In this respect it is an interesting example of direct collaboration between the government white-collar employees and government manual workers.

The Council of Professional Associations covers seven professional organizations within the Commonwealth public service. Most of the organizations in this council are also affiliated with the High Council of Commonwealth Public Service Organizations, but, in recent years, the relatively young professional associations in the Commonwealth public service have felt the need for collaboration among themselves. This is a fact of some significance, signifying the increased union activity of professional employees and their tendency to feel that their interests are in some respects distinct from the interests of clerical employees. The unions of public servants employed by state governments are federated in the Australian Public Service Federation, but this is much more of a consultative than a representative body. It functions mainly to keep the associations of public servants in the six states in touch with their progress in terms of wages and conditions and does not itself represent these associations in any industrial proceedings. (The High Council of Commonwealth Public Service Organizations does appear in proceedings before the Commonwealth Public Service Arbitrator.)

A similar body, the Australian Teachers' Federation, performs a similar function for the Teachers' Federations in the six states. These very strong associations maintain contact and consult with each other through the Australian Teachers' Federation to endeavor to ensure that conditions for teachers in any state remain reasonably close to those achieved in the other states.

The development of staff associations in the Australian universities has been largely a post-World War II phenomenon, although such associations did exist in some universities earlier than this. These associations are now strong in practically all the ten Australian universities and their constituent colleges and affiliated institutions. In the 1950's, these associations formed the Federal Council of University Staff Associations of Australia, which is a purely consultative body with no powers over its constituent associations. In 1964 it appointed a full-time research officer but previously its work was carried on entirely by voluntary labor as is true of all the universities' staff associations.

As indicated by the above account, white-collar unions in Australia have been strongly established for some time, particularly in government employment, and have been growing recently in private employment. They have achieved a considerable degree of coordination between the various associations and, in recent years, between those in the government and private sectors. Until recently, however, the white-collar unions in government seem to have taken little interest in the activities of white-collar unions outside the government. The present situation indicates that coordination between the activities of the unions in the government sector and those in the private sector will continue to grow.

FACTORS RESPONSIBLE FOR THE GROWTH OF WHITE-COLLAR UNIONS

Among the factors that have influenced the development and organization of white-collar unions in Australia, the first has been the general strength of the trade unions and the labor movement in this relatively young country. This in turn may be attributed to four influences: the nature of the people who settled in Australia, the economic environment, the social climate, and the compulsory arbitration system.[5]

Many of the people who settled Australia in the nineteenth century were actively connected with trade unions or other social reform movements in Great Britain. Some of them were compulsorily transported to Australia because of such activities but many others had radical sympathies (some were Irish rebels and others were Chartists). Others who had not openly identified themselves with any of the

[5] For a fuller account, see my chapter on Australia in Walter Galenson, ed., *Comparative Labour Movements* (Englewood Cliffs, N.J.: Prentice-Hall, 1952).

reformist movements which developed in Britain in the first half of the nineteenth century had left their country to escape want and insecurity and were sympathetic with those who expressed a dissident outlook on social questions. In this class-conscious, reformist climate of opinion, trade unions were a natural growth.

The economic environment did not favor the small independent businessman, which tended to place the Australian settler in the group of employees at an early stage. Geographic factors demanded large-scale utilization of the land and made it difficult for the small settler to succeed. In the cities, government enterprise or the large corporation played a dominant role at an earlier stage than in many countries owing to slow population growth and the method of colonization which was, very largely, government sponsored. A limited economic horizon thus confronted the individual worker almost from the beginning. Rather than being a land of opportunity as America claimed to be, Australia was essentially a land of equality where the frugal gifts of nature were at least to be shared fairly.

The social climate was also favorable to unionism. Urbanization proceeded more rapidly in Australia than in America, for example, and the absence of many foreign immigrants of different national backgrounds made it relatively easy to achieve cohesion in the labor force. The wide dispersion of the settlers encouraged the development of centralized government and weakened local government and local initiative. The necessity to organize in order to influence the central government was a dominant factor in this social environment. In a fluid social structure dissidents were in the majority and individuals who had been uprooted from the network of traditional group relations in Britain were free to embrace new affiliations. Local and familial affiliations were at a minimum and occupational groupings were more sharply defined in the new country. In Britain, where there was the same if not greater limitation of economic horizon as in Australia, the dissident elements were a smaller proportion of the population. They had to contend with a social structure strictly defined by tradition where the individual worker was enmeshed in a web of established group relations extending beyond occupational groupings. In America, by contrast, pressure for social advancement expressed itself in a wider economic horizon in the urge to individual economic success through free enterprise and upward economic mobility. In Australia, people of dissident temper hemmed in by a limited horizon of economic opportunity turned to a form of collective organization familiar to them from Britain and found few practical obstacles to the building of strong organization. Thus in historical perspective the Australian labor movement appears as a stream diverted from the main flow of social reform in Britain, the accumulated pressure of which carried it forward over the relatively unresisting terrain of the new society.

The fourth factor encouraging the development of trade unionism in Australia was undoubtedly the establishment of compulsory arbitration. Interest in compulsory arbitration had been growing in the latter part of the nineteenth century before it was established following the big strikes of the 1890's, when the employers sought to prevent the unions establishing collective bargaining in the sheep-raising industry and other central industries in the economy. The intransigent attitude of employers who refused to meet unions in conference did not sit happily with the community's conception of fair play and justice. Compulsory arbitration appealed to the Australian community as a just solution of the impasse created by the employers' insistence upon the legal right of employer and employee to make individual contracts of employment. By establishing a tribunal to resolve the issues between organizations of employees and employers, recognition could be given to the principle of collective bargaining without the community surrendering completely to the assertion of union power. It also seemed that compulsory arbitration would provide machinery which would overcome the deadlocks that had prostrated the economy in the big strikes of the nineties.

The influence of the compulsory arbitration system upon the growth of Australian trade unions has been twofold. On the one hand, there has been the guarantee of union security and the right of collective bargaining which a union gains when it registers as an industrial organization under the system, and on the other hand there has been the attraction of the improved conditions which may be gained by arbitration without resort to a strike. The attitudes of Australian unions to the working of the compulsory arbitration system have always been mixed and in general the unions have felt that they have not gained all they would wish from the tribunals. Union leaders have pointed out that a number of unions have "been born out of and have grown strong as a result of arbitration and would as quickly fade and die if the arbitration protection were withdrawn and they were forced out of the enervating atmosphere of the Court into the hard work-a-day world of industrial and economic strife, where the ability to hurt is the most cogent argument."[6] Strong

[6] J. Hooke, *Is Arbitration Enough?* Symposium organized by Workers' Educational Association (Sydney, 1946), p. 1.

unions may have felt that the arbitration system has put a brake on their powers, but weaker ones have gained.[7] The attitudes of white-collar unions to this aspect of arbitration will be referred to below, but at this point it is necessary to explain the relationship between an Australian trade union and the state as it is governed by various legislation.

Three types of legislation define the relationship of the trade union to the state in Australia. These are: (a) the laws establishing tribunals for the settlement of industrial disputes which, for the most part, provide for the registration of unions, a process whereby the unions give up certain powers over the regulation of their internal affairs in exchange for guarantees of union security and collective bargaining; (b) other legislation, under which trade unions may register and gain legal status; and (c) coercive legislation controlling stoppages of work in certain industries or in certain circumstances.[8]

The Commonwealth and state governments have experimented with various forms and procedures of government machinery for the settlement of industrial disputes since the experiments in these directions began early in the twentieth century. The arrangements vary considerably between the states and the Commonwealth and will not be described here. In general, the state tribunals have jurisdiction only within the borders of their state and interstate disputes may be settled by the machinery established by the Commonwealth government. The legislation of the Commonwealth and four of the six states provides for organizations of employees and employers to be registered with the tribunal, a procedure which enables them to apply for awards if they are unable to settle disputes in their industry and to make private agreements between unions and employers legally enforceable by having them registered by the tribunal.

By far the majority of Australian unions are registered with a federal or state tribunal. It is possible, however, for a union to register under other legislation which predates the legislation establishing industrial tribunals. For the most part, it is based on the legislation

[7] On the effects of the arbitration system, see my article: "Arbitration in a New Key," *Economic Record,* XXXIII (1957), 60-71; and D. W. Oxnam "Industrial Arbitration in Australia: Its Effects on Wages and Unions," *Industrial and Labor Relations Review,* IX (1956), 610-28. See also D. W. Oxnam, "Arbitration in Perspective—A Further Comment," *Economic Record,* XXXIV (1958), 96-103.
[8] See J. H. Portus, *The Development of Australian Trade Union Law* (Melbourne: Melbourne University Press, 1958).

of Britain late in the nineteenth century and has the effect of giving a registrant union corporate status and of protecting it from being considered an unlawful combination. The industrial disputes machinery carries legal regulation of the internal affairs of Australian trade unions much further, and registration under such machinery is of considerable legal significance. As stated in a judgment of the Australian High Court,

It must always be remembered that an "Organization" such as the responding organization is a creation of the Act and simply incidental to its great purposes. Those who become members of such an organization, and particularly those who undertake the duty of managing its affairs . . . take a part more or less responsible in an organization which is not merely a convenient method of obtaining their just rights but is also a public instrument for effectively administering an important statute of public policy for the general welfare. Such an organization secures rights and privileges, but it also has duties.[9]

The obligation to refrain from strikes is, of course, the most important of the duties imposed on a union by Australian industrial arbitration laws. Nevertheless, Australian trade unions have always been prepared to strike against an award which they regard as unsatisfactory and they seem to have proceeded on the assumption that some strikes are necessary to keep the arbitrators on their toes. At times, severe penalties have been imposed on unions which persisted in striking against awards, including jail sentences upon union leaders. Despite these efforts to outlaw strikes, and the steps taken at times to break strikes by the use of the army, the general attitude of the community has been tolerant of illegal strikes. As the president of the Queensland Industrial Court said in 1924: "The difficulty of enforcing penalties against strikes is partly political, partly practical. The punishment of large numbers of strikers by prosecutions is in practice a difficult matter. The enforcement of the penalties is usually opposed by one or other political party. In practice the deterrent against strikes is the recognition of the fact that, since arbitration has been on the whole beneficial to the unions, deprivation of access to the industrial tribunals is a substantial loss, and strikes endanger such access." [10]

Although the Australian attempt to abolish strikes and lockouts by legislation must be judged a failure, it should be noted that Aus-

[9] J. Isaacs, in the High Court, Australian Commonwealth Shipping Board and Federated Seamen's Union of Australia, 35 *C.L.R.*, pp. 475-76.
[10] T. W. McCawley, *Industrial Arbitration* (Brisbane: Queensland Government Printer, 1924), p. 83.

tralian industrial relations are very peacefully conducted and violence has been relatively rare.

The development of Australian white-collar unions has been fostered not only by the general strength of the Australian labor movement, but also by its strongly political character. Again, the sources of this characteristic lie in the ideological backgrounds of those who formed the labor movement in the nineteenth century, together with the importance of government in Australia and its centralized form. The general dependence of the community on the central government in each state encouraged trade unions, like other bodies, to engage in political activity at a relatively early date. The absence of established political parties when the unions became strong and the fact that a number of general social and political issues remained to be settled at the end of the nineteenth century made it natural for the unions to become deeply involved in politics. Political power was a more feasible goal for labor in Australia than in America. There were fewer governments to be captured and there was no ancient tradition of government nor any long-established political parties. Basic issues such as civil liberties and constitutional structure were still to be resolved and labor policy naturally embraced these as well as matters closer to labor's specific interests. The practical problems of political organization were much less in Britain and America and the scope for making rapid gains was correspondingly greater.

Against this background the growth of white-collar unionism, particularly in the government sector of the economy, appears very natural. The idea of unionism and of submitting one's claims for improved employment conditions to a government system of compulsory arbitration was fairly widely accepted in the Australian community. Trade unions did not confront such a hostile environment as in America and, at the same time, the social distinction between the various classes in the community was not so strong as in Great Britain. The idea of joining a union in order to further one's economic aims was therefore not so repugnant to the middle class Australian as in some other countries.

Nevertheless, most of the Australian white-collar unions came slowly to acceptance of arbitration. The Commonwealth Public Service white-collar unions, for example, resisted the establishment of arbitration arrangements for them, holding the view that it should be unnecessary for them to go before an arbitrator. They considered that in public employment, where the community was in effect the employer, legislation combined with collective bargaining and negotiation should be sufficient to establish proper employment conditions. They moved slowly to use the Commonwealth arbitration system when it was forced upon them until they found that the tribunal was awarding conditions of employment better than those provided by the Commonwealth Public Service Commissioner. A similar process can be seen in the recent history of the attitudes of the University Staff Associations to arbitration. In the last ten years these associations have gradually moved more and more to acceptance of the principle of arbitration, although this has still not yet achieved general assent. Support for submission of claims to some form of arbitration tribunal has grown because members of these associations have felt that their salaries and conditions have not kept pace with the improvements in conditions in other sections of the economy. They have turned towards arbitration in the hope that this will maintain their relative position. Fears that submission of claims to arbitration would involve the imposition of rules such as the public service has on the signing of timebooks and the keeping of strict hours of duty, etc., have been removed by the failure of these fears to be substantiated following experience of awards by the New South Wales Industrial Commission for staff of the University of New South Wales in recent years.

In summary it may be said that where Australian white-collar workers have developed the attitudes which favor the formation of a union, circumstances for most of them in Australia have made it relatively easy for them to establish a union organization and achieve recognition by employers and the community. Government employees, in particular, found few obstacles to access to an industrial tribunal when they reached the point where they wished to form a union for this purpose, although the unions of professional employees have experienced more difficulty. White-collar unions in private industry have had a harder struggle.[11]

What factors have fostered a "union attitude" among white-collar workers in government employment and certain kinds of private employment? Why has this "union attitude" been extending in recent years in private industry and among professional workers in the government?

It may be suggested that such attitudes were fostered fairly early among government employees and among employees in banks,

[11] See the history of the Australian Journalists' Association, *Crusade for Journalism,* G. Sparrow, ed. (Melbourne: The A.J.A., 1960).

insurance companies, and trustee companies, because in all these cases large numbers of employees carrying out similar duties are collected together and confronted by a small number of employers. The most extreme case is that of government employees who really have only one employer to deal with and who are in a special position insofar as there is no true distinction between the managerial group and the rank and file. Within the administrative division of the public services any officer has the legal right to rise to the very top of the organization and, in fact, at least until after World War II, most of the heads of departments in Commonwealth Public Service had begun their careers in lowly occupations such as telegraph messengers. Thus the employees who formed public service unions were negotiating with men who themselves had come up through the ranks, and had perhaps been active in the union themselves. In these conditions many factors favored the development and progress of the union.

In the Australian banking system there are only a few banks, each with many branches, and government banks compete with private banks over the whole range of banking services. The large homogeneous work force confronting a few employers kept its eyes on the trend of employment conditions in the government service, for this tended to provide a model for the government banks and thus set the pattern for the private banks. Many of the officers of the private banks campaigned actively against the nationalization of the banks proposed by the federal labor government soon after World War II, but this did not prevent them striving to maintain or improve the relationship between their conditions of employment and those in the government banks.

The spread of a "union attitude" in other sections of private industry probably arises from the inflation following World War II and the success of the manual workers' unions in gaining for their members a number of the fringe benefits such as sick leave, annual leave, long-service leave, and superannuation (retirement pay) which previously distinguished white-collar workers from manual workers. Working hours per week, which used to differ by at least four hours, now differ by only about two and one-half. Physical working conditions in factories have been greatly improved. The white-collar worker's economic position has suffered under inflation, and his status in the community has been jeopardized.

This point was put rather graphically by an official of the Professional Engineers' Association as follows: "Pre-war days have a glamour for the clerk. That was the period, recruits were told, when their seniors built their *crédit foncier* home in Glen Iris and employed part-time domestic help. At the (recent) meeting of Bank Officers . . . an official said that as a group Bank Officers are living far worse than plumbers next door. Mr. O'Dea commented: 'I would suggest that the more weighty grievance is that the plumbers *are* now living next door.'"[12] As this comment might suggest, some of the dynamic of the modern white-collar unions is provided by the sense of a loss of status. Naturally, the white-collar unionist's interest in better salary conditions is not restricted solely to status, but this aspect should not be ignored. Some of the benefits of white-collar employment compared with factory employment, such as use of a different entry to the plant, use of different cafeteria premises and employee facilities, longer periods of engagement, longer holidays, etc., have in the past been some compensation for a lower pay packet than that of the skilled worker. Under inflationary conditions such as have obtained in Australia for the most part since World War II, however, the gap may become so great as to disturb the white-collar worker's sense of justice and he then demands an increase in tangible reward in addition to his other marks of status. This, however, brings us to the objectives of the white-collar unions.

OBJECTIVES OF THE WHITE-COLLAR UNIONS

In the earlier days of white-collar unionism in Australia it seems likely that the white-collar unionist in government employment and the pioneer white-collar unions in private employment, particularly the Australian Journalists' Association, were directly concerned with the absolute level of their salaries and conditions. More and more, however, it seems that the white-collar unions have been concerned with relative rewards rather than the absolute level of economic reward.

Table 3 shows the responses of the officials of 50 Australian white-collar unions to a questionnaire regarding the objectives of their union.

The principal objectives are improved salaries and "wage justice." While the latter objective is a favorite slogan of the Australian trade-union movement, it has particular relevance for the white-collar un-

[12] L. G. Matthews, The Growing White Collar Unions, Paper delivered to 10th Annual Industrial Officers' Convention of Victorian Employers' Federation, 1961, p. 4.

Table 3. Objectives of 50 White-Collar Unions, 1963

	Percentage of Unions
Higher wages	94
Relative wage justice	92
Shorter hours	62
Rearranged hours	52
Seniority rule in promotions	44
Seniority rule in retrenchments	34
Promotions appeal tribunal	60
Union representation on or before disciplinary tribunal	58
Collection of membership subscriptions by deduction from pay	50
Compulsory unionism	26
Preference for unionists in employment	56
Better physical working conditions	78
Recognition of organization by employers	70
Cooperation with employers	72
Formal joint consultative machinery	72
Protection against victimization	70
Recognition by public	58

ions, particularly in more recent years. In general it would seem that many white-collar unions, especially those of professional employees, are not so much engaged in a direct struggle for "more" as concerned to *restore* their relative position in the community structure of salaries and conditions. The dynamic of the modern white-collar unions includes the sheer improvement of their conditions, but focuses on the restoration of what they feel to be their just relative position in the community structure of economic reward. The notion of justice seems to have particular appeal to the modern white-collar unionists. Many of them would be happy not to worry about trade unionism and campaigning for improved conditions provided they could be assured that by some formula their conditions would be kept in their relative standing in the community pattern of wages and conditions.

While there are no comparable data for manual workers' unions, it seems likely that manual unions would place more emphasis on compulsory unionism and preference to unionism. This may merely indicate that the achievement of such an aim would be so difficult that most of the white-collar unions have not bothered about it for the most part.

The white-collar unions have also been particularly concerned with justice in the opportunity for promotion. Seniority as applied not only to retrenchments but more particularly to the opportunity for promotion, has been a favorite objective of the government white-collar unions as of the manual workers. The white-collar unions in government service have also fought for the establishment of tripartite appeal boards to deal with promotions, disciplinary cases, and in some instances, salaries.

Formal joint consultative machinery has been another objective of white-collar unions, particularly of the government unions. Increased participation by employees in management has also been favored by these unions. In Table 4 it will be seen that only 28 per cent of the leaders of white-collar unions in the survey referred to above think that "unions should restrict themselves to getting fair wages and working conditions for their members and keep out of the management of industry." Eighty-nine per cent think that "employers should do more to encourage their employees to make suggestions about their work." Ninety-one per cent think that "employers should consult the unions more." Fifty-nine per cent think that "employers and union leaders should see more of each other off the jobs," and seventy per cent think that "the average union leader has as much ability as the average employer." It should be noted, however, that the leaders of white-collar unions do not differ significantly from the leaders of manual workers' unions in these opinions.

ATTITUDES AND TECHNIQUES OF WHITE-COLLAR UNIONISTS

Table 4 shows the opinions of samples of business executives, personnel officers and the leaders of manual workers' and white-collar unions respectively on seventeen issues related to industrial relations. The table also shows the questions on which the leaders of the white-collar unions differ from the other groups. It will be seen that there are seven items on which the leaders of the white-collar unions differ from the leaders of manual unions to an extent which makes it unlikely that the difference could be due to chance. The first of these is Item 1: "Most employers take a real interest in the welfare of their employees." Half the white-collar union leaders endorse this statement, and share the views of business executives much more than do the leaders of manual unions, or even personnel officers. The leaders of white-collar unions are much more prone to agree that "Most

Table 4. Opinions of White-Collar Union Leaders, Manual Union Leaders, Personnel Officers, and Business Executives on Industrial Relations

	Percentage Agreeing				*Statistically Significant Differences* [a] *Between*			
Statement	*White-Collar Union Leaders (N = 46)*	*Manual Union Leaders (N = 107)*	*Personnel Officers (N = 140)*	*Business Executives (N = 255)*	*White-Collar and Other Unions*	*White-Collar Unions and Personnel Officers*	*White-Collar Unions and Executives*	*Other Unions and Executives*
1. Most employers take a real interest in the welfare of their employees	50	28	57	65	Yes	No	No	Yes
2. Employers should consult the unions more	91	96	75	51	No	Yes	Yes	Yes
3. Most employees cooperate with their employer	89	67	73	67	Yes	Yes	Yes	No
4. Labor usually gets a fair return for the work it does	43	23	85	88	Yes	Yes	Yes	Yes
5. Most foremen treat their workers fairly	83	73	81	89	No	No	No	Yes
6. A union could make satisfactory progress without striking	50	24	58	61	Yes	No	No	Yes
7. Employers and union leaders should see more of each other off the job	59	64	62	58	No	No	No	No
8. Anyone with ability who is willing to work can get to the top	50	43	78	85	No	Yes	Yes	Yes
9. Most workers loaf if they know they can easily get another job	9	8	19	36	No	No	Yes	Yes

10. A firm that makes big profits is usually more efficient than other firms	26	51	45	62	Yes	Yes	Yes	No
11. The average union leader has as much ability as the average employer	70	82	30	29	No	Yes	Yes	Yes
12. Most employees take pride in their work	91	86	62	50	No	Yes	Yes	Yes
13. Extra pay for extra work is the best way to get more output from workers	46	59	47	69	No	No	Yes	Yes
14. Employers should do more to encourage their employees to make suggestions about their work	89	97	96	96	No	No	No	No
15. Industrial relations would be more peaceful without the arbitration system	9	23	12	9	Yes	No	No	Yes
16. Unions should restrict themselves to getting fair wages and working conditions for their members and keep out of the management of industry	28	39	58	69	No	Yes	Yes	Yes
17. The difference between the lowest and highest incomes in Australia is too big to be fair	63	87	30	8	Yes	Yes	Yes	Yes

[a] A statistically significant difference is one which would occur by chance not more than once in 20 times (.05 level). In all but one instance in this table, the significant differences would occur by chance not more than twice in 100 times, and mostly only once in 100.

employees cooperate with their employer" (Item 3) than any other group. The leaders of white-collar unions seem to be more identified with employees than the leaders of manual unions and personnel officers. The leaders of white-collar unions do not share the views of personnel officers and business executives on Item 4 ("Labor usually gets a fair return for the work it does") but they endorse this statement significantly more frequently than do the leaders of the manual unions. On Item 10 ("A firm that makes big profits is usually more efficient than other firms"), the white-collar unions are distinguished by the low proportion (26 per cent) who endorse this statement. They differ significantly from the other three groups on this item. Half the leaders of white-collar unions agree that "A union could make satisfactory progress without striking" (Item 6), a significantly higher proportion than among the leaders of manual unions. On this item the white-collar union leaders do not differ significantly from personnel officers or business executives.

On Item 15 ("Industrial relations would be more peaceful without the arbitration system"), the leaders of white-collar unions agree exactly with the business executives. Significantly fewer of them endorse this view than do leaders of the manual unions, but the proportion of white-collar union leaders agreeing with this statement is not significantly different from the proportion of personnel officers or business executives who agree with it.

Leaders of white-collar unions also differ significantly from all three groups in their support for the statement that "The difference between the lowest and highest unions in Australia is too big to be fair" (Item 17). Fewer white-collar leaders agree with this statement than leaders of manual unions, but the proportion (63 per cent) is significantly below the proportion in the personnel officer and business executive groups.

In general, the results of this survey show that on socio-economic issues the leaders of white-collar unions tend to fall between the leaders of manual unions on the one hand and personnel officers and business executives on the other, but they are more doubtful of the efficiency of firms making big profits than any of the other three groups. They stress the cooperative tendencies of employees more than any other group, and they share the views of personnel officers and business executives on the goodwill of the employer and agree with these groups' opinions in favor of the peaceful conduct of industrial relations and the use of arbitration.

In the original study,[13] which compared the opinions of business executives and the leaders of trade unions, nine items discriminated significantly in each of two samples of union leaders and business executives. These were Items 1, 2, 4, 6, 8, 9, 11, 12, and 17. When scored in the pro-union direction (that is, in the direction in which the majority of union leaders answered them) these items can be taken to form a pro-unionism scale. The white-collar unions come more or less midway between the leaders of the manual trade unions and the personnel officers in their pro-union score on these items. The mean score of the leaders of manual trade unions was 14.2, while that of the leaders of white-collar unions was 12.8 and that of the personnel officers was 9.2. These differences are all statistically significant at the 1 per cent level.

To what extent do these differences in the opinions and attitudes of the leaders of white-collar unions reflect differences in the attitudes of their rank-and-file members? Some light is cast on this question by a comparison of the answers of a sample of 145 male white-collar workers in Perth to a job attitudes questionnaire which had previously been answered by 554 workers in five organizations in Perth, most of the members of the latter sample being employed in manual occupations.[14] In the white-collar sample, a significantly higher proportion desire more say in what goes on in their jobs and a significantly higher proportion want more responsibility. A substantially lower proportion (55 per cent) feel that their present job is satisfying in the extent to which it gives them a chance to show what they can do. A significantly lower proportion of white-collar workers than of the manual workers feel free to set their own work pace. A significantly higher proportion than among the manual workers (52 per cent compared with 39 per cent) feel that they have a great or good deal of influence in what goes on on the job, but a significantly higher proportion than among the manual workers (66 per cent compared with 50 per cent) desire still more influence on the job. The proportion of the white-collar workers' sample who consider that their immediate

[13] K. F. Walker, "Attitudes of Union Leaders and Business Executives to Industrial Relations, *Occupational Psychology,* XXXIII (1959), 159-65. See also K. F. Walker, "Conflict and Mutual Misunderstanding: A Survey of Union Leaders' and Business Executives' Attitudes to Industrial Relations," *Journal of Industrial Relations,* I (1959), 20-30.

[14] See K. F. Walker and J. Lumsden, "Employees' Job Satisfaction and Attitudes: A Survey," *Business Review,* (February and March, 1963), 12 pp. I am indebted to Dr. N. F. Dufty for collecting the white-collar data.

supervisor has a great deal or a good deal of influence on what goes on on the job is significantly less than among the manual workers' sample (53 per cent as against 63 per cent). These are the only statistically significant differences between the two samples, which in other ways express very similar views.

There is clear evidence here of a stronger desire among the white-collar workers for interesting work and more control over what happens on the job. Significantly fewer of them mention interest in the work, or physical working conditions, among the good things about their job and significantly fewer of them mention pay and the boss as the worst things about the present job.

Further light is thrown on the attitudes of rank-and-file white-collar workers by Dufty's study comparing attitudes expressed by members of the Western Australian Railway Officers' Association towards their union with those expressed by one hundred members of the Carpenters' Union and an engineering union.[15] Dufty found that the white-collar sample expressed equally positive feelings towards the union as the blue-collar sample. Over half of them favored compulsory unionism and a third favored preference in employment of unionists. The remainder said that a person should be free to join the union or remain out. These opinions did not differ significantly from those of the blue-collar workers. Similar opinions were held by the white-collar workers and the blue-collar workers on the gains which might be won by a strike but the white-collar workers were less inclined to favor the use of the strike and felt less need for protection of their working conditions by the union than did the skilled tradesmen in the manual unions. They also were more inclined to think the strikes were only used as a last resort compared with the blue-collar workers, who, of course, had rather more personal experience. Two-fifths of the white-collar workers in this sample thought that the union did, in fact, strike only as a last resort and this was twice the proportion who expressed this view in the sample of skilled tradesmen. A third of the white-collar workers were against striking in any circumstances whereas only a quarter of the sample of manual workers held this view. White-collar workers were also less likely to look for militant characteristics in their officials and on the whole they were more satisfied with the operation of their unions. They expressed less critical comments about officials, fewer of them thought that the union dues were too high, they were more satisfied with the

[15] N. F. Dufty, "The White Collar Unionist," *Journal of Industrial Relations,* III (1961), 151-56.

way in which union funds were spent, and on the whole more of them were content with the link between the union and the labor party.

The opinions of the rank-and-file members of one white-collar union on the use of the strike weapon seemed to be reasonably consistent with those expressed by the union leaders reported in Table 4. The opinions of the rank and file in one union also seemed consistent with the expressed opinions of the leaders of white-collar unions on the influence of the arbitration system on industrial relations (Item 15 in Table 4).

The picture of the white-collar unionist which emerges from the above data from leaders and rank and file is that of an employee interested in his job, ready to cooperate with his employer, and although conscious of his solidarity with his fellow workers, disposed to defend and advance his interests by negotiation and resort to constitutional procedures.

These opinions both of rank-and-file members and of the leaders of white-collar unions are consistent with the known actions of white-collar unions in attempting to achieve their aim. There are hardly any recorded strikes in which white-collar unions have played a leading part although, at times, white-collar workers who have been members of unions principally constituted of manual employees have joined the manual workers in a strike. True white-collar strikes, however, have been exceedingly rare. In the survey of 50 white-collar unions referred to above, only 4 reported that their unions had participated in a strike. These were the Australian Journalists' Association, the Australian Air Pilots' Federation, the State School Teachers' Union of Western Australia, and the Western Australian Civil Service Association. Actually, the last two unions joined together in the one strike.

The Australian Journalists' Association is one of the most interesting of the Australian white-collar unions. Organized in 1910, this union achieved registration with the Commonwealth Arbitration Court in 1911. In 1912 the Western Australian branch of the union called their members out on a strike against the *Daily News* in an effort to force the employer to agree to rates of pay agreed to in other states. This is probably the first recorded strike by a white-collar union in Australia, and was successful. Two bigger strikes in which the AJA was involved occurred in Sydney, one in 1944 and one in 1955. Both of these disputes developed when the proprietors of the various Sydney newspapers desired to produce a composite paper as an emergency to overcome the difficulty caused by a strike of printers. Members of the AJA reported for their normal duties but refused to work on the composite paper which was to be a joint production of the four newspapers which had been struck by the printers. Journalists who refused to work on this composite paper were then suspended by their employers. Together with the Printing Industry Employees' Union the AJA then brought out their own newspaper for Sydney, called *The News*. In the editorial to the first issue the heading was: "Sydney Newsmen Keep Faith." It said: "*The News* carries on where the Sydney newspaper proprietors left off. They are on strike. We are at work." *The News* was a great success, selling over one-hundred-thousand copies per day for the five days during which it was produced. The organization of the printing and distribution of this paper was a major achievement.

A dispute which also originated between the newspaper proprietors and the printers occurred in 1955 and involved the AJA in much the same way. Again the AJA and the printers' union produced a rival newspaper to the composite paper which the newspaper proprietors were endeavoring to produce, and this paper (entitled *The Clarion*) sold in very large numbers for the three days during which it was produced. *The Clarion* made about £1,000 per day profit which was shared equally between the two unions.

The State School Teachers' Union of Western Australia went on strike in association with the Civil Service Association in that state from the 10th to 28th of July 1920, over salaries and the composition of proposed appeals boards which were to arbitrate on conditions and grievances. The unions wanted the boards to include a representative elected by their members and succeeded in having an elected representative included, although he was to be elected by all the staff concerned, whether they belonged to the union or not. The unions were appointed, however, as constitutional representatives of the staff concerned and given the right to approach the board on behalf of all the staff.

In 1934 the Teachers' Union in Western Australia held a regulation strike in which they remained at work but refused all duties beyond those strictly defined in the regulations. This action followed many protests against government economy measures which required the teachers to make sacrifices of salaries and conditions which they felt to be disproportionate compared to other civil servants.

The principal technique of white-collar unions is undoubtedly negotiation and, where appropriate, arbitration. For the most part relations with the representatives of employers are quite friendly. In the survey of 50 white-collar unions 45 union leaders answered a question on the quality of personal relations between the union leader and representatives of employers. Fifteen classified such relations as very friendly and 26 classified them as friendly. There seems little doubt that the success of the white-collar unions in the process of negotiation is facilitated by the fact that for the most part they are negotiating with people of background and training similar to their own.

Whereas manual unions tend to use strikes or stop-work meetings to back up their negotiations (and even their arbitration proceedings), the white-collar unions tend to use the public meetings and newspaper publicity as their supplementary weapons. Only a few white-collar unions have engaged in stop-work meetings (out of the 50 unions covered in the survey mentioned above only 5 report having had a stop-work meeting). Newspaper publicity has been used by 31 of these 50 unions and 21 of them have held public protest meetings.

Some of the newspaper publicity is quite ambitious. For example, the *Sydney Morning Herald* of September 21, 1963, carried a half-page advertisement inserted by the New South Wales Teachers' Federation which in a big headline showed the salaries paid to the Chairman, Deputy Chairman, and members of the New South Wales Public Service Board. The announcement went on to say in large type:

> These are the annual salaries of members of the Public Service Board fixed by Parliament on September 5th in an Act which validated the payment of these rates from 1st January, 1962.
>
> Teachers do NOT ask Parliament to fix their salaries.
>
> But they do seek effective negotiations so that they may "receive salaries commensurate with the wonderful service they give the community" (Mr. Heffron's words at an earlier date). As evidence of our bona fides, we have even proposed that the Premier arrange for negotiation between the Public Service Board and the Teachers' Federation under the Chairmanship of the President of the Industrial Commission.
>
> The Government which FIXES the salaries of members of the Public Service Board CAN ARRANGE NEGOTIATIONS that are likely to lead to SALARY JUSTICE for teachers.
>
> A government based on the trade unions should have as much *concern* for government *employees* as for members of the government *employing authority.*

An officer of one white-collar union (R. J. O'Dea of the Professional Engineers' Association) has suggested that "much of the tactics in industrial relations of white-collar organizations must, I suggest, be placed more in the category of the public relations activity of a pressure group than in the conventions of militant trade unions. There is a close parallel between the white-collar protest meeting and that of the outer suburban Progress Association protesting against indifference to their needs on the part of water, sewerage, and road-making authorities. There is a recognition by both that impersonal bureaucracies have one sensitive area, their public relations."[16] The public protest meetings organized by white-collar organizations are essentially of the same character.

It is a small step from newspaper publicity of the sort described above to direct political campaigning on behalf of one party or another, or campaigning to ensure that political parties shape their programs to cater to the needs of white-collar workers. During the election campaign of November 1963, for example, the Public Service Association of New South Wales ran an advertisement in the *Sydney Morning Herald* measuring 7¼ inches by 4¼ inches with a headline in 7/16-inch type: "Means test is a penalty on thrift" and referring to the fact that there is no means test in New Zealand, Canada, Great Britain, and the United States. "What do our political leaders say in their policy speeches?" the statement goes on to ask. It then lists the leaders of the three parties: "The Liberal Party, the Hon. Sir Robert Menzies—not mentioned in his speech; Australian Labour Party, the Hon. A. A. Calwell—'we will abolish the means test progressively and as opportunity offers'; Australian Country Party, the Hon J. McEwan —not mentioned in his speech." The statement ends "DEMAND A CLEAR STATEMENT FROM YOUR CANDIDATE ON THIS VITAL ISSUE."

In some elections, particular white-collar associations have campaigned directly for one party rather than another, usually for the Labour Party. Government white-collar organizations, for example, have tended to support the Labour Party and to campaign on its behalf at various times. White-collar organizations tend to do a good deal of informal canvassing of politicians trying to influence them in favor of policies which the associations consider will contribute towards their objectives.

The general question of the link between Australian trade unions and the political wing of the labor movement is very complex. It seems clear from the extent to which nonlabor governments have been able to stay in office over long periods, particularly in recent years, that not all members of Australian trade unions vote labor. Many trade unions,

[16] Quoted by L. G. Matthews, *op. cit.*, p. 4.

however, contribute to the funds of the Australian Labour Party and many are affiliated with it. White-collar unions have been much less ready to link themselves with the Australian Labour Party than the manual unions. Out of 50 unions included in the above-mentioned survey only 8 are affiliated with the A.L.P. and with one exception these are all unions of government employees. Even in the case of the exception a large part of the membership is employed by a government instrumentality. It is generally thought that white-collar unions have refrained from affiliation with the A.L.P. and even the ACTU for fear that such affiliations would discourage some white-collar workers from joining these unions.

ACHIEVEMENTS OF WHITE-COLLAR UNIONS

How much progress have Australian white-collar unions been able to make by the use of these methods, relying as they do so heavily on negotiation and public relations procedures rather than industrial warfare? Their basic objective has been to maintain or where necessary restore the relative position of their salaries and conditions compared with other groups in the community. In the 1957 campaign the formula developed by the ACSPA for a general white-collar salary increase aimed at raising salaries to four or five times the prewar level, on a number of grounds. The first ground was that the real purchasing power of salaries had deteriorated substantially through the rise of prices and to this point was joined a second ground that increased direct taxation coupled with heavy indirect taxation had further reduced the real purchasing power of salaries. Third, the council maintained that the white-collar workers were entitled to a restoration of their share of the national income on the grounds that they had not received an equitable and just share of the increased national productivity since prewar days.

To these three arguments were added two arguments more familiar to Australian industrial tribunals: first, a claim that salaries should be raised because of increased "work value" arising from the need for greater skill and the discharge of greater responsibilities, and second, that the actual level of white-collar salaries had declined in relation to other salaries and should be adjusted to preserve "relative wage justice."

The first three grounds put forward in support of the claim for a rise in salaries are relatively novel in Australian wage-fixing. Emphasis on the role of taxation is an argument almost peculiar to the white-collar unions. The attempt was also made in supporting statistical analysis to argue that salaries should have kept step with the average personal consumption of the nation. The analysis showed that the higher levels of white-collar employment had not experienced salary rises sufficiently great to keep in step with the increase of average personal consumption. It was shown, for example, that the rate for a 21-year-old male clerk, bank official, or insurance officer who received £200 gross in 1938-39, had risen by 3.2 times or even 3.9 times in some cases and had thus more or less kept pace with price rises between 1938-39 and 1957. Salaries for higher paid white-collar jobs, however, had not risen proportionately. A job carrying £1,250 per annum in 1938-39, for instance, had risen by less than 2.5 times to £3,066. In the Commonwealth Public Service, the ratio of the highest salary to the adult male basic wage was 13.6 to 1 in 1901 and 9.4 to 1 in 1961.

In fact, in the proceedings before the federal arbitration tribunal in 1959 the white-collar unions were content to rely on grounds put forward by the ACTU for increases in the metal industries. These were restoration of the pre-1954 relativities, loss of purchasing power and the general economic capacity of the community to pay higher rates. An interim decision gave an increase of 20 per cent in the margins above the basic wage [17] and settlements were then reached between many individual white-collar unions in private industry and their employers, some unions being able to obtain marginal increases of over 28 per cent (this being better, therefore, than the increase of 28 per cent in margins of manual workers awarded by the federal tribunal). Presumably the white-collar unions were prepared to settle for something now rather than persist in their claim for the full settlement of their case for much higher rises. Perhaps the bird in the hand was made the more attractive in those cases where it amounted to something more than the manual workers got.

In the Commonwealth Public Service, the clerical and professional unions had great difficulty in pressing their claims for a 28 per cent increase in margins to carry right up to the highest positions. The tribunal took the view that it was in order to expect that generally speaking where living standards rise, poorer groups will tend to catch up on the richer groups. They thought that the purchasing power of

[17] Australian wage-fixing tribunals divide wages into the basic wage, which is the level paid to the unskilled worker, and "margins for skill." These are extra amounts paid to skilled workers according to their skill. These two elements in the wage structure are negotiated and arbitrated separately.

high salaries covers things nearer to items of luxury and investment than sheer needs to meet a minimum standard of living. It may be concluded, therefore, that Australian industrial tribunals have as yet been reluctant to accept the basic arguments put forward by the ACSPA for a restoration of the white-collar position in the community structure of economic rewards. As noted earlier, the fringe benefits which previously differentiated white-collar workers from manual workers, have been progressively extended to manual workers and there seems no likelihood of a restoration of the white-collar workers' advantages in this field.

Perhaps the most important gain on the part of the white-collar group was the making of a "work value" award for professional engineers in 1961.[18] This case first came before the federal arbitration tribunal in September 1957. The award set national minimum salaries payable by all employers of professional engineers, displacing federal and state awards, registered agreements, and private contracts of 29 employee organizations with employers as diverse as the Commonwealth and state Public Services, Commonwealth and state instrumentalities and private industry employers in industries such as metal industries, aircraft, gas, oil, automobiles, and engineering consulting. The Association of Professional Engineers itself was formed by the federation of a number of state organizations to replace the 29 organizations previously capable of acting on behalf of professional engineers registered under federal and state industrial legislation. The Association was registered with the federal tribunal in 1948 and its efforts to obtain an award for professional engineers met with various legal and constitutional problems which will not be considered here.

This case also raised important issues regarding the relative role of the Commonwealth and state industrial tribunals. Although the engineers' case has often been regarded as a test case for white-collar workers, the position of this case in relation to other claims before the federal industrial tribunal on behalf of other white-collar unions became rather complex and was not generally understood. Eventually, however, the engineers' claim for an award based on the work value of the engineers' professional functions was separated clearly from the claim for adjustment of margins for white-collar workers on the general grounds referred to above.

[18] My account of this case is based on the following two articles: R. J. O'Dea, "Some Features of the Professional Engineers' Case," *Journal of Industrial Relations,* IV (1962), 90-107; P. C. Molhuysen, "The Professional Engineers' Case, *Australian Economic Papers,* I (1962), 57-78.

In its case, the Association of Professional Engineers mentioned that it was asking the tribunal "to step out of the normal routine of assessing wage rates and salaries by simple process of comparison and to undertake a re-evaluation of the social worth of a professional class." This social worth was to be based not on current salaries, but on what ought to be paid in the light of educational requirements, the professional nature of the work done, the overall relative position of engineers in comparison with manual workers and skilled tradesmen, and an appropriate standard of comfort "representing the social stratum to which the professional man should belong." Booklets on "The Education of Professional Engineers in Australia" and "The Development of the Content of Professional Engineering Courses 1918-1958" were produced by the association and many distinguished professors and other professional men gave evidence on the nature of the work of the professional engineer. One of these professors of engineering had previously qualified as a barrister and gave evidence of the comparative difficulty of the two disciplines. A neuro-surgeon and a physician, both previously engineers, gave similar comparative evidence in relation to the professions of engineering and medicine. The Association of Professional Engineers conducted a comprehensive survey into salaries and living standards of engineers in 1955 in which it obtained 6,500 returns. A sample of 1,000 of these returns was analyzed and the result submitted to the tribunal in an attempt to show that current salary levels were producing an "unprofessional standard of living."

Although the association did not succeed in its full claim, the tribunal did award substantial increases for the qualified engineer with a university degree or technical college diploma. Employers, however, were very slow to give consequential increases to engineers above the level of the so-called "experienced engineer" who had had a number of years' experience following his initial professional qualification. The case relating to the salaries of more senior engineers was therefore brought before the tribunal following the failure of attempts to negotiate agreements with major government employers of engineers. Some gains were made when the decision was made in 1962 but it is still too early to determine the full effect of the engineers' award. The cost of the proceedings and campaign to the Association of Professional Engineers has been reputed to be £50,000.

The extent to which the Engineers' Award will set a pattern for the consideration of the work value of other professional groups cannot yet be assessed. In its judgment, the tribunal stated that it was not concerned to make a detailed assessment of the work of various professions and to arrange them in a hierarchy of relative values. In coming to the conclusion that professional engineers had been substantially underpaid it expressed no view on salaries of other professions, either in themselves or relative to the salaries of professional engineers. It stated that there was "no sound ground for the belief that there should be a consequential review of the remuneration of other employees whether professional, executive, or clerical and even though, in the case of professionals, employed on similar work."[19] Other classes of employees were to be required to make claims for salary increases depending on proper proof of the value of their own work as they would not apparently be entitled to make comparisons with the work of engineers the main basis of their case. When a public service union presented a case for increased salaries for scientific officers in 1962 it was held that this union could not rely on the rates awarded in the Engineers' Case as any guide for the purposes of the scientific officers, despite the fact that the case claimed to be based on the work value of the scientific officer. In fact, the union tried to avoid comparing scientists with engineers and the whole case was decided without reference to the engineers. In 1962 the Commonwealth Legal Professional Officers' Association brought a work value case which made extensive reference to the Engineers' Case and it clearly was based on a desire of the legal officers in the Commonwealth Public Service to restore the relationship of their salaries to that which they had previously had with the salaries of engineers in that service. This association, like the Association of Professional Engineers, brought a great deal of evidence from professors and leading members of their profession to try to establish the value of the work done by legal officers, the difficulty of their course of training and so on. In his decision the Public Service Arbitrator said, "It is evident that certain of the factors affecting the decision in the Professional Engineers Case are appropriate to a consideration of Legal Officers and, no doubt, other professional officers, but it is just as evident that other factors can have no bearing. Further, where there are common factors, the weight to be applied may differ materially."

The whole concept of "work value" in Australian wage-fixing by arbitration tribunals is confused and complicated and the approach of the various tribunals has differed at various times.[20] Obviously,

[19] Commonwealth Arbitration and Conciliation Commission Judgment (Print A.7855), p. 96.

[20] See J. R. Kerr, "Work Value," Presidential Address to the Industrial Relations Society (Sydney: August 14, 1963), 18 pp. (mimeo.).

some of these tribunals have endeavored to formulate decisions and principles underlying such decisions in a way that will minimize the repercussive effect of the engineers' and other work value awards upon the salary claims of white-collar workers in other professions. All the experience of the working of the Australian industrial relations system, however, suggests that the tribunals' attempts to avoid repercussive effects will be doomed to failure, although they may succeed in slowing down the spread of wage movements arising from such decisions. The federal tribunals' decision on the work value of the professional engineer was undoubtedly of great significance for the future of salary fixation of the white-collar group, even though it may take years before its repercussions have made their impact on the whole of the white-collar working population.

As noted above, the white-collar unions have always been concerned not only to maintain the position of the white-collar worker in the community structure of economic reward, but also, particularly in the public services, to exert some degree of control over managerial powers in promotions and transfers. Their efforts to achieve this objective have taken two main forms. One is the traditional trade-union attempt to establish a seniority rule in promotions (and also in retrenchments) and the other is the attempt to set up tripartite machinery before which the claims of individual officers could be argued by the union and perhaps by legal counsel. On the whole, the white-collar unions have been very successful within the government sector in their attempts to penetrate the managerial function in this respect. Of the 50 unions included in the survey referred to above, 27 report that they operate under a tripartite Promotions Appeals Tribunal and 22 report that they work with a seniority rule for promotions, without any promotions appeal machinery.

Promotions appeal machinery is practically entirely restricted to the government sector, but seniority has been accepted in agreements in some other industries. Usually, the seniority rule relating to promotions provides that, where other considerations are equal, the more senior officer shall have preference. The effect of such a rule is to throw the onus on management to prove that one officer is more efficient or more suited to the job than another. Before such tribunals, unions have tried to argue that an officer is entitled to a trial in the job carrying higher responsibility provided his efficiency in the lower job has been at least equal to that of his rivals. The appeals tribunals have not usually accepted this line of argument where they were convinced that the management had good reasons for its view that the less senior officer would be more efficient in the post carrying higher responsibilities.

The growth of such tripartite machinery and the acceptance of seniority are natural concomitants of the acceptance of unions in the government sector and of the relatively harmonious negotiation which takes place between the unions and those charged with the management of government departments and agencies. A very small proportion of promotions has been upset by such tribunals, but the existence of the tribunals leads those responsible for promotions to make sure of their ground before acting.

In addition to tripartite appeals boards, white-collar unions, especially government unions, have sought to establish broader formal joint consultative machinery. In the Commonwealth Public Service, one of the major ventures in joint consultative machinery in Australia has developed in the form of the Joint Advisory Council on which representatives of the Public Service Union meet with representatives of the Commonwealth Public Service Board, to discuss various aspects of employment. This body does not negotiate agreements or awards but it provides a convenient setting in which such issues may be discussed without prejudice to actual proceedings before an arbitrator. In the Australian industrial environment, where experiments in joint consultative machinery are almost unknown, the existence of this rather elaborate joint consultative procedure stands out as unusual. Again, special features are no doubt responsible for its being established in government employment.

PROSPECTS FOR WHITE-COLLAR UNIONISM

It was suggested above that in Australia unionism among white-collar workers grows fairly easily once a "union attitude" develops. The critical factor in the future prospects of white-collar unions in this country will therefore be the extent to which such a union attitude grows among the white-collar workers. The growth of such an attitude will be affected by the extent to which the forces of supply and demand change the white-collar workers' relative position in the community, the impact of technological change, and the vigor and efficiency of the white-collar unions themselves.

The heterogeneity of the white-collar workforce makes it difficult to assess the strength of supply and demand in this labor market. Hughes and Rawson [21] have estimated that the ratio of white-collar

[21] H. Hughes and D. W. Rawson, "Collective Bargaining and the White-Collar Pay Structure," *Journal of Industrial Relations,* II (1960), 75-89.

workers to manual workers rose slowly by five per cent between 1921 and 1946, and conclude that white-collar employment has not expanded very much as a proportion of the work force since 1946. Government agencies have tended to meet any shortage of suitably qualified staff by dropping entrance standards rather than bidding up salaries, and the supply of persons educated for white-collar occupations has been rising steadily.

Demand for white-collar workers will be affected by the growth of industries employing a large amount of clerical labor and by technological changes affecting the amount of clerical labor in these and other industries. If the trend of the last 30-35 years persists, the former factor is not likely to produce a dramatic increase in demand.

Technological changes, insofar as they affect office work, will probably weaken the demand for less skilled white-collar workers and increase the demand for professionally trained staff. As Hughes and Rawson point out, Australian industry tends to be technologically dependent upon overseas countries and this limits the demand in private industry for the technically qualified white-collar workers needed to develop new technologies. A higher proportion of research is carried on in government agencies than in some countries, and this should favor unionization.

Overseas research [22] on the impact of automation on office work suggests that in general it tends to make office work more like factory work. Shift work tends to develop, and while many routine clerical jobs are eliminated, the jobs that remain demand more precision, more adherence to deadlines and quality standards, greater interdependence on one another's work, and more accountability for errors. Promotional ladders are disrupted, with some rungs in middle management disappearing. These changes increase with the increasing degree of automation. In general, these changes may be expected to encourage a union attitude, with office workers turning to unions to protect them from the impact of technical changes of a magnitude which the present generation of office workers has not previously experienced.

While automation may not proceed so far in industry in Australia as in countries with larger manufacturing potential, it appears likely to extend widely in clerical work.[23] Further growth of unions among white-collar workers in private industry thus seems fairly certain.

[22] See F. C. Mann, in *Automation and Technological Change,* J. T. Dunlop, ed. (Englewood Cliffs, N.J.: Prentice-Hall, 1962), chap. 3.
[23] See K. J. Creek, "Electronic Computers in Australia: Employment and Personnel Aspects. I. Extent of Use of Computers," *Personnel Practice Bulletin,* Vol. XVIII, No. 3 (1962), pp. 29-37.

A final factor in the growth of white-collar unionism will be the extent to which the unions themselves can make membership attractive to white-collar workers who begin to consider the desirability of joining a union. It seems that the unions will have to project an image of respectability, embodying some of the traditional middle class attitudes, if they are to increase their appeal to some types of white-collar workers. In view of the heterogeneous character of the white-collar group and their relative commitment to their jobs, the union appeal may have to be aimed very specifically at the interests and objectives of particular classes of employees. The tendency for professional workers to form their own unions and their own interunion bodies has already been mentioned, and even within a general professional union such as the Commonwealth Professional Officers' Association, members of individual professions have found the need to organize their own groups. Whether such needs will lead to the growth of further professional unions will depend on the members in various professional groups and on the extent to which the general professional unions cater to their needs.

There seems little doubt that there will be opportunities for vigorous unions to capitalize on the dissatisfaction of particular groups of white-collar workers. Such opportunities will arise when major technological changes affect substantial numbers of office workers, or where the salaries and conditions of a particular group are allowed to deteriorate markedly in relation to the rest of the community. (Hughes and Rawson give the example of nurses working under the New South Wales Hospitals Commission whose number doubled between 1946 and 1956 but whose relative salaries fell from 220 per cent to 150 per cent of the female basic wage. Interest by nurses in salaries and conditions has traditionally been regarded as "unprofessional," but such a situation appears to offer an opportunity to astute union leadership.)

It should be noted, however, that many of the younger white-collar workers will not be much disturbed by a relative decline in salaries. These are the ones who would not have obtained white-collar jobs at all had they been in the labor market a generation ago. They have had better educational opportunities than their manual worker parents and have been able to take advantage of such opportunities more readily because their parents have had more continuous and better paid employment while the children were of school age. These "newly arrived" white-collar workers may be too pleased with their own upward occupational and social mobility to worry about a relative decline in salaries compared with 10-15 years or more ago. Against this, their parents' identification with the working class and trade unionism may be strong enough to influence these new white-collar workers towards unionism.

It seems unlikely that Australian white-collar unions will become more strongly identified with the Labour Party unless that party moves further to the center and develops very specific appeal to the white-collar worker. In recent years the nonlabor parties have been able to meet any challenge in this direction by offering similar benefits and appealing to the conservatism of the middle class.

If Australian society becomes more and more affluent, and more bourgeois in outlook, manual unions may shrink in social importance and the white-collar unions may be cast in a more crucial social role.

WHITE-COLLAR UNIONS IN AUSTRIA

BY ERNST LAKENBACHER

AUSTRIA AND ITS WORKING POPULATION

The Republic of Austria was all that remained of the Austrian-Hungarian monarchy after it was divided following World War I. At the present time, the Austrian Republic is only slightly larger than the state of Maine, 83,849 square kilometers; it is divided into nine autonomous provinces. This area is inhabited by 7,067,432 people (census of March 1961) which just about corresponds to the population of the state of Michigan.

A comparison of the census figures for 1934 (6,730,233) and 1951 (6,933,905) indicates a relatively insignificant six per cent increase in total population. On the other hand, more significant changes are evident when the figures for number of persons dependent upon various branches of the economy are compared. In 1934 that part of the population receiving its livelihood in agriculture and forestry (self-employed as well as those employed and the family members they support) numbered 1,842,450, or 27 per cent of the total population. In 1951,[1] only 1,515,945 people belonged to this category, or not quite 22 per cent. On the other hand, the number of persons earning a

[1] The 1951 statistics have to be used since the results of the census taken in 1961 had not been compiled at the time of writing.

livelihood in industry and trade increased from 2,100,461 (1934) to 2,585,587 (1951), or from 32 to 37 per cent.

The statistics of the social security agency, which in Austria covers all workers, employees, and civil service personnel in private as well as public employment, indicate that the trends mentioned above have continued at an even more rapid pace. Austria is involved in a process of continued industrialization with an accompanying increase in the number of employees in trade and service jobs. In 1951 a total of 128,344 people (workers and employees) were employed in trade; by 1960 this number had increased to 214,607, or 67 per cent. In other service jobs the numbers of employees increased from 293,900 to 392,225, or 34 per cent, in the same span of time.

THE EMPLOYEE IN THE AUSTRIAN EMPLOYEE MOVEMENT

The problem of defining "employees"[2] consists in differentiating them from workers. At first employees were thought of as "intellectual" workers as opposed to "manual" workers, but the Austrian employee movement early encountered a few experiences in regard to the intellectual work as the mark for differentiation which advised against the further use of this distinction.

The first special law for private employees, the pension insurance law of December 16, 1906, defines as in need of insurance all those employed, "who either have, depending on their position, a *Beamte* character or do regularly perform mainly intellectual work." The decision about what is to be considered intellectual work was up to the administrative court which has jurisdiction over appeals regarding the interpretation of laws by the administration.

In a basic decision,[3] the administrative court arrived at a not unexpected formulation. In essence it claims that the manual worker cannot do his work entirely without "a certain help of his intellectual

[2] The word "white-collar worker" has no completely adequate translation in Austrian terminology. In the following study the workers who are its subject will be called "employees." We will differentiate between those "privately employed" and those "publicly employed." The latter are usually called "civil servants" (*Beamte*). In linguistic usage, some categories of the privately employed are also called *Beamte* (those working in banks and insurance companies, for example) because the employment guarantees of these privately employed categories are very similar to those of the publicly employed.

[3] Decision of the VGH (Verwaltunsgerichtshof—Administrative Court) of May 20, 1910, No. 4160, cited in Dr. Hubert Korkisch, *Kommentar zum Pensionsversicherungsgesetz; Verlag Manz* (Vienna, 1915), pp. 130-31.

capacities" and that "intellectual work hardly ever occurs without any physical participation." For instance: Do clerks in retail stores perform mostly intellectual tasks? No. In general, the waiting on customers involves "physical labor," but "knowledge of the merchandise, foreign languages, skill, etc., . . . should be classified as intellectual services."

It lists further as not eligible for insurance—clerks in book stores, cashiers in retail stores, persons working with the stocks of a certain commodity, and finally also some of the categories of supervisors.

In the mind of the employees of all categories as well as in the mind of the public, there has never been any doubt that clerks are employees. At the time of the judgment they represented the largest group of employees and were most active especially during the development of the employee union movement. If the interpretation of "mostly intellectual services" had remained a criterion for being classified as an employee, then two groups would have emerged. This development was avoided when a new law was enacted, setting equal minima to be observed regarding wages and working conditions of all employees.

When the law on wages and working conditions was codified in the "law concerning the service contracts of employees in trade and other workers in like positions" of January 16, 1910, the effect on the pension insurance law could be anticipated. Under the influence of the by then active employees' trade union and a strong social-democratic parliamentary party—elected on the basis of general and equal suffrage—this law was to govern "the service relationship of persons who were employed in the business of a merchant [and in a number of other "businesses," listed in the law] and will to a large extent be asked to perform commercial or higher non-commercial services or office duties." This definition has proven itself. The experiences of half a century have confirmed that it includes all persons who are thought of as employees by the trade unions. Finally, the range of the pension insurance of the employees was extended to include them. There remains no more doubt as to who belongs to the employee group in Austria, either in questions related to the unions or in the law.

The dominant unions among Austrian employees before 1934, to which the majority of organized employees belonged, were organizationally and ideologically closely associated with manual labor. They belonged to the same union federation and were pledged to socialism, as were other unions in the federation. In 1945 the union movement was reorganized on a new basis, combining all political currents in one labor federation. The employees' trade union in private enterprise is affiliated with the new federation, and it is again largely under socialistic leadership.

Among the civil servants of the First Republic (1918-34) there also existed organizations with the character of trade unions, some of which were affiliated with the federation of the free trade unions of workers and employees, and some which kept their distance. In the Second Republic (since 1945) the trade unions of the civil servants belong to the unified trade-union center, the Austrian Federation of Labor.

STATISTICS OF EMPLOYEES AND CIVIL SERVANTS IN THE ECONOMY

Just as in all other countries where industry is developing rapidly and is accompanied by an equally rapid expansion of trade and service occupations, the employees and civil servants are growing more numerous within the Austrian labor force. Table 1 summarizes findings of the occupational census, which, in Austria, is taken following the overall census. The table clearly indicates the increase in the number and proportion of employees and civil servants.

Table 1. Employees and Civil Servants Within the Austrian Labor Force

Year	*Labor Force* [a]	*Employees and Civil Servants*	*Index of the Increase of Employees and Civil Servants*	*Percentage of the Employees and Civil Servants Within the Labor Force*
1923	2,684,773	329,693	100	12⅓
1934	2,590,984	470,473	143	18⅙
1951	2,754,062	674,693	205	24½

[a] The number of employed persons is stated after "helping family members" have been subtracted. Over nine-tenths of the latter are working on farms. The occupational census includes those unemployed. They have been entered according to their last job. Apprentices in trade were added to the employees and civil servants since they are being prepared for work in these categories. In 1923 they numbered: 11,692; 1934: 10,234; 1951: 11,923.

Source: *Statistische Handbücher für Österreich* (Vienna: Verlag der Österreichischen Staatsdruckerei, 1928, 1935, and 1953).

Even though the criteria for classifying employees in the categories of the civil servants and employees were different for each of the three occupational censuses, Table 1 nevertheless pictures the trend of the development correctly. Employees and civil servants made up one-eighth of the labor force in 1923; the number increased so much within a quarter of a century that in 1951 they represented one-fourth of the entire labor force. Between 1923 and 1951 their number more than doubled while the size of the labor force changed hardly at all. Even the insignificant increase in the labor force of 1951 over 1923, following the decrease in 1934, can be accounted for by the increase in the number of employees and civil servants. If the latter

Table 2.[a] Employees, Civil Servants, and Workers in Various Branches of the Economy

Branch	*Findings of the Occupational Census (1934, 1951)*		*People Who Work, According to the Statistics of the Association of the Austrian Social Insurance Institutes (1951, 1960)*	
	Employees and Civil Servants			
	1934	*1951*	*1951*	*1960*
Agriculture and forestry	11,484	9,464	7,913	9,668
Mining, industry, handicrafts	104,241	145,359	127,791	188,479
Trade, transportation, banking, insurance	178,913	245,224	192,124	282,819
Other service jobs	100,872	129,686	43,959	68,122
Public service	56,474	131,187	225,036	257,779
Total	451,984	660,930	596,823	806,867
	Workers			
	1934	*1951*	*1951*	*1960*
Agriculture and forestry	348,000	219,371	217,325	133,282
Mining, industry, handicrafts	781,483	951,796	900,286	1,009,972
Trade, transportation, banking, insurance	125,623	89,310	103,581	124,841
Other service jobs	112,475	113,753	82,080	131,060
Public service	63,426	16,016	57,640	51,568
Total	1,431,007	1,390,246	1,360,912	1,450,673

Sources: The findings of the occupational census are taken from the *Statistische Handbücher für Österreich* (Vienna: Verlag der Österreichischen Staatsdruckerei, 1935 and 1953); the statistics of the Association of Austrian Social Insurance Institutes are taken from *Wirtschaftsstatistisches Handbuch 1960* (Vienna: Chamber of Labor, 1961).

[a] This table calls for some comments. (Continued on page 42.)

number is subtracted from the total labor force, a decrease from 2,355,080 to 2,079,369 persons over the 28-year period can be noted.

How employees and civil servants are distributed among the various branches of the economy can be seen in Table 2. The figures from the occupational census of the year 1923 cannot be used since entire groups of employees (e.g., supervisors in some industries such as textiles, and clerks in other industries such as retail trade) were not counted as employees but rather as workers.

The findings of the occupational census of 1961 have not been compiled as of the time of writing this report. Even so it is possible to follow the development up to the present. The entire labor force—workers, employees, and civil servants—is registered by the Health Insurance of Austria since every person working in any capacity is by law subject to health insurance. The statistics of employed and there-

1. Workers and employees (the number of the latter is rather small) employed in households and related jobs and the employees and workers in cases where it was impossible to determine their specific branch have not been included in this table.
2. For the year 1951 the figures had to be listed twice on the basis of the occupational census and the statistics of the Association of Austrian Social Insurance Institutes. For a number of reasons these two statistical compilations do not agree. The most important causes are:

A. The occupational census also includes the unemployed; they are listed according to their last occupation. The statistics of the social insurance count only the employed.

B. The occupational census does not differentiate strictly between persons publicly and privately employed. Only those employees and civil servants listed under the heading "Public Service" in the occupational census are without exception public employees. In all other branches of the economy the *Beamte* and employees are listed together. In the branch "trade and transportation" there appear the civil servants who work for federal and municipal communication systems such as railroad, streetcar, post office, telephone, and telegraph; the *Beamte* of federal monopolies such as tobacco and salt are classified under "mining, industry, handicrafts." The yearbook for 1933-35 of the Chamber of Labor in Vienna lists 176,893 public employees, three times as many as the occupational census in 1934. Nearly all public employees are combined under "Public Service" in the statistics of the social insurance, since they have special social insurance institutes and can therefore be registered separately.

3. Noticeable also in the occupational census is the apparently great change in the number of persons classified as civil servants and workers in public service in 1934 and in 1951. This can be explained by the fact that many persons in public service were classified as workers in 1934, but in 1951, according to changed legislation, they were on equal status with the civil servants and therefore included in that category in the statistics.
4. The division of the working force into employees and workers is more precise in the statistics of the social insurance than in the occupational census since the employees and workers belong to different insurance institutes. At the time of application the decision has to be made whether the person employed is to be classified as a worker or employee. The application has to be signed by the employer as well as the person being employed and is also submitted to the works council of the workers or employees for review. Since belonging to the social insurance institute for employees involves benefits in service and social insurance which do not apply to workers, the employees are concerned about being registered with the proper institute. On the other hand, it is the employer who sees to it that workers are not registered with the social insurance institute for employees. If no agreement as to the proper institute can be reached, the administration will decide the case, which can be appealed to the administrative court.
5. The occupational census lists apprentices separately. In Table 2 apprentices in trade and communications, who are being trained for vocations as employees, were added to the number of employees, but apprentices in all other branches were included in the figures for workers, as is generally done in the statistics of social insurance.

fore insured workers, kept by the Association of Austrian Social Insurance Institutes, divides those insured according to the different branches of the economy on the one hand and classifies them as workers, employees, or civil servants on the other.

In 1934, the year of the last occupational census before the occupation of Austria by German troops, the crisis in the economy of the country, which had started in 1929, still prevailed. On the average there were 405,745 unemployed[4] registered with the employment offices; about 200,000 unemployed persons who had not been registered could be added to this total. In the figures of the occupational census the unemployment rate is not noticeable since even the unemployed are classified according to the last jobs they performed. In addition, however, and not included in the figures were thousands of young people who could not find jobs after finishing their education.

Between 1938 and 1945, the time of the German occupation, the administration made numerous changes in the economy to eliminate inefficient small businesses and to encourage development of industry. This proved profitable for Austria after the liberation of the country. Help through the Marshall Plan started pouring into Austria in 1948. The reconstruction of industries that had been destroyed during the war—mainly heavy industry, as well as the transportation and communication systems—advanced rapidly. As a result, in October 1951, the year of the first occupational census in the Second Republic, the highest number of employed persons (workers and employees including civil servants) since 1918 was reached—a total of 2,050,000.

Employees benefited especially from this development. As can be seen in Table 2, the number of employees and civil servants rose during the years 1934-51 from 451,984 to 660,930, an increase of 208,946 or 46 per cent. The number of workers did not change.[5] Average unemployment during 1951 was only 117,500; of these 17,800 were employees.[6]

From 1951 until the present day, except for 1952 and 1953, Austria has experienced a boom leading to a complete exhaustion of the available labor reserves. In 1960 only 87,196 unemployed were registered, among them, on the average, 11,231 employees. This average

[4] *Wirtschaftsstatistisches Jahrbuch 1933-35* (Vienna: Chamber of Labor, 1935).
[5] The decline in the number of workers which appears in Table 2 can be explained by the classification of workers and employees in public services and federal communication services.
[6] *Wirtschaftsstatistisches Handbuch 1960* (Vienna: Chamber of Labor, yearly).

quota of unemployed results mainly from seasonal unemployment during the winter months (December-March) in agriculture, construction, and tourist trade.

According to the statistics of the Association of Austrian Social Insurance Institutes, which records only those actually working, the number of employees rose between 1951 and 1960 from 596,823 to 806,857, an increase of 210,034 or 35 per cent. The number of workers rose 6.6 per cent during the same period.

The increase in the number of employees and civil servants from census to census represents a real increase only insofar as employees are concerned. The jump in the number of civil servants in public services from 1934 to 1951, however, constitutes only partly real growth. As already mentioned, it is due to the transfer of people working for the state from the category of workers to that of civil servants. The growth in the number of employees changes drastically the ratio between workers and employees as can be noted in Table 3.

***Table** 3.* Employees per 1,000 Workers

	According to Occupational Census		*According to Social Insurance Statistics*	
	1934	*1951*	*1951*	*1960*
In all branches of the economy	316	457	439	556
In mining, industry, and handicrafts	103	153	142	187
In trade, transportation, and communication	1424	2764 [a]	1855	2265

[a] This growth, too, is in part due to the change of categories of those employed in public transportation. How noticeable this regrouping is can be seen by comparing the number of employees and civil servants in trade, transportation, banking, and insurance during the occupational census in 1951 (245,224) with their number in the statistics of the social insurance (192,124). In the latter the civil servants in the federal transportation industry are not listed in the column "trade, transportation, etc.," but rather under the heading "public service."

When using these figures one has to keep in mind that between 1934 and 1951 there is a span of seventeen years, but between 1951 and 1960 only nine, just about half as many. Yet in the most important branch of the economy—mining, industry, and handicrafts—the proportion of employees rose 50 units during the seventeen-year period and in the following nine-year period just about as much—45 units. This means that the proportion of employees grows more and more rapidly with the progress of time.

The increase in the number of employees during the period 1951-60, but not from 1934 to 1950, was obtained, as shown in Table 4, by a comparatively rapid increase in the number of women working as employees. It should be mentioned that in the occupational census taken in 1934, 151,978 of the total of 451,984 employees and civil servants were women; this amounts to 33.8 per cent. Table 4 shows that in 1951 only 32.2 per cent of the employees were women, a decrease. In 1960 female participation amounted to 37.7 per cent.

Table 4. Employees in Austria According to Sex

Year	*Total*	*Men*	*Women*
		Employees and Civil Servants	
1951	596,823	404,714	192,109
1960	806,867	502,541	304,326
Increase	210,044	97,827	112,217
		Workers	
1951	1,360,912	964,124	396,788
1960	1,450,673	989,167	461,506
Increase	89,761	25,043	64,718

Source: *Wirtschaftsstatistisches Handbuch 1960* (Vienna: Chamber of Labor, yearly).

From 1951 to 1960 the number of women employees increased by 58 per cent; the number of the male employees increased only 24 per cent. The increase at the worker level was also notably higher for women than for men, 16 per cent as compared to 2.6 per cent, but both remained considerably behind the rate of increase for employees.

THE RE-ESTABLISHMENT OF THE UNION FOR PRIVATE EMPLOYEES IN LIBERATED AUSTRIA

On April 10, 1945, troops of the Russian Marshal Tolbuchin entered the outer districts of Vienna. This event marked the beginning of the fight for liberation of the Austrian capital which was occupied by specially selected SS troops. The struggle lasted for several days, and at one time there was danger that large districts of the badly destroyed city might be recaptured. On April 13, while the fighting was still going on, five Socialist leaders of the dissolved free unions met in private quarters to discuss the re-establishment of the union movement. One of them was Anton Gottlieb, representative for the employees and former leader of the *Zentralverein der kaufmännischen Angestellten Österreichs* (Central Association of Commercial Employees in Austria). Representatives of the Communist and Christian workers' organizations, with whom there had already been some contact during the resistance movement, were included in later meetings.

The free unions began their reconstruction by taking over the basic ideas of the illegal unions which functioned during the war years. In place of the pre-1934 strict craft and political orientation, which divided the movement into numerous politically split trade groups, the new movement was to build upon the concept of politically independent unions divided into branch organizations. In their relations with the government, the unions would represent the members' interests in economic and social affairs; in relations with employers, they would represent the workers on wage issues.

In the beginning it was impossible for the members to elect leaders since there were no members yet. They had to be recruited first. But there were leaders known to the workers and employees from the past who still enjoyed their confidence, and above all there were the previously illegal shop stewards in the factories. About these Klenner reports:

> During the entire time of the fascist regime there had been illegal leaders working in all sizable organizations, besides the officially appointed leaders. And it was the former who had been the real shop stewards. They had the guiding influence, and to them the workers turned for advice and council. Unnoticed, they held all the strings in their hands, guided the actions, and kept alive the hope for the renewal of democracy. In April, 1945, the illegal union members re-appeared. . . . The appearance of the union members provided direction and a goal for the workers.[7]

Whenever possible these shop stewards were included in the rapid succession of conferences which had the re-establishment of the unions as their goal. It was these shop stewards who endorsed the leaders in their positions or elected them to their posts.

Gradually the different "sections" of the union were established: commercial, industrial employees, those in banks and savings institutions, social insurance, and insurance companies, etc.

In the course of the following three years all branch unions of the new Austrian Trade Union Federation conducted legal elections of their top leaders. The first Congress of the Austrian Trade Union Federation met from May 18 to 23, 1948.

[7] Fritz Klenner, *Die Österreichischen Gewerkschaften,* II (Vienna: Verlag des Österreichischen Gewerkschaftsbundes, 1953), 1597.

At the first Congress, the chairman of the Austrian Trade Union Federation (ÖGB—Österreichischer Gewerkschaftsbund) at that time, Johann Böhm, spoke about "organizational tasks of the Trade Union Federation" among which he briefly mentioned the recruitment of private employees. He pointed out that the Trade Union Federation had as one of its goals the realization of the principle of organization according to industrial groups. Naturally this goal could not be completely realized in 1945; for organizational purposes exceptions had to be allowed. "For instance, we agreed that the private employees were better combined in one of their own organizations than divided into various industrial unions." [8] This sensible point of view of the founders and leaders of the unions of manual workers provided the impetus for the union of the private employees after 1945.

New systems of organization were introduced throughout the branches affiliated with the Austrian Trade Union Federation (ÖGB). In the white-collar field, the new system involved the establishment of a unified trade union.

Prior to 1934, the occupation of the employees was the organizational principle of the employees' trade union. At the time of their dissolution in 1935 there existed seven such unions: commercial, industrial, insurance, banking, social insurance, press, and printers.

The Austrian Trade Union Federation (ÖGB), formed by sixteen trade-union branches, was established as a largely centralized organization. This kind of organization was made possible by the fact that in the vacuum left by the National Socialist dictatorship, the trade-union movement had to be rebuilt from the ground up. It is organized according to the principle that related branches of industry can be combined into one industrial group; thus sixteen industrial unions replaced the fifty occupational groups that had existed prior to 1934. Now in every firm there is one trade union which represents the interests of all those employed in the same firm without regard to their professional status. For instance, the leather workers, paper hangers, and carpenters who are employed in an automobile factory belong to the metal workers' union which represents the firm. There is only one exception to this principle; in private industries, the employees do not belong to the industrial organizations but rather to the trade union for all private employees.

This rigid centralization extends to the internal organization. The separate unions are actually only branch offices of the top organiza-

[8] *Ibid.*, p. 1638.

tion, the ÖGB, which alone has authority as far as the law is concerned. The ÖGB decides on the constitution of the various trade unions. It employs the people who work for them and assigns their duties. The various trade unions can sign contracts with the employer only in the name of the ÖGB, and the ÖGB decides on union policies to which the unions are subject. The membership fee has to be transmitted to the ÖGB, which decides what portion the various unions can retain.

The highest court of the trade-union movement is the Congress of the Austrian Trade Union Federation, which convenes every four years and is composed of delegates of all trade unions. The Congress of the Austrian Trade Union Federation elects the executive committee which guides and directs the affairs of the ÖGB. The committee names the secretaries of the Federation. Every four years, prior to the meeting of the Congress, the sixteen trade unions hold their meetings, at which time the executive committees for the various trade unions are elected.

The Trade Union Federation is a nonpolitical organization which serves workers, employees, and civil servants without regard to their political affiliation. Outside the Trade Union Federation there remains only one organization, that of agriculture, which is thought of as a "yellow" organization by the Federation.[9] Each Austrian political party forms its own unit within the Trade Union Federation, and membership on the executive committee of the ÖGB and of its sixteen member unions is apportioned according to the strength of the political party.[10]

Table 5 shows the membership of the sixteen trade unions.

At the time these membership figures were compiled, there were 2,377,806 Austrian workers registered with the health insurance organization.[11] According to those figures, about 64 per cent of all working people are members of the ÖGB.

The reorganization left only one trade union of the employees in private industries (*Gewerkschaft der Angestellten in der Privatswirtschaft,* GAP). This implied the rejection of an organizational arrange-

[9] The term "yellow" means in Austrian labor parlance roughly the same as "company union" in the U.S.

[10] The apportionment is determined by the result of the elections to the Chamber of Labor. At the last election (1959), the candidates of the Austrian Socialist Party received 74 per cent of the votes, the Austrian People's Party (Catholic-conservative) 13.9 per cent, the Communists 7.3 per cent, the Austrian Liberty Party (German nationalist) 2.9 per cent, and those free of all party ties 2 per cent of the votes.

[11] *Wirtschaftsstatistisches Handbuch, 1962* (Vienna: Chamber of Labor, yearly), p. 86.

Table 5. Trade-Union Members, December 31, 1962

Trade Union	*Membership*	
	Total	*Women*
Employees in private businesses	239,548	104,815
Public employees	118,017	36,262
Municipal employees	119,771	40,640
Art and free professions	16,142	5,203
Construction and wood workers	189,794	7,108
Workers of the chemical industry	66,055	17,342
Railroad workers	123,616	6,606
Graphic and paper handicrafts	25,869	8,855
Workers in trade, transportation, and communication	25,913	7,198
Workers in the hotel and tourist trade	14,502	8,968
Workers in agriculture and forestry	56,531	13,601
Workers in foods and delicacies	58,375	21,633
Workers in metal and mining industries	285,870	46,831
Workers in textile, garments, and leather industries	102,804	74,302
Post and telegraph employees	51,641	10,667
Workers for personal services	23,678	22,205
ÖGB Total	1,518,096	432,146

Source: *Wirtschaftsstatistisches Handbuch 1962* (Vienna: Chamber of Labor, yearly), pp. 154-55.

ment which had been of great importance in the former separate occupational associations, based upon loyalty to the occupational group. This feeling had been strong in some professions, especially among persons working for banks and insurance companies.

There is no doubt that the new organizational form presents advantages so noticeable that some disadvantages have to be accepted. On the administrative side there is the advantage of the big organization as opposed to a small one; the unified trade union can make use of all modern facilities in administration which would remain out of reach for the various small organizations. The large organization has financial resources, enabling it to establish some welfare programs for its members which naturally add to the attractiveness of the trade union. Some of these welfare programs involve vacation and recuperation homes; an effective home-building producers' cooperative; qualitative, high-level cultural activities (theater tickets at very reduced prices); occupational and general education courses; recreational facilities; trade-union establishments; and similar benefits. As far as trade-union functions are concerned, the unified organization constitutes an impressive force much regarded by the public, thus bestowing benefits upon all occupations incorporated within it. It is not of little importance that the big trade union of employees constitutes an impressive proportion of the entire trade-union movement in which the extensive industrial branches of the workers dominate.

But there are also some disadvantages. Such a big organization produces, quite naturally, some red tape. It loosens the ties of the individual member to his union so that he feels robbed of any direct influence on its tactics and policies. The trade union concentrates upon maintaining contact with the shop stewards. Thus, there arises a certain estrangement of the members who tend to see the organization as an institution similar to the social security institutes which owe them a certain service for the membership fee they pay.

The second principle which found realization within the GAP, as in the ÖGB, is political independence. Basically the trade unions of the ÖGB are not united through common political and social views; workers and employees of all political persuasions are represented. In the workers' trade unions, however, where there is a strong representation of Socialist members, the ideological tradition of the free trade unions remains alive to a high degree; political independence is much more apparent within the ranks of the GAP because of the rather sizable group of Christian employees, and far stronger, though not organized, group of employees without any political ties who demand some consideration.[12]

As far as the employees' trade union is concerned renunciation of the strong ties which the closed political community represents is balanced by an expansion of the scope of the trade-union movement to include all employees without regard to the *Weltanschauung* and also by elimination of the discord between the free trade unions and the associations of employees whose religious and political views stood contrary to the free unions and impeded their progress prior to 1934. The GAP also benefits by the fact that it does not take a strong political stand in opposition to the organizations of the employers as the social-democratic free trade unions of the employees once did. The trade union has more or less ceased to be an organization of people with like mind. It is now an institution, especially in the case of the GAP, representing the social and economic interests of its members vis-à-vis the employers, or, if need be, the workers.

[12] The employees without party ties have no official representation within the governing body of the GAP, since they are not organized.

There was a strong temptation after 1945 not to establish a separate trade union for the private employees, but to observe strictly the principle of organization of industrial branches and to include the employees in the ten trade unions of the workers, according to the economic branches to which they belonged. The leaders of the ÖGB resisted this temptation, but not without a struggle. It took some persuasion to get them to recognize a need for a separate union of employees. The discussion about how the private employees should be classified dragged out until 1951. The end of the discussion came on February 15, 1951, when the executive of the ÖGB issued guidelines for the boundaries of the organization. They read:

1. The first principle for the organization of the trade unions is the organization of unified industrial branches.
2. Within the individual branches, the first principle is the uniform works organization. Until that goal is realized, only one trade union for the workers and one for the employees is permitted in a given firm. The decisive factor is that the industrial branch represents the majority of the people working for the firm.
3. The realization of these principles should be worked out step by step and in accordance with all unions concerned. If no agreement is possible, the decision rests with the executive committee of the federation.

There are still union members who view this decision as provisional and accept it for tactical reasons only. An expression of this view is the following comment in the official *Handbuch des Österreichischen Gewerkschaftsbundes*: [13]

The decision of the executive committee of the ÖGB provided an occasion for some employees to express themselves rather heatedly in the press. The goal of a common organization for employees and workers of one industrial branch is, of course, the most natural thing. Employed within the same firm, sometimes advanced from worker to employee, where would there be a reason for a special organization? The union for the municipal civil servants includes directors of the city of Vienna as well as all communal workers. Has that had any ill effects for anyone? In the last resort they are all protected by the same service law. And therefore hope exists that the step-by-step procedure of following the guidelines for the organizational division according to the principle of the branch organizations will prove itself advantageous for all union members and their organization.

The fact is, however, that the employees' union in private firms (GAP) has grown to be the second strongest among the sixteen trade unions which form the ÖGB and is only surpassed by the union of the

[13] *Handbuch des Österreichischen Gewerkschaftsbundes* by Anton Proksch, Generalsekretär of the ÖGB, Schriftenreihe des Österreichischen Gewerkschaftsbundes No. 2, second revised edition (Vienna: Publishing House of ÖGB, 1954). (Since 1956 Anton Proksch has been minister for social administration.)

metal and mining workers. The GAP has increased its membership during the ten years from 1951-60 from 144,400 to 217,926. On August 1, 1961, the statistics of the social security agency showed 446,864 employees in private firms. Thus, 49 per cent of all employees are organized in a trade union. Sooner or later GAP will also leave the metal workers' union behind as far as membership is concerned since it is apparent that the number of private employees increases faster than the number of workers. The practical view of the leaders of the ÖGB which led them to overcome their theoretical hesitation to set up a special organization of private employees has thus had good results.

An analysis of the number of employees registered with the social security agency shows that it includes many people who are registered as employees as far as the social security agency is concerned but who do not belong within the organizational framework of the GAP or who cannot be included. Several groups of employees in public service belong in the first category who, according to the law, are classified with the same health insurance group as the workers and employees of private firms to provide them, in the absence of another suitable insurance agency, with the services of pension, sickness, and accident insurance. The second group includes people in executive positions with considerable influence in the affairs of a firm—managers, directors, deputies, who are, according to the new social laws, excluded from the realm of the collective agreements. In this category belong also family members who help out in small businesses and often set up a working contract to insure themselves of the services of the social insurance. Finally there are persons whose employment is of a transitional character, like temporary help during vacation time, high school students, retired people, housewives, etc. If one could subtract the unknown figure of the organizationally unqualified people from the 446,864 insured, the percentage of union members among employees would rise considerably.

Within the organizational framework of the GAP are also the single employees of the small firms in handicrafts, trade, and transportation whose recruitment for the union is difficult. The recruitment of members for the trade unions is in the main the work of the shop stewards and work councils that have been elected according to the works council law (*Betriebrätegesetz*). Work councils, however, are elected in firms having at least 20 people regularly employed, including workers and employees. In firms having 5 to 19 employees, one or two shop stewards are elected. Therefore, employees working in firms with less than five employees are difficult to enroll.

The percentage of employees affiliated with trade unions varies, therefore, with the size of the firm. It is higher in large and medium-sized firms and becomes smaller as the size of the firm and the number of employees decreases. But there are also great differences among the various branches of the economy. Bank and insurance company employees are the most thoroughly organized. In banks organization amounts to about 80 per cent. Within the big banking and savings institutions with headquarters in Vienna, it amounts to 90 to 100 per cent. This percentage often declines with the size of the towns and in the co-op banks of the rural areas it is considerably lower. The concentration of personnel in the banking institutions of the federal capital creates a favorable climate for organization, while the isolation of employees in smaller local institutions is a hindering factor.

The industry and handicrafts section (handicrafts in Austria include mostly those smaller firms in which the work process is largely a manual operation) of the GAP estimates in its report to the fourth general meeting of the section in Vienna (June 1962) "that at the end of 1961 about 67 per cent of all eligible employees in industry and handicraft firms are members of our organization" and remarks, "We have, therefore, a comparatively much higher proportion of union members [in industry and handicrafts] than the trade-union movements in other European countries." The large nationalized industries of mining, chemical, and electrical industries have the highest percentage of organization. Next come the large firms of private industry. The least well organized are the handicraft firms, especially outside of larger cities, whose employees are difficult to organize from the administrative point of view. The GAP leaders have such an extensive work load in the larger firms that they cannot find time to do the time-consuming recruiting among the employees of the small firms which would be necessary to bring them into the fold.

The report of the GAP trade section at its fourth general meeting in Vienna (May 1962) includes an interesting statistical breakdown of firms according to the number of employees. The figures are particularly relevant to the problem of organizing employees of smaller firms. According to this report, in 1961 there were 37,782 trading firms which employed others in addition to the owner; 15,372 employed only one outside person (worker or employee); 15,121 employed two to five workers; 6,929 firms employed more than five. Only 84 firms employed 100 or more people. The report shows a total of 157,020 employees in trade for the year 1961, of which 30,330—just about one-fifth—were apprentices. At the end of 1961 the section had 59,619 members,

10,804 of them being minors. In private insurance companies there are two strictly divided groups of employees, one being the people working in offices and the other those working as salesmen or traveling representatives. The insurance office workers group is the best organized of the GAP and is also the most successful in collective bargaining. Membership in this group reaches 95-98 per cent, and includes officials of the highest ranks. It is noteworthy that the GAP insurance section continues uninterrupted the tradition of organization and loyal union membership which flourished among the free trade unions of the employees before 1934.

GAP leadership estimates that about 60 per cent of the potential members of the union are organized. This estimate is by no means exaggerated since the health insurance statistics show that of all employees registered, 49 per cent belong to a trade union. Such a high percentage has not been reached in any other country. This phenomenon calls for an examination of what special circumstances in Austria made this possible.

We find the starting point in the past. During the First Republic, before the crisis in the economy and political pressure reduced the number of union members, the free trade unions of Austrian employees were able to organize a far larger proportion of employees in their categories than the unions of other European countries.

During the time of the annexation of Austria to Germany, the employees, especially those in larger industries, were more or less forced into the *Deutsche Arbeitsfront* (DAF), the national-socialist substitute for unions. As paradoxical as it may seem, this organization in a sense left a heritage for the GAP. At the time of the postwar reestablishment of unions, leaders of GAP found large organized groups of employees, held together through membership in the DAF, and succeeded in taking them over. During the seven years of German occupation, the employees, including those rather unwilling to be organized, had become used to belonging to an organization and to regular payment of membership dues. Today the GAP leadership finds that the younger generation of employees who did not experience those occupation years are more difficult to win and retain as union members than the older ones.

In many firms during the Nazi period, employees continued to seek council from illegal shop stewards whose tenure could be traced to the days of the free trade unions. After the liberation, those "unofficial" shop leaders were in a position to take over the posts of the

DAF people, and they were the ones responsible for the establishment of the new trade unions in their respective firms.

The GAP was organized entirely by former leaders of the employees' free trade unions who started to work right after the liberation. These leaders had had to step aside in February 1934 when the free trade unions were dissolved, but they had never faltered in their resolution: "We are coming back!" When their moment came, they began with great enthusiasm to organize again a powerful employees' union, a task they had been planning for many years. Their enthusiasm was catching. Scattered in various firms were tens of thousands of employees who had participated in the earlier free trade-union movement and who had longed for its re-establishment for more than a decade. Now they formed the foundation of the new organization, determined to make it stronger, more closely knit, and larger than the one destroyed in 1934. The new movement, which included employees from all occupations, provided an impressive experience which received enthusiastic support.

The strength of the Austrian trade union of employees also has political connotations. Even without party ties, the trade-union movement has its strongest support from the Austrian Socialist Party (SPÖ). In a national election, the SPÖ receives 45 per cent of the votes when between 90 and 95 per cent of the voters participate. Among the male voters, it receives an even 55 per cent. The votes of women, which decreases the total Socialist percentage, are mostly those of housewives. The SPÖ percentage varies unevenly throughout the country. It is much higher in urban and industrial regions than in rural areas. Votes of a sizable number of employees would necessarily have to be included to account for the high SPÖ percentages. The party has seven hundred thousand members paying membership fees; only one-third of those voting for the party are party members. It is mandatory for party members to be affiliated with a trade union, but affiliation is also expected from every employee who identifies himself with the party and its policies by voting for the party. Among the SPÖ members and followers, the employees' free trade-union movement found a solid membership and its most active shop stewards. The fact that the Austrian trade-union movement has been organized on a nonpolitical basis since 1945 has had no effect on this association. Yet, union independence from party ties makes the union attractive to those employees not favoring the SPÖ.

A complete change of position toward the employees' trade union has been noted among the Christian employees, who form the second strongest group within the GAP.[14] Before the war, Christian employees had formed an organization to counter the employees' free trade unions although its membership was not very large. Under the present changed circumstances, the Christian group of members and followers of the Austrian People's Party (ÖVP) is very much interested that all employees with political opinions similar to theirs become members of trade unions, since the strength of their following within the GAP assures them of a part in leadership and policy-making. The Christian members and leaders of the GAP have proven themselves to be loyal trade unionists.

The Christian trade-union members find membership in the trade union considerably eased because of the friendly attitude of the Austrian church leaders, especially of high Catholic officials, toward the ÖGB. The ÖGB itself also benefits from this attitude. During the First Republic the relationship between the church and the free trade unions was pronouncedly hostile. More recently it caused a public stir and gratification within union circles when the Cardinal Archbishop of Vienna, Dr. König, accepted an invitation to the congress of the ÖGB and participated as a guest.[15] It also attracted attention when the president of the ÖGB, Franz Olah, a Socialist member of parliament, on the occasion of a visit to Rome, was received by the Pope in audience.

The political and religious neutrality to which the GAP strictly adheres has opened wide areas previously closed to the employees' unions, not only among the Catholic employees but also among those with no party ties. True, numerous employees without party ties belonged to the employees' trade union before 1934. Otherwise the high percentage of organized union members in many occupational

[14] The third group is formed by the Communists, who form the opposition within the ÖGB and its trade unions. Because of their small minority they exert little influence, especially since the ÖGB acted to exclude some Communists from leadership positions because of lack of discipline. Among those expelled was the Communist vice-president of the ÖGB. As a result, no Communist is a member of the executive committee of the ÖGB. The Communists had the support of the Soviet occupation as long as the eastern zone of Austria was occupied by Russian troops, but this is no longer the case. Within the ranks of the GAP the Communists are even less influential than within the other trade unions affiliated with the ÖGB.

[15] "Cardinal König," reports the Socialist *Arbeiter-Zeitung* (September 6, 1962), in large print, "conducts regular meetings with shop stewards and leaders of the trade union which he suggested while visiting firms. The Cardinal agreed to the suggestion to invite other trade-union leaders also. . . . Those participating are not asked as to their political or religious views."

branches before 1934 could not be explained. Yet, the independence of the trade unions from any political party has broken down many restraints. Employees not affiliated with a political party are also attracted by the simplicity of the organizational structure which includes employees of all kinds. In addition, some employees, especially in big firms, may fear being looked down upon by co-workers of the two organized groups who belong to the union, or even being passed over for advancement should they remain outside the union. It is difficult to remain outside the tide of organization when colleagues of two politically opposite views are members.

Not only within the realm of church-related life, but also in the entire social and political structure, a great change has taken place in the Second Republic in comparison with the atmosphere of the First Republic. The chasm which divided the classes before 1934 has been bridged at many places. Contributing to the change were not only pressure of the national socialistic dictatorship and the wounds of the war, but also a recognition that sharp political cleavages led to the civil war of 1934. Politically, this meeting of minds finds expression in the coalition government of the two big Austrian parties, the SPÖ and the ÖVP. The relationship between the employers and their organizations and the trade unions has adapted itself to the new style. The valiant reconstruction work of workers and employees has a part in this changed relationship as does the strong anti-communist stand of the union leaders, exemplified in October, 1950, when socialists and trade unionists under the leadership of Franz Olah defeated an attempted communist coup.

Of importance also is the fact that the organizations of the employers who confront the trade unions at meetings and negotiate collective agreements are of a far different character in the Second Republic than in the First. During the First Republic they were independent organizations of the employers; now they are statutory Chambers of Commerce. Before the free organization of the employers had had a chance to get reorganized following the war, the Chambers of Commerce, which had existed for one hundred years, were put on a new basis by law. This legislation received the support of the socialists, without whose agreement it could not have been established, both in government and parliament. Now the Chamber is an official institution, including all branches of the commercial, industrial, and handicraft economy; all firms are required to belong. Sections were established for industry, the handicrafts, transportation, banking credit, and insurance agencies. According to the law, only this institution has the right to conclude collective agreements.[16]

The Chamber of Commerce, led by a large staff of officials under the present system, is backed by the tradition of a century. Its field of action is not restricted to questions of workers and employees, as had been the case with the free organizations of the employers, but rather reaches into every aspect of economic policy. Such an institution naturally develops a different style in its relationships with the trade unions than was used by the former employers' organizations, which concentrated on fighting the union movement, especially among "their" employees. Add to this the facts that the officers of the numerous economic branches of the Chamber of Commerce meet frequently with the representatives of the Federation of the Trade Unions and the Chambers of Labor, and that the representatives of both groups often combine their efforts to solve national economic problems. The old employers' organizations were once hard to convince that trade unions and their right to settle work issues collectively should be recognized. It was only during the First Republic that this right was granted to most of the employees' trade unions; employees in industry were refused the right until the end. This recognition has not been an issue in the Second Republic.

The enterprises in heavy industry and mining, which had been the hotbed for antilabor agitation, were nationalized in the Second Republic. While they fought the employees' trade unions with every possible means, organized "independent" unions to counter the union movement, and finally terrorized the trade unionists during the First Republic, they did not object to the organization of employees into trade unions in the Second Republic.

The GAP is profiting more than other union groups from this new style of relationship between the organization of employers and the trade unions since it knew how to adapt to the situation and make the best of it. For the point of this discussion, the extent of organization among employees, it is of vital importance that belonging to a trade union, with some exceptions, has ceased to be a danger for employees with regard to the stability of their employment contracts. Within the part of the economy from which the union recruits its

[16] It should be mentioned that the Federation of Trade Unions declined an offer of an analogous monopoly position. It prefers to remain an organization based on the voluntary membership of workers and employees and to gain the right to sign collective agreements through the confidence of an overwhelming majority of workers and employees.

members, union membership no longer constitutes a reason for persecution or a hindrance in professional advancement. Nor are the shop councils of employees kept from performing their tasks for the union within or outside the firm—with some exceptions. All of the elements mentioned—the unions' lack of political ties, the favorable view of the church, the changed relationship towards employers—naturally mean a considerable easing in the atmosphere surrounding the recruitment of members and the maintenance of union membership.

The trade-union organizations in Austria are built upon shop councils and the shop steward system.[17] The shop councils, in turn, need the backing of a strong—if possible an all-inclusive—trade union in order to strengthen their position. This support is essential not only in negotiations with the employer; in industrial firms the shop council as well as the individual employee needs the backing of a strong employees' trade union in relation to the often collectively organized workers. This is especially true for employees in the production section of a firm, who have constant contact with the workers. Out of day-to-day events in the firm, conflicts may arise between the shop councils of the workers and those of the employees, as well as between individual employees and workers. The trade union can intervene and a peaceful and friendly settlement can be achieved on the union level. Thus, affiliation with the trade union provides an additional benefit for employees in the industrial field to replace what was at one time a source of tension in the trade-union movement for employees.

The seemingly stronger propensity of the Austrian employees to organize in trade unions, as compared with employees in other lands, is promoted through the fact that they no doubt have taken a realistic view concerning their sociological position as independent wage earners. This consciousness has evolved over time. Today it is surprisingly solid. They realized how much their way of life depended upon salaries when, during the successive inflations during and after the two wars, their assumed "middle class standing" was reduced to that of the proletariat. They shared the workers' lack of security of employment during the painful period of crisis in the Austrian economy which was chronic at first but became acute in 1929 and lasted for two decades. They also did not forget what the loss of freedom to

[17] The councils, elected according to the law by all workers and employees in the shop, are primarily concerned with individual grievances and observation of labor legislation in the plant. See below, pp. 62 ff.

organize, after the enforced dissolution of their trade union, meant for their livelihood and their remuneration. They learned their lesson of history. Their inclination to include themselves in the middle class has been lessened, and the consciousness of their dependence upon their salaries has been strengthened. Now Austrians of all professional categories favor the idea of organization. Farmers, professors, artisans, industrialists, and merchants of all ranks have been organized into professional interest groups for a long time. The political organization of Austrians of the various party hues is considerably stronger than in other countries.

Because employees long held the view that they might surrender their higher status if they organized like "common" workers, they accepted the principle of organization much later than workers. Such thoughts belong to the past, and the free unions of the years prior to 1934 have to be credited with the change. Two circumstances contributed to this recognition: A higher evaluation of the social position of the workers, resulting from the influence of their trade unions, provided a strong stimulus for the organization of unions among employees. For once, good examples spoiled bad customs. Second, the development of social legislation in favor of the employees which quite obviously occurred under the influence of the employees' trade union. The special law for employees gave them job security and protection against risks, as did the social insurance law for employees, which lessened their fear of not being able to earn a living because of sickness and becoming an invalid and provided security for their retirement and support for those whom they left behind. Unemployment insurance lessened their fear of the consequences of losing their jobs. The entire legislation, however, was a result of their social position as dependently employed persons, who needed the protection of the law—the type of protection an employer has by means of his property.

All these facts combined have resulted in the Austrian trade-union movement for employees reaching a degree of organization unequaled in any other country in the Western Hemisphere.

THE ORGANIZATIONAL STRUCTURE OF THE EMPLOYEES' TRADE UNION (GAP) IN PRIVATE ENTERPRISES

"The Trade Union of the Employees in Private Enterprises is an organization of all technical, commercial, and administrative employees in private enterprises in Austria [with the exception of the free professions for whom a separate trade union (art and free professions) is appropriate] insofar as they are subject to the regulations of the law for the employees, or have the same legal rights as other employees. In addition it is entitled to recruit members among other groups as declared appropriate by decision of the Austrian Federation of Labor (ÖGB)."[18] Thus does paragraph 1 of the GAP charter define its organizational mandate.

The extensive jurisdiction of the GAP, which includes twelve of the sixteen branches of the ÖGB, necessitates a rather complicated organizational structure. This structure has two streams which join only at the top. One stream organizes the members, according to location, into local groups which are combined into federal branches. The other stream organizes members according to occupational sections. The local groups include all members employed in one location without regard to their occupational status. Their tasks are therefore more general. The charter states as its foremost task to "spread and intensify the trade-union idea within its area." The winning of members, training, education as to goal and purpose of the trade union, collection of membership fees, arrangements for get-togethers and meetings of members at which lectures concerning questions of interest to union members and topics of general interest are being discussed, belong among the tasks of the local organizations. The leadership of the local group consists of the chairman, two deputy chairmen, the treasurer and his deputy, the secretary and his deputy, and, depending on the size of the membership, two to twelve additional board members. The election is by ballot according to proportional representation.

Local groups are combined into state organizations. Each local group may send at least one delegate to its state conference; local groups with more than one hundred members send more delegates. The state conference meets at least once a year to elect its leaders, to hear their activity report, and to name delegates who will represent the state group in the Trade Union Federation. The leadership of the state organization, chairman, treasurer, and secretary as well as a deputy for each and from four to twelve members are elected for a four-year term.

The plant section is the smallest group in the organizational structure of the GAP. In every firm where there are at least five mem-

[18] *Business and Election Procedures and Organizational Structure of the Trade Union for Employees in Private Enterprises* (Vienna: Selbstverlag der Gewerkschaft, 1959).

bers, a section is formed which, in accordance with the shop council law, is led by elected shop councils and shop stewards—of course only when they are members of the union. In this way the law-based system of shop councils and shop stewards is built into the organization of the union. Thus the shop council members and stewards are integrated into the leadership of the trade union. The elected union leaders come from among the shop councilors since they dominate in the local organizations, both local and state-wide.

The plant section is governed by a section meeting which convenes semi-annually according to shop council law. The proposed date for this meeting has to be reported to the trade union, and the union leaders are authorized to take part in these section meetings.

The second stream of the organizational structure of the GAP is formed by grouping members into professional branches and sections, depending on the sections of the economy to which they belong. The six sections of the GAP are: 1. industry and handicrafts; 2. trade and transportation; 3. banks, savings and loan institutions; 4. private insurance companies; 5. social insurance agencies; 6. agriculture and forestry.

Since some employees do not belong in any one of the listed categories within the framework of the GAP and are not large enough to justify a separate section, the charter specifies that they be added to the trade section. The sections are the actual agencies for trade-union activities. They negotiate the collective agreements with the respective employer organizations.

The sections enjoy a far-reaching autonomy, primarily because their goals and the methods used to achieve them are very different. The charter of the GAP contains the following statement with regard to section autonomy and the influence of the central trade union:

> Matters of concern only to the members of a section will be—as far as they are not issues of principle—taken care of by the section and within their respective locality. In spite of this, though, the section is subject to the guiding principles of the ÖGB and the trade union. If a particular issue concerns questions, whose solution may be of importance to other sections, it has to be handled with the agreement of the union as a whole.

The organizational foundations of the sections are the professional groups. The division of the sections into professional groups corresponds to the structure of the employer organization, which is the union's opposite in negotiating collective agreements.

The sectional organizations of similar enterprises join together to form state-wide professional groups which, in turn, may organize into federal professional groups for all of Austria. Leaders of the professional groups and sections are elected by the shop councils of their own section. Professionally related groups may organize state professional leagues and federal professional leagues. The shop councils and stewards meet in a state-wide shop council conference. At this conference from three to eight members, depending upon total membership, are elected to the federal professional group and its executive committee; delegates to the general conference of the section are also elected. Only shop councilors and stewards who are members of the trade union are eligible to vote. The executive is elected by a similar procedure. The professional groups combine into state sections, and the state groups into a section for the entire country. The chairman of the state section is elected by a shop council conference of all the professional groups represented in the state sections. The leadership of the section is elected by the general assembly of the section. The leadership consists of the chairman, his deputy, and a number of other members depending on needs.

Outside of the local sectional structure of the trade union there are departments for women and young people. They are locally constructed units with two primary tasks: (1) to gain members and to explain the union idea to them, and (2) to represent their special interests within the trade union. Arrangement has been made for them to be represented through delegates in the various decision-making bodies of the organizations.

The top agency of the entire trade-union movement is the convention (*Gewerkschaftstag*) which usually meets every four years. Delegates represent the local as well as the professional organizations and the women's and youth departments.

As complicated as this structure of the employees' trade union in private enterprises and its leading rule-making groups may be, some deficiencies remain. Several significant professional groups within the ranks of the employees are not organized as special interest groups—for instance, the industrial engineers and the salesmen and representatives in trade and industry. Such professional groups are valuable in that they strengthen the ties of the members to the union, especially in cases where the professional groups have been difficult to convince of the value of the trade-union idea. They exert a modifying influence in the negotiations of collective agreements by pointing out their own special needs. Their absence in the organizational structure of the trade unions may result in the failure to include some clauses in the agreement covering the people involved.

Terms of office for the elected officers in the GAP are usually long. Representatives at the lowest level of the two organizational streams, the local and the state-wide professional groups, are elected for two years. The terms in the higher level usually are for four years. The advantage of this election system is that sufficient time is given the elected officers to acquaint themselves with their duties and to get to know the permanent staff. It also gives the trade union stability in leadership. Long terms of office are favored by the permanent leadership. On the other hand, of course, changing needs of the membership and prompt attention to new problems in the organizational and economic life may encounter some personal obstacles.

The elected officers of the union have been able to maintain themselves in office for long periods. This trend has been strengthened by the complicated organizational system of the GAP. An additional reinforcement comes from the fact that direct election of officers through members occurs only on one level—in the local group. Whether or not too much right has been given to the desire for continuity in leadership is open to question.

The GAP has in addition to its elected officers a staff of permanent paid officials. The elected chairman of the trade union is at the same time a paid executive secretary. The chief secretary is at the same time deputy chairman and executive secretary. Three other secretaries share the work of the trade union with the chief secretary. The chief secretary is responsible for the most important department, the negotiation of collective agreements and organizational questions. His position requires naturally that he may use his influence in the other departments. One secretary is assigned to each of the following departments: social politics and social insurance; education, press relations, and other publications of the trade union; finances, dues, and membership. Each secretary is assisted by a number of employees of the trade union.

One chief secretary heads the administration of each section. He, too, has a staff to assist him.

Further down the hierarchy, each state-wide group has a state secretary and, depending on the size of the membership within the state, an appropriate number of staff members. The office of the state-wide union also has to take care of the state-wide professional groups and the state-wide sections. The State of Vienna, which has the largest membership, has the smallest office force, since its management is restricted by the charter. The affairs of the State of Vienna are administered, in most cases, by the staff of the central office. It is presently in the hands of a woman secretary. The two "departments," for women and youth, also have secretaries (female for the women's department).

When nominating candidates for an election of officers or when appointing paid officials, the GAP leadership at all times has to take into consideration the strength of the three political groups which constitute its membership. Therefore, the chairman at each organizational level has two deputies, one of whom is appointed from the ranks of one of the minority groups.

THE ORGANIZATION OF PUBLIC EMPLOYEES

While employees in private industry are organized into their own trade union, separate from the trade union for workers, there is only one organization for people working in public services, from the lowest to the highest level and without regard to the kind of work they perform, manual or intellectual. This organizational form was chosen because under Austrian law they all have the same terms of employment. Public service workers, manual workers included, are either classified as "civil servants" on permanent status, in which case they cannot be given notice and have a legal title to a pension for themselves and their survivors, or they are on indefinite appointments, in which case they can be given notice according to a contract defined in the law which gives them more rights than the employment law grants private employees. Public employees on indefinite appointment are in a minority. Many times a public employee with this type of a contract is on a temporary assignment pending the time when he will be promoted to permanent status.[19] Public employees, clas-

Table 6. Trade-Union Membership Among Public Employees

Trade Union	*Members*
Civil servants	118,017
Municipal employees	119,741
Railroad employees	123,616
Post and telegraph employees	51,641
Total membership	413,015

Source: *Wirtschaftsstatistisches Handbuch 1962* (Vienna: Chamber of Labor, yearly), pp. 154 and 155; census of December 31, 1962.

[19] The service law for civil servants and temporary employees of the railroad, post office, and telegraph is the same as the service law of the civil servants and temporary employees of the federal government.

sified according to membership in four trade-union divisions, are listed in Table 6.

The public employees' trade union is divided into 26 different sections. Seven sections enroll civil servants of the federal government according to service branches, including employees with contracts: (1) territorial administration; (2) economic administration; (3) education; (4) justice; (5) finance; (6) agriculture and forestry; (7) social administration. The civil servants and employees of the state are organized in two sections: (8) state and district administration; (9) state institutions and public utilities. The educators form five sections: (10) grade school teachers; (11) junior high teachers; (12) teachers in vocational schools; (13) secondary school teachers; (14) teachers in professional institutes. The agencies of public security form five sections: (15) security guards; (16) police; (17) customs officials; (18) detectives; and (19) guards in jails and law courts. The other sections are: (20) employees of federal institutions and enterprises; (21) employees of public chambers and corporations established by law; (22) pensioners; (23) judges and public prosecutors; (24) public construction officials; (25) federal army officers, sergeants, and civil servants of the army administration; and (26) employees in offices of unemployment insurance and employment services. The 22nd section includes the pensioners from all of the 25 other sections.

All trade unions of public employees have the right to strike, just as do the private employees' groups. In the conservative circles of Austria, this right is being protested vigorously.

During the summer of 1962 when the police went on strike over a wage issue and the customs officials organized passive resistance, conservative lawyers, through the press, called public attention to a ruling by the emperor on July 25, 1914, in which public employees participating in strikes or passive resistance were threatened with severe punishment. This ruling was released on the eve of World War I to protect the federal government during the war. The Socialist minister of justice entered the discussion on August 24, 1962, with a statement saying that the ruling was never sanctioned by parliament and no longer applied. This decision, it was said, had already been made in a circular of the Chancellor of July 7, 1946. This was reinforced through the law of July 6, 1954, concerning extension of the "liberty to work and assemble" to include the public employees. Thus public employees received the same union rights as the rest of the working force.

Statistics of the social insurance agency for public employees, according to branches, are shown in Table 7.

Table 7. Public Employees Registered for Social Insurance, by Branches

Civil service (federal, state, and community)	314,668
Transportation (including private workers and employees)	160,165
Education, culture, art, and entertainment (including employees in private institutions)	38,982
Health (including employees in private institutions)	42,553
Total	556,368

Source: *Wirtschaftsstatistisches Handbuch 1962* (Vienna: Chamber of Labor, yearly), p. 86; census of August, 1962.

If one compares the total number of organized public employees (413,015) with the total in Table 7, the percentage is 74. It would be even higher if one could exclude the private employees in the last three categories. The ÖGB as a whole has organized only 64 per cent of all dependently employed, and this figure would be even lower if the public employees were excluded. There is a reason for the higher percentage of organization among public employees. They are far more localized, in the larger cities, and are concentrated in a comparatively few large enterprises. They are subject to only one employer, which makes it easier to recruit them. The employer of public employees is bound by law to respect the employee's right to join the union. Actually, the same holds true for the private employers, but they often don't respect it, especially in the smaller and privately owned firms. In private enterprises it often happens that an employee is at a disadvantage because of union membership. This is very seldom the case in public service. Should it happen, the matter is taken up by parliament and quickly settled. This freedom to join the union is especially noticeable among civil servants in higher positions. In private enterprises it is difficult to recruit employees of that type for union membership, but in public services they are under no restrictions from the employer. Finally, the influence of the Socialist majority among the leadership of the unions in private enterprises is not as noticeable in the public services. Within the trade union of the public servants and the post and telegraph employees, the Austrian People's Party has a rather strong hold. Therefore, the ideological reasons, which in other occupational groups keeps some employees and workers from joining the union, do not exist here.

The union activity of the organizations of public employees is concentrated, even more than in other trade unions, on the question of remuneration, since the law has provided them with generally satisfying working conditions. The constant rise in living expenses through creeping inflation is far more difficult to keep up with in the public services than in private enterprises which can convert a pay increase into higher prices for goods and services. Increases in taxes and tariffs, on the other hand, are subject to decisions of the parliament, and the representatives in the National Assembly have understandably little inclination for such unpopular measures. Public opinion, represented by the press, puts pressure on them. In addition, the federal budget, as well as those of most of the state and city governments, suffer from chronic deficits which can only be wiped out through difficult financial manipulations. The trade unions of public employees fight for higher wages in the shadow of the private employees and workers and follow them without being able to achieve the same results.

SOCIAL LEGISLATION

Employees in Austria are covered by every kind of social legislation designed to protect the working population and assure their security, including even those laws which were previously meant to be only for the workers. Thus, employees are protected by safety laws against accidents and health-endangering chemicals. There are legal restrictions on working hours as well as work at night and on Sundays and holidays. Other restrictions cover work by young people as well as by women, pregnant women, and mothers of small children. Sick leave and accident and unemployment insurance are guaranteed by law. The shop council law grants the right of representatives elected by persons working for a firm to participate in meetings concerning personnel and management of the enterprise. Another law establishes the legal basis for the Chambers of Labor, as the elected and official representatives of the interests of workers and employees, to participate on an equal basis with the Chambers of Commerce in advising on the social, cultural, and economic legislation of the Austrian Republic, its states, and its municipalities.

Where necessary, special clauses were inserted to cover employees, e.g., regulations regarding Sundays as days of rest and daily closing hours in the offices and in wholesale and retail businesses, the law for shop councils, and the law regarding the establishment of Chambers of Labor.

In addition, special legislation for white-collar employees, originating in laws of the Empire (1910), was enacted during the First Republic (May 11, 1921). This covers dismissal notice, which varies from six weeks during the first two years of service to five months after 25 years, dismissal pay, vacations, sick pay, etc. Its main emphasis is on employment security. In this regard, the law has been successful. During the recession of 1952-53 when employment of workers declined, employment of white-collar workers remained constant.[20]

Hours of work are regulated by a collective agreement concluded between the union federation and the federal Chamber of Commerce (*Bundeswirtschaftskammer*). This agreement is supplemented by a special agreement regarding overtime pay of the industrial white-collar employees. The special legislation, which earlier covered social security for white-collar employees, has been merged with the system for manual workers in the joint general social security law of 1955, though the special retirement fund of white-collar workers continues to exist.

LEGAL REPRESENTATION OF THE INTERESTS OF THE EMPLOYEES

The Austrian employees (and workers) have three legal institutions to represent their interests: the trade unions, the shop councils, and the Chambers of Labor. All three received their legal basis during the revolutionary period at the end of World War I when employers were willing to make extensive concessions to prevent the

[20] It should be mentioned that the legislation for shop councils also includes prohibitions against arbitrary dismissal. Prior to each dismissal, the owner has to inform the shop council. The shop council has three days to reply and the employer may not legally dismiss a person during the interim. The shop council as well as the employee (or worker) have the right to contest the dismissal, if it means social hardship for the person concerned or if the dismissal is not based on the regulations of the enterprise. The final decision on a contested dismissal is made by a judicial institution, the so-called arbitration court (*Einigungsamt*), set up under Austrian labor law. The court consists of a judge, a representative of the employers, and a union representative.

In case of dismissal the person concerned may within two weeks file a petition against it if the shop council, after a fruitless intervention with the employer, confirms that the dismissal was made by the employer to avoid the procedural regulations for dismissal.

spread of Bolshevism into Austria. This legislation helped to keep the First Republic a democracy.

Trade unions and shop stewards who had been elected spokesmen by the union members within the firms and in agreement with the leadership of the trade union had been in existence as free institutions before 1918. Even before this there was also some discussion concerning the establishment of Chambers of Labor. The legal basis was provided within the short period from 1918 to 1921 when social democrats participated in the government. The authoritarian system of 1934 changed these institutions to political instruments within the system by replacing the free election through appointment of officers. Soon after the inauguration of the dictatorship of the National Socialists in Austria all these institutions were abolished completely. The Second Republic reinstated them, and it was possible at that time to improve the legislation on the basis of past experience. Rights of shop councils and Chambers of Labor were extended considerably, and the legislation on the organizational rights of the trade union was so stated that "yellow" organizations were excluded from the right to negotiate collective agreements guaranteed to genuine trade unions.

The three institutions—trade unions, shop councils, and Chambers of Labor—have been working together closely and amicably from the beginning. The trade unions lead and link together the organizations. The shop councils are the agencies of the unions in the work places. The Chambers of Labor are joined with them through their elected officers and the officers of the trade unions and fulfill the functions of a public-legal agency within the trade-union movement which is available for replenishing of intellectual weapons.

The federal law of February 26, 1947, which sets forth the rights and procedures of collective bargaining on conditions of work and pay forms the legal basis for the most important task of the unions, the negotiating of collective agreements. This law gives negotiated agreements the binding legal character they did not have under the monarchy and establishes what type of organization of workers and employees is permitted to conclude collective agreements.

The law states, "Permitted to conclude collective agreements are the legally competent representatives of the employers and the employees." According to this definition, these representatives are the federal Chambers of Commerce on the side of the employers and the Chambers of Labor for the employees. While the Chambers of Commerce make use of this right and exclude the free employers' organizations in most economic sectors from concluding collective agreements, the Chambers of Labor do not use their right. Instead they leave the field to the trade unions.

Permitted to conclude collective agreements are "also those occupational organizations of the employers and employees depending on voluntary membership and who according to their articles see it as one of their tasks to regulate working conditions within their respective area, provided that they have an extended realm of interest in regard to occupation and area, and that their membership and activities are economically important and independent of one another." Whether or not an occupational organization should be granted the right to conclude collective agreements is decided by a special board with legal characteristics. The chairman is a judge or high legal official; he is assisted by an equal number of committee members from both the employer and the employee organizations.

The law defines the irrevocable legality of collective agreements as follows: "The regulations in collective agreements, as far as they refer to relations between employer and employee, cannot be restricted through a work order or service contract. Special arrangements, if they are not entirely excluded through the collective agreement, are possible only if they are of greater advantage to the employee or concern a matter not covered by the collective agreement." Further: "The clauses of the collective agreement are regulated, as far as they regulate relations between the employer and the employee, as part of service contracts which are signed between employer and employees as partners of collective agreements."

The consequence of the latter clause is that terms of a collective agreement can remain in force even though the collective agreement might terminate. This legislation serves an important function in times of crisis. It keeps the work contracts from losing their effectiveness beyond the term of the collective agreement. In such situations it may be even more advantageous for the trade union not to push for a new collective agreement if this would only result in achieving conditions less desirable than those of the old agreement.

Because the federal Chamber of Commerce is a contract partner on the employer side and because every enterprise must belong to the federal Chamber and to one of its smaller economic-sector branch organizations, all enterprises, without exception, are subject to the collective agreements for the sector to which they belong. On the employee side, the law states precisely that "the collective agreement is also legally binding upon those employees who are not members of the trade union making the agreement." Because of these two circumstances, the contract monopoly of the employers' organizations and the legal extension of collective agreement to include nonmembers of the union, nearly all Austrian employees benefit from the collective agreements.

The institution of the shop councils in Austria is an illegitimate child of the Russian revolution. The fact that councils of workers and soldiers acted as the government in the beginning of the Russian Revolution had long-lasting repercussions in the labor movement of Central Europe. In Germany these repercussions led to a civil war. In Austria, following a successful struggle for general suffrage in parliamentary elections, a democratic tradition took root within the masses, and the leadership of the labor movement and especially the union leaders were unwilling to abandon the democratic way. When the council movement came to Austria it was guided into legal channels by the shop council law which was passed by the constitutional National Assembly on May 15, 1919, seven months after the establishment of the republic. The draft for this law had been worked out by the federal commission for socialization and not by the federal ministry for social administration. The law on collective agreements was enacted in December of the same year, and the law establishing the Chambers of Labor only in February 1920.

The present shop council law, BGB1 No. 96, concerning the establishment of plant representations was enacted March 28, 1947, and requires the election of shop councils in the plants in which at least twenty people, including workers, employees, and apprentices, are permanently employed. In plants employing more than fifty people, the employees elect a separate council if they number at least twenty. If the employees of a particular firm number at least five but less than twenty, there must be a combined council with at least one of the members being an employee.

The shop councils are the agencies for the participation of the employed in affairs of the firm, including recruitment, transfer, presenting of notices, and the dismissal of fellow workers and employees. Shop councils are authorized to see that collective agreements are observed and that laws concerning the protection of the employees are enforced. They also have permission to check the payroll of all employees as well as pertinent documents and to control the payment of salaries and wages. The employer can take disciplinary measures toward individual employees only with the consent of the shop council.

The shop council may suggest improvements in the plant. The

owner is obligated upon demand of the council to discuss management objectives and improvements within the firm. In larger enterprises, the shop council may request a copy of the balance sheet and the profit-and-loss statement, and the company officials must make any requested or necessary explanations. The administration is also obligated, if requested, to furnish information concerning the financial status of the business, kind and volume of manufactured goods, orders on hand, sales, and measures taken to improve the productivity of the firm.

In joint-stock companies, two members of the shop council attend the meetings of the board of directors and enjoy the same rights as directors elected by the stockholders.

The Chambers of Labor are the representatives of the working population in formulating the economic, social, and cultural legislation of the federal republic and the various states. There is a Chamber of Labor in every state; the nine chambers are combined into the Austrian Chamber of Labor convention under the leadership of the Viennese Chamber. In every state, the people covered by health insurance who are working in industry, mining, handicrafts, trade, and transportation, and those in service jobs elect the members for the plenary session of the Chamber. These sessions usually take place twice a year, and members discuss the budget and the financial report and accept the activity reports. Out of these sessions emerge the operating agencies, the presiding committee, the directorate of the Chamber, and the working committees for the various branches of chamber activity.

The labor force is grouped in three different bodies—workers, employees, and civil servants in public transportation—which elect members to the plenary sessions. Representation is proportional depending upon the number of eligible voters in each of these groups within the state. The same proportional method is used to elect the directorate at the plenary sessions.

The special body of electors for employees is all that remains of their once-favored position when they had a special section of employees within each Chamber of Labor in each of the nine states.

The Chamber of Labor law of July 20, 1945, the first in the Second Republic, reads: "The chambers divide into sections of workers and employees," and for each section there is formed a "special body of electors."

On May 19, 1954, the National Council passed a new Chamber of Labor law which no longer recognizes the sections, but only three separate bodies of electors for elections to the plenary sessions.

The influence of the Chambers of Labor upon legislation and administration is ensured by the law which requires the federal and state governments to consult the Chambers on any change in the legislation which might touch the interests of the working population. On both levels, consultation must be undertaken before the legislation can be put before the legislative assemblies or a decree made public. Supplementing the required consultation is the right of the Chamber to make suggestions and reports to the administration and the legislative bodies.

The Austrian Labor Council (*Öesterreichische Arbeiterkammertag*) is under the leadership of the Viennese Chamber. Its president is at the same time president of the Council, and the office of the Viennese Chamber is assigned its management. The Chambers of Labor have the right to collect from all workers and employees a fee amounting to one-half of 1 per cent of the monthly pay up to a limit of 2,400 Austrian shillings to finance a wide variety of activities and the employment of trained personnel.

The Chambers of Labor work closely with the trade unions. Numerous laws, especially in the area of economic legislation, allow for combined commissions with representation of both employers' organizations and workers' and employees' organizations. As far as the latter are concerned, the Austrian Labor Council is usually the nominating body. Elections to such positions are always made in agreement with the Austrian trade-union federation, and important decisions and their application are always made with the agreement of the federation. The nominations for the boards of the social insurance institutes are made on the basis of suggestions which the Chambers of Labor submit to the Minister of Social Administration, the Chamber always keeping in mind the needs of the trade unions.

Candidates for the election of delegates to the Chambers' plenary sessions are named from the ranks of the Austrian political parties. The candidates are nominated from the political groups within the trade-union federation; in this way personal identity is established between the leading officers of the trade unions and the officials of the Chambers of Labor. The influence of the Socialist group is predominant in the elected plenary sessions of the chamber. As a result of the last elections (1959), the Socialist candidates had 563 of the 810 available seats. Of the remaining seats, 161 went to the Federation of Austrian Workers and Employees, which is part of the Catholic-Conservative Austrian People's Party, 40 to the Communists, 31 to the Liberty Party (German Nationalist), and 15 to those without party ties. Socialists received 68.4 per cent of the valid votes; the People's Party (ÖVP), 18.6 per cent; the Communists, 6 per cent; the Liberty Party, 3.7 per cent; and those without party ties, 2.7 per cent.

In the employees' body of electors, the Socialists have 49 per cent of the votes and hold 81 of the 164 mandates. The ÖVP received 34.5 per cent of the votes and 60 mandates, the Communists 3.7 per cent and two mandates, the Liberty Party 7.4 per cent and 14 mandates. Those without party ties won 5.3 per cent of the votes and seven mandates.

The Socialist group of the Chamber keeps close contact with the Socialist groups of the trade unions and the party leadership. Since the two groups, the Socialists and the Austrian People's Party, generally work together harmoniously in both unions and Chamber, the decisions of both groups are usually made with the consent of the other.

The Chambers of Labor are distinct Austrian institutions which have been copied in few foreign countries: Luxembourg and two German states—the Saar area and Bremen. One of the valuable and remarkable traits of these institutions is that they can remain more independent of the special interests of the members in the different branches than can trade-union headquarters. In the trade-union federation, the large industrial groups have the major influence, and in some instances on questions concerning economic legislation, they may put their special interests first. The Chambers of Labor also carry more weight in public opinion than the Chambers of Commerce, which are divided into branches frequently differing in their views and controlled by the large corporations. Thus in regard to economic legislation, the Chambers of Labor are often more representative of the public interest in the Austrian economy—beyond the interest of the branches as well as of individual members. This notion lends weight to the opinion and point of view expressed by the Chambers of Labor.

COLLECTIVE BARGAINING POLICIES OF THE TRADE UNION OF THE EMPLOYEES IN PRIVATE ENTERPRISES

Right after the war, Austria found itself in a serious economic situation with its factories either destroyed or dismantled by occupation forces and also with a shortage of machines and raw materials to make a new start. Other factors were the low level of agricultural production insufficient for the needs of the population and an inflation which threatened to take a dangerous turn.

The most urgent problem proved to be the procurement of food, housing, and fuel for the population. All the powers of the trade-union movement were concentrated on providing these needs. It secured help from the occupation forces for the most urgent needs. This was followed by relief shipments of the United Nations through UNRRA. Marshall Plan aid began in 1948. The Austrian trade-union federation requested and received the right to voice its opinion on the administration of Marshall Plan assistance.

In this situation there was little room for separate policy on collective bargaining of the various trade unions. Collective agreements were negotiated centrally by the trade-union federation.

Wages and salaries were decided upon in five wage and price agreements, in which the government assisted. Each new agreement was generated by the attempt of private enterprises, especially in the farm sector, to achieve higher prices for their products. At that time a large part of the prices, especially those for vital necessities, were officially controlled, and an increase could be made only with the consent of the government. The government also supported prices of important goods, like food, through subsidies to the producers. The ÖGB tried hard to prevent wages and salaries from lagging behind the rising costs of living. This was a task it could not completely accomplish. It was possible to balance the officially permitted price increases of agricultural and industrial products as well as the increases in charges for public services against the rise of wages and salaries. But against the secondary price wave of the great variety of non-controlled goods, initiated through the price and wage agreement, the trade-union federation was just as helpless as it was against the lack of discipline and the greed of the producers and dealers.

The wage agreements were approved by the ÖGB in the form of collective agreements applicable in all of Austria and nearly all branches of the economy. A shortcoming was that they were based on the least productive enterprises, an objective of the contract partner for the employers, the federal Chamber of Commerce. These contracts left the workers and employees of larger and more productive firms unsatisfied. They paralyzed the individual trade unions and threatened to diminish the loyalty of some union members who felt that their unions had no active part in decisions concerning wages. The agreements effected a leveling of the wage and salary structure by emphasizing the principle of subsistence and neglecting the principle of achievement. This leveling effect extended to the employees and completely distorted the traditional salary structure within the hierarchy of the firms.

After the fourth agreement increasing dissatisfaction among the workers and employees became noticeable and led to a general strike movement in October 1950, promoted by the Communists. This movement went as far as a Communist uprising in the part of Austria then occupied by the Russians.

Only in about 1951-52 did the individual trade unions again gain full freedom of action, when the ÖGB abandoned its central direction of wage movements.

The GAP took advantage of its opportunity immediately by taking action to counter the trend toward leveling of employees' salaries. On one hand, the salaries of the employees had lagged behind the wages of workers. On the other hand, the differential between the salaries of the lower and the higher categories of employees had diminished considerably.

In March 1957, a new element entered the collective bargaining policy of trade unions. In the beginning of 1957, prices increased considerably, and the danger of a rather painful decrease in the purchasing power of wages and salaries emerged. In this situation the ÖGB requested the establishment of a board to adjudicate prices and declared its willingness to submit the control of wage movements to this body. After long and difficult discussions with the employers' federal Chamber of Commerce, the "Bi-lateral Wage and Price Commission" was established. It is composed of an equal number of representatives of workers and employees, and of employers. The partners are obligated to submit intended price increases or demanded wage increases to this commission. This obligation has been adhered to strictly as far as the unions are concerned, and they have been forced to drop or postpone several wage demands because the commission did not endorse them. The discipline on the side of employers has been rather weak. But in general this commission has, in spite of its purely voluntary nature, fulfilled its purpose and its effects have been noticeable until 1961-62. It has kept the prices within a tolerable range which, with the favorable business cycle situation and full employment, has not always been easy.

At the end of 1961, price increases appeared to slip away from the commission's control, but early in 1962, under pressure from the trade unions, the parties reached a new agreement. Under the new agreement, stricter control was possible, which actually stopped the price climb. Of course, the trade unions, including the GAP, had to accept the check on wage increases which the existence of the commission represented. Yet, agreement of the commission to a wage hike provided a strong moral support for the trade unions in the negotiations with the representatives of the employers' organization. The GAP has used this technique most effectively. The employees' trade union has, thanks to the nature of its membership, a closer view of the financial position of the firms. The GAP has always pursued a well-thought-through set of proposals for collective agreements which it could support with serious and impressive arguments. No other trade union has, for instance, such complete statistics, kept for more than a decade, of the salaries actually paid in the various firms. In 1958, the union executive could report to the congress of the GAP: "The commission has naturally had an influence on our activities concerning collective agreements, but in May 1958 we could point out in a report to an ÖGB conference that we have been able to use the new situation to the interests of the private employees."

Among the regulations governing the Price and Wage Commission, one on collective agreements is especially important for the trade unions: it established a subcommittee to consider wage questions. The subcommittee has a period of not more than six weeks to deal with requests to open negotiations on wages. If this time passes without a decision, the application is automatically handed on to the plenary commission. If no decision is reached in the commission within five weeks, the application is considered approved and the trade union has permission to begin negotiating on wage issues. Thus the slowing down of the wage movement has been limited in time.

In the numerous wage movements which the GAP conducted since 1958, it was not satisfied with merely keeping up with constantly rising prices. It achieved a substantial increase in the level of real salaries in all branches, even for the economically and numerically weaker branches. The GAP stuck to the motto of "solidaristic wages policy" in spite of the criticism of its members in those professional groups who, thanks to favorable business conditions, might have been able to achieve greater increases in their salaries. The GAP weighs wage rate increases against one another so that the employees in the economically less favored branches also benefit from them. This type of wage policy is favored by the range of collective agreements which often extend over all of Austria and may combine a number of branches under one contract. Even where this is not the case, an important collective agreement will provide a standard for agreements in other related groups or areas. This necessitates a certain toning down of the demands in these pattern-setting contracts to make it possible for others to reach approximately the same results—thus "solidaristic wages policy." The GAP further did not lose sight of its goal to re-establish differentials among the salaries of the employees.

The climate in which collective agreements of the GAP were negotiated since 1958 was one of full employment and increasing productivity. One result is that the employers often find it necessary to offer the infrequent applicants for new positions, especially technically trained personnel who often receive tempting offers from abroad, higher salaries than are called for in the salary schedule. At the same time they have to give pay increases to their qualified personnel to prevent their changing to other firms—again over and above what is called for in the salary schedule. The industry section reported to the fourth congress on this problem:

> The employers try, by keeping the minimum salaries [of the schedule] as low as possible, to exclude the influence of the trade unions in regard to effective salaries. Our statistics show us that the salary scale for employees in industry with its minimum salaries and in relation to the individual occupational groups, has become unrealistic. Over-payment as against the collective agreement occurs, especially during the first year of employment, in every group subject to the contract, far above the minimum salaries. The additional amount paid employees with more than 10 years of service is comparatively very low.

The fact that employees with longer service years enjoy only small income differentials results from the low mobility of people in the higher age group of employees. Their hesitant attitude toward changing positions is reinforced by the consideration that they have most of their service years with the same firm which entitles them to longer vacations, extended sick leave with pay, higher severance pay in case of dismissal. They are reluctant to give up these acquired rights. The employers are cognizant of this attitude and try to use it to their own advantage, thus effecting savings on their total payroll.

The unrealistic situation with regard to the pay scale, as established by the industry section, does not mean that the various increases in basic wage scale, put into effect between 1958 and 1962, did not affect the effective salaries. The industry section achieved not only increases in the minimum salaries but also noticeable general increases which resulted in raising the effective salaries of all employees. The impact of a hike in the minimum salaries on the effective salaries is that every employee who thinks himself at least partially qualified (and which employee does not?) measures his value within the hierarchy of the firm in terms of the differential between his effective salary and the minimum salary applicable to him. As soon as the minimum salary receives a boost, he will push for the re-establishment of the former differential. In the climate of full employment, he will succeed, either individually, if his position in the firm is a strong one, or by joint action with other employees which occurs regularly after every wage settlement of the occupational group in the trade union; such an action has to be submitted to the shop council in an effort to adapt the effective salaries to the new minimum salaries. This is how the unrealistic pay scale arises.

The union is now in the process of devising means to adjust the minimum rates of different categories to the average effective rates as ascertained by the union.

WORKERS AND EMPLOYEES IN AUSTRIA

When one views the relationship between the workers and employees and their trade unions over the decades since the turn of the century, one will note a change in the relationship between the two. The workers learn to know the employees in the first place as employees in industry, in the daily plant routine. And it is especially here that a change has occurred which has influenced the mutual relations.

Before World War I the workers viewed the employees only as agents of the employers. Most of the employees at that time had not yet grasped the meaning of trade unionism. They viewed the slowly increasing power and influence of the workers' trade unions from a distance and maybe even with some misgivings. In cases of labor disputes the employees kept neutral at best, but often they took sides with the employer. They were even willing to be used as strike-breakers by taking over the duties of the striking workers or by supervising other strike-breakers hired by the employer.

After the collapse of Austria in 1918, a noteworthy change took place. The political revolution, the democratization of political life, their own needs resulting from the war, and the enormous rise of the cost of living through inflationary price hikes drove the employees of industry toward trade unionism. Many times the workers of the enterprise showed the way to their co-workers in the offices. Thus a fraternal relationship began which suffered some setbacks when, contrary to expectations, the social revolution according to the Russian pattern did not occur following the political revolution. Yet the estrangement of the prewar years did not return. The later depression hit workers and employees alike. The fear of unemployment, the sight of thousands of unemployed in both camps, and the pay reductions caught both and were uniting factors.

Then followed the seven years of the Nazi regime in Austria. The Austrian workers had much to suffer during this time. They were the only class of society which resisted National Socialism to a considerable extent. Passive and sometimes active resistance against the pressure of fascism, including sabotage within the plants which were now working at capacity to supply war needs, resulted in imprisonment, concentration camps, and death for many victims from the workers' ranks.

The employees both voluntarily and involuntarily carried out the orders of the tyrant within the firms. They handed on the orders of the Nazi administration. They had to put into practice the whole system of speed-up, work during long extra hours, and "voluntary" abandonment of holidays. The industrial enterprises as such offer, even under normal circumstances, sources for irritation between workers and employees. Before the war, the trade unions concerned on both sides cooperated by discussing these issues and, if possible, solved them without involving the management of the enterprise. This had been a medium for compromise which the DAF (German Labor Front of *Deutsche Arbeitsfront*), organized on the "leadership" principle, could not offer. Thus the years of Nazi occupation were not conducive to a friendly relationship between workers and employees.

After the decline of the Third Reich, the free trade-union movement began again. This time the employees' trade union underwent a considerable change in its ideological point of view. It was no longer a Socialist group, but a community of people with the same interests and without party strings. After the war there was also the rapidly expanding mechanization of the industrial enterprises, especially those firms employing a great number of workers and employees.

Between the two wars, the foremen, having close contact with the workers, were the persons by whom the workers judged the employees. The foremen, though, were mostly former colleagues who through diligence, intelligence, and painfully achieved technical training had advanced to their position. They never quite rid themselves of the signs of their background. They also very easily found the right tone to deal with those under their supervision. The "rationalized" firms often eliminated the position of foreman. The employee now confronting the workers is a staff technician or engineer. He comes from a background strange to the worker. He does not have his roots in the working class and has reached his position through schooling. Now, very often the orders reaching the worker are given no longer in a personal, oral way by the supervisor, but impersonally in written form through an office whose occupants know the workers only from a distance. On a higher technical level, the staff relationship between the worker and the employee in industry, which existed before World War I, is in a way being restored. At the same time the gap between workers and employees is becoming wider. Especially the older workers, who set the tone within the circle of their co-workers and who can tell them what conditions used to be, realize the change.

At the same time democracy in a political and social sense provides the workers with growing self-confidence. They demand and quickly achieve the same kinds of social legislation and social insurance as the employees; lately they are reaching for their last goal—the complete legal assimilation of their position with that of the employees. This makes the worker especially sensitive for his relationship to others employed in his place of work.

Against this background must be viewed the relationships between the organizations of the workers and those of the employees. Viewed historically, the employees' trade unions are a result of the struggle and success of the labor union movement. Before World War I the workers' unions already had considerable strength and influence, while the employees' trade unions were just taking their first steps. That the latter gained remarkable influence after World War I is due in great measure to the unselfish work of the labor movement, its trade unions, and its political party. Without their support, the employees' union would not have achieved its privileged position in the area of labor legislation and social insurance. During that period the trade unions of workers looked upon the organization of employees as a little brother they had to care for. They used their power unselfishly for their benefit because they felt that they were strongly united through the trade unions, by common political views, with a socially and professionally higher level of people. The joining of the employees' trade unions with the general Socialist trade-union center indicated a commitment to the same views. At the same time, the workers in the firms were sensitive to the fact that when the employee unions entered within the community of the free (Socialist) trade unions this implied a renunciation of middle class society, which the employees could belong to, and a proclamation of solidarity with the working class. That employees in banks, insurance companies, industry, and trade acknowledged belonging to the working class filled the workers with pride and satisfaction. In their eyes this was the first breakthrough of unionism into a higher social level, traditionally separated from labor by background, education, and habits. It meant a victory for the Socialist idea, their idea.

In the Second Republic, the tie of political mutuality between the workers and employees in the trade-union movement no longer exists. People of all political currents represented in the republic can be and are union members. The trade unions have become a fellowship of people with like interests. Among the workers, the Socialist current is strongest, but such is not the case in the employees' trade unions. Here the Socialist group is forced to work much more on a nonpartisan basis.[21] The Socialist workers who had shown so much interest and willingness to help the employees during the First Republic now display a certain aversion. Changed also is the position of the employees' trade union. It has become the second strongest union within the Austrian federation. In public life it enjoys the same respect as the trade unions of workers and has a powerful position in industry. This position is as stable as that of the strongest union of manual workers. Its careful, tactful, and skillful leadership has brought it the respect of the employers and also considerable success in achieving union goals without much struggle. In place of the relationship of protector and protected, there is now a matter-of-fact relationship between the workers' and the employees' organizations, sometimes influenced by an uncertain feeling of jealousy, perhaps even envy.

[21] The different strength of Socialist views among the workers and employees becomes clear in the elections for the Chambers of Labor. During 1959 they showed the following results:

Body of Electors for Workers

Valid Votes	*SPÖ*	*ÖVP*	*German Nationalist*	*No Party*	*KP (Communist)*
641,618	465,251	87,260	18,023	12,859	45,661
Percentage	74.0	13.9	2.9	2.0	7.3

Body of Electors for Employees

Valid Votes	*SPÖ*	*ÖVP*	*German Nationalist*	*No Party*	*KP (Communist)*
230,067	110,761	77,999	16,649	12,055	8,315
Percentage	49.0	34.5	7.4	5.3	3.7

SPÖ—*Sozialistische Partei Österreichs* (Austrian Socialist Party)
ÖVP—*Osterreichische Volkspartei* (Austrian People's Party)

While three-fourths of the valid votes among the workers were for candidates of the Socialist group in the trade union, not quite half of the valid votes of the employees were for Socialist candidates. Among the workers, the middle class conservative groups (ÖVP, German National, and Independent) combined received 18.8 per cent of the votes. The same group received 47.2 per cent among the employees.

This changed relationship is enhanced by the conspicuous change in the numerical relationship of the two groups. Within the last years the workers have had occasion to witness this change in their own work places. The change has caused a more vigorous demand on the part of the workers for equal rights with regard to labor law and insurance. The privileged position of the employees in these areas was easier to take when 5 out of 100 people employed in a firm were benefiting than when the proportion is 25 out of 100. The workers see how the modernization of the firms, mechanization, and especially automation of the production processes cause a depopulation of the production line in a plant while the technical, commercial, and administrative offices expand. Hand in hand with this comes the realization that the value of their occupational abilities and skills is being transferred to the organization of the firm itself, directed from the office.

If any differences between the unions of the workers and those of the employees occurred during the First Republic—by an action of the employees' union which also affected the workers, for example—great care was taken that the public would not learn about these frictions. In the Second Republic this kind of discretion is no longer practiced.

Differences between workers and employees on wages policy have arisen during the two stages of the economic development since the end of the war.

During the first years after the war when there was a shortage of goods—even food—and the purchasing power of money was declining, all unions achieved little more than a minimum existence for their members. Wage adjustments for all were conducted by the Austrian Federation of Trade Unions, excluding the individual branches, so that no special recognition of the employees' salary scale was possible. Such a wage agreement usually called for an increase by a certain number of shillings which all the employed people received in equal amounts plus a percentage increase with an upper and lower limit. Workers in the lowest income bracket received a higher percentage of the increase and employees in the higher salary brackets in turn received a correspondingly lower increase. The consequence was a strong trend toward leveling of employees' salaries. When they compared their pay with that of the workers, they felt at a disadvantage.

During the second stage, a period of near full employment and when shortages of qualified employees were developing in some booming industries and trades, the employees' unions were able to make up for their past disadvantages. The employers were even forced to pay higher salaries than were called for in the union scale. In this stage, the employees' trade union was able to gain more than the workers' union. The employees concentrated their efforts on the achievement of a thirteenth and fourteenth supplement which soon amounted to the equivalent of two full months' salary for all employees. The workers' unions followed this example, but the employers granted their demands only very reluctantly and step by step; extra pay in addition to the regular pay was a completely new development in the wage system for workers while Christmas bonus and vacation pay for employees were just reinstatements of benefits that had already existed before the war. Now the workers felt at a disadvantage, not because of the employers but because of the employees. They felt that the employees' union was dipping with a bigger spoon into the common paypot and was leaving there less than what they considered their share. In this stage it could happen that the leaders of the workers' unions would intervene, for instance, by demanding the same concessions for their members before the employer could make another offer to the employees.

The differences over pay adjustments were still smoldering under the surface when the workers' unions demanded social equality with the employees, a move which brought the estrangement before the public.

The employees' unions had done pioneering work in wages and social legislation for the manual workers, too, but no acknowledgment came from the leadership of the workers' unions, at least not publicly. In the area of wage adjustments, the example of the thirteenth and fourteenth monthly payment has been cited, and in social legislation there are a number of obvious examples of this kind.

The employees have legal assurance of continuous pay for six or more weeks in case of illness; the workers' unions in their collective agreements have won employer supplements to the legal sick pay under social insurance. Thus the sick worker will receive, from both sources combined, nearly his full pay. Legislation allows employees 12 work days of vacation per year during the first 5 years of service, 18 days after 5 years, 24 after 10, and 30 after 25 years of service. A vacation law for workers was worked out according to the same pattern and with the same number of days except for the thirty-day period. As to retirement insurance, an employee must be unable to perform his professional duties before he can receive a disability pension, while the general social insurance legislation in its original form requires a more stringent disability test—inability to perform any work—for a worker. This is, wrote the *Arbeiter-Zeitung*, "one great injustice since employees under the same circumstances find it much easier to receive pension payments." [22]

The demand was granted. The ninth revision of the social insurance law granting disability pensions to skilled workers—not to unskilled personnel—is patterned after the presently applicable regulation for employees; it has been in force since the beginning of 1962.

It would have been natural, and without doubt tactically the right thing to do, had the workers' unions continued along this line, trying to achieve step-by-step parity with the rights of the employees. But they chose a different way. The Austrian Federation of Trade Unions had requested at the time of the fourth federation meeting in 1955 that the entire body of labor legislation, a collection of regulations scattered through a variety of laws, be codified. That alone would not have helped the workers. The concept was therefore extended. The goal was to be not only a systematic collection of laws but also a unification of the regulations on the highest level attained in any special legislation. This would have achieved the objective of extending the special privileges of the employees to the manual workers. Connected with this request was the false notion that the assimilation of the workers and the employees under the law would also eliminate the social differences between them. Anton Proksch, former secretary general of the trade-union federation, undertook this assignment after he was named minister for social administration (1956). In 1960 the first part of the codified law was ready in draft form. In this draft the assimilation of the workers to the legal status of the employees was to a great extent provided for so that no distinction was made between "workers" and "employees." Instead the collective term "employed people" was used. The draft of the law caused considerable public discussion. The organizations of the employers and their publications rejected it, denouncing the proposed additional burdens in the social field.

The workers' trade unions and their publications defended the draft. Their arguments failed to support the demands—longer vacation, continued payment of wages in case of illness, settlement for dismissal, etc.—as a positive world-wide social need of workers in the period of the third industrial revolution. Rather they confined

[22] *Arbeiter-Zeitung*, Vienna, March 1, 1961.

themselves to arguing that their demands had to be met because the employees were enjoying the privileges in question.

For instance, the New Year's message of the Federation of Trade Unions reads:

The ÖGB tries to achieve that step by step all workers will receive four weeks pay as a Christmas bonus and four weeks additional vacation pay. There is no reason why there should be considerable legal differences in the social sector between workers and employees. Protection in case of dismissal, and the vacation legislation should also be improved and severance pay in case of dismissal should also apply for the workers.[23]

Soon thereafter the directorate of the Austrian Chambers of Labor had the following to say on the subject:

One of the most important tasks is the assimilation of the social legislation of the workers with that of the employees. Many employers already realize that it is not right to pay dismissal pay to an employee who has only been working for three years in the same firm and nothing to the worker, even if he has been working 30 years for the same firm. But that is only one example of the nonsensical differences that are still being made in the social realm between workers and employees. Further differences are for instance the payments to sick employees. It is time to put an end to this unequal treatment.[24]

The GAP took part in the discussion, but with restraint necessitated by its unusual situation. The basis for its belonging to the Federation of Trade Unions with all its consequences is the idea of solidarity between workers and employees in the union struggle, derived from common interests in their relationships to the employer. The workers' trade unions do not endanger the unity of their members if they view this principle somewhat from the light side, but the employees' union cannot do that. Its aim is to unite a group of working people whose members do not accept this principle as a matter of fact; on the contrary, they have to be made aware of it again and again. A not unimportant part of the education the employees' union has to provide consists of trying to convince its members that solidarity with the workers is the right way to represent their interests.

The comments made by the GAP were confined to two publications, as far as they became known to the public. The executive committee of the employees' union in December 1960 favored "the plan to codify the entire labor legislation. . . . In agreement with an old and practically proven principle which it acknowledges fully, it sup-

[23] *Gewerkschaftlicher Nachrichtendienst,* issued by the ÖGB, No. 934, Vienna, December 31, 1959.

[24] *Pressedienst der Arbeiterkammer,* Vienna, February 18, 1960, No. 943.

ports the desire for assimilation of less privileged groups to improved rights of other groups." On the other hand, the committee is "at the same time of the opinion that in the interest of general progress in the field under discussion, the better situated group should nevertheless have the right to try with all available strength to achieve further improvements"; it thus rejected the one-pot theory—from which the employees are said to withdraw more than the manual workers—of the trade union of the workers.

Friedrich Hillegeist, president of the employees' trade union, in a broadcast discussion [25] took sides a little more definitely and critically. He expressed the view that "elimination of the existing differences between workers and employees, especially in the area of wage and labor legislation . . . is their [the workers] legal right and we [the employees] cannot oppose it." But he added: "Yet, I am definitely against a merger of workers and employees into one and the same organization, since such a forced unit would tend to disturb rather than promote the working relationship of both groups which is in the interest of social progress." This was followed by a critical remark concerning the method of argument of the workers' trade unions: "I personally think it rather questionable, if some representatives of the unions of the workers think that they have only to request the assimilation with the reasoning that since the employees have it they have to have it too. In my view, the basis for such a demand must only be founded in the necessity, in the social needs of the group in question and must be substantiated as such."

Since 1962 these divergences have no longer manifested themselves in public. Anton Proksch, Minister of Social Insurance, has renewed the distinction between workers and employees in the second part of his draft of a new labor code. The unions of manual workers have once again embarked upon a course designed to reduce the differences between their status and the legally determined rights of the employees by way of collective agreements. In the area of vacations and holidays, they have already succeeded to a considerable extent. Similarly, a demand that their members receive a month's pay each at Christmas and at vacation time, as the employees do, has been accepted fully or in part in many collective agreements. In this way the differences have been reduced. Both sides have recognized that their common interests are stronger than those that separate them and that public discussion can only harm both of them.

[25] Printed in the agent of the union, *Der Privataugestellte,* 15 year, No. 430, Vienna, November 1960.

While this evolution went on in the trade-union camp, employers' organizations have accentuated their opposition to the trade unions. This led, of necessity, to a stronger sense of solidarity between workers and employees.

WHITE-COLLAR UNIONS -- THE CASE OF FRANCE

BY MICHEL CROZIER

White-collar unions in France may be viewed from two perspectives. On the one hand, they are very similar to white-collar unions of other industrially developed Western countries, since the character of a union ultimately depends on the situation and role of the worker-members. The situation and role, in turn, are quite closely determined and shaped by the same technical evolution and changing processes of production and by the same growing diffusion of the ideals and practices of mass-consumption society that are blurring class and status differences in many countries. On the other hand, however, there are still some striking dissimilarities based superficially upon the accident of their history and more deeply upon peculiarly French cultural factors. Inasmuch as white-collar work primarily involves human relations, white-collar employees are indeed much more under the impact of such factors than blue-collar workers whose work situation is more technically determined. This is especially important in France where the delicate synthesis of bureaucratic and anarchistic traits that characterize French social relations seems to have persisted, even within modern organizational techniques.

Before beginning an analysis of the history of French white-collar unions, of their methods and practices, of the problems of unionization, and of the general prospects of white-collar unionism, it is necessary to examine carefully the general framework under which French white-collar unions must develop.

THE FRENCH WHITE-COLLAR WORKERS' SITUATION WITHIN THE GENERAL TREND

The situation of French white-collar workers is almost identical to that of their English and German neighbors, but when it is compared with that of the American white-collar group, a time lag is apparent in four main aspects: the growth in numbers, the increase in the percentage of women, the narrowing of the wage differential, and the change in job content. I shall not stress this perspective since I do not want to repeat what is described elsewhere, but it will be useful to present some concurring evidence and to discuss possible distortions of the general trend in France.

In France, as elsewhere, the growth in the numbers of white-collar workers is the most spectacular and the most widely publicized feature of the social evolution. This trend is most easily seen in the case of the clerks and salesworkers who form the core of the white-collar labor force.[1] These two groups are also most amenable to unionization.

In 1960, these groups numbered together 2,300,000 people, i.e., 25 per cent of the nonagricultural salaried labor force,[2] as against 36 per cent in the United States.[3] Their growth has been steady and spectacular all through the last century from a bare 1 per cent of the total labor force up to around 11 per cent.[4] But comparison with the United States raises an interesting question. The growth of the American white-collar labor force seems to have reached its peak in the middle 1950's and we now are witnessing a leveling off. A similar

[1] They are also the only categories that can be easily compared across countries. The category of professional, technical, and related workers is not yet very homogeneous; and as regards the category of administrative, executive, and managerial workers, it cannot be distinguished in the present statistics from the category of proprietors and managers. In a country like France, the general trend toward the increase and professionalization of the managerial labor force is completely blurred by the slow decline of the small bosses of the handicraft sector of the economy.
[2] Computed from the first analysis of the 1960 employment census the figure for 1956 was 2,040,000; it covers both the public and the private sector of the economy.
[3] Computed from the *U.S. Statistical Abstracts 1959,* p. 218.
[4] Estimate of the French labor department statisticians.

leveling off seems to have taken place in France where the ratio of white-collar to blue-collar workers in the private sector of industry has remained quite stable over the past ten years, progressing only from 22.9 per cent to 23.1 per cent between 1955 and 1960.[5]

Shall we expect, therefore, the French white-collar labor force to stabilize at a level lower than the American, or shall we hypothesize it will grow again until it reaches the present American level? The second alternative, we believe, is much more likely, although from now on the rate of increase may be much slower than the earlier American rate and the stabilizing point in say twenty years may be somewhat lower than the present American figure which probably will have declined during the same interim.

France's historical sluggishness in keeping pace with the modern industrial sector prepared the way for the spectacular growth of the past ten years which has brought about an increase in the blue-collar labor force even if this increase, because of gains in productivity, was much lower than proportional. If we take into consideration the fact that the size of the white-collar labor force was seriously inflated at the beginning of the period when related to the general state of the economy, we can understand how it could remain stable in a period of sweeping modernization and rapid progress of the economy.

The development of the French white-collar labor force may be looked at as having preceded industrial development. Industrial growth could be achieved, therefore, with a relatively stable white-collar force, although this stability may hide many far-reaching transformations. Thus we can hypothesize that the possibilities of expansion will still be great when the readjustment is finished. If we look at the differences industry by industry, we still can foresee the growth that will have to take place to dispose of the present disparities. Some examples of such quick transformations can already be found in the present statistics: in the metal-producing industries from 1955 to 1960, the number of white-collar employees increased from 12,600 to 22,600 and the ratio of white- to blue-collar workers from 7.5 per cent to 13.2 per cent.[6] A still more spectacular development can be expected in some key sectors of predominantly white-collar activities, such as banking and insurance, that have been lagging behind in

[5] Computed from Statistics given by the INSEE (National Institute for Statistics and Economic Studies). See *Bulletin mensuel de Statistiques,* No. 21, April 7, 1962. Another series computed by the INSEE show actually a decrease, but it bears on the number of households whose head is a white-collar worker and is not very significant of employment trends. See *Le Monde,* April 29-30, 1962.

[6] See *Bulletin mensuel de Statistiques, op. cit.*

France up to now. During the past five years, notwithstanding the introduction of automation in many firms, the total number of white-collar workers in these two fields has risen from 126,800 to 151,300, i.e., by almost 20 per cent as against an average 13 per cent for the whole private and semipublic sector.[7]

Coming later and in a changing technological environment, however, the growth of white-collar work will be taken care of in large part by the development of automatic techniques, which means that the social problems of the new "administrative revolution" that is following the former industrial revolutions will be kept at a minimum in France, at least regarding employment.

At the same time as elsewhere in the Western world, but maybe even more quickly, both the numbers and the proportion of supervisors, technicians, and professional salaried workers in the total population have increased tremendously. A sample survey of the National Institute of Statistics indicates that the number of households whose heads may be classified in this group has risen 31 per cent during the past six years.[8]

The increase in numbers, however, is only one aspect of the changing situation of the French white-collar worker. The other aspects—the rapid increase in the proportion of women in the labor force, the decline of wage differentials, the change in job content, and the narrowing of class differences in the mass-consumption society—are all related and tend to correct the superficial interpretation one is tempted to give of the growth in numbers. They have a tremendous importance for unionization, but there again France is no exception to the general trend.

First of all, the increase in the proportion of women in the white-collar world must be examined. One hundred years ago an almost exclusively male group, the clerical and sales force is now shifting more and more rapidly from predominantly male to predominantly female. Over-all in the private, semipublic, and public sectors combined, men still outnumber women, but women already outnumber men significantly in the private sector during the past ten years. The shift is becoming especially rapid now: for example, the last figures from 1956 to 1960 show the fastest rate of increase of the proportion

[7] *Ibid.*

[8] Together with the managers and proprietors and with the white-collar employees as in America, they are as numerous as the blue-collar workers. But the comparison may be misleading since many more members of the proprietors group in France are only independent blue-collar workers.

of women, from 49 per cent to 53 per cent, in the private and semi-public sectors.[9]

Regarding wages, the over-all differential is now around 11 per cent in favor of the white-collar group, having decreased from 12 to 11 per cent in the past five years. But the differential would still be sizable if white- and blue-collar wages within the male group (17 per cent) and within the female group (39 per cent) were compared. The decrease is very significant, compared with the past,[10] but the contrast between France and the United States where the average pay differential of white- and blue-collar workers has been about the same since 1944,[11] is still apparent. More elaborate comparative inquiries, however, may show that the French differential is due primarily to the weight of the least developed part of the economy. The evolution, although it has come much earlier in the United States, has followed about the same trend in all Western countries.

Finally, the change of the job content may temper and correct the conclusions one would like to draw from the other points. A definite downgrading of the white-collar jobs has accompanied the advance of women and the relative loss of pay. Conversely, many jobs that were once considered "employés" jobs are now classified as supervisory or technicians' jobs. People who correspond more closely to the old line white-collar workers have now been upgraded to new, more professional jobs. The too easy comparisons that lead to the notion of the proletarianization of the white-collar world should be avoided. What may be called the white-collar world is undoubtedly more proletarian than it was fifty years ago, but it does not cover the same status groups. The old white-collar strata in France, as in America or in Great Britain, are being more and more split into a growing minority of the better educated, better paid, and predominantly male groups of supervisors and technicians and a slowly decreasing majority of routine operators, mostly female. The shift may be newer and not yet completed in France where the old line "employé aux écritures" (bookkeeper) is still holding on in many branches. But it is definitely on the way.

The coming of a mass-consumption society has a decisive although indirect impact on the status of the white-collar worker in France as

[9] In the civil service for the lower grades a sample survey in 1956 showed still the predominance of men (66 per cent).
[10] Henri Mercillon, *La Remuneration des employes* (Paris: Armand Colin, 1955).
[11] Robert K. Burns, "The comparative economic position of manual and white-collar employees," *Journal of Business of the University of Chicago*, Vol. XXVII, No. 4 (October 1954).

well as in the rest of the Western world. The white-collar worker drew his prestige mostly from physical and intellectual proximity to the managerial group. As improved communication techniques make the mores, the way of life, and the culture of the upper groups easy for all groups, even the lower ones, to observe, the status advantage of the white-collar worker is gradually disappearing. To be sure, he knows a little more about the inside of our modern organizational culture, but this is nothing to compare with the advantages he once possessed over a blue-collar worker completely cut off from the mainstreams of national culture.

THE PECULIARITIES OF THE FRENCH SITUATION

If the factors we have listed and briefly described were operating in a vacuum, there should not be many differences among industrially developed countries. White-collar workers should have the same view of basically identical situations and should show the same propensity to engage in trade-union activities. Yet, a comparison of the actual attitudes of white-collar workers toward the labor movement in France and in Germany or the United States and also of the way white-collar unions behave in these three countries discloses surprising differences, all the more noticeable by contrast with blue-collar workers and their unions. The latter seem to react almost homogeneously, and at least some unions with particular individuality, such as the miners, the sailors, and the printers, have drawn on the same traditions and have had long parallel histories.

A general explanation can be found in the importance of the human relations content of the white-collar job. Human relations arrangements are much more culturally determined than are technical arrangements.[12] Every one of the Western societies has developed patterns of its own to take care of its managerial problems and of the white-collar activities that are associated with them, and the status and possibilities of action of the white-collar workers may be quite different, according to the place they may be assigned in such patterns.

Let us now consider the French case in this perspective. Three series of variables seem to be important:

1. The resistance of French society to mass consumption; its general pattern of status stratification.

[12] Technical arrangements, of course, are not by any means independent of cultural variables. It is only a matter of degree.

2. Centralization of power, prestige, and cultural activities in Paris.
3. Deep-seated conflict between white-collar workers of the private sector of the economy and those who are members of the civil service.

The coming of a mass-consumption society should ultimately level off all class and status differences. Should people participate on a basis of equal access to all cultural products and should only earnings discriminate between them, no significant differences would persist between white- and blue-collar workers. This is still far from being the case, especially in France where mass consumption has not been entirely achieved. First of all, French society long resisted the trend toward mass consumption, and it is still lagging behind in some respects. This resistance may have slowed its economic development,[13] but the requirements of an advanced industrial society are not so clear-cut that one can not imagine, at least, a successful industrial society keeping a pattern of social relations and status differences out of tune with the mass-consumption economy.[14] Second, and perhaps more important, older cultural patterns can persist within the new society and accommodate very well to new conditions. New differentiations can be worked out, enabling the society to maintain its status system. This was apparent in surveys made in 1956-59 among bank and insurance clerks in Paris.[15] The persistence of the old fears and prejudices of the nonmanual workers against the manual workers was apparent all through the interviews. The importance of the cultural barrier was shown indirectly by the attitudes of the people from the working class who were more likely to be apathetic and to refuse to participate even in trade-union and political matters than their better established colleagues. Finally, leisure-time activities were considered as a way to assert one's own ranking in the class system; the products of mass-consumption society were used very skillfully as devices of discrimination.[16] Magazines, of course, were very well stratified; theater attendance was a prerequisite of bourgeois status, and even within the world of the movies consistent efforts at discrimi-

[13] As some economic historians have claimed: see, for example, David Landes, "French Business and the Businessman: A Social and Cultural Analysis" in ed. E. M. Earle, *Modern France* (Princeton: Princton University Press, 1951).
[14] The Japanese society could be the best case in point.
[15] Michel Crozier, *Le monde des employés de bureau* (Paris: Le Seuil, 1965).
[16] See Michel Crozier, "Employés et petits fonctionnaires; note sur les loisirs comme moyen de participation a la culture bourgeoise," *Esprit* (June 1959).

nation could be recognized. Only TV was catering to all strata, but it was still very much resisted.[17]

To understand the meaning of these attitudes, precise comparative studies across countries would be needed. Unfortunately, nothing serious has been done yet and we can present only some tentative explanations. In our view status and behavior of the white-collar workers depend primarily upon the communication system between social classes and social categories. The more difficult the communication, the more prestige and privilege go to that part of the lower groups than can communicate. Possibilities of easy communications are increased by the tremendous development of the new technological world and by the diffusion of education,[18] but significant differences are introduced by the patterns of social distance and authority relationships prevailing in a country.

Let us compare, for example, the French situation with the German and the English ones. In Germany, where social distances are greater and authority relationships harsher and accepted in a more submissive way, communication between social groups is still more formal and difficult, and the white-collar worker has retained a more distinct position in a more rigid stratification system. The vocabulary has recognized it in the word *Angestellte*, a very specific title. His trade unions were traditionally separate, and even now that most white-collar workers are in the DGB, there is still a very strong feeling of group cohesiveness and a lack of common allegiance between white- and blue-collar workers. In England social distance may still be great, but blue-collar workers long ago won recognition of their strength and the privilege of communicating easily with management groups. Intermediary groups, such as white-collar workers, therefore, never got the same attention from the upper classes and they did not solidify into a class-conscious group. They did not even acquire a generic name and must be referred to by awkward designations such as *black-coated* or *white-collar* workers. Their trade unions are not part of a separate federation; they follow the lead of the manual workers' unions.

[17] One of the reasons may have been its situation as a state monopoly and the insistence of its managers to use it in an educative perspective and to refuse to yield to "vulgarity."

[18] In market terms the privilege of the white-collar worker can be analyzed in reference to the rarity of people with the education necessary to achieve the white-collar rank, but such an analysis fails for all wide-enough comparisons across countries and in the long periods because the criterion that is used is much too narrow.

In France, the picture is quite different. Social distance was not as great as in Germany and authority was not accepted submissively, so that there was no segregation of the white-collar worker who did not side with the bourgeoisie. Social communication, however, could not be resolved by bargaining, as in America, but required the intervention of the state and very long and frustrating detours. The white-collar workers and especially the civil servants, although they do not have a recognized hierarchical ranking, benefit from their central position in the social and political bargaining process. This explains the fact that their trade unions were and still are comparatively vigorous, although they never were separated from the rest of the labor movement. This also explains their traditional alignment left of center politically whereas their German counterparts would side right of center. The vocabulary reflects this intermediate position since the term Frenchmen use, *employés,* is not a specific and generic term like *Angestellte;* it can designate, just as the English term does, all the personnel of an enterprise. It is not an image like *black-coated* and *blue-collar* and its connotation has been fairly constant over time.

The second distinctive trait of the French white-collar worker is his concentration in the Paris area and his close association with the pattern of centralization that prevails in the country. More than one-third of the French white-collar workers are employed in the Paris area.[19] Everywhere, of course, white-collar workers are more numerous in large cities, but the unique disproportionate importance of Paris in French society adds a new dimension to this usual distribution. It means that a much greater and strategically important segment of the French white-collar group borrows social prestige from living in close contact with the recognized center of everything worthwhile socially, politically, and culturally. They are in a certain sense members of an elite.[20] The development of modern mass media somewhat weakens this privileged status since physical proximity is no longer as necessary for vicarious participation as before. But a good deal still persists and it is one of the decisive factors that helps account for the social status of the white-collar worker in France and the country's discriminatory use of mass-consumption techniques.

[19] Although only one out of six Frenchmen live in the same regional unit.

[20] The social patterns of diffusion of information, fashions, and new models of behavior seem to be as follows: 1. professional and managerial groups; 2 supervisors, technicians; 3. white-collar workers; 4. small business and handicraft; 5. industrial workers; 6. peasants. The introduction of the Parisian pattern variable would still greatly enhance the position of the Parisian white-collar worker.

The third and even more original trait of the French situation is the existence of a deep rift and strong opposition between the private and public sectors. To be sure, there are differences and opposition everywhere, but nowhere else are they as sharp as in France. It seems that this is not superficial group solidarity but that there coexist actually two opposing systems of participation and integration into society—a paternalistic type, to which the white-collar people of the private sector belong, and the egalitarian type of the civil service. Both types, of course, operate within the general model we have described, but there is a considerable gap between them that is one of the more important facts of French social and political life. Two different sets of roles and two opposite views of the world correspond to these psychological situations. They revolve basically around promotion systems, one based on competitive examinations, with a strong emphasis on equality, impersonality, and the anticlerical spirit, and the other based on paternalistic relationships.

To be sure, we are now far from the system of patronage that once flourished. What managers now require is nothing compared with the moral allegiance that was demanded by their predecessors. Yet there is still a "right type" for bank employees and for sales clerks, and personnel departments still inquire about the family of the applicant and may carefully reject those who show any working class solidarities.[21] Selection and promotion depend very much on recommendations and on a respectable appearance and demeanor. Public administration ignores these subtle pressures for conformity but social barriers are not altogether absent; they have only become formal and academic. Other criteria of social conformity rather than actual achievements are relied upon. The civil service system does not differ from the private sector because of its lack of stratification but rather because of the values on which stratification is based. In the private sector we find particularistic paternalist values; in the public sector, universalistic abstract cultural values.

These differences are decisive for the possibilities of trade-union development as well as for political alignments. The civil service unions are traditionally *laique*[22] and anticlerical. The white-collar

[21] This was still standard practice in one of the best known Parisian department stores a few years go.

[22] The term *secular* is an unsatisfactory, though literal, translation of *laique*. The French word, embodying as it were the spirit of the French revolution and of the struggles over the issue of the separation of Church and State, which divided France for almost two centuries, carries a profound emotional connotation. (Ed. note.)

world of the private sector has long been the stronghold of the Catholic unions. The hold is slowly diminishing in strength, but it remains one of the important factors of union politics and even of politics in general.

In the light of this general picture and the cultural background, the history of white-collar unions in France will be easier to understand. Conversely, the historic approach will permit us to see on a more operational basis the working of the forces we have just described. The present division of the white-collar world is not new; indeed, it was apparent long ago. Yet if one looks beyond first impressions, it seems that there is some slow progress toward unity. History, then, will let us understand better the models of collective action that are used in the white-collar world. These models, similar in many respects to the models used by the manual workers' unions, determine the present structure, methods, and practices of white-collar unions.

We will focus on five periods only: the origins, the turning point of the early twenties, the great upsurge of 1936, the postwar liberation period with its nationalization measures, and the strikes and other events of the fifties.

THE ORIGINS

From the beginning there were three sources of unionism in the French white-collar world: the Parisian department stores, the postal workers and grade school teachers within the lower grades of the civil service, and the Catholic vocational schools.

The great Parisian department stores date from the 1850's and 1860's. The earliest ones in the world, they introduced an unheard-of concentration and revolutionary practices to a traditional Parisian field of activity. Their promoters were self-made men of modest origin, ruthless and authoritarian capitalists of the pioneering type with no respect for the feelings of their personnel. Their paternalism was of the crudest kind. Hours were long, conditions of work very difficult, and discipline very harsh. Women had to eat in separate dining rooms and were locked in during their short meal times. Dress and demeanor were constantly checked. The personnel did not wait long to react. There were attempts at organization as early as the 1860's. Friendly societies and mutual benefit associations developed first,[23] but from the very beginning there was agitation about Sunday rest. After a

[23] Mutual benefit associations in France, one has to recall, were at that time the great scheme of such foremost socialist thinkers as Proudhon.

series of meetings at the masonic *Grand Orient,* a *Chambre Syndicale des Employés de Commerce* (a trade-union center for commercial employees) was formed in 1869, just at the time of the creation in Paris of the section of the *First Internationale.* The masonic influence, which was then republican and anticlerical in France, was strong and lasting. After the war of 1870, the Commune, and the social setback brought on by its failure and repression, the organization of sales clerks subsided, and we have to wait until 1882 to see the foundation of the *Chambre Syndicale Fédérale des Employés* which was the first stable organization in the field.[24] Yet the clerks were not by any means trailing behind other labor organizations since their union was among the first to be re-established after the catastrophe of 1871. The *Chambre Syndicale* campaigned for the eight-hour day and Sunday rest; its membership was wholly Parisian. In 1893 a national federation was set up, but it was more or less a paper organization since very few substantial groups outside the Parisian *Chambre Syndicale* affiliated. During the 1890's and 1900's many conflicts and discussions developed among these organizations, partly based on the political opposition between anarchists and socialists and among the different socialist groups. The importance of the left-wing influences should be noted. The *Chambre Syndicale* was not a conservative group; it participated in the founding of the *Confédération Générale du Travail* (CGT, French trade-union confederation) in 1895 and was open to the same currents of thought as the blue-collar workers' unions. It, too, was a minority group, and a militant and fiery one. Some strikes of department store workers were famous, the one at Dufayel in 1905, for example.[25]

The second main source of white-collar unionism was among the lower grades of the civil service, primarily the postal workers and the primary school teachers. Theirs was a somewhat more prudent and less anarchistic union, but also a more powerful one. It drew its characteristics and its strength from roots in the work environment. From the beginning it was not a minority movement, as the department store unions and the manual workers' unions of the period were.

[24] In 1879 the anarchist leader Emile Pouget, who was to become the second in command of the CGT in the "heroic period" of the Charte d'Amiens (from 1902 to 1908), had already organized a union of sales clerks. He was himself at that time a sales clerk in a Parisian *magasin de nouveautés.*

[25] For a history of this movement there are scattered elements in Edouard Dolléans, *Histoire du mouvement ouvrier français, II, 1871-1920* (Paris: Armand Colin, 1953), but the only comprehensive account is a union publication, *Historique de la Chambre Syndicale des Employés de la Région Parisienne* (Paris: CGT, 1938).

It was much broader in scope, but neither its militancy nor its receptivity to anarcho-syndicalist ideas was thereby lessened.

The postal workers were the most vocal. After participating in friendly societies for a long period, in 1900 they formed two general associations, one for the *agents* and one for the *sous-agents* (a lower grade). Millerand, the socialist leader turned minister, assisted with the organization. At the time, the postal recruitment and promotion systems were already egalitarian and democratic. What was at stake for the employees was to win protection against the arbitrary influence of politics since the most political authority in the administrative world, the prefect, could interfere with promotion policy. Postal workers were highly successful at organizing and by 1903 they claimed to have enlisted three-quarters of the *agents*. They were rather moderate in their views and had open and clandestine contacts, through masonry, with the higher state authorities. But the situation was very fluid, and they also maintained contacts with the revolutionary CGT and even contemplated affiliation. Direct pressure from the government prevented this action, and in 1905 there was a general hardening of the attitude of the state toward civil service organizations.[26] In 1906 a Committee for the Rights of State Employees to Organize held meetings all over France under the guidance of Griffuelhes, the general secretary of the CGT. The *sous-agents* of the postal services was the first of several groups to strike. In Paris three thousand letter carriers stopped work; three hundred of them were immediately fired, and after a week the strike was lost. This event took place under the government and authoritarian leadership of Clemenceau and of his Under-Secretary Simyan. In 1907 another two hundred agents were fired. In 1909 Simyan tried to impose a drastic change of the promotion system. A major conflict developed. A strike broke out in March at the Parisian Telegraphic center and police brutalities ensued. A general strike was voted by the national organization and provincial groups responded to the strike call. Clemenceau felt obliged to negotiate. With only half-promises, he succeeded in persuading the workers to return to their jobs. He retained Simyan and the hard line, and after the First of May celebration, militants were fired again. A strike was voted a second time, but the momentum was lost. The CGT launched an appeal for solidarity of the working class, but to no

[26] The strike of the postal workers of 1909 was one of the most famous episodes of the heroic period of French "Syndicalism." There was born a deep-seated allegiance of the civil servants to the working class that has not been broken ever since although the memories of the event have long faded away.

avail. The postal workers had lost. The price to be paid was heavy: eight hundred firings and many sanctions. One month later the Clemenceau government fell and with it the authoritarian "reforms" disappeared. In the end the srtikers won, and the postal workers, although not officially members of the CGT, had achieved their place as one of the most influential groups within the labor movement.[27]

The other civil service organizations were pale indeed compared to those of the postal workers. Lower grade civil servants formed friendly societies (*amicales*) and associations and maintained contacts with the CGT, but they were weaker and retreated early. The teachers, however, were powerful and militant. Like the postal workers, they were a distinct and cohesive body recruited under a democratic and egalitarian system, the operation of which was hampered by undue political influences. Moreover, they had already played an important role in the 1880's in the establishment of the Republic whose storm troops they had been. They had durable links with masonry and with radical republican circles. Although their struggles were not, at that time, as spectacular as those of the postal workers, they were another thorn in the flesh of the Clemenceau government. Their leaders were fired along with those of the postal workers in 1906 and 1907. Quickly more radical elements came to the fore. In 1912 the teachers' union was dissolved for having passed an antimilitaristic motion at its convention. This is the time when socialist and antimilitaristic ideas were replacing the old republican creed among teachers of the new generation—the seeds of the pacifist movement of the twenties and thirties.[28]

The third main source of white-collar unionism, supported by the Catholic church, was extremely different from the other two in the beginning and was regarded by the bulk of the labor movement as "yellow" company-unionism. What was to become a powerful and militant trade-union confederation, the present CFTC, was born as a paternalistic employment service founded in 1885 by the *Frères des Écoles Chrétiennes,* a religious order in charge of Catholic vocational schools. The *Syndicat des Employés du Commerce et de l'Industrie,* that succeeded the employment service in 1892, was formed in cooperation with Catholic employers' associations. Catholic opinion was then extremely hostile to trade unions, but the small group had the

[27] Postal workers were not formally recognized as civil servants until 1929.
[28] For historical sources one could consult Edouard Dolléans, *op. cit.*; B. Laurent, *Poste et Postiers* (Paris: Octave Doin, 1922); Georges Duveau, *Les Instituteurs* (Paris: Editions du Seuil).

support of Pope Leo XIII whose Encyclical letter *Rerum Novarum* had been issued in 1891. The S.E.C.I. was to suffer for a long time from its origin as a religious friendly society whose aims were to secure employment and promotion for trustworthy Catholic youngsters. At the same time, in the North, similar groups were used deliberately by the employers to oppose the CGT. The S.E.C.I. grew slowly and could claim only two thousand members in 1900. In the 1910's, however, a new generation brought new objectives and a new approach. The aftermath of the Dreyfuss affair was fading and Catholic liberals such as Marc Sangnier were campaigning for a reversal of the conservative policies of the church. In that climate S.E.C.I. decided to become the focus of all Christian workers and to engage in a policy of expansion. In 1912 a *Fédération Française des Syndicats d'Employés Catholiques* (French Federation of Catholic White-Collar Unions) was founded. The report of the Executive of 1913 emphasized the dangers if trade unionism were too closely under the control of the church hierarchy. In that period of intense intellectual discussions one could see the harbingers of the great transformation of the Catholic unions that took place in 1919 and 1920 after the shock of the World War.[29]

THE TURNING POINT OF THE TWENTIES

Nothing much can be said of the white-collar unions during World War I. All activities were interrupted during four long years. The introduction of progressive labor legislation in the armament industries was no compensation. Yet this suppression of all channels of expression did not prevent thinking. There were teachers and postal workers in the Zimmerwald group,[30] and their revolutionary philosophy had a profound impact on their colleagues soon after peace was restored. Opposition to war was to become the official philosophy of the civil trade unions.

Reconversion from the war was indeed a decisive turning point for the labor movement and especially for the white-collar unions. In the great strikes that shook France as well as many other Western countries in 1919 and 1920, the white-collar people played an impor-

[29] For historical sources see Verdin, *La Fondation du Syndicat des Employés du Commerce et de l'Industrie 1886-1891* (Paris: Edition Spes, 1929); R. P. Stephane Piat, *Jules Zirnheld, president de la CFTC* (Paris: Bonne Presse, 1948).

[30] An antiwar meeting of Socialist and trade union leaders held in Zimmerwald (Switzerland) during World War I to oppose the patriotic attitude of the leaders of the Socialist majorities in most countries on both sides in the war. (Ed. note.)

tant role. They participated in the general strike of the First of May, 1919. In May and June most of the great Parisian department stores were struck, one after another. The movement was on the whole successful. Collective contracts were signed. Banks—up to that time very difficult for union militants to penetrate—opened up for the first time. On May 5, fifteen thousand bank employees stopped work. For the first time also the Christian Federation endorsed a strike movement. Unity of action seemed to be in view. Success, however, was only temporary. No stable organization was built during the struggle and members quit as quickly as they had joined. In October 1919 the general strike of the Parisian department stores, although impressive by its magnitude and its length (it lasted a month) ended in partial defeat. And in 1920 the labor movement, torn by dissension, moved from one defeat to another.

During that period of intense agitation, postal workers, teachers, and civil servants were not in the forefront. They supported the strike movement and affiliated with the CGT in defiance of government orders. Their point was won easily. In 1924 the famous *Circulaire Chautemps*—an order issued by Minister Chautemps—recognized their complete freedom to organize.[31]

Results of the movement of 1919-20 may seem meager, but from a historical point of view they mark a very important turning point, at least for the white-collar workers. The solid allegiance of the white-collar world to working class unity dates from this period. The Catholic unions, that were up to that time a factor of dubious value, had shown that at the decisive moment they would side with the strikers. One of the strongholds of bourgeois respectability, the banks, had given up.[32] The civil service unions at the same time got *de facto* recognition and their place within the labor movement could not be contested.

With the split of July 1921 and the founding of the CGTU (*Confédération Générale du Travail Unitaire,* communist-led trade union federation), affiliated with the Red International of Trade Unions, the French labor movement entered a long period of decline and later stagnation. The white-collar unions suffered along with the blue-collar unions; only the civil service groups prospered and consequently their importance for the labor movement as a whole increased. During this

[31] This was an administrative circular of the then Minister of Interior which was for a long time the only legal protection of the civil service unions. It could not be really called into question. One had to wait for the 1946 constitution to see the existence of the civil service unions recognized by law.

[32] The insurance companies, however, stood up and joined the union side only in 1936.

period another major characteristic of the French labor movement developed: its peculiar type of relation with the centralized state. It had been prepared by the *Union Sacrée* of the war period [33] and took its roots in the alliance of the majority CGT, purged of its communist-inclined elements (which had formed the CGTU), and the left-of-center governments of the twenties. The CGT became a major respectable force in the Third Republic. The civil service unions played a significant role in all of these activities. They made a decisive contribution to the 1924 electoral campaign that brought the *Cartel des Gauches*—an alliance of the Radical and the Socialist parties—to power. Their numerical strength within the labor movement had risen; in 1932 their three main unions (*Fédération Générale des Fonctionnaires, Syndicat National des Instituteurs, Fédération Postale*) accounted for 35 per cent of the total membership of the CGT. They were the only section of the labor world that could reasonably claim to represent a working consensus of employees. Equally important at least was the number of educated and responsible militants they could provide for the movement. Protected by the rules of the civil service, they were the only unions able to supply a great number of militants with enough free time to a movement that desperately needed help since it had to rely on unpaid labor to survive. Their members very often held the key jobs of secretaries of *unions departementales* and *unions locales* (department and city federations). Their roles as intellectuals, educators, and mediators with the political world were central for the whole movement. Even in the communist CGTU, their contribution was not overlooked.

THE 1936 UPHEAVAL

The alliance that had been forged in the strikes of 1919-20 was tested and confirmed in the major crisis of 1936 that saw white-collar workers occupy department stores and insurance companies as well as factories.

In 1934 threats of the right-wing and fascist groups had been brought to a stop by a general strike. The deflationary measures of the Laval government were met by civil service strikes, and the whole labor movement reunited in October 1935. Each branch negotiated its separate fusion during the following months. In every white-collar union, *confédérés* (the majority noncommunist organization) were in charge of the new organizations. The first sitdowns took place before

[33] An informal internal political and social peace agreement during World War I. (Ed. note.)

the elections of May 1936, which gave a substantial majority to the Popular Front. But the wave of strikes broke in earnest after the electoral victory. By early June it had become irresistible; in Paris most of the large department stores were occupied, and so were half a dozen large insurance companies and innumerable business houses. Hundreds of collective contracts were signed after the famous *accords Matignon* of June 8, 1936.[34] Sitdowns continued, however, during a good part of June in some department stores until complete victory could be won.

The department stores were the stronghold of the white-collar movement of 1936. For the first time the workers of the insurance companies joined the strike. The bank employees, however, won a collective contract without striking. No representative of the Christian Federation took part in any of the department store negotiations; it could secure a representative only in the discussions with the insurance companies and with the banks.

In most industries scattered white-collar workers were organized with the blue-collar people. Only after the victory did they eventually join white-collar unions. The civil service employees remained quiet. During the strikes and the Popular Front period, the leadership of the labor movement was clearly taken away from them by the blue-collar workers and their self-appointed representative, the Communist Party.

The years 1936-37 were ones of triumph for the *Chambre Syndicale des Employés de la Région Parisienne* (Trade Union Center of White-Collar Employees in the Paris Area). It had more than one hundred thousand members,[35] thirty thousand of whom were in the department stores and more than twenty thousand in the banking and insurance fields. In the provinces, people were rapidly joining. The leadership was confident and aggressive. In April 1937, employees of a great business house, *La Soie,* occupied the offices after ten of their leaders had been fired. They were to sitdown for 155 days in one of the longest and bitterest strikes of the period. But the ebbing of the tide soon came, and defeat in the general strike of November 1938, which the CFTC refused to join, marked the end of the movement. Membership of the *Chambre Syndicale* declined quickly and it could not survive as an organization during the war years.

[34] An agreement between the employers association and the unions providing for union recognition, brought about by Prime Minister Leon Blum under the pressure of the sitdown strikes.

[35] They had, at that time, more than a third of the whole membership of the union.

What was finally the outcome of this great popular upheaval for the white-collar people and their unions? It was to have first, as we have already stated, a great influence on their collective reactions and their psychology. It had put to a test and reinforced their solidarity with the blue-collar people, already established in 1919-20. Right-wing groups, and especially the *Croix de Feu* and its offshoot, the *Parti Social Français,* made strenuous efforts to organize *syndicats professionnels* (unions based on craft or profession). White-collar people were their favorite target, but apart from a few cases where they made some inroads with the support of the employers, they were generally unsuccessful. Whatever their own reservations about blue-collar workers, the white-collar people were on the side of the strikers. Not only were they sympathetic, but they wanted to act, too.

Second, on the political front the upheaval provoked a realignment of the union forces. The united CGT benefited from the irresistible appeal of a successful movement from which the Christian unions were deliberately excluded. The CFTC was surprised and could not break the monopoly its adversaries held as representatives of a fighting working class. Even in the white-collar world, where before the strikes the CFTC had as strong and often stronger positions than the CGT, it had to give up its leadership. It was skillful enough, however, not to oppose the movement but to attack the CGT only on its closed shop practices and to fight for a worker's freedom to join the union of his own choice. This moderate course was appropriate to the mood of the white-collar strikers who wanted to be part of the action but did not want to be committed to the socialist and communist orientation of the CGT. Very soon the CFTC regained all the influence it had lost. At the same time the blue-collar unions became more and more dominated by militants of the Communist Party and disassociated themselves from civil service unions under the control of socialist elements. The antagonisms within the labor movement that were to produce the present divisions were already well under way. On the one side, the blue-collar workers identified themselves to a large extent with the Communist Party; on the other side, the white-collar workers were split between socialist and secular tendencies (overwhelmingly preponderant in the civil service) and Christian ones (most influential within the private sector of the white-collar world).[36]

On the material side, finally, the gains of the white-collar workers may have been on many issues less spectacular than those of the

[36] They also had very important regional influences, especially in the North and in Alsace.

blue-collar workers, but they were often of decisive importance and more durable. The white-collar workers first of all duplicated the blue-collar workers gains of salary increases, paid holidays, and the right to elect shop stewards, but they also won special advantages. For example, the salary differential between men and women was drastically reduced; it fell from more than 30 per cent to 10 per cent and less, and complete equality was actually achieved in some branches. They won protection against layoff and provisions for substantial severance pay. The bank employees imposed important provisions with regard to seniority and promotion in their collective contract, similar to some of the civil service statutes. Everywhere careers and promotion lines were systematized.

THE WAR YEARS, THE LIBERATION, AND THE NATIONALIZATION MEASURES

During the war years, the labor movement fell into lethargy. The Vichy regime dissolved labor confederations and national unions and tried to integrate the labor movement in its corporatist *Charte du Travail,* but few leaders and militants cooperated. Stronger efforts were made to eradicate union solidarity from the civil service, but with little avail. Meanwhile, resistance movements were organized around the former networks of political and union friendships. This revival was decisive in selecting a new generation of leaders and militants. Many of the new leaders at all levels of the organization were white-collar unionists from the civil service and from the private sector. A sizable number of the new political personnel in the postwar period had their start in the resistance movement.

The Liberation period brought a triumphal revival of the labor movement with thousands of workers flocking into unions even more rapidly than in 1936. But accompanying this revival was a violent struggle for power, especially in the white-collar world. The Communists, who regained and consolidated their hold on the major blue-collar unions, tried to invade the white-collar field, especially the civil service. During their two and one-half years in the government, they used all available means to eliminate their opponents.[37] The postal workers federation was one of their major objectives, but their high-handed methods raised such opposition that a schism was unavoidable. The strike of the postal workers of 1946 against their "pro-

[37] A Communist was Minister of Labor, and Maurice Thorez as Vice-President of the government was in charge of the civil service (a minor post which he tried to use).

ductivist" policy was one of the Communists' major setbacks and resulted in the emergence of an autonomous federation of postal workers. This federation joined the CGT-FO (*Confédération Générale du Travail—Force Ouvrière,* General Trade Union Confederation—Labor and Strength) in 1948, a few months after the founding of the anti-Communist confederation.

The nationalized industries established in 1945-46 were a major battleground. The Communists succeeded fairly well in controlling the white-collar as well as the blue-collar workers in the new Gas and Electricity Authority, and somewhat less well in the mining industry; in the banking and insurance fields they had to contend with the CFTC which had always been very powerful in these areas. The fight went on at several levels since there were many jobs available in the *conseils d'administration* (supervisory board of nationalized industries), management as well as union posts. A few leaders began business careers while many others were given sizable political and administrative rewards. The rush for political payoff produced ill-feeling among the rank and file and contributed to a general loss of confidence in the labor movement.

The postwar years brought many important social measures such as social security legislation, but the major alteration in the balance of forces was brought about by the nationalization laws. Nationalization of industry has been the focus of much of the attention and enthusiasm of the union militants, and the failure of these measures on the social side, notwithstanding their economic success, was discouraging to their supporters. This was especially marked in the banks and insurance companies where the departure of the former owners brought about almost no change as far as the employees were concerned. Within a few years, nationalization was viewed with complete indifference, if not with cynicism. After the Communists left the government in 1947, the failure of their revolutionary strikes of 1947 and 1948 resulted in a rapid decline in membership and a loss of influence on the part of the unions almost comparable to the disaster of November 1938.

THE CONTEMPORARY MOVEMENTS

With return to normalcy in the late forties and in the fifties, the hopes of a coming social revolution vanished and the labor movement settled down as an extremely vocal but not too powerful minority group. In this new context of moderation, the well-organized civil service unions again came to the forefront, but they were partially overshadowed this time by the unions of the nationalized industries—the railroads, gas and electric utilities, public transportation, and mines. Yet one of the major social events of the period, the civil service general strike that paralyzed the whole country in August 1953 and later brought down the government, was initiated in the postal service.

In the private sector of white-collar occupations, a change similar to the one in the blue-collar field has taken place. The leadership has shifted from the department stores to the nationalized banks and insurance companies. Two major strikes, in 1947 and in 1957, were those of bank employees.

The bloody repression of the Hungarian revolt in November 1956 and the coming to power of General de Gaulle in 1958 were blows to the Communist influence, blows that were less easily recouped in the white-collar field where Communist influence was small to begin with. But such losses were of only partial benefit to the non-Communist unions. The labor movement as a whole suffered, and the revival that is manifest since 1961 merely tends to re-establish the former pattern.

Let us now analyze the structure, methods, and patterns of action of present-day white-collar unions. The brief historical sketch has already shown us a few general traits one could see running throughout the past of the movement:

a. French white-collar unions are in the main stream of the French labor movement; they are not separatist unions and they seem to have solved their problems of allegiance long ago.

b. They have been consistently Parisian-run and Parisian-minded.

c. They have always been profoundly divided between civil service unions and unions catering to the private and semipublic sectors.

d. Just like the rest of the French labor movement, they are weak, but they are not the weakest part. They are not trailing behind; on the contrary, the civil service is the only well-unionized sector of the economy.

e. Their patterns of action, like those of the rest of the French labor movement, are unpredictable and even erratic; great waves of agitation are succeeded by long periods of lethargy with very little conscious policy-making.

f. Like the rest of the French labor movement, they are divided along ideological lines among the CGT, CGT-FO, and CFTC, the Communist-inclined, Socialist-inclined, and Christian confederations. But these ideological divisions reflect both group consciousness and class cleavages. CGT-FO is most powerful among civil servants, CFTC in the private sector; CGT is now often in the minority, although it is usually the dominant force among blue-collar workers in the industrial field. [CFTC has dropped the reference to its religious ideology and now calls itself CFTD (Confédération des Travailleurs Démocratiques —Democratic Labor Federation). A minority has refused to accept the change. Ed. note.]

THE EXTENT OF UNIONISM IN THE DIFFERENT BRANCHES

Let us give first a general picture of the extent of unionism in the different branches of the white-collar world.

The Civil Service

The civil service is by far the best unionized sector of the French economy. The proportion of union members is generally estimated as 40 per cent of the employees compared to an average of 20 per cent for private industry. Moreover, this percentage is remaining stable while the proportion is constantly declining for all other branches.[38]

The members are divided among a great number of national unions (almost 400 of them) grouped into a few *Fédérations* that belong to the three main confederations; some unions are independent and some, mostly in the postal service, have joined a *Fédération* of autonomous unions. On top of these *Fédérations* are *cartels* or a *Fédération Générale,* as in CFTC and FO, or a *Union Générale des Fédérations,* as in the CGT. There are also confederate sections by department[39] and federations of central administrations in Paris. In most ministries there are two, three, or even five different competing unions, each affiliated with one of the three *confédérations* or with an autonomous body. The whole civil service seems to be, therefore, a mosaic of small corporate groups, jealous of their autonomy, upon which the ideological dividing lines are only partially superimposed.

This complexity is certainly a peculiar trait seldom encountered in the rest of the French labor movement whose structure is usually, theoretically at least, rational.

From the results of the elections to the joint administrative boards, it seems that the CGT and the CGT-FO have about the same influence (each receives about a third of the ballots) while the CFTC

[38] Such figures are only guesses since unions keep them a well-guarded secret.
[39] The territorial units of France's administration between an American state and an American county.

gets 20 per cent and the autonomous unions around 10 per cent.[40] But this over-all distribution covers extremely different situations. The CGT's greatest influence is in the lower categories; besides organizing the bulk of the blue-collar workers of the civil service, it has a majority among some of the lower grades of white-collar workers such as the letter carriers. It is the major force in some big departments or branches, such as the Administration of Indirect Taxes and the penitentiary services that traditionally have a more "proletarian" orientation within the civil service and that remained united within the CGT after the scission. In neither of these cases, however, are the CGT unions dominated by Communist leaders.

In contrast, FO seems to cater principally to the middle grades. It has the majority in many services and is the majority union for a number of large departments that have a tradition of greater "respectability" than those influenced by the CGT (such as the Treasury Department and the Direct Taxes). The influence of FO, however, is much greater than its sheer numbers would suggest. It usually has the most strategic influence because of its traditions, its connections with the higher authorities, and its influence on promotions. No movement can succeed without the FO, and whenever a campaign is launched there is a good chance that FO will be actually in charge of preparing the settlement. For these reasons it is often criticized as being secretive and stuffy. By trying to be the governing body of the civil service, very often it has lost touch with the personnel. The rise of autonomous unions whose leaders and militants come from FO is an ominous sign, although these unions have not been too successful except among the postal workers.

The CFTC is much newer in the field, except for the female personnel it had already organized in the twenties. It made some inroads during the postwar period due to the general climate of tolerance that softened the traditional anticlerical orientation of the service, the increase in female personnel, and its greater militancy compared, at least, to the new and often complacent FO.

The Teachers

Teachers should be set aside from the rest of the civil service since they are a unique example in France of a group organized by one union alone, which shares almost all the potential membership with only one small competitor.

[40] This is for the whole civil service, the teachers excepted.

Because of this unique feature, the FEN (*Fédération de l'Education Nationale*) is a great power. With its 200,000 to 250,000 members, it is the most important union in France. It has been autonomous since 1947, i.e., it is not affiliated with either the CGT or the FO. Its members can affiliate with the confederations individually, if they wish. As to currents of opinion expressing themselves in the conventions and in union journals, the majority tendency since the beginning seems to be FO-inclined.

The FEN is a federation of about forty unions, but the largest of them, the SNI (*Syndicat National des Instituteurs*—grade school teachers) accounts for 60 per cent at least of its members and is its dominant force. Grade school teachers are 90 per cent organized, while organization in the other categories, secondary and technical school teachers, and university professors, is only 50 per cent or less.

The power of the SNI and of the FEN comes from its control of the promotion system (supervisors are all members of the union) and the services it gives its members—mutual benefit societies, social security, trade information, correspondence courses, pedagogic advice. It is occasionally criticized as being a huge and slow-moving, conservative, corporatist body. It feels especially uneasy about the new reforms that are beginning to transform the French educational system.

The minority union, the SGEN (*Syndicat Général de l'Education Nationale*) is a small group of active and devoted unionists who have played an important role within their confederation, the CFTC, as an intellectual and training center; it is not very influential among the teachers themselves, although it is able at times to introduce new issues.

The Department Stores

Parisian department stores, that were once the hotbed of white-collar unionism, have ceased to be in the forefront of the labor movement. The personnel is now quite apathetic and new; more sophisticated managements have been able to hold the unions in check while conforming strictly to the letter of the law.

Comités d'entreprise (plant committees)[41] are operating, but they have no influence besides overseeing social work within the

[41] Joint labor-management committees provided for by law, with primarily consultative functions, extending under the law to the technical and business aspects of the enterprise. In fact, however, most committees concern themselves primarily or even exclusively with welfare matters. (Ed. note.)

enterprise, holiday camps, and recreational activities for the personnel. When employees elect representatives to the *comités d'entreprise* and to the social security boards, it is possible to measure accurately the respective influence of the three *confédérations*, but there are no practical results regarding decision-making and the number of actual dues-paying members is small.

By tradition, department stores are a preserve of CGT and CGT-FO; FO has more members in the provinces and especially in the Southwest, the CGT is stronger in Paris and in some cities, as for example Marseilles. But each department store is a special case, some being more FO-oriented and some more toward CGT.[42] The CGT has lost more membership proportionately in white-collar than in blue-collar occupations since 1956, and for once FO seems the more aggressive and virile confederation.

The Banks, Insurance Companies, and Social Security

The CFTC, which is a minority organization in the department stores, is the leading one in the banks and insurance companies where, oddly enough, unionism seems now much more powerful than in most blue-collar branches. Nationalization, as we have pointed out, is responsible. It has made it impossible for the management of the newly nationalized companies to oppose unions, and it has set the tone for the frightened smaller non-nationalized companies that did not want to stay in the forefront of news, at least during the first fateful postwar years. Employees generally are now well protected, they have gained increments by seniority, some promotion rules must be respected, and anti-union discrimination is difficult to practice. By contrast, wages often lag behind other sectors. Management must wait for administrative decisions, and employees are forced to strike if they want to be heard. This is a kind of trade unionism that is not unlike civil service unionism. It is, however, much less organized and powerful because it lacks tradition and leadership. Most of the 1936 leaders are now in managerial or political jobs. The middle grades, contrary to what takes place in the civil service, are not very well unionized, and the lower grades do not have the means of planning and implementing a consistent policy. Moreover, the division among the different unions is a greater hindrance here than in civil service where it took place only after unions had achieved a position of strength.

[42] One of the two biggest Parisian department stores is CGT-dominated (Le Printemps) and the other FO (Galeries Lafayette), but this does not seem to disturb one or the other management.

Banks, insurance companies, and the social security organization (which is a semipublic corporation) are about 30 per cent organized, with a great deal of variation between individual enterprises. In a survey made in 1957 in six Parisian insurance companies, it was found that about 20 per cent of the personnel of three companies were union members, while the three others were 40 per cent, 50 per cent, and 60 per cent organized, respectively. Employees who operate data-processing equipment are usually the most aggressive and union-oriented segment of the labor force.

CFTC is the majority union for France as a whole, but CGT is often more powerful in Paris and FO may be dominant in some units, especially in the social security and stock exchange. Bank and social security employees formed autonomous unions within the CFTC in 1950 and 1954. They united in a new *fédération des employés* in 1964. In FO and in the CGT, they are part of the over-all federations.

Other Fields

White-collar unions have organized a great number of scattered fields—the retail trades, the clerical help of the professions, publishing houses, the newspapers, import-export businesses, middlemen, and so forth. Workers in these fields are usually not very well protected, although the publishing house and newspaper employees have won very good collective bargaining contracts. On the whole, one may argue that the white-collar world in France is comparatively well organized. Unions are weakest for white-collar people in retail trade and in industrial branches where they now belong to federations of blue-collar workers.

SUPERVISORS AND PROFESSIONAL WORKERS

Technicians are usually organized in autonomous groups within industrial unions. Supervisors and managerial personnel have separate unions within the three main *confédérations,* the largest being the CFTC's *Fédération des Ingenieurs et Cadres.* But there exists a fourth confederation, the *Confédération Générale des Cadres,* that caters only to supervisory personnel and is usually the majority organization. Unionism among supervisory and professional employees has developed primarily because of the necessity of presenting candidates for the elections to the *comités d'entreprise.* The CGC is a corporatist and narrow-minded body that works mostly apart from the rest of the labor movement, while the other supervisory unions are small minority organizations, the most active, once again, being the CFTC. Supervisory and professional people are organized mainly as a pressure group and wield an influence that should not be overlooked. Often this influence runs counter to that of the other unions.

STRUCTURE AND GOVERNMENT OF WHITE-COLLAR UNIONS

Structure and government of French white-collar unions follow the general pattern of the French labor movement. They are centralized organizations run from the top down by a few full-time officials; they operate on a very low budget, with limited assets and liabilities and with heavy reliance on unpaid ideological help. Leaders stay in office indefinitely as in other countries, but their freedom of action is very much limited by the existence of competing unions, their lack of power, and their low social status.

The first and paramount trait one has to take into account is what is called in France *pluralisme syndical,* the existence of several competitive unions. Nowhere can one find an enterprise, a plant, a government department, or even an office where one union represents all the members of the unit. The law gives protection and even a practical advantage to minorities so that in every unit, whenever it is important enough, one will find two or three competing local unions affiliated with the three main unions that have jurisdiction in the field and representing the three *confédérations.* If one union is not strong enough to start a local (section) officially, it will have one or two correspondents in a unit. When it insists on having a *section,* nobody will be able to prevent it, even if it can enroll only half a dozen members. Plant elections encourage the establishment of splinter groups since they are, in practice, political elections where the Communist Party, the Socialist Party, and other parties are fighting each other under the union flags. Political loyalty is, therefore, easy to appeal to and one will find almost any place people representative of each significant political tendency. Almost every union is present everywhere, and save for the exceptional case of the FEN, the success of a union in one field is no reason for other unions to renounce organizing in the same field. On the contrary, such success seems to work as an incentive. This division and the ever present competition is extremely burdensome for union work inasmuch as it puts a premium on irresponsible actions and does not allow for serious and efficient leadership. Employees in general, and white-collar workers especially, feel that in this way they have two or three sets of spokesmen at their disposal. They do not want to commit themselves to one alone, and they try to play one against the other. Moreover, the union militants have become more and more a separate caste of politically minded people who do all the union work and who do not have much contact with the rank and file.

Another peculiar trait is centralization. This also is traditionally French and linked with *pluralism.* The emphasis put on the *confédéral* affiliation (if asked about the name of their union, workers will answer CGT or CFTC and will probably ignore the actual name of their own national union or *fédération*) does not allow local groups to entrench themselves and to take root. There are certain local and regional tendencies, but they are very minor indeed compared to what one can find in America or in Germany. All the unions we have described are run from Paris by people living mostly in Paris. The only full-time officials, with very few exceptions, live in the metropolis. Furthermore, for white-collar people, their sheer concentration in the Paris area has the natural consequence not only of their leaders being in the Paris area, but also of their organizational basis and their possibilities of action being there so that people everywhere wait for their lead.

French white-collar unions are run by a general secretary and a permanent secretariat. Conventions are usually held every two years; in between an executive committee meets twice or three times a year and a *bureau* (board) every month. Organized opposition seldom exists outside the *confédéral* level. Not too many members are able and eager to fill union jobs that are not especially rewarding; as a result, leaders stay in office indefinitely. The present general secretaries of the *fédération des employés* CGT, of the *fédération des employés* FO, of the postal workers FO, and of the most important civil service unions have been in office since the founding of their organizations in the present form in 1945-47. Some leaders of the FEN, who were of advanced age when they took office, have retired, but the leadership has always remained in the hands of a small inner circle. The only union that has changed a great deal is the *fédération des employés* CFTC; once the stronghold of the conservative and clerical forces in the CFTC, the federation came later under the control of a moderate so-called majority group until the victory of the left minority groups in 1958 finally brought in younger and more energetic leadership.

Unions in France are usually organized along "industrial" lines.

In the industrial branches, white-collar people are distributed among the different industrial unions of the CGT and of the CGT-FO. There remain in the *fédération des employés* only the employees of department stores, whether they are blue- or white-collar workers, those of banks and insurance companies, and those of miscellaneous industries. Up to the present the situation was different in the CFTC where the *fédération des employés* grouped white-collar people from all sorts of industries and was, therefore, especially in the North, a sort of catch-all general union. A decision reached in 1962 will finally break down this last remnant of the class-conscious Christian origin of the CFTC. White-collar members will belong to their respective industrial unions, but those for whom no industrial union exists will stay in a new *fédération des employés* with the former autonomous unions of bank and social security personnel.

French white-collar unions are very poor. The FO *fédération des employés* has only five full-time organizers, as has the CGT federation. The CFTC *fédération des employés* is somewhat better off with seven full-time officials. If one remembers that there are no other full-time officials in the organizations, the comparatively small number of organizers means that there is only one permanent official for several thousand members. The ratio would be even greater if one compared the number of officials with the number of people in the branch of industry the union serves.

The situation is much better in the civil service, although here, too, the number of paid officials is very small. The FO postal workers have twelve officials, but the largest single union, the SNI, has only four. However, the local and departmental secretaries of the powerful unions, such as the teachers, the postal workers, and the finance department employees, have complete freedom to take time off to manage the affairs of their unions. This means, though, that they must depend on the tolerance of the administrative authorities. Marginal offices may also serve as a kind of substitute for a union office: The mutual benefit societies are, in a certain sense, union jobs; positions on their national boards or committees help pay expenses for union work. On the whole, one cannot help but be impressed by the very small budgets some apparently powerful bureaucratic organizations rely upon. They have no research facilities whatsoever; their archives are very scanty. They get some legal advice and some training facilities from their confederations, but they have to depend almost entirely on the good will of their militants or on unpaid outside help if they want to do more than merely manage their day-to-day business.

The CFTC unions have tried to promote new young organizers who are to devote a great deal of their time to training activities. The *fédération des employés* FO is working in that direction, too. But the FO and CGT civil service unions are very complacent and so, in another way, are the teachers' unions. The lack of research activities is especially dangerous in a period of constant transformation where new problems, brought on by the coming of automation and the revolution in education, are going to alter completely the situation of French white-collar people. Unions, up to now, ignore change and stick to their moral and ideological positions; they are extremely radical in principle and quite conservative in practice.

Unpaid militants are the key men in the situation. Without their relentless efforts, unions would crumble; in order to survive, the unions must do their utmost to attract and retain these people. This dependence upon militants makes constructive leadership extremely difficult. Militants are motivated only by idealistic incentives, and the leaders are prisoners of the demagogic appeal that seems to be the only way to keep the militants active. The primacy of these idealistic incentives imposes revolutionary dogmas upon the organizations, fostering division and internal quarrels while making it impossible to overcome conservative corporatist pressures. Leaders very often would like to appeal directly to the common sense of the rank and file, but they have no way to break through. Militants, on the other hand, are very much separated from the rank and file because of the esoteric character of their activities; they are suspected of playing partisan politics. The influence of the Communists has been decisive in bringing about this impasse, but it is now an independent factor whose weight can be felt even in situations where the CGT is rather weak, as in the white-collar area.

METHODS AND PATTERNS OF ACTION

French white-collar unions have patterns of action in many ways similar to those of other French unions. Only the civil service unions have very distinctive features, and even among them, one can discover the same basic reactions. The pattern can be analyzed as follows: there is a façade of official and rather conservative action pursued by each union in a more or less cooperative way, and there are unpredictable explosions imposing changes. Unions use these explosions as their starting points and their sources of authority, but they can neither mobilize this popular strength for their own aims nor prepare or even predict the outbursts and use them when bargaining with management.

The façade of official action exists at different levels. It is especially developed, however, at the higher ones. Union leaders, in the civil service as well as in the private sector, participate on many boards and committees at a national and state level. These activities are time-consuming and burdensome for organizations whose human resources are limited. Yet they seem to take first priority, since the political and social status they give union leaders permits them to be well informed and to exert a certain amount of bargaining power (many people, especially at the higher state level, are obliged to make efforts to convince trade unionists to go along with their programs). The outside activities might also be considered as necessary rewards for underpaid people. They keep open channels of social promotion for the leaders and permit them to keep in touch with a political world into which some of their predecessors found entrance by their trade-union activities.

With employers, of course, bargaining is less perfunctory, but one should not view it as an actual concrete confrontation. Free collective bargaining was re-established only in 1950, and the long years of state controls in a country that never really accepted free collective bargaining left many persistent habits. The state is still indirectly the dominant authority, since unions may expect it to extend the content of an agreement to a whole branch even when only a minority of the union people have signed.[43] Contracts, furthermore, are not detailed. Rather, they are vague and abstract and come only indirectly to grips with basic problems. For most enterprises, they do not set wages but impose a minimum and propose new wage patterns only by inference. In certain industrial branches more realistic firm-wide agreements, which do go into details, have been signed, but this has not been the case in the white-collar area. Nor are trade unions very eager to have detailed contracts. They are organized only at the national level and do not have enough experts to negotiate at the level of the enterprise. The CGT, moreover, does not really approve of collective contracts and prefers to fight for new coercive legislation. FO and CFTC would like employers to agree to discuss more collective contracts, but they do not have either the means or the will to campaign strenuously on this issue. They still rely quite a lot on the action of the state to which they constantly appeal.

[43] This is most often the case since the CGT refuses to sign most of the time.

Another portion of the time of the union organizer is absorbed by the endless job of policing his branch of industry to enforce compliance with the law and contractual obligations. Grievances are channeled through special agencies such as the *Prud'hommes* [44] or through state bodies such as the Labor Inspectorate. This function requires a lot of attention and political connections.

At a lower level one finds the activities of the numerous plant committees whose role may vary from establishment to establishment but never gives union militants real responsibility. The administration of the social welfare activities of the enterprise enables them to make contacts and gather information, but it does not go very far and has not been, save for a few exceptions, a good training ground for local leaders.

What are the forces French white-collar unions rely upon now? They are not shying away from strikes, although their rank-and-file members are not very sold on them.[45] They are using strikes in a very peculiar way. A strike is not the last weapon they will resort to in a bargaining situation; rather, it is an advance warning, a sort of demonstration to influence not only and not even primarily the employers but also the public and especially the state. The only strikes unions have been able to organize in the white-collar world are demonstrations or *journées d'action* (action days) whose influence has always been indirect; they force the state to exert pressure for a settlement. The government is too vulnerable to allow agitation to continue very long.

Such a pattern of action is possible only because the state fears stronger explosions. The major strikes, and the only ones whose influence has been deep, were unplanned and uncontrolled actions; unions then rushed in to use the strikes for their own purposes, but they could not have predicted the events. The most extraordinary example is the general strike of the civil service of August 1953 that found most of the union leaders on their holiday.

There are important differences between the civil service and private sectors, due mostly to the strength of the civil service unions, to the protection their members enjoy, and to their proximity to the omnipotent state. We find, in general, the same institutional system in both sectors, but it is more elaborate and more perfected in the civil

[44] See William H. McPherson, "Les Conseils de Prud'hommes," *Droit Social* (janvier 1962). (Ed. note.)

[45] Interviews of white-collar workers in insurance companies have shown that strikes are still widely regarded as a means of action lacking in respectability.

service. Demonstration days are easier to arrange and more frequent. They also have a more direct impact on what has become more concrete bargaining. Curiously enough, it is in the civil service, where bargaining is not allowed since the "sovereign state" can take only unilateral action, that salaries are more directly discussed and decided upon.[46] At least one explanation is that civil service salaries are lagging behind—which creates constant frustration—and the protection the civil service unions enjoy enables them to express these frustrations. Yet, why are they not able to force the state to grant better conditions? It is, after all, a paradox to discover that pay is the lowest, comparatively, where the unions are strongest. To understand it one must take into account the divisions among the unions and the links some of them have with politics. One union, usually the FO, does not want to embarrass the state too much, and even a half-day strike can succeed only if the three *confédérations* agree. Then there are the extremely complex differences between classes of employees, the protection each of them enjoys, and the advantages obtained through indirect upgrading. Lower and upper grades are certainly underpaid. But the middle grades may be quite well off, and they are the most influential in the bargaining process. State authorities have long experience in dealing with union action; they use delaying tactics but always agree to some settlement. Unions are further weakened because they are not really organized on the job; instead they are organized to defend different groups while their means of action are functional units. This discrepancy is reinforced, at the same time, by the prejudices of the employees themselves who are extremely conscious of the status differences of categories and by the policy of management, which will negotiate only at the higher level, i.e., at a level where unions are obliged to present together the contradictory claims of different units and groups.

The existence of such a bargaining process makes it possible to understand that, in spite of appearances, civil service unions are not as powerful as they seem to be. They are powerful only in a conservative and negative sense. They can prevent any questioning of the advantages and protection civil servants have already won, but they have little success in realizing advances and taking advantage of the opportunities of an economy in expansion.

[46] Union activities and the right to strike are officially recognized in theory in the 1946 Constitution. The necessary legislation, however, has never been passed, but an almost complete tolerance has always seemed a political necessity, even in de Gaulle's regime.

Banks and insurance companies are, in a way, in the same predicament. The management in these industries is always pretending that the state prevents it from increasing salaries and reorganizing job classifications. Demonstration days have been organized by the unions, and explosive strikes have broken out. Bargaining is not very realistic, but progress has been made because of the greater freedom of action of management, compared to the civil service, and because of pressure upon the public sector of these industries to remain competitive with the private sector.

In other white-collar occupations and especially the department stores, unions cannot easily follow such demonstrative patterns of action because of their own weaknesses, but they still try to obtain more at the bargaining table by making the best of the contacts they have at the higher levels and of the threats of demonstrations and strikes they can engineer at the lower level. Employers, however, have a very easy situation to handle since they have retained complete freedom of action and bargain only about principles. This permits them to give the union token satisfaction without making real concessions. The personnel, not well paid by any means, has lost much of its former combative spirit because of a decline in job qualifications and resulting loss of status.

Issues discussed in current white-collar bargaining in France relate primarily to wages. Conditions of work, discipline, layoffs, and job protection are usually covered by legislation and, in general, have vanished from the bargaining picture; they are brought up only when these rights and other comparable ones seem to be seriously threatened (as in August 1953 for the civil service). After a long period, hours of work are becoming a problem again in the retail trades because of the methods the department stores are using to increase productivity. Automation should be a major issue, but unions are so concerned with day-to-day problems and are so lacking in research facilities that they have followed a negative and conservative approach of prudent opposition that has been easily appeased by employers' promises to renounce any layoffs. It is quite probable that such promises will be kept if economic expansion continues. But the opportunity of gaining substantial advantages by bargaining for joint consultation at the beginning of this new industrial revolution has not yet been realized. The same negative approach is used by the civil service and especially the teachers as regards the impending reforms of their functions in society.

CONCLUSION

Let us now turn, in conclusion, to the problem of the unionization of the white-collar world. In some other Western countries the feeling may be that further progress of the labor movement will depend to a considerable extent on its ability to organize this growing and strategic section of the labor force. This does not seem to be the case in France at all. French white-collar unions are not weaker than the unions of blue-collar workers. White-collar workers may be moderate and not very strike-prone, but they have struck quite often and there does not seem to be any necessity for them to break psychological barriers to join labor's ranks. These barriers were broken a long time ago, and if white-collar workers have not built very powerful unions, neither have blue-collar workers.

Another problem, however, may have great influence upon the future prospects of French white-collar unions, that is, the problem of the peculiar influence the civil service unions have achieved within the labor movement. We have analyzed this influence both in historical perspective and in its present form as it affects patterns of labor action.

Could it not be argued that such patterns, although they may be efficient in the short run and in the civil service, act as a brake upon the labor movement as a whole? We have indicated already how conservative the unions seem to have become in their failure to take advantage of the opportunities a growing economy may offer. As to the labor movement as a whole, the unions seem almost totally unable to dramatize simple popular objectives; public reactions to their demonstrations are remarkably hostile. One may conclude that their favorite pattern of action, which consists of deliberately disturbing the functioning of public services in order to force the state into action, has compromised the labor cause and has acted as a brake on union development. In the last few years, trade-union activities have taken the form less of collective bargaining or of labor conflicts with industrial employers but rather of demonstrations against the public and the state. Although the objectives they are pursuing are by no means regarded unfavorably, their activities are barely tolerated and they only rarely obtain positive results.

Union progress is also held in check by the lack of enthusiasm of its own members. Since all of these factors are distinctive traits of the white-collar world, a reasonable conclusion would be that the labor movement will progress only if blue-collar workers take the lead again and propose new patterns of action to the movement. If there is a new potential in France for the labor movement, it should not be looked for in the offices and sales rooms but in the industrial workshops. Blue-collar workers are not without influence and even power, but their instruments, especially the Communist Party, are hopelessly inadequate. They have no real protection on the job and cannot enter into any responsible partnerships. Their rejection of the communist dream and their coming to maturity may bring a new social crisis, but it will be the only way the labor movement can be rebuilt. White-collar workers will not hinder such a development; they will react favorably and will follow any lead of this kind, but one should neither count on them to initiate such action nor think that white-collar problems are a major issue for the labor movement. Even the issue of automation does not seem to cause any stir within the conservative processes we have described. Probably private employers and the state will not meet any real challenge on the part of the unions, whose only objective will be to preserve the vested interests of their members.

The central problem of the French labor movement finally seems to be its capacity to find an easy and responsible system of communicating with its rank and file. Workers distrust the militants; the militants distrust the leaders and refuse to give them means to build responsible organizations. Weak unions try desperately to maintain the façade that enables them to speak in the name of an active, aggressive, and unruly working class. The detours of state and political intervention make it possible to play such a game, and this is why the white-collar world, and especially the civil service, exemplifies the successes and failures of such a system of action. White-collar emphasis on protective rights has made the members especially conservative and deeply identified with the system. The white-collar unions, whose role has been extremely exaggerated by contrast with the long passivity of the blue-collar unions, cannot be relied upon to break away from a system that gives them such prominence. Even in the CFTC, the renewal has come not from the white-collar but from the blue-collar unions; white-collar workers as individuals, however, have played a decisive role within this movement.

IV

GERMANY

BY GÜNTER HARTFIEL[1]

THE RISE OF THE WHITE-COLLAR EMPLOYEES[2]

During the first third of this century numerous efforts were made to solve the rather difficult problem of determining the size of the white-collar work group.[3]

[1] This chapter consists of excerpts from the author's book, *Angestellte und Angestelltengewerkschaften in Deutschland* (Berlin: Duncker and Humblot, 1961). This study is Issue No. 1 in "Soziologische Abhandlungen," O. Stammer, ed. Special permission to translate and reprint these excerpts has been granted by the publisher.

[2] The word "white-collar worker" has no completely adequate translation in German terminology. In the following study the workers who are its subject will be called "employees." We will differentiate between those "privately employed" and those "publicly employed." The latter are usually called "civil servants" (*Beamte*). In linguistic usage, some categories of the privately employed are also called *Beamte* (those working in banks and insurance companies) because the employment guarantees of these privately employed categories are very similar to those of the publicly employed.

[3] Among the studies were: Emil Lederer, "Theoretische und statistische Grundlagen zur Beurteilung der modernen Angestelltenfrage," dissertation (Tübingen, 1912); Emil Lederer, *Die Privatangestellten in der modernen Wirtschaftsentwicklung* (Tübingen, 1912); AFA-BUND, *Die Angestellten in der Wirtschaft* (Berlin, 1928); Gertrud Fromke, "Die Angestellten in der Statistik," dissertation (Leipzig, 1934); Fritz Fischer, "Die Angestellten, ihr Bewegung und ihre Ideologien," dissertation (Heidelberg, 1931); Otto Süssengut, "Die Angestellten als Stand und Klasse," dissertation (Heidelberg, 1930); Emma Sträter, "Die soziale Stellung der Angestellten," dissertation (Bonn, 1933); Manfred Dittrich, *Die Entstehung der Angestelltenschaft in Deutschland* (Stuttgart and Berlin, 1939).

Emil Lederer's study, which was written only a few years after the results of the occupational census of 1907 were published, concerns itself with finding an explanation for the rapid growth of the white-collar movement in the years around the turn of the century. At that time he could not yet discern the quantitative importance which the white-collar group achieved in later years. He saw merely their then special position as a group of employees concentrated in a few large industries and major trading companies, and, from the numerical point of view, he did not attribute much importance to them.[4] Studies in the twenties and thirties were largely restricted to the elaboration of Lederer hypotheses which the authors tried to confirm with the help of the 1925 occupational census. Again they attempted to account for the increase in the number of white-collar employees by claiming it was the result of the concentration of offices accompanying the development of large-scale operations. Apart from these observations the numerical growth of the employees was attributed also to a relatively more intense development in the sector of service, trade, and transportation occupations compared with other branches of industry. Furthermore, these works stressed the increased employment of commercial and administrative personnel in industries resulting from their organizational regrouping—which in turn sprang from the trend toward large-scale operation and the need for coordination arising from it. Dittrich, writing a few years later, also included the results of the 1933 occupational census in his consideration.[5]

We do not intend here to write a critical review of these largely undocumented studies of the thirties. The statistical part of our discussions of the development of the German white-collar movement is limited to a further interpretation of the available statistical sources which were extended into the present.

Table 1 presents an over-all view of the increase in the number of dependently employed persons in the German Reich and the German Federal Republic. The breakdown of the dependently employed into "social classes," that is "according to their status in their profession," shows an especially rapid increase in the percentage of employees and civil servants since the first systematic occupational census of 1882. According to that census, the share of the white-collar employees and civil servants then amounted to only 2.5 per cent of the entire work force. Up to the time of the last occupational census, September 13, 1950, this number had increased eight times to 20 per cent.

[4] Lederer, *Die Privatangestellten. . . , op. cit.*, p. 46.
[5] Dittrich, *op. cit.*

Table 1. Employed Persons in the German Reich (and in the German Federal Republic) According to Occupational Status

Occupational census, professional taxonomy, and geographic situation at the time	1882 [a]		1895 [a]		1907 [a]		1925		1933		1939		1950		1958	
	Numbers in 1,000	in Per Cent	Numbers in 1,000	in Per Cent	Numbers in 1,000	in Per Cent	Numbers in 1,000	in Per Cent	Numbers in 1,000	in Per Cent	Numbers in 1,000	in Per Cent	Numbers in 1,000	in Per Cent	Numbers in 1,000	in Per Cent
Self-employed	5,544	31.4	5,934	28.6	5,490	20.5	5,538	17.3	5,303	16.4	5,678	14.3	3,258	14.9	3,308	13.5
Helping family members	—	—	—	—	—	—	5,437	17.0	5,312	16.4	6,747	17.0	3,184	14.4	2,720	11.1
Civil servants									1,481	4.6	2,090	5.2	879	4.0		
	444	2.5	818	3.9	3,029	11.2	5,274	16.5							6,318	25.7
White-collar workers									4,032	12.5	5,270	13.2	3,524	16.0		
Manual workers	11,644	66.1	14,019	67.5	17,836	66.5	14,434	45.1	14,950	46.3	20,007	50.3	11,229	50.7	12,203	49.7
Household employees	—	—	—	—	472	1.8	1,326	4.1	1,218	3.8	—	—	—	—	—	—
Total labor force	17,632	100.0	20,771	100.0	26,827	100.0	32,009	100.0	32,296	100.0	39,792	100.0	22,074	100.0	24,549	100.0

[a] In the classification of the census in 1882 and 1895, the groups later classified as "helping family members" and "household employees" were counted as "manual workers."

Source: For 1882 through 1939, *Statistik des Deutschen Reiches:* 1882 and 1895, CXI, 62; 1907, CCIII, 4-5; 1925, CDVIII, 108; 1933, CDLVIII, 18; 1939, Vol. DLVI, Book 1, pp. 2-3. For 1950, *Statistisches Jahrbuch der Bundesrepublik Deutschland,* Vol. 36, Part 1, Book 3, p. 25. For 1958, result of the microcensus, *Wirtschaft und Statistik,* 1960, Book 1, p. 22.

If one adds the percentage of "workers," "helping family members," and "household employees" in the years 1925, 1933, 1939, and 1950 (Table 2), thus making the statistics for those years parallel with those for the years 1882, 1895, and 1907 (when "household employees" and "helping family members" were classified as "workers"), the percentage of the "workers" group is almost unchanged.

***Table* 2.** Percentage of Self-Employed, Workers, White-Collar Employees, and Civil Servants in the Entire Working Force According to the Occupational Census of:

	1882	*1895*	*1907*	*1925*	*1933*	*1939*	*1950*
Self-employed	31.4	28.6	20.5	17.3	16.4	14.3	14.8
Household employees Helping family members Workers	66.1	67.5	68.3	66.2	66.5	67.3	65.2
White-collar employees and civil servants	2.5	3.9	11.2	16.5	17.1	18.4	20.0
	100.0	100.0	100.0	100.0	100.0	100.0	100.0

Source: *Angestellte und Angestelltengewerkschaften in Deutschland* (Berlin: Duncker and Humblot, 1961), p. 30.

The increase of the proportion of "white-collar employees and civil servants" seems to correspond to the relative decrease in the number of "self-employed." While the percentage of "white-collar employees and civil servants" in the entire work force increased from 2.5 per cent to 20 per cent between 1882 and 1950, the proportion of the "self-employed" dropped from 31.4 to 14.8 per cent during the same period. The absolute numbers also indicate this development. While the work force nearly doubled between 1882 and 1939, the number of "white-collar employees and civil servants" increased sixteen fold. At the same time, the number of "self-employed" increased only infinitesimally.

White-collar employees and civil servants in leading positions are counted among the "self-employed for the years 1907-1933." [6] In comparison with the censuses of 1939 and 1950, this group of "self-employed" has to be divided and included in the number of "white-collar

[6] Described in the earlier censuses as a_3 persons; in the census of 1933 as s_3 persons.

employees" or "civil servants," respectively, since in both years no persons in dependent positions, no matter what kind or whether they belonged to "higher or lower levels," were included among the "self-employed." That the "white-collar employees" and "civil servants" were not added to the number of "self-employed" in 1939 and 1950 can only be attributed to technical difficulties during the census which in earlier surveys, too, had been responsible for arbitrary classifications. The decision was often difficult to make whether or not a higher employee, e.g., a person with some authority or an executive, had the characteristics of an entrepreneur which made him an employee in a "leading" position. The results of the various censuses lead one to suspect that from one census to the next different rules for classification prevailed.[7] A reclassification as white-collar employees of those in leading positions listed as "self-employed" in 1907, 1925, and 1933 causes the percentage for the "white-collar employees and civil servants" in the total number of dependently employed to show no important changes.[8]

Up to the occupational census of 1925, official occupational statistics in grouping the working population according to "social classes" did not separate white-collar employees and civil servants. Their economic and social standing was viewed as so similar that it seemed unnecessary to make a statistical distinction. It is characteristic for this view that even in 1934—one year after the first occupational census of 1933 which differentiated between "white-collar employees" and "civil servants"—one dissertation expresses the view that "civil servants and white-collar employees are hardly different when it comes to function and employer."[9] Establishment of the first separate classi-

[7] The occupational censuses of 1907 and 1925 interpreted the meaning of employees and civil servants in "leading" positions rather broadly (for 1907: "Alphabetische Berufsliste," *Statistik des Deutschen Reiches* (*St.d.D.R.*), CCII, 131; for 1925: "Alphabetisches Berufsverzeichnis," *St.d.D.R.*, CDII, 177, and thus came up with a considerably higher number of employees and civil servants in "leading" positions than the census of 1933, which applied stricter definitions. The statistically determined number of employees in "leading" positions declined about two-thirds (while the working force remained the same) from 1925 (250,335) until 1933 (88,837). Compare *St.d.D.R.*, CDVIII, 111, and *St.d.D.R.*, CDLVIII, 37, 40.

[8] By adding the white-collar employees and civil servants in leading positions, the percentage for the civil servants and white-collar employees compared with the total number of dependently employed could be adjusted as follows: 1907—from 11.2 per cent to 12.1 per cent; 1925—from 16.5 per cent to 17.3 per cent; 1933—from 4.6 per cent to 4.7 per cent (for civil servants); 1933—from 12.5 per cent to 12.7 per cent (for white-collar employees).

[9] Fromke, *op. cit.*, p. 8.

fication for "white-collar employees" and "civil servants" in 1933 can be attributed to a large extent to the slowly emerging recognition that civil servants and white-collar employees differ extensively in spite of their to all appearances similar work duties and their economic and social positions. Kurt Wiedenfeld, especially, pointed out shortly before the occupational census of 1933 the differences between the work situation of the civil servants and the white-collar employees.[10] Thus the civil servant as agent of the sovereign powers of the state has to devote at all times his entire life to his tasks and receives in return the guarantee of unlimited tenure of his means of livelihood through the permanency of his position and through his remuneration which is set according to a status principle of an adequate standard of living. The white-collar employee, on the other hand, is similar to the worker—a true member of the capitalistic economy and as such subject to the changes and uncertainties in the labor market of the free economy. The laws of the market decide whether a person is needed and how much should be paid for his services.

Separation of white-collar employees and civil servants on the basis of the published statistics of the occupational census from 1882-1925 is thus not possible. For 1925 the Statistische Reichsamt estimates the number of civil servants at 1,524,000, or 4.8 per cent of all the dependently employed persons accounted for in the occupational census of 1925. A comparison of the number of "civil servants" and "white-collar employees" in Table 1 shows a constant growth, but at a slower rate, in the percentage of white-collar employees since 1925 in relation to the entire working population; as for the civil servants, their share of the total labor force has been nearly an invariable constant except since 1950 when it tended to decline.

Some professional groups, which have been included in the column "white-collar employees" since 1925, were listed as "workers" in earlier censuses. For instance, "foremen and similar supervisory functions"—who today are even referred to as qualified white-collar employees—were included in the other group, the so-called "c" schedule, in 1822. A quantitative separation of these people cannot be made since the census of 1882 did not subdivide the "c" group as has been done in later studies.

All the clerks were also included in the "workers" column in 1882 as well as in 1895 and 1907. In the framework of the occupational

[10] Kurt Wiedenfeld, *Kapitalismus und Beamtentum* (Berlin and Leipzig, 1932), p. 139.

census of 1895 and 1907, these persons were singled out in the "workers" column ("c" persons) as "c_2" persons.[11]

If one attempted to view the various occupational groups of the present white-collar force in their quantitative development, one would have to regroup some employees who were included among the workers in earlier occupational censuses, and now, according to the present view, should be listed as the white-collar employees. Only then, with a proper starting figure for the turn of the century, could the development in the white-collar field be presented in isolation as it resulted from the development of certain professional groups. But the fact that fifty years ago functions such as clerking in stores, today listed under the white-collar heading, were included in the "workers" category, shows nevertheless that the development in the white-collar field has not just consisted of the growth of certain occupations and activities. For statistical purposes and therefore for the "white-collar employee" and "worker" figures of the occupational census, the classification of a given professional occupation was done mainly on the basis of its social evaluation at the time. This evaluation has undergone great changes.

Following the occupational census of June 16, 1933, the official statistics have changed the results of earlier censuses according to the occupational scheme for 1933 and its subdivisions. This led to the remarkable conclusion that the percentage of white-collar employees and civil servants, as a proportion of the entire working population, did not change from 2.5 per cent (1882) to 17.1 per cent but rather from 7 per cent to 17.1 per cent (see Table 3). The rate of growth of the white-collar group, or better, of the professions looked upon as white-collar occupations today, has not been as great by far as indicated by the figures, which do not take into account the later transfer of large professional groups from the "worker" to the "white-collar" status.

WHITE-COLLAR TRADE UNIONS TODAY

1. The Structure and Organizational Form of the New Trade Unions

Reconstruction of the German trade-union movement following World War II could not be undertaken in a unified way; instead it was largely influenced by the intentions and the ideologies of the re-

[11] *St.d.D.R., op. cit.*, CDVIII, 139.

Table 3. Employees and Civil Servants and Their Share in the Labor Force in Germany (1882-1933)

	Territory of Classification at Time of Census		*For all Censuses, Territory and Classification of 1933*	
Year	*Employees and Civil Servants (in 1,000)*	*As Per Cent of Labor Force*	*Employees and Civil Servants (in 1,000)*	*As Per Cent of Labor Force*
1882	444	2.5	1,183	7.0
1895	818	3.9	2,115	10.7
1907	3,029	11.2	3,311	13.2
1925	5,274	16.5	5,442	17.0
1933	5,513	17.1	5,513	17.1

Source: *Angestellte und Angestelltengewerkschaften in Deutschland* (Berlin: Duncker and Humblot, 1961), p. 34.

spective occupation forces with regard to the state, the economy, and society. As the entire economic and social life in early postwar Germany was shaped through directives and regulations of the occupation forces, so also was the structure of the trade unions.

For Berlin and the Russian Zone, Order No. 2 of the Russian military administration of June 10, 1945, opened the way for the establishment of a central trade-union federation, the Free German Trade Union Federation (FDGB). On June 15 of the same year the "Planning Committee for the Trade Union," made up of representatives of all leading trade unions that had existed before 1933, issued an appeal for the formation of a union. As early as July 1945 state and district organizations were being formed in Berlin and all parts of the Russian Zone, and on February 11, 1946, at the "first general delegates conference of the Free German Trade Union Federation," the founding congress of the FDGB, all state and district organizations were combined into one central federation. Until the various trade-union organizations were dissolved or "brought into line" with the *Deutsche Arbeitsfront* (DAF) during the months of May until July 1933, the German trade unions had been organized with emphasis on occupations; now the movement stressed the industrial union and the motto "one enterprise—one trade union." Only one exception was made—the case of the white-collar employees—because a "merger of the white-collar employees and the manual workers did not seem advisable since contracts and social legislation were traditionally different." In addition to the industrial unions for workers, the Trade Union for Commercial, Office and Administration Employees and the Trade Union for Technicians and Foremen were established.

Developments in the western parts of occupied Germany were different. The first official announcement was made by the military government in the British Zone in August 1945; it informed all interested parties that the military administration would view in a positive manner the establishment of trade unions. The right to organize trade unions was granted to all groups of employees "who were united through a common interest in regard to their work."

In contrast to policy in the Russian occupied territory, the western occupation forces regarded it as a necessary condition for the development of a democratic union that local and plant-wide organization come first. Industrial Relations Directive No. 16 of April 12, 1946, which prescribed the detailed regulations for admission and establishment of trade unions, clearly stated that the development of trade unions had to be pursued on a "local basis" first. All attempts to extend trade unions to include larger areas were subject to the permission of the military administration. As far as the organizational structure of the trade unions was concerned, an earlier announcement of August 30, 1945, emphasized that "the military government desires that the German people decide for themselves what form of trade union they want." Industrial Relations Directive No. 16 also pointed out that it was not a task of the military government to "establish trade unions or insist on a certain structure they would have to follow. . . . The officers of the military government were to report any signs should trade unions try to suppress rival trade unions." This directive further stated: "Like other German workers, the white-collar employees receive the right to organize and select the kind of trade union they desire."

The organizers of the new trade-union movement in the western part of Germany held the unanimous view that:

1. "This reconstruction can be undertaken only on a democratic basis and that the trade unions in the future social and economic order should represent a factor of vital importance."

2. The new movement should be established free of political party, ideological, religious, and occupational ties, nor should there be any discussions concerning the establishment of trade unions, or professional organizations of a particular persuasion.

3. The consequences of these ideas should be support for a new organizational form and, if at all possible, establishment of trade-union

units which would include all workers, white-collar employees, and civil servants.

The organizational efforts of the trade unions then centered upon the establishment of large industrial unions which were to be combined into one strong federation. At first the isolated local efforts to establish unions ran into great difficulties. The aims of the new trade-union officials to achieve quickly a central labor federation above the local bodies was at first made impossible by the Directive No. 16 which prescribed three phases for the development of trade unions which had to be strictly adhered to.[12]

Trade unions were established in different organizational forms in the various states and towns according to the views and intentions of the local founders. Along with general trade unions, which organized employees of all professions and industrial branches, there appeared industrial unions and unions for just one enterprise. Widely different opinions were held, especially with regard to organizing white-collar employees and civil servants. The leading labor union officials tried therefore to have district and zone meetings promptly since "the different views of the military governments concerning the kind and volume of work of the trade unions, variations in the application of directives and regulations through local administrations as well as the influence of the respective economic structure on the local and district level, had led to a variety of organizational forms and areas."

By the middle of 1947 seven trade-union federations had been established as representatives of the new trade-union movement within the territory of the three occupation forces:

1. *British Zone.* German Trade Union Federation (with 15 trade unions in the zone), established April 22-25, 1947, in Bielefeld.

2. *American Zone.* Bavarian Trade Union Federation (with 14 local trade unions), established March 27-29, 1947, in Munich. Trade Union Federation Württemberg-Baden (with 16 local organizations), established August 29-September 1, 1946, in Kornwestheim. Free

[12] *Die Gewerkschaftsbewegung in der britischen Besatzungszone, Geschäftsbericht des Deutschen Gewerkschaftsbundes (britische Besatzungszone),* 1947-49 (Köln, 1949), pp. 16ff.: "The organizing of trade unions should be subdivided into three phases: 1. The introducing, proving, and planning stage; 2. The period of preliminary development; 3. The period of growth which follows the establishment of a sound constitutional basis." Only in the third stage, with trade unions established, could unions apply to the military government for permission to merge.

Trade Union Federation Hessen (with 15 local organizations), established August 24-25, 1946, in Frankfurt-Enkheim.

3. *French Zone.* General Trade Union Federation Rheinland Pfalz (with 17 local organizations), established May 2-3, 1947, in Mainz. Trade Union Federation Baden (with 16 craft and industrial unions), established March 1-2, 1947, in Freiburg. Trade Union Federation Südwürttemberg-Hohenzollern (with 14 local craft organizations), established February 15-16, 1947.

Unified organizational forms for the trade unions already existed within the various federations. In the British and American Zones, industrial trade unionism had taken root. In the French Zone, craft unions had been established following the pattern of unionism until 1933. "As yet there was no agreement in regard to the question of organizing the white-collar employees." [13]

2. White-Collar Unions and Industrial Trade Unionism

The question, "Should and must employees march in organizational unity with the workers in the trade unions?" had already been raised at the time of the early trade-union work in white-collar circles and had, in the following decades, often been the topic of heated discussions.

For the vast majority of the craft unions of white-collar employees, joining with trade unions for workers was out of the question. The occupational unions of the white-collar employees had always seen as their special task the cultivation of professional ideas and the struggle for special legislation and privileges for the members of the professional unions they were representing. Only during the last phase of World War I did these organizations accept the trade-union idea in their work program. As representatives of a "new middle class," they devoted special attention to a clear separation from the "proletarian" working class. The older associations of "assistant merchants" did not feel a common social status even with the later developing associations of "plant employees" (*Betriebs beamte*), technicians, and foremen. Testimony for this idea can be found in the efforts at that time of the clerical workers' union in opposing the notion of a "unified employee legislation" as propagated especially by the organizations for technicians of the Study Group of the Free White-Collar Unions, and in struggling for special privileges for clerks.

[13] *DGB-Geschäftsbericht,* 1950-51, p. 35.

The social position of the white-collar employees was viewed differently by the free trade unions. When the Central Union for the Clerks and the Union for Office Workers joined the General Commission of the Trade Unions [editor's note: the forerunner of the DGB in Imperial Germany], they showed a willingness to cooperate with the trade unions of the manual workers. This was at a time when there was no thought of establishing a common central organization for manual labor, white-collar employees, and civil servants.

Only with the Auxiliary Service Law of 1916, especially the regulations about plant commissions of white-collar and manual labor, did more intimate cooperation between the trade unions of workers and the white-collar unions begin. The middle class–oriented white-collar unions established contact with labor unions of similar ideologies. This approach found its organizational conclusion in the years 1919-21, when the "three columns" of the labor movement, manual labor, white-collar employees, and civil servant unions joined with their counterparts of similar orientation with regard to union and politico-philosophic matters to form federations. These, then, combined independent unions of white-collar employees with craft and industrial trade unions of the workers and with civil servant unions.

When, at the time of the reconstruction of the trade unions after 1945, the "formation of a unified trade union movement" was demanded, the intention was not only to organize one independent trade union for all without political, religious, or ideological ties, but also to achieve an organization free of professional interest groups, in the conviction that at this time it "would also be understood by the civil servants and white-collar employees that there is no longer any room for the reconstruction of the earlier professional and status unions since these circumstances were completely different." [14] The organizational form of the occupation-based union was to be replaced by the industrial union although both organizational forms had coexisted until 1933. The affiliation of an employee to a trade union should no longer be determined by his occupation (occupational union); rather it was to be done without regard to his professional or legal position but according to his being employed in a given industrial or economic branch (industrial union). Reconstruction of the trade unions commenced in the British Zone proceeded according to this precept. Later, it became the standard for trade unions in the entire Federal Re-

[14] *Die Gewerkschaftsbewegung. . ., op. cit.*, p. 10.

public and is the organizational scheme which is still in effect today.[15]

Consistent application of the industrial union principle by all trade unions would have meant that the white-collar employees would have to abandon their organization. But events followed a pattern similar to the developments after World War I. Even then an organization such as the Central Union of the White-Collar Employees, which was in favor of a closer working relationship between white-collar employees and the manual workers, rejected the idea of a merger of the white-collar and industrial unions. This was suggested at that time by the chairman of the Metalworkers Union, Robert Dissmann. Similarly, after World War II, many officials of the white-collar unions opposed the exclusive application of the principle of industrial unionism.

In Hamburg, which has a high percentage of white-collar employees because of its economic structure, the following decision was arrived at during the establishment of new local trade unions after 1945: "The basis for the trade union movement should be the independent trade unions with their own administration and financial sovereignty organized on the principle of industrial organizations while the white-collar employees are to be united in one unified white-collar organization."

In accordance with the decision made in Hamburg, the German Trade Union for White-Collar Employees (DAG) was founded on July 1, 1945, and later extended its territory to include the entire area of the British Zone. Friction over questions of jurisdiction with the developing industrial unions, which also accepted white-collar employees, was unavoidable. When the organization of white-collar unions spread to other zones in the West, especially the French Zone, discussion about the problem of organizational enrollment and inte-

[15] In 1949, shortly before the founding of the German Trade Union Federation for the territory of the Federal Republic, the German Trade Union Federation (British Zone) was composed of the following fifteen industrial trade unions: Building, Quarrying, and Building Materials (Industrial Union, IG); Mining and Power (IG); Chemicals, Paper, Ceramics (IG); Printing and Paper (IG); Timber (IG); Metal (IG); Textiles, Clothing, and Leather (IG); Food Production and Catering (IG); Education and Science (TU); Union of German Railwaymen (TU); Market Gardening, Agriculture, and Forestry (TU); Commerce, Banks, and Insurance (TU); Union for Music, Stage, Artistic Work, and Film (TU) [today: Art (TU)]; Public Services, Transport, and Traffic (TU); Union of German Postal Employees (TU). The sixteenth industrial trade union of the German Trade Union Federation is Textiles and Clothing, which split from the industrial union Leather. *Ibid.*, pp. 56-57.

gration of the white-collar employees into a trade union, which was generally desired, began to attract much attention.

In spite of extensive discussions about the organizational problem of the white-collar employees, records of the meetings of the German Trade Union Federation (British Zone) as well as of the German Trade Union of White-Collar Employees (DAG) from the time of the establishment of the DGB contain only a few guiding principles as to the point of view of the advocates of industrial trade unions or of independent trade unions for the white-collar employees.

On both sides, in the industrial unions and in the DAG, the opinion was expressed that the new German trade-union movement should become the "pillar of a new social order" and that for the achievement of this goal it would be necessary to "consolidate into one trade union federation." There was never any thought "to make the German white-collar organization an independent top organization (federation)," but rather to "try under all circumstances to establish a trade union for white-collar employees in concert with the DGB."

It was necessary, therefore, "in the interest of a united trade union movement to find a way which would make it possible for the white-collar employees to become active as part of the central labor force in the German Trade Union Federation (of the British Zone)." However, there were different opinons about the way this could be accomplished.

The motto of the new industrial union was: "One enterprise, one trade union." For the employees of such plants and economic branches in which white-collar employees are employed alongside the manual workers, the existence of an independent trade union for white-collar employees is equal to a violation of the basic principle of industrial unionism. Such a violation can only be avoided if the groups of white-collar employees, which are in a minority, are organized in the industrial unions.

Representatives of the unions of white-collar employees argued that the principle of the industrial union was not a workable solution in all situations; it could not be applied to all occupations. "This principle has its limitations somewhere, where the occupational aspect becomes very obvious." "Only an autonomous organization of the white-collar employees can . . . represent the interests of the white-collar employees. . . . Because of their structure the Industrial Trade Unions are not in a position to represent the interests of the white-collar employees." The following line of reasoning was stated in support of this view:

The industrial union disturbs the organizational link of professional solidarity. White-collar employees would thus be scattered in various industrial unions and remain a minority with the manual workers in the majority. No industrial union could avoid setting up special secretariats to take care of members with white-collar standing. The different professional and departmental interests of the commercial and technical white-collar employees would make it necessary, in turn, to establish subdivisions among the white-collar employees. So why not begin with a separate organization for the white-collar employees?

The industrial union would be a handicap in the settlement of collective bargaining conditions for employees. Splintering of the white-collar groups and their annexation to the various industrial unions would raise the question of whether the industrial trade unions would conclude uniform wage agreements for manual and white-collar employees or whether there would be a special contract on working conditions for members with white-collar status. In the case of uniform wage agreements for white-collar employees and manual workers, the advocates of an independent trade union for white-collar employees feared that every time the workers reached a wage agreement, and representatives of the white-collar group were dissatisfied with the results, the white-collar employees would not be able to find sufficient support for their interests among the manual workers in the industrial union since they would be in the minority and their opinions would not carry much weight. Therefore, it would be necessary to establish expensive secretariats for the white-collar employees to represent their minority interests. Furthermore, the collective agreements for the white-collar employees could be established uniformly for several or all industrial branches in many districts, but the organizational division into industrial trade unions would necessitate setting up a coordinating agency which would have to combine the splintered groups in order to win new wage agreements. (In a way that would be a substitute for the special branch organizations of the occupational trade union.)

The industrial union would make the professional and union training of the white-collar employees more difficult. Not only wage movements but also all other questions of social policy and labor legislation as well as the tasks of trade-union propaganda, of professional and labor education, and of youth work would have to be carried out by various industrial trade unions instead of through one central organization for the white-collar employees. Moreover, the opinion was voiced that only an independent trade union for the white-collar employees would create the union ties among its members and thus provide motivation for actions not only on issues of social and economic policy but also in the area of the cultural and social life of the white-collar employees.

The industrial union would also necessitate undesirably frequent changes in union affiliation. Since white-collar employees change jobs far more often than do specially trained workers and can substitute for each other much more readily, the principle of industrial unionism would require of white-collar employees unnecessary changes in the union affiliation every time they changed employers. Such a change would weaken the feeling of professional solidarity which must exist in order for a union to operate satisfactorily.

The industrial union, it was claimed, would prevent the rational use of the officers of the white-collar unions. In most industrial unions, white-collar employees are in a minority. In view of the dispersion of the white-collar group, the number of officers taking care of their interests would either have to be increased in each industrial union out of proportion to the number of members served or, if officers of the manual workers added this work to their other duties, the interests of the white-collar group might then be neglected.

It was also argued that industrial unions have no attraction for the white-collar employees. This is so, it is said, because of the special group consciousness of the white-collar employees which still exists today and the fact that their view on social questions is basically different from that of the organized manual workers.

3. The German Trade Union Federation and the German Trade Union of the White-Collar Employees (DAG): The Course of the Split in the New German Trade-Union Movement

A few months before the founding congress of the German Trade Union Federation for the area of the German Federal Republic (October 12-14, 1949, in Munich), the trade-union council and the Planning Commission for the Founding Congress made the following decision with regard to the problem posed by white-collar union organization: "it becomes more and more obvious that the attitude of the DAG can no longer be brought into harmony with our views on trade unionism, and that these ideological differences make further co-operation impossible. As this development becomes clearer all the time, it is the opinion of the trade union council that there is no possibility to incorporate the DAG into the coming west-German trade union federation. . . ."

As a result of this decision, the German Trade Union for the White-Collar Employees and its members were excluded from the merger of all West German industrial trade unions into the new unified German Trade Union Federation (DGB).

A review of the historical events surrounding the trade-union movement since 1945 shows the dispute between the industrial and the white-collar unions defeated all attempts to achieve a unified West German trade union at the conclusion of the reorganization of the trade unions.

When the first local trade unions were established, the unsolved problem of what to do with the white-collar employees disturbed the new movement. The leading officials of the trade union were therefore anxious to call meetings for the districts and the various zones as soon as possible. At these meetings they hoped not only to solve the white-collar employee problem but also to discuss the task of coordinating all local trade unions during their re-establishment and in their further work.

The first meetings of representatives of the trade-union movement in the British Zone on a regional level, which had great influence in the further development of the trade unions, were scheduled for September 1945. The first official conference, convened with the permission of the military government, was held from March 12 to 14, 1946, in Hannover. Officials of the trade unions of all districts within the British Zone were invited. "A decision in regard to the future organizational form (of the trade unions) was not yet made; the time did not seem ripe for that as yet."

Only at the conference at Bielefeld from August 21-23, 1946, was some groundwork done, when it was decided that further organization of the trade-union movement should proceed in accordance with the principle of industrial unionism. For the first time following the war, delegates to this meeting were properly elected by their union members.

At the trade-union conference in March 1946 in Hannover a temporary council for the zone was elected, composed of the chairmen of the various districts.[16] Furthermore, a zone commission was formed and given the task of bringing "the question of the organizational form closer to clarification."

At the meetings of the temporary zone commission and the zone

[16] District Nordrhein, Hans Böckler; District Westfalen, Hans Böhm; District Niedersachsen, Albin Karl; District Hamburg, Franz Spliedt; for white-collar employees (DAG), Wilhelm Dörr; for civil servants, Hans Jahn.

council, bodies where both the DAG and the industrial unions were represented, the differences in opinion concerning the organizational form of the trade union for white-collar employees became more and more apparent. A special commission was called at Nienburg/Weser on December 4, 1946, for the purpose of discussing existing differences. This commission was to seek an agreement between the various industrial trade unions and the DAG to be valid until the establishment of the proposed trade-union federation. The commission succeeded in reaching an agreement which received the consent of both the zone council and the zone commission on December 5, 1946. This agreement reads in part:

> both views (regarding the organization of white-collar employees) are at present still so far apart that the suggestion of the organizing commission in this matter as well as the suggestion of the DAG did not result in a reconciliation. The members of the commission agreed that they should avoid a break in the discussions since otherwise the DAG will remain outside of the German Trade Union Federation and that would greatly endanger the unity of the German trade union movement. Representatives of the industrial trade unions and the DAG will discuss the question within their own organizations. . . .

"To avoid further separation," for the time being, it was agreed that one group would not try to raid the other and that leaflets and letters should not be sent in which either organization or persons and their actions would be attacked or ridiculed.

Difficulties standing in the way of an agreement arose again two months later when a decision regarding methods of organizing the white-collar employees was made at the first congress of the DAG from February 12-14, 1947, in Nienburg. In the same official way in which the industrial unions at their first congress in Bielefeld (August 21-23, 1946) had decided to accept the principle of industrial unionism, the DAG now demanded that one unified organization should combine all white-collar employees: "the white-collar employees demand . . . a central white-collar trade union as the organization for all white-collar employees in Germany. They reject the principle of industrial unionism which would include the white-collar employees and call upon white-collar employees of all professions to unite in the German Trade Union for the White Collar Employees."

Similarly, the white-collar unions in the other occupation zones, especially the French, now proceeded to reject officially the principle of industrial unionism. The First Congress of the Trade Union for White-Collar Employees in Württemberg-Baden rejected in a resolution the idea of "organizing the white-collar employees into industrial trade unions as unadvisable and unsuitable." Representatives at this meeting were of the opinion that "if the white-collar employees were organized in various industrial unions, they would represent a variety of minority groups and would thus be hindered in pursuing their professional interests effectively."

Preparations then starting for the establishment of trade-union federations for each zone made it necessary for the existing autonomous trade unions for the white-collar employees of West Germany to express themselves definitively about the way they expected to cooperate with the other unions and how they conceived their organizational incorporation into the proposed federation which was to be devoted to the principle of industrial unionism. As a result of a conference of representatives of all trade unions for the white-collar employees (March 11-12, 1947, in Frankfurt), the statement was made in the form of the *Frankfurt Agreement.* Basically, a resolution recommended in principle "the establishment of trade unions for the white-collar employees in the framework of the trade union federation." The representatives of the white-collar employees declared:

that the ultimate goal must be seen in the organizational unification of all workers. The tasks at hand which have to be fulfilled by the trade unions, in pursuing their objective of establishing industrial democracy, force the manual and white-collar employees to create even now a unified organization for all workers and employees in their place of work in those enterprises that have become public property or are about to be transferred to public ownership. A unified organization of all workers and employees is also the goal in public administration and enterprises, as well as in public institutions. Agreements to this effect should be made in the following industries especially: mining, chemicals, steel and iron, power, public administration and enterprises, as well as other public institutions. To realize the established principle, the constitutionally competent bodies of the federations must reach agreement with the trade unions concerning their respective jurisdictions. The industrial unions or the trade unions for the white-collar employees, which are competent in each particular case, are obligated to enroll all employees in the establishment (manual workers, white-collar employees, and civil servants).

This declaration shows the readiness of the white-collar unions to compromise. They declared their willingness to leave jurisdiction over the white-collar employees in basic industries and in public enterprises and administrations to the industrial trade unions, but demanded the exclusive right to organize all economic branches which were primarily in the white-collar field. This appeared to be a temporary abandonment of their stated principle, to "establish alongside the industrial trade unions an autonomous trade union for the white-collar employees of all professions." This temporary abandonment can only be explained by the concern of the then-controlling officers of the white-collar employees that the formation of an all-inclusive trade-union federation should not be allowed to fail because of special wishes of a minority group.[17]

The Frankfurt decision was presented as a "recommendation" to the industrial unions at the founding congress of the German Trade Union Federation for the British Zone (April 22-25, 1947, in Bielefeld) and was accepted after a vote. The majority of the representatives of the industrial unions accepted the suggestion of the white-collar unions. For the time being unity among the trade unions was preserved, and the DAG remained in the trade-union federation.

The problem of organizing the white-collar employees in those industrial branches not mentioned in the "agreement" as basic industries was still unresolved. The result was that the industrial unions as well as the DAG tried to recruit the white-collar employees in these industries, and the issue of organizing foremen and technical and commercial white-collar employees rekindled the conflict. It reached a peak when the executive of the new federation and the advisory committee of the Trade Union Federation of the British Zone issued the following statement on August 28, 1947: "Industrial Trade Unions and the DAG have equal rights to recruit among the white-collar employees."

This statement would have been understandable had the point been that the white-collar employees themselves were to decide this question instead of, as previously, only the union officers. Such a decision could have been based on the decrease or increase in membership of the industrial unions or the DAG. The statement of the advisory committee of the federation read further: "The recruitment has to be limited to those white-collar employees not yet organized. Attempts to attract members already enrolled in another organization are not permissible and must be avoided under all circumstances. Exceptions can be made only if the union losing the member has given

[17] The *Frankfurt Agreement* was never thought of as a final solution by the representatives of the white-collar unions but only as a necessary compromise because of "circumstances." One year later the chairman of the DAG, Wilhelm Dörr, declared at the second extraordinary congress of the DAG (May 22-23, 1948, in Bielefeld): "We have expressed (i.e., in the *Frankfurt Agreement*), that we do *not* desire to have in one organization the entirety [of the white-collar employees] *right away* since we know very well that one cannot hasten developments which have to ripen. . . . The Frankfurt decision is a compromise." Minutes, DAG-Bielefeld, 1948, p. 43.

its consent. Members which give up their membership in order to avoid this regulation shall not be accepted."

The individual member's freedom of choice thus continued to be suppressed, and the rivalry between the trade unions for the white-collar members received official sanction from the then highest level in the union movement. This sanction was, of course, restricted to the "unorganized."

The compromise stated in the *Frankfurt Agreement* seemed to have been forgotten when the DAG's second extraordinary trade-union conference also emphasized in a statement on the question of organization that the DAG would organize henceforth "into its ranks the commercial and technical white-collar employees in trade and industry, in banks, savings institutes and insurance companies, in public administrations and firms, in shipping enterprises as well as in *all* other enterprises employing white-collar employees."

A further attempt to solve the white-collar problem and bring about some understanding between the industrial unions and the DAG was supposed to get under way at the Special Federation Congress of the DGB (British Zone) from June 16 to 18, 1948, in Recklinghausen. The federation's executive committee and advisory council felt it advisable to call this special session to consider a number of difficult matters which had been confronting the federation for some time. The fifth item on the agenda was Problems of Organization in the DGB.

Rather than to try to work out a new compromise in the face of almost insurmountable problems, when it was put into practice the leadership posed the question of principles at the beginning: "occupational or industrial unions?" Jurisdiction over white-collar employees in the primarily white-collar enterprises like banking, savings, marketing and insurance, trade, publishing, and several service branches were to be left entirely to the DAG. This was not seen as a break with the newly established principle of industrial unionism. "The organizing problem of the DGB," as far as white-collar employees were concerned, was the fact that the DAG demanded "an area of authority in industry," while the industrial unions insisted upon "respect for the principle of the industrial union without any concessions."

In spite of the warning of the chairman of the DAG, Wilhelm Dörr,[18] not to conclude "that the DAG should have no right to organ-

[18] Dörr was at the same time a member of the federal executive of the DGB (British Zone). He resigned, however, after the DAG left the DGB on August 30, 1948.

ize and recruit in industry," the congress accepted by a large majority (153 to 20) a "resolution to regulate the relationship between the DAG and industrial trade unions" which opposed any compromise. Wilhelm Dörr had also warned that such a resolution would pre-empt a part of the sphere of jurisdiction of the DAG which it believed it had a right to claim and which it would claim, and that such a decision would eliminate every possibility of an agreement. The DGB consented to leave the realm of the primarily white-collar enterprises to the DAG, but rejected the DAG's demand that it concede on any part of the industrial union principle.

At a meeting of the advisory council of the DGB (British Zone) on July 20 and 21, 1948, the federation received a message from the DAG stating that it rejected the Recklinghausen decision and felt in no way bound by it. Thus was the relationship between the DAG and the industrial unions "settled." By rejecting the Recklinghausen decision and the renouncing of further participation at meetings of the advisory council of the federation, the DAG severed its membership in the federation.

The third phase of the dispute between industrial and white-collar unions was introduced in discussions about founding a trade-union federation for the entire area of the German Federal Republic.

The conference convening in Rod an der Weil on March 12 and 13, 1949, between the advisory council of the industrial unions and the DAG, with Hans Böckler as chairman, seemed to bring about still another turning point. A joint press statement reported "a willingness in both camps to reach a solution in the debated question." They agreed to work together in the area of economic and social legislation. With regard to conducting wage negotiations, they recommended letting all legitimate trade unions participate in the negotiations. The press statement assured in closing that "the negotiations were conducted in a conciliatory mood and will be continued in the near future."

This conference occurred on March 29 and 30, 1949, in Münster am Stein. Although the advisory council of the trade unions as well as the presidents of the various industrial unions negotiated with the representatives of the DAG, the industrial union presidents showed no willingness to accept as a basis for the discussions the request for an autonomous trade union for the white-collar employees within the framework of the Trade Union Federation as proposed once again by the DAG. Representatives of the DAG asked the frank question,

"Is the advisory council, or the representatives who are meeting here, of the opinion that the soon-to-be-established Trade Union for White-Collar Employees will have a place in the new Trade Union Federation?" The spokesman for the industrial trade unions, the chairman of the DGB (British Zone), Hans Böckler, answered "No." He explained further that "a Trade Union for White-Collar Employees with the structure and functions of the DAG could not belong to such a federation."

A few days later, at a meeting on April 12 and 13, 1949, in Stuttgart-Bad Cannstatt, delegates of the trade unions for white-collar employees of the British and American Zone voted for a merger agreement which resulted in the formation of a central organization of white-collar unions for those two zones. Now the trade unions for the white-collar employees had achieved federation extending beyond the boundaries of a zone at a time when the industrial unions were still concerned with the preparations for the founding of the German Trade Union Federation.

When the Planning Committee for the Founding Commission of a future German Trade Union Federation ultimately made the decision not to accept the DAG into the federation at a meeting on July 27, 1949, it came as no surprise since it had already been forecast through the events during the months prior to this meeting. As Albin Karl, chairman of the DGB (British Zone) stated in a letter of July 3, 1949, to the members of the advisory council, the events indicated that "the DAG's behavior was damaging for the trade unions." [19]

[19] On July 4, 1949, this statement was sent out by the executive committee of the DGB (British Zone) as circular letter No. 122/49. In it Albin Karl directed the attention of members of the trade-union council and the industrial unions to some of the events that had led to open dispute between the DAG and several district branches of the industrial unions.

On May 5, 1949, the Münster County court issued a temporary order, at the request of the DAG district office, against the district office of the Commerce, Banks, and Insurance industrial union. In this order the latter organization was prohibited from publicizing in recruiting efforts that the DAG was not authorized to conduct wage agreements, that members of the DAG were not entitled to benefit from collective bargaining, and that the DAG would thus not be in a position to represent the interests of its members successfully. The cause for this dispute over a recruiting campaign was the fact that a wage agreement had been concluded between the Commerce, Banks, and Insurance and the Food Production and Catering industrial unions on one side, and the cooperative societies of Nordrhein-Westfalen on the other.

In two further instances, at the beginning of June 1949 in Marienweiler bei Düren and at the end of June in the area of Bielefeld, the DAG had remained aloof in strikes of the Textiles and Clothing union, and by not participating in the strike "endangered the common labor struggle," in the opinion of DGB officials.

Paragraph 3, Section 2a of the charter adopted at the founding congress of the German Trade Union Federation, stated the following as a prerequisite for admission of a trade union into the federation: "That no one of the member organizations of the federation already has jurisdiction for the same group of employees or that the appropriate organization has no objections to the admission of the competing organization."

This requirement made it impossible to include the DAG among the founders of the DGB since it sought the membership of the white-collar employees and since the Planning Committee, applying the principle of industrial unionism, had already promised the jurisdiction to other trade unions. For the time being unity of the new German Trade Union Movement was not accomplished because of the unwillingness to compromise on the part of both the Trade Union for the White-Collar Employees and the industrial unions. Those officers of the industrial unions who were willing to compromise could only regret that the majority of the member organizations of the federation did not indicate an equal willingness to "give up the principle of industrial unionism to the degree that a trade union might be granted the right to claim for itself as members all or substantial numbers of the white-collar employees in all industrial unions."

The German Trade Union for the White-Collar Employees remained an independent organization outside the new Federation. The founding congress of the DGB on one hand set up "guidelines for work among white-collar employees in the German Trade Union Federation" and recommended, on the other hand, that the main executive committees of the trade unions affiliated with the DGB "devote more time to the representation of the white-collar employees who are members of their trade unions and, should such formal representation not already exist, set up secretariats for the members with white-collar employee status in order to achieve a systematic representation of the interests of the white-collar employees in the trade unions." "To assure a uniform and energetic representation of the interests of the members with white-collar status of all trade unions in the German Trade Union Federation," the founding congress also requested that on all levels of organization special offices be set up for the white-collar employees. In due course this was accomplished. This development made the DAG and the DGB, as far as the organization of the white-collar employees was concerned, competing trade unions, a situation that has remained unchanged until the present.

4. Programmatic Differences in the Present German White-Collar Movement

a) *German Trade Union Federation and German Trade Union for White-Collar Employees.* A comparison of the charters and the basic programs of the German Trade Union Federation and the German Trade Union for White-Collar Employees does not reveal any important differences which would justify two separate trade unions.

The DGB as well as the DAG wants to promote and maintain, "on a democratic basis without regard of party-political and religious goals . . . the economic, social, professional, and cultural interests of its members." As far as economic legislation is concerned, they both work for the "transfer of key industries to common ownership," and in social legislation they voice the demand for "social justice through appropriate shares for all employees in the entire economic proceeds and the granting of sufficient income for those unable to work because of age, invalidity, or sickness." Unanimity also exists in the demand for "a voice for the organized employees in all personnel, economic, and social questions in the realm of economic policy and development."

The basic program of the DAG shows that apparently only the organizational differences mentioned in the last section led to the division. The program emphasizes: "The solidarity growing out of the social interconnection of two equal partners—DAG and DGB—means more than the mere acknowledgment of the one or the other organizational form. The organized white-collar employees are therefore fully aware of their common interests with manual workers."

In spite of very similar programs, the arguments voiced by the two organizations during election campaigns for the autonomous organizations of social insurance and workers' councils, at meetings, and during recruiting campaigns for new members, affirmed the point of view of each organization and led to a deepening ideological separation as well as the organizational division.

In defense of the principle of industrial unionism, the DGB and its member organizations emphasize especially that the white-collar employees, "isolating" themselves within a so-called "organization of status (*Standesorganisation*)," will not succeed "alone and without help to achieve the deserved acknowledgment and the necessary legal position in legislation and public life. . . . For instance, never would the DAG alone have been able to achieve a voice in the affairs of the basic iron and coal industries and a still regretfully insufficient voice in the Works Constitution Law." Furthermore, they say that white-collar employees live in a kind of dream world which is neither in accord with their economic and social position nor with their actual social status. "The tragedy of the white-collar employees" is that in their circles there are efforts to keep up a "middle class ideology" and an "out-of-date pride of status," and even to revive them. The progress toward equal labor legislation and advancing rationalization and automation have rendered fluid the boundaries between white-collar employees and manual workers, and for all those employees "advanced to professions of white-collar standing through self education or other means . . .," differences of status between manual workers and white-collar employees will cease to exist. In addition, the wave to rationalize, which is following automation and is especially noticeable in white-collar occupations in offices and administrations, is a great threat to the white-collar employees. "If the white-collar employees—individually or as a group—do not want to suffer in the age of automation which has already begun, if they want to see to it that they, too, benefit from these new technical developments, they will have to bring their social image in line with their economic and social position. That means they will have to acknowledge that they are employees who can represent their interests and hopes only together with the manual workers in one common trade union." The organization suitable for these tasks in this age of automation is the industrial union.

To counter the argument of communality of interests of white-collar employees and manual workers emphasized by the industrial unions, the DAG tries to prove that white-collar employees have a special function which makes an independent trade union necessary. The supporting evidence for this thesis, however, has not always been presented in the same way.

One statement reads:

> The functionally meaningful role which is played by the white-collar employees to an increasing degree in the economic world and in public administration has led to the emerging of the white-collar employees as a completely separate group with their own consciousness, value system, and world view, within the entire class of dependently employed persons which includes also manual workers and civil servants. The individuality of white-collar employees is derived from their peculiar training based upon a professional education lasting several years and an especially keen drive for further development of their professional skills.

These formulations strongly remind one of the equalization of work for white-collar employees and skilled labor. Thus we can read in the same place: "This does not exclude the possibility, perhaps even the necessity, that certain groups of skilled workers whose working conditions and view of life have come close to those of the white-collar employees will join the ranks of the white-collar employees." Instead of a grouping of employees according to wage systems and insurance techniques, it is the opinion of the DAG that in the future the classification will more than ever depend only on functional criteria.

Elsewhere is the admission that advanced technology and increasing mechanization has changed white-collar functions in many instances and that the various rationalization measures in the large firms have caused noticeable changes in the labor market, especially as far as white-collar employees are concerned. Yet the statement avoids suggesting, in accordance with the view expressed above, a regrouping following "functional criteria" and does not talk about an assimilation of the working conditions of many white-collar employees and manual workers. Instead, the following point of view is adopted: "The use of technical devices where before only manual work was employed should not result in a discrimination against the employee, just as holding a routine job should not be interpreted as evidence of lack of ability in the person performing those duties. The more or less mechanical work in the performance of a partial function has therefore nothing to do with the criteria of white-collar work." After testing and approving the analysis of Fritz Croner,[20] reference is made to his "function and delegation theory" as proof for the "functional individuality of the white-collar employees," and it is stated:

> The division of labor in the modern economy has also caught hold of the one-man functions of the owner and thus made the white-collar employees the functional carriers of the leadership [in the enterprises]. . . . Viewed socially, the white-collar employees are, in spite of their functions at their place of work, employees who offer their skills in exchange for a salary on the labor market. But the dependent relationship of white-collar employees is overshadowed by their awareness that each task of a white-collar employee reflects on the employer. For in no stage can the function of a white-collar employee in its performance be separated from the purpose and goal of the firm. No matter if he is given simpler or more responsible tasks, the white-collar employee has a certain freedom of movement and independence in his professional actions.

As a result, the DAG takes a position in opposition to all actions [of the industrial unions] "which propose the leveling of the white-collar employees into the social group of manual workers." The main

[20] Fritz Croner, now active in the Swedish white-collar movement but originally a German, has written extensively on white-collar problems. One of his latest major works is *Die Angestellten in der modernen Wirtschaft* (Frankfurt-Vienna, 1954), also published in Swedish (Stockholm, 1951).

goal of the DAG as a professional organization, which has caused the industrial unions to accuse it of trying to maintain "middle class ideology" and "out-of-date pride of status," is rather: "The importance of the social and social-political role of the white-collar employee in the state and the economy must, according to the value of his function, be given its deserved recognition."

b) *The Christian-National Trade Union for White-Collar Employees.* After the political collapse in 1945, officials of the former Pan-German Association of Clerks (DHV) watched "with keen awareness and great concern the faulty development of the central trade unions [DGB and DAG] since 1946 and their political captivity in the Marxist camp." To restore the tradition of the emphatically antisocialistic Pan-German Association of Clerks (DHV), the organization was re-established under the name German Association of Clerks on October 1, 1950, in Hamburg following the necessary preparation and a "gathering of all former members."

The objective in establishing the association was "to unite the German clerks on a Christian-national basis for the purpose of raising their economic and social position." In contrast to the DGB and DAG, who pursued their aims without religious goals, the new DHV, continuing the tradition of the Christian white-collar movement, is "religiously not neutral, but above denominational level and acknowledges national characteristics and Christendom." Christendom and national characteristics give direction to its educational work.

Everybody should view the nation to which he belongs as a fundamental fact. But national characteristics can be developed only in the merger with "Christendom," since "its ethical principles cannot be differentiated from the moral concept of the national culture." Elimination of all order always accompanies the decay of religious zeal, without which there can be no common interest since the nation too needs a religious basis.

With reference to the difficult tasks in the modern economy for which "commercial collaborators with knowledge, know-how, and experience" are needed and "for whom no office technique can be substituted," the concept of the profession is central to this trade-union organization. It is also stated "that these white-collar employees in various professional branches must show more responsibility, more accuracy, deeper-seated professional conscience [than the manual workers] to accomplish their tasks as co-workers of the entrepreneur."

The occupational and status element is derived from the common profession which provides common ties and from the continuing tradition of the DHV until its "assimilation" [by the Nazis] in 1933; now it again controls the organization. The "essence of the occupational status," which manifests itself in the common attitude towards the basis of our national life, economy, and culture, is conceived of as all members striving to orient their claims on the requirements for the whole [the community], and not only voicing claims but also recognizing their personal duty. This attitude of the DHV differs basically from that of other trade unions, which see as their objective the pursuing of a one-sided "group-egoism" without taking into account the "organized social order" and which always try to get more than their share at the expense of other people.

Similar to the idea of a "working community of entrepreneur and employee" as espoused by the Christian trade unions until 1933, the DHV views the abolition of the class struggle and of collectivism as the social-ethical task of our generation and supports the idea of social partners in which equals may freely and independently strive for social and economic progress. The most important basis for a true partnership is the true order of precedence of person and matter. The employee in the company—and especially the white-collar employee—does not want to be an hourly wage earner but rather a coworker. There is no doubt that such a partnership would result not only in rights for the employee but also in duties. In the conviction that the economic success of the entrepreneur depends largely on the skill and training of the "co-workers," the DHV as an occupational organization makes membership in its ranks dependent upon the proof of "proper professional training."

In pursuing this economic and political program which makes social partnership the central factor of the order to be established in the plant and in the economic system, the DHV rejects a "socialistic economic order to be achieved through collectivization of property or transfer of key industries into common property or through planned direction of production and requirements."

In the six decades of its existence since 1893, the DHV, as can be inferred from its name, "Association of Clerks" has been mainly interested in a tightly circumscribed occupational representation of white-collar employees in trade. Developments in the last years show that an extension of the organizational framework is being considered because of the increasing importance of other work areas for commercial and office employees. On January 14, 1956, the DHV decided to change its name from German Association of Clerks—Trade Union for the Commercial Employees to German Association of Commercial and Industrial White-Collar Employees, and in the new charter of October 1958 the DHV also calls itself (in paragraph 2) a professional trade union "of administrative employees in public service." With these changes the DHV approaches more and more the organizational structure of the DAG which it first rejected as a "unity trade union." This approximation is all the more important as some district administrations of the DHV also take care of the business and interests of the formally independent, but, as far as membership and trade-union influence is concerned, unimportant Christian-National Technicians and other occupational associations.[21] The tendencies in the development from a strictly limited professional trade union to an association of white-collar employees and thus a unified organization for extremely heterogeneous occupational groups will within the predictable future confront the DHV with great difficulties in its efforts "to foster professional ethics in order to strengthen the human personality."

Since the middle of 1951 the Association of Female White-Collar Employees (VWA) according to an old tradition—"guided by the thought of national solidarity, carried by the spirit of Christian ethics" —has again taken up the representation of the "professional and social interests of the female white-collar employees." As the only German trade union exclusively for women, the association sets for itself the assignment of "training the female white-collar employees in citizenship" in addition to performing the tasks of a trade union, such as "improvements in the working and pay conditions of its members through conclusion of collective agreements with the associations of the social partners" by means of peaceful agreements. The main points of its social program (according to Paragraph 1 of the charter) are focused on the goal of achieving improvements in unsatisfactory occupational conditions and pay for white-collar employees. Thus the VWA demands a prompt reworking of the basic agreement (*Manteltarif*) for female white-collar employees including a "proper classification," "possibilities of advancement to the higher positions in public administrations"; in addition, the organization stands for the "representation and participation of the female white-collar employees according to their growing importance in all self-governing organizations of social insurance, labor administration, and all economic and social-political institutions."

The top organization "for the occupational trade unions for male

[21] Association of the German Technicians (VDT)—Trade Unions of the Technicians; German Association of Foreman; German Association of White-Collar Employees in Agriculture and Forestry.

and female white-collar employees working on a Christian-national basis" is the *Gesamtverband Deutscher Angestelltengewerkschaften* (GEDAG). Since April 1, 1959, the following organizations have united "while retaining their organizational and financial independence": German Trade Union for Commercial and Industrial White-Collar Employees, Trade Union for Female White-Collar Employees, Association of German Technicians, German White-Collar Employees in Agricultural and Forest Enterprises.

It was hoped that this merger would create "further prerequisites for the proposed establishment of a central organization of all Christian trade unions in Germany." This intention was realized on June 27, 1959, when the Christian Trade Union Association of Germany (CGB) was established.

PRESENT SITUATION AND PERSPECTIVES

The main problem at present for all trade-union organizations of white-collar employees is the fact that employees, in contrast to manual workers, are not sufficiently interested in the work of trade unions. A comparison of employment figures with those of union membership (Table 4) shows that the trend to organize into trade unions is much stronger among manual workers than among the white-collar employees. The DGB, the DAG, and the DHV have tried to arouse the supposedly latent interest of the employees in trade-union affairs by stressing their different principles of white-collar unionism; yet, all together, they have not succeeded in persuading more than one-fourth of the white-collar employees to join a trade union. A comparison of the membership figures of 1950 and 1958 shows that the increased degree of organization among manual workers is not close to being paralleled among white-collar employees, in spite of vigorous recruiting campaigns of all the professional trade unions. The willingness to organize into trade unions is especially low among the female white-collar employees.

Neither the DHV's promise to work to preserve and defend "the status and position of white-collar employees in the modern mass world," nor the DAG's emphasis on the "economic and professional recognition of the white-collar employee" whose interests can be represented successfully only through an organization independent from other labor groups, nor the idea of the commonality of interests of all dependently employed persons—manual and white-collar—advanced by the DGB industrial unions have been able, up to now, to

Table 4. Employees and Trade-Union Members in the German Federal Republic in September-October, 1950 and 1958, According to Sex and Status in the Profession

		Trade-Union Members	
	Labor Force	*Number*	*Percentage of Labor Force*
1950:			
White-Collar Employees			
Male	2,011,474	583,878	29.0
Female	1,512,046	213,552	14.1
All	3,523,520	797,430	22.6
Manual Workers			
Male	8,034,632	3,523,032	43.9
Female	3,194,619	611,074	19.1
All	11,229,251	4,134,106	36.8
1958:			
White-Collar Employees			
Male	2,505,000	792,473	31.6
Female	2,518,000	388,428	15.4
All	5,053,000	1,180,901	23.5
Manual Workers			
Male	8,668,000	4,346,917	50.1
Female	3,535,000	824,740	23.3
All	12,203,000	5,171,657	42.4

Sources: WWI, *Deutschland in Zahlen,* 1950 (Cologne, 1951), pp. 90-91; *Statistisches Jahrbuch der Bundesrepublik Deutschland,* 1959, p. 128; *Wirtschaft und Statistik,* 1960, Book 1, p. 22.

interest the majority of white-collar employees. If one asks the white-collar employees themselves the reason for their lack of interest, one learns that they view the trade union as an organization for manual workers only. They see joining a trade union also as incompatible with their "social status," and they view the union as an organization fighting against the company. To them the employer represents such a high authority that they would not think of rebelling against it as manual workers do when entering a trade union.

Both the professionally oriented trade union for the white-collar employees and the "unity trade union" for white-collar employees have an advantage only over the industrial unions enrolling both white-collar employees and manual workers. They can tell their members, which they recruit among professional groups with a great variety of special qualifications, that all white-collar employees are entitled to a higher or at least "different" social position from manual workers because of their special function in economy and administration. This approach is not available to the industrial unions. In all their actions they must emphasize the common trade mark for all employees and manual workers—the fact of being dependently employed—and thus reject the claim for a different social position for the two groups. It is easy to see that an organization with such a motto, which runs counter to the well-entrenched notion of the higher value of the white-collar employees, will not find it easy to win wide popularity among them, at least not until the white-collar employees are convinced that their economic and social situation is essentially the same as that of other dependently employed persons. Because of this, and because they are accused by the competing white-collar groups of promoting what they reject as a "leveling attempt," the industrial unions do not dare to campaign for an assimilation in labor and social legislation in their white-collar work. Instead, in recruiting, they weaken their "uniformity" program, probably for the purpose of making some concessions to the traditional white-collar ideology, and speak instead of "openness of work situation and professional status" as typical for white-collar professions and of the possibility for white-collar employees to influence their position in the enterprise and their careers through "personal effort." Thus the industrial trade unions acknowledge a functional speciality of all white-collar professions which has to be taken into consideration in the daily work of the unions.

A trade union which does not wish to be primarily a home for the political, ideological, religious, or professional ambitions of its members, but rather restricts itself to the "classical" tasks (that is, to exert influence upon the economy and its operation and the conditions on the labor market in favor of the employees) can work successfully only when it is able to make clear to its members and to those not yet organized that the professional and material situation of the individual is largely decided in the impersonal labor market. With the tendency toward scientific management, job evaluation, and other forms of objective characterization of many tasks of white-collar employees, universally applicable theoretical training and know-how can be procured and the suitable applicants for each job can be found in large numbers. The knowledge concerning specific conditions in the company and the special relationship of one plant to other units of the economy, which white-collar employees or civil servants were required to have in earlier years, is being replaced more and more by the technical aspect of the operation which requires only a certain "formal knowledge" of the employee. This development is, next to the formulation of many routine jobs for the employee, the main reason for the well-advanced functional approximation of the working conditions of white-collar employees and manual workers. In a period of expanding size of enterprises and the tendency toward more anonymous hierarchies of personnel, the divided representation of interests of two groups of employees—divided functionally in what appears to be an arbitrary fashion—among several trade unions will hardly make sense. The so-called "white-collar employee problem" can be solved by the trade unions only if they succeed in demonstrating the change in functions in most white-collar occupations and the present functional and economic situation of the white-collar employees resulting therefrom.

The trade unions face a truly functionally conditioned "white-collar employee problem" only with regard to those employees whose professional duties are not exhausted by merely applying knowledge and know-how, as transmitted to them in theoretical and practical training according to the requirements of job descriptions. For such employees an impersonal labor market does not yet exist. The functions of "decision-making" and "preparing" are so specialized within the establishment that they are tied to the person of the individual employee. Such employees are not so easily replaceable, and the result is that the position in the company and the work performance of these employees are subject to an individual appraisal by the employer which is beyond the influence of the trade union and outside its evaluation. For such employees a trade union can only become interesting if it helps them to achieve a set of special legislative regulations reflecting their needs for security which they could use as a basis from which to develop their functional positions in "personal initiative."

APPENDIX

Table 5. Technical, Supervisory, and Commercial Personnel in Agriculture, Industry, Trade, and Transportation (According to the Occupational Census of 1895-1933 and the Salary and Wage Structure of 1951-52)

Year and Branch	*Technical Employees (Percentage)*	*Supervisory Personnel (Percentage)*	*Commercial Employees (Percentage)*	*All Employees (Percentage)*
1895:				
Agriculture	59.3	37.2	3.5	100.0
Industry	18.6	40.1	41.3	100.0
Trade and Transportation [a]	—	—	—	—
1907:				
Agriculture	54.9	40.5	4.6	100.0
Industry	18.3	35.2	46.5	100.0
Trade and Transportation [a]	—	—	—	—
1925:				
Agriculture	76.2	12.7	11.1	100.0
Industry	15.8	20.5	63.7	100.0
Trade and Transportation	21.6	2.7	75.7	100.0
1933:				
Agriculture [b]	85.3		14.7	100.0
Industry [b]	36.5		63.5	100.0
Trade and Transportation [b]	11.8		88.2	100.0
1951–52:				
Industry	23.9	14.5	61.6	100.0
Trade and Transportation	3.0	1.3	95.7	100.0

[a] No subdivisions possible.
[b] Technical employees and supervisors shown only together.

Sources: For 1895, *St.d.D.R.*, CXI, 72; for 1907, *St.d.D.R.*, Vol. CCIII, Dept. II, Book 1, pp. 4-20; for 1925, *St.d.D.R.*, CDVIII, 110; for 1933, *St.d.D.R.*, CDLVIII, 25-33; for 1951-52, *St.J.d.B.R.D.*, XCI, 15.

Table 6. Labor Force (Including White-Collar Employees and Civil Servants) in the Various Branches of the Economy in the German Reich and in the Federal Republic from 1882-1950

Year	*Agriculture*		*Industry and Handicrafts*		*Trade and Transportation*		*Public Services and Private Service Occupations*	
	Number	*Percentage of Labor Force*	*Number*	*Percentage of Labor Force*	*Number*	*Percentage of Labor Force*	*Number*	*Percentage of Labor Force*
1882:								
Total labor force	8,236,496	—	6,396,465	—	1,570,318	—	—	—
White-collar employees and civil servants	66,644	0.8	99,076	1.5	141,548	9.0	—	—
1895:								
Total labor force	8,292,692	—	8,281,220	—	2,338,511	—	—	—
White-collar employees and civil servants	96,173	1.2	263,745	3.2	261,907	11.2	—	—
1907:								
Total labor force	9,883,257	—	11,256,254	—	3,477,626	—	—	—
White-collar employees and civil servants	98,812	1.0	686,007	6.1	505,909	14.5	—	—
1925:								
Total labor force	9,762,426	—	13,239,223	—	5,273,502	—	3,734,049	—
White-collar employees and civil servants	161,777	1.7	1,452,293	11.0	2,220,818	42.1	1,439,344	38.5

1933:								
Total labor force	9,342,789	—	13,052,982	—	5,932,069	—	3,968,238	—
White-collar employees	97,878	1.0	1,300,818	10.0	1,784,161	30.1	849,488	21.4
Civil servants	16,744	0.2	22,613	0.2	548,537	9.2	892,898	22.5
1939:								
Total labor force	10,847,516	—	16,504,041	—	6,850,883	—	4,068,137	—
White-collar employees	89,550	0.8	1,846,255	11.2	1,974,678	28.8	1,338,577	32.9
Civil servants	19,309	0.2	31,017	0.2	660,439	9.6	1,379,144	33.9
1950:								
Total labor force [a]	5,113,700	—	9,339,400	—	3,443,000	—	3,694,000	—
White-collar employees	32,400	0.6	1,106,100	11.8	1,204,100	35.0	1,135,700	30.7
Civil servants	7,400	0.1	2,900	0.0	350,000	10.2	518,300	14.0
1958:								
Total labor force [a]	3,936,000	—	11,681,000	—	4,748,000	—	4,184,000	—
White-collar employees and civil servants	28,000	0.7	1,796,000	15.4	2,380,000	50.1	2,114,000	50.5

[a] To make possible a comparison with earlier census figures, the labor force, white-collar employees and civil servants of the "economic branches" following the census of 1950 are classified as follows: Agriculture—economic department I; Industry and handicrafts—economic departments II to V; Trade and transportation—economic departments VI and VIII; Public services and private service occupations—economic departments VII and IX.

Sources: For 1882 and 1895, *St.d.D.R.*, CXI, 61; for 1907, computed from *St.d.D.R.*, CCIII, 4-5; for 1925, *St.d.D.R.*, CDVIII, 24, 110; for 1933, *St.d.D.R.*, CDLVIII, 25-33; for 1939, *St.d.D.R.*, DLVI, 2-3; for 1950, *St.J.d.B.R.D.*, Vol. 36, Part 1, Book 2, p. 44; for 1958, results of the microcensus, *Wi.u.St.*, 1960, Book 1, p. 22.

Table 7. The Membership Movements in the Trade Unions for White-Collar Employees (1950-58)

Members	*As of September 30, 1950*	*As of September 30, 1954*	*As of September 30, 1958*
White-Collar Employees in the German Trade Union Federation (DGB)	490,554	641,001	690,724
Among them in the industrial union for:			
Building, Quarrying, and Building Materials	8,808	16,898	14,778
Mining	35,509	45,916	45,690
Chemicals, Paper, Ceramics	33,004	34,570	37,551
Printing and Paper	6,724	5,620	6,101
Union of Railwaymen	2,152	4,027	4,720
Union of Education and Science	911	2,944	2,713
Market Gardening, Agriculture, and Forestry	1,822	982	1,914
Commerce, Banks, and Insurance	37,402	80,636	100,954
Timber	2,033	3,417	2,777
Art	34,505	36,970	30,954
Leather	2,860	2,746	2,267
Metal	87,790	108,994	126,544
Food Production and Catering	20,952	25,920	31,725
Public Services, Transportation, and Traffic	186,136	232,310	252,125
Union of German Postal Employees	17,837	26,171	17,836
Textiles and Clothing	12,109	12,880	12,075
German Trade Union For White Collar Employees (DAG)	306,877	406,473	438,142
Among them:			
Commercial Employees	127,905	177,875	188,840
Banks and Savings Institutes	20,023	27,415	30,248
Insurances	22,289	27,037	27,194
Public Services	71,216	85,919	91,578
Technicians	32,445	43,812	54,286
Foremen	27,005	30,227	32,379
Shipping Enterprises	5,994	7,294	7,917
Others (1958: Saar Area)	—	6,894	5,700
German Trade Union for Commercial and Industrial Employees	—	25,865	52,035

Sources: For 1950, WWI, *Deutschland in Zahlen,* 1950 (Cologne, 1951), pp. 90-91; for 1954, *St.J.d.B.R.D.* (1955), p. 126; for 1958, *St.J.d.B.R.D.* (1959), p. 128.

V

WHITE-COLLAR UNIONS IN THE UNITED KINGDOM[1]

BY GUY ROUTH

Traditionally, the white collar has been the symbol of respectability, the mark of moderation. It was a guarantee of its owner's conservatism, of that unswerving loyalty to the *status quo* that qualified him as custodian of the firm's secrets and set him apart from the muscle-using process worker and craftsman.

To those who see the need for social improvement, the much-publicized increase in the proportion of white-collar workers is thus a somewhat depressing phenomenon. Will it entail a slowing down of progress—in particular, the transformation of the trade-union movement into a docile appendage of the personnel department? In Britain, the answer has come from the white-collar unions themselves—not in words, but in a series of unusual actions that have enlivened the trade-union history of the recent past. Savings bank managers have marched at the head of their staffs, civil servants paraded in Whitehall, teachers balloted for direct action, clerks and television actors struck, postmen and counter clerks worked to rule. In short, an abundance of clinical material has been produced that may help

[1] The United Kingdom of Great Britain and Northern Ireland has three major administrative areas: (1) England and Wales, (2) Scotland, and (3) Northern Ireland. Official statistics sometimes relate to all three, sometimes to (1) and (2), sometimes to only (1).

us to see, albeit somewhat hazily, the lineaments of the society of the future.

OCCUPATIONAL CLASS STRATIFICATION

That it is to be a future dominated by white-collar workers is clear enough. In 1951, the gainfully occupied population of Great Britain was distributed as follows:

Table 1. Occupational Stratification

		Numbers (in 1,000)	*Per Cent*
Higher Professional		434	1.9
Lower Professional		1,059	4.7
Employers and Proprietors		1,118	5.0
Managers and Administrators		1,246	5.5
Clerical Workers		2,404	10.7
Foremen, Inspectors, Supervisors		590	2.6
Shop Assistants		1,111	4.9
Manual Workers:	Skilled	5,616	25.0
	Semiskilled	6,227	27.7
	Unskilled	2,709	12.0
		22,514	100.0

The last three groups made up 75 per cent of the workforce in 1911, 65 per cent in 1951. No one can complain that this rate of change is immoderate, yet the social impact of a shift of even one percentage point is very great, affecting more than two hundred thousand workers and their dependents. Pre-1911, the rate of change was much slower; post-1951, it has speeded up. The professional groups have been expanding at a compound rate of 3 per cent per year, clerical workers at 2.4 per cent. Since 1951, engineers have increased by 5 per cent per year (between 1881 and 1901, the rate of increase averaged 1 per cent per year), scientists by over 6 per cent, laboratory technicians by between 5 and 6 per cent, and draftsmen by between 7 and 9 per cent. By contrast, the number of coal miners, agricultural workers, textile workers, and domestic servants has been substantially reduced.

Yet even at this rate of change it will be another quarter-century before manual workers are in a minority.[2] Not that there is anything magical about that moment. It is true that there is a marked correla-

[2] Assuming the continuance of current industrial and occupational trends.

tion between occupational class and political allegiance, but a substantial minority of the manual workers vote for the Conservative Party; a large number do not vote at all; only about half are members of trade unions. Yet the process of conversion from "working class" to "middle class" is continuing inexorably, with all that it implies in changed values, orientation, and behavior.

The social effect of this changed occupational distribution is greater than one might think, because it is of necessity concentrated into the lower end of the age scale. Adults are loath to go back to school, so the need for more educated manpower must be met by an educational redeployment of the young, and there are many indications that this is taking place—on a scale small when measured by what is socially desirable, but very big when measured against the achievements of the past.

So, in England and Wales in 1938, there were only 50,000 sixteen-year-olds still at school; in 1960, the number was 136,000. In May 1951, 19 per cent of the age group 15 to 19 (inclusive) were in full-time education; in May 1959, 25 per cent. The university population has more than doubled compared with prewar:

Full-time University Students
United Kingdom

1938-39	50,000
1962-63	118,000

The Education Act of 1870 empowered local authorities to provide compulsory education and so broke the privileged position of the clerk; a similar revolution is now taking place with regard to higher education. Paradoxically, it is now easier for the bright child of a poor parent to get a university education than that of a rich one, for the former will get a public grant sufficient to see him through college, while the means test will make the latter dependent on the generosity of his parents.

In fact, the maximum advantage of the provisions of the welfare state comes at about the level of the skilled craftsman and the clerical worker; here, the child's chances of scholastic success are not impaired by the low literacy or obscurantism of the parents, and he will get the full benefit of the public grants. But even those who do not get scholarships pay fees that are much less, relative to costs, than their fathers paid, for universities are much more heavily subsidized now than they were before the war. The result was a shortage of university places, with students applying for admission to half a dozen or more universities in the hopes of getting into one. The ensuing chaos has forced the universities to establish a central clearing house, through which applications are now made, with a maximum of four choices per student.

This release of intellectual energy is a salubrious spectacle; but it has disquieting features. Its splitting off of an intellectual elite from the mass of ordinary people has something about it of the determinism of the beehive. It is here that the effects of social inequality are most active. The children of professional and managerial parents have a much better chance of getting into Grammar Schools than the children of other workers. Clerical and other nonmanual workers also get more than their fair share of places, skilled manual workers rather less than their share, semiskilled and unskilled workers much less than their share.[3]

And when the children of manual workers do succeed in getting grammar school places, the bulk of them leave before turning 17 (85 per cent of the children of semiskilled and unskilled workers, 75 per cent in the case of skilled workers). Thus the social class of those destined for white-collar jobs is partly predetermined, a high proportion being children of fathers who were themselves white-collar workers. Insofar as they are shaped by the schools, the shaping process begins very early, at the age of seven or eight. At that age, the process of segregation begins, those children who seem most amenable to teaching being put in different classes from the more backward. A series of tests follows at the age of about eleven, when the top 30 per cent are given places in Grammar Schools, while the rest are relegated to Secondary Modern Schools (or the appropriate streams of Comprehensive Schools). The Grammar School children are groomed for the universities, though, as we saw, those from working class families have a particular propensity to fall out before they get there. The Secondary Modern children reach an educational peak about their second year and then a decline sets in. In their fourth and final year, they have forgotten much of what they once knew; at the end of each term, those who have turned fifteen leave to look for work, watched enviously and sullenly by those whom the law compels to remain behind.[4]

[3] The Secondary Grammar Schools prepare children for the General Certificate of Education, passes in which are a prerequisite for admission to universities, teacher training colleges, and to many forms of higher employment. *15 to 18*, a report of the Central Advisory Council for Education (Government Stationery Office, 1959), reports on a number of inquiries into parents' occupation in respect to children in the various sorts of schools.

[4] Adam Smith might have been describing this system when he wrote, "The difference between the most dissimilar characters, between a philosopher and a

Modern society is much more lavishly equipped with passive, nonintellectual entertainment than that of fifty years ago. The pangs of physical hunger have been stilled, many causes of anxiety eliminated, and amusement (canned or boxed) mass produced to fill the intellectual void. Most people feel that lectures, meetings, theatres, churches—and even books—are not for them.[5]

On the other side, those who enter the professions or subprofessions renounce this bucolic life for a lifetime of study: exams must be passed, certificates accumulated, and until the very end of the career, new techniques absorbed. The furrow that separated the two children at the age of seven has become a chasm.[6] It is a pretty formidable chasm, but it is not unbridgeable. We shall return to the bridges later and now observe the trade-union organizations of those who have succeeded in escaping from the necessity for manual labor.

THE SCOPE AND MEMBERSHIP OF WHITE-COLLAR UNIONS

There were 9,872 trade unionists belonging to 623 unions in the United Kingdom in December 1962.[7] The total number of employees was 23,000,000. It is not possible to get an accurate industrial or occupational breakdown of these figures, because there is a large area of overlap between different unions, most of which sprawl across a variety of industries and occupations.[8]

Thus there are clerical workers in the Amalgamated Engineering Union, the National Union of Mineworkers, and the general unions as

common street porter, for example, seems to arise not so much from nature as from habit, custom and education. When they came into the world, and for the first six or eight years of their existence, they were perhaps very much alike. . . . About that age, or soon after, they come to be employed in very different occupations. The difference of talents . . . widens by degrees, till at last the vanity of the philosopher is willing to acknowledge scarce any resemblance." (*The Wealth of Nations,* Everyman edition, London: Dent, 1910, p. 69.)

[5] Of 377 workers in 4 factories interviewed by Ferdynand Zweig, 152 did not read books, 25 read them occasionally, 48 read only Westerns or thrillers. See *The Worker in an Affluent Society* (Heinemann, 1961).

[6] The social upgrading that is required by the expansion of white-collar employment itself brings secondary problems involved in the transfer of allegiance and change of values, with some of the most ardent supporters of the *status quo* being themselves new entrants to the middle class from a working class milieu. Thus, paradoxically, increased mobility tends to accentuate class stratification. See Jackson and Marsden, *Education and the Working Class* (Routledge, for the Institute of Community Studies, 1962).

[7] *Ministry of Labour Gazette,* December 1963.

[8] Collective bargaining is usually done by a federation or panel of unions with overlapping interests.

well as in the Clerical and Administrative Workers' Union. The National Union of Railwaymen organizes hotel and catering workers and seamen employed by the British Transport Commission, and the Transport and General Workers' Union and the National Union of General and Municipal Workers have members in every industry and almost every occupation in the country. Some of the unions do classify their members, but then it is generally by negotiating group rather than industry or occupation, so it would be a formidable task to discover how trade-union members fit into the categories of the official classification of occupations or industries.

We can get a first (and very rough) approximation of the extent of white-collar organization by looking at the extent of union membership in industries dominated by white-collar workers (Table 2).

Table 2. Number of Men and Women in Trade Unions and Their Percentage of All Employees in Predominantly Nonmanual Industries, United Kingdom, December 1962

	Numbers in Thousands [a]					
	Men		*Women*		*Total*	
	Number	*Percentage*	*Number*	*Percentage*	*Number*	*Percentage*
Distributive trades	234	16	171	11	405	13
Insurance, banking, and finance	136	40	60	22	196	32
Educational services	190	58	227	32	417	40
All other professional and scientific services	109	25	141	18	250	20
Cinemas, theatres, radio, sport, betting, etc.	72	55	23	20	95	38
National government service	254	66	134	73	388	68
Local government service	350	57	227	(100)	577	70
	1,345	36	983	25	2,328	31

[a] Parts and totals sometimes differ because of rounding. Women organized in local government unions represent more than the total of women in local government employ because of overlapping membership of their unions.

Union members attributed to each industry represent total membership of those unions who have the bulk of their members in the industries concerned. In most cases, the actual number of trade unionists in the industry concerned is in fact higher than shown, because the Ministry of Labour is unable to distinguish the members of the two great general unions [9] by industry. Further, organization in local government is exaggerated at the expense of professional services, for a large number of the members of the National and Local Government Officers' Association and the National Union of Public Employees actually work in the Health Service.

None the less, the figures do show that the numbers organized in national and local government and in education are very much above the national average, and those organized in the distributive trades and in banking, insurance, and finance, very much below.

We may note immediately that a major distinction with regard to density of organization relates to whether employment is in the public or private sector. In the nationalized coal mining industry, workers are 95 per cent organized, on the nationalized railways, 85 per cent. Paper and printing, and metal manufacturing and engineering, despite the power and maturity of their unions, are only between 50 and 60 per cent organized.

While there is a multitude of white-collar associations, some affiliated to the Trades Union Congress, some not even registered as trade unions, very few have more than a handful of members or have any influence on the national scene. The major white-collar unions are shown in Table 3.

Table 3. Major White-Collar Unions, Membership, 1961

	Number of Members, 1961 (in 1,000)
Mainly Clerical Workers	
Clerical and Administrative Workers' Union	60
Civil Service Clerical Association	140
Transport Salaried Staffs Association	87
Clerical and Manipulative Workers	
Union of Post Office Workers	166

[9] The Transport and General Workers' Union and the National Union of General and Municipal Workers.

	Number of Members, 1961 (in 1,000)
Clerical Workers and Officials	
Association of Post Office Controlling Officers	13
Confederation of Health Service Employees	54
Guild of Insurance Officials	18
Inland Revenue Staff Federation	41
Ministry of Labour Staff Association	11
National and Local Government Officers' Association	285
National Federation of Insurance Workers	37
National Union of Bank Employees	53
Professionals and Technicians	
Association of Scientific Workers	12
British Actors' Equity Association	10
British Medical Association [a]	71
Draftsmen's and Allied Technicians' Association	67
Electrical Power Engineers' Association	18
Institution of Professional Civil Servants [a]	60
Musicians' Union	28
National Association of Schoolmasters [a]	27
National Association of Theatrical and Kine Employees	22
National Union of Journalists	16
National Union of Teachers [a]	230
Society of Technical Civil Servants	9
Mixed	
Association of Supervisory Staffs, Executives and Technicians	25
National Union of Public Employees	200
Distributive Trade	
Union of Shop, Distributive and Allied Workers	355
Total	2,115

[a] Not affiliated to the Trades Union Congress.

The above classification illustrates the difficulty of analyzing British trade unions by the occupation of their members. They are free of religious or political divisions; in the main the larger ones are affiliated to the TUC or at least cooperate with it, and they are free of most other sorts of divisions as well. But, there is a great deal of rivalry between them in the recruitment of members, though the Bridlington Agreement is designed to prevent poaching.[10] In fact, it is only in the National Government Service that lines of demarcation are fairly clear. This is helped by the fact that the Civil Service unions are affiliated to the Civil Service National Whitley Council and that the government, as a rule, recognizes only one union in respect of each grade in the Civil Service.

In local government and in the National Health Service, there is a great deal of overlapping: a worker has the choice of joining the National and Local Government Officers' Association, the National Union of Public Employees, the National Union of General and Municipal Workers, one of a score or more specialized associations, or, for manual workers, the appropriate craft or occupational union.

In insurance and banking, there is again strong rivalry, but this time mainly between the broader unions and the staff associations that are attached to most of the big companies. In the wider world of commerce and industry, it is only the draftsmen and the co-op employees who are strongly organized, while managers, scientists, engineers, clerks, and foremen, with some notable exceptions, are hardly organized at all.

THE ORIGINS OF WHITE-COLLAR UNIONISM

There are many examples, in the last half of the nineteenth century, of white-collar workers who combined in order to remedy a grievance.[11] In a way, it was easier for them to do this than it was for manual workers. They were closer to their employers, more nearly of equal social status; they were literate and articulate and could con-

[10] This was a code of procedure adopted at the annual Trade Union Congress at Bridlington in 1939, in terms of which no union may accept a member of another union without consulting that union. No member who was under discipline, engaged in a trade dispute or in arrears with his contributions may be accepted. No union may commence organizing in any establishment where a majority of the relevant grade of workers belong to another union and have their conditions negotiated by that union. See B. C. Roberts, *Trade Union Government and Administration in Great Britain* (London: Bell, 1956).

[11] O. G. Pickard gives a concise history in "Trade Unions among Clerical Workers," *British Management Review* (April 1955), pp. 102-20.

spire together in working hours without being found out. Also, since they were gentlemanly in appearance and behavior, they did not inspire in their employers' minds the same fears of revolution as did combinations of manual workers. Finally—and this was something of great importance—some of them had the vote, and could thus influence parliamentary elections.

This last was a peculiarly effective weapon in the hands of civil servants. The Lords of the Treasury issued a minute on May 2, 1867, in which they observe "with great regret a growing practice on the part of gentlemen employed in the public service to endeavour to influence this Board to accede to their applications for increases of salary or additional retiring allowances by means of the private solicitation of members of Parliament, and other persons of political influence." Public officers were warned that such action would be treated as an admission that the case was not good upon its merits and would be "dealt with by their Lordships accordingly." [12]

An official witness to the Ridley Commission in 1886 criticized the creation of common classes in the Civil Service. The Lower Division, he said, was a united, compact body. "They have already brought their influence to bear upon members of Parliament, and there have been important meetings held at which a number of members were present, who, I venture to think, had not closely examined the grounds upon which the claim was put forward. . . ." By the institution of service-wide grades, he maintained, "you are creating a trade union—I am not using the word at all in a critical manner—it is perfectly natural that it should be so; but the trades union that you are creating will probably be too strong for the Government, and probably too strong for Parliament." [13]

Sometimes civil servants appeared before official commissions or committees not as individuals but as representatives of organizations —the Salaries Increase Movement or the Writers' Association—and were received with curiosity but not open antagonism. The Writers' Association, in fact, scored some signal successes for its members, who were temporary copyists originally hired by the government from an agency at 10d. an hour, but many of whom had had themselves attached to particular departments at higher rates.[14] The Treasury at one stage decided to eliminate the agency and hire them directly at

[12] *Report of the Royal Commission into the Civil Establishments,* the Ridley Commission (1886), Appendix (3), p. 417.

[13] Ridley Commission, *op. cit.,* para. 10742, *et seq.*

[14] A "temporary" civil servant may have his employment terminated and is not entitled to a pension.

a uniform rate of 10d. an hour and staged what was really a lockout in order to do so. So vigorous was the Writers' reaction that the Treasury was forced to confirm them in their special terms. Lowe, one-time Chancellor of the Exchequer, testified to the effectiveness of their action: "One thing which we overlooked was the danger of collecting a very large body of persons together, having friends all over the country, having a particular interest, and that interest being to obtain better terms from the Government." [15]

In 1886, the Writers actually persuaded the government to distribute bonuses amongst them, an initial vote of £6,000 being increased (after some vigorous agitation) to £14,000.[16]

The British Medical Association was established in 1832, though it assumed its present title only in 1856. It led a vigorous life, protecting and furthering its members' interests and, with the extension of salaried employment with the growth of public medicine, assumed some of the functions of a trade union. In 1910, after its application for a charter had been refused, it look legal opinion as to whether it could register as a trade union: the ruling was negative, since it was an association neither of workmen nor masters.[17] However, in fact, if not in law, it plays the role of trade union in its negotiations with the government for doctors' pay in the National Health Service.

Teachers, too, were organized early in the century, though the National Union of Elementary Teachers, forerunner of the present-day National Union of Teachers, was established only in 1870.[18]

Despite these early manifestations of the will to combine, it was really not until the 1890's that trade unionism spread from the skilled journeymen to the unskilled laborers, on the one side, and the white-collar workers on the other. The forerunners of many modern unions were established about that time: the National Amalgamated Union of Shop Assistants, Warehousemen and Clerks, the Amalgamated Union of Co-operative Employees, the National Union of Clerks, the Municipal Employees' Association, the Postmen's Federation, the Second Division Clerks' Association, the Association of Tax Clerks, the Customs Officers' Federation. The Railway Clerks' Association followed a few years later, in 1897.

[15] Royal Commission of 1874, *Evidence,* para. 3-4, *et seq.*

[16] Miss B. V. Humphreys, in *Clerical Unions in the Civil Service* (London: Blackwell & Mott, 1958), describes these early organizations and lists thirteen that were formed between 1857 and 1898.

[17] Employers' associations are trade unions in British Law.

[18] See Asher Tropp, *The School Teachers* (London: Heinemann, 1957), chap. VIII.

INTO ACTION

But once established, what then? The unskilled workers won some signal successes because they were desperate enough to strike, needed little strike pay because their earnings were so miserable, and because their newly publicized sufferings excited great public sympathy.[19] The nonmanual workers, who were regarded as socially superior even to the craftsmen, had much more to lose and could expect no such sympathetic public response.

A strike of telegraphists in 1868 had ended in failure and a strike of postmen in 1890 was even more disastrous.[20] The idea of a strike was not seriously raised again in the Post Office until 1913, when, in a period of general trade-union militancy, a conference of 23 Post Office unions was held, with a general membership of 100,000. At this meeting the principle of amalgamation was agreed upon, which led, though not till after the war, to the formation of the Union of Post Office Workers. G. H. Stuart-Bunning was one of the advocates of the invincibility of an all-grades strike, but this, too, was interrupted by the war, at the end of which he became one of the leading advocates of joint consultation in the Civil Service.[21]

A trade union that cannot strike is like a muzzled dog—however fierce its noises, no one is really afraid. But as every organizer knows, white-collar workers are extraordinarily difficult to get out on strike; it goes against some deeply held feelings—their sense of social equality with the boss, their privilege of payment for time lost through illness, their semipermanent attachment to the firm, their sense of responsibility for the performance of their work (which accumulates while they are away), their hopes of promotion, their superiority to the manual workers. When to this is added the small and scattered distribution of the units in which they are frequently employed and the geographic dispersion of their homes, a strike becomes almost impossible.[22]

[19] The London dockers were paid 5d. an hour for their irregular employment before their great strike of 1889. Nearly £49,000 was collected in Britain for their strike fund by public subscription and a further £30,000 telegraphed from Australia. See Sidney and Beatrice Webb, *The History of Trade Unionism* (London: Longmans, Green, 1920), pp. 403-4.

[20] See H. G. Swift, *A History of Postal Agitation* (London: Pearson, 1900), p. 221.

[21] Stuart-Bunning was one of the most picturesque of the early leaders. His name was really Stuart, but he added the "Bunning" as a mark of extra distinction. In the Post Office, many legends still circulate about him.

[22] Though, as we shall see, not completely so.

In the main, these unions, before 1914, occupied themselves in propaganda, fact-finding, parliamentary pressure, and mutual encouragement. The National Union of Clerks published *The Clerks' Charter,* reviewing the decline in the pay and status of clerical workers that had followed the introduction of the General Education Act of 1870. "Thousands (of women) are being turned out every year by business training colleges, schools, typewriter companies, and second-hand typewriter dealers. One well-known firm of the last-named category advertises constantly that they will send out machine and operator for 15s. a week. That they sweat their girls is patent and the secret of how they make a profit is given away by the advertisements appearing in the *Daily Mail* for girls to come and earn 2s. 6d. a week, while learning. Having finished such an apprenticeship I have known girls to offer their services through a labor exchange at nothing a week, in order to get into a real office and make a start."[23]

The Shop Assistants' Union conducted an elaborate study of wages and conditions, collecting information from several thousand workers.[24] This showed the chaotic nature of the wage structure in the distributive trade, with rates for similar work ranging from 2d. to 1s. 4d. an hour. The average for 3,171 assistants aged 17 to 50 was £1. 8s. 6d. per week of from 47 to 91 hours.[25]

A great deal of loving effort went into the production of union journals. The British Medical Association, of course, produced the *Medical Journal,* a widely read weekly magazine that dealt (and still deals) with everything from the science of medicine to doctors' pay. The National Union of Teachers published *The Schoolmaster.* Others were *The Shop Assistant, Red Tape, The Civil Service Gazette, The Post, The Telegraph Chronicle.*

A favorite form of activity was the canvassing of parliamentary candidates or Members of Parliament. In 1892, the Postmaster-General prohibited postal employees, in combination or otherwise, from extracting promises from parliamentry candidates in connection with their pay or position,[26] but this injunction was ignored and the Fawcett Association circularized all candidates in the subsequent general election asking them if, in the event of election, they would support

[23] Quoted by F. D. Klingender in *The Condition of Clerical Labour in Britain* (London: Martin Lawrence, 1935), p. 22.
[24] See P. C. Hoffman, *They Also Serve* (London: Porcupine Press, 1949), p. 78.
[25] To convert £'s of pre–World War I value into £'s of 1960 value, multiply by 4.5.
[26] *Post Office Circular,* June 17, 1892.

the appointment of a Parliamentary Committee to inquire into postal pay.[27] In 1900, the Postmen's Federation, Fawcett Association, and Postal Telegraph Clerks' Association directed a campaign at all Members of Parliament. "We may have a General Election during the autumn, and in any case candidates and Members will soon be among their constituents. Local branches should arrange interviews with both political parties; they should explain the grievances and try and obtain definite assurances. This is the *only* road to success and no centralisation of work can possibly be of the same value." [28]

The Association of Assistant Clerks (precursor of the Civil Service Clerical Association), which was formed in 1902, had as its seventh object the appointment of a commission of inquiry into their conditions of service, in support of which they organized a petition in 1906, which was signed by 376 M.P.'s. When their campaign succeeded (six years later), *Red Tape,* the Association's journal, reported, "A continuous repetition of grievances, much spilling of printer's ink, and the spending of wearisome months in the 'Lobby' of the House of Commons have at length achieved what will prove, we all hope, the first step towards a contented Civil Service."

The National Union of Teachers, too, had a long history of parliamentary actions that involved canvassing, lobbying, and (in 1890) the compilation of registers recording for future reference election promises made by M.P.'s respecting education.[29] In 1895, two sponsored candidates were elected to Parliament—one a Conservative, the other a Liberal—thus ensuring that the Union's voice would be heard in the House and, at the same time, preventing political controversy within the Union. This is a form of political nonpartisanship that the Union has preserved to the present day.

But the result of these parliamentary maneuvers was not always happy. In 1912, a Parliamentary Select Committee, appointed on the insistence of the National Joint Committee of Post Office Unions, reported, "Your Committee finds it extremely difficult to compare the conditions of Post Office Servants with those in any outside employment. In spite of several challenges to the witnesses on behalf of the staff no evidence was adduced to support the proposition that Post Office Servants suffer any disadvantage in the matter of wages as compared with persons engaged in other occupations. Moreover . . .

[27] The Fawcett Association was named after the blind Postmaster-General who did much to improve the lot of the postal workers.
[28] *The Telegraph Chronicle,* August 3, 1900.
[29] Tropp, *op. cit.,* pp. 139-43.

there is no difficulty in recruiting a sufficient number of persons competent for the duties they have to perform." [30]

The indignation of the staff was epitomized by a prayer recited by a subpostmaster at a mass meeting in Dundee: [31]

Lord, hear our earnest cry and prayer
Against the Holt Committee there;
Thy strong right hand, Lord, mak' it bear
  Upon their heads.
Lord, weight it doon—and dinna spare—
  For their misdeeds.

Lord, in the days of vengeance try them,
Lord, visit them who did employ them,
And pass not, in thy mercy, by them,
  Nor hear their prayer,
But for Thy people's sake destroy them,
  An' dinna spare.

Direct action was beyond the scope of most white-collar unions, but it was used effectively by the shop assistants and by the teachers. Numbers of strikes in retail stores were aimed against the living-in system.[32] The discipline exercised against the shop assistant was severe, his life hedged about by rules breach of which was punished by fine or dismissal. Many employers refused to employ married men, so that those who wanted both wife and job had to keep their marriage a secret.

Hoffman records how he participated in a campaign in 1901. To advertise a meeting, he and twelve other assistants hired sandwich boards, pasted posters on to them, and paraded through the West End of London dressed in top hats and frock coats (which, of course, was standard going-out dress for those in their station): "We were frightfully shy over it and huddled together for comfort and failed to conform to the regulation that sandwichmen must keep 30 paces apart, for we should have felt very lonely 30 paces apart. . . . When shortly afterwards I entered the employment of Peter Robinson's, assistants from all over the house came into the silk department to shake my hand." [33]

The meeting was a thundering success, the chapel packed, hundreds turned away. Demonstrations followed in many parts of the

[30] Report of the Holt Committee, 1912-13.
[31] *The Telegraph Chronicle,* December 19, 1913, p. 15.
[32] See Hoffman, *op. cit.*
[33] *Ibid.,* p. 48.

country. At first, concessions were made, fines abolished, rules relaxed, but, in 1907, the system itself came under heavy fire. A public committee was investigating the truck system and heard evidence about living-in. A number of large department stores (many of which are still flourishing today) abolished the system. The first strike against living-in took place that year and ended in the closing down of the store concerned; another strike continued for sixteen weeks in a large drapery store in Kentish Town, London,[34] and after that the system was abandoned in shop after shop until, by 1914, it was virtually at an end.

In 1910, the Shop Assistants' Union adopted a schedule of minimum rates and negotiated with firms in many parts of the country for their acceptance, achieving some success. Hoffman records eight strikes (other than those to do with living-in) between 1904 and 1914.

The national conference of the National Union of Teachers had first adopted a resolution in favor of a strike fund in 1893, the proposal being that each member should contribute 3s. However, this was rejected by the local associations by 6,354 votes to 1,172. Education was under the management of local authorities (county councils) who fixed their own salary scales, and the most the NUT could do was to circulate information on the subject and try to channel teachers from low-salary to high-salary areas. The first skirmish came in 1907, when the West Ham Council decided to reduce salaries. But, while white-collar workers are prepared to suffer low pay with nothing more than verbal protests, attempts to cut their pay excite the same passions in them that they do in other workers. The Union prepared for strike action. "It held public meetings and conferences in the Borough, 'black-listed' the authority, began to withdraw teachers from the schools and threatened 200 resignations."[35]

The dispute was settled to the teachers' satisfaction, but a more serious action was fought in Herefordshire in 1913, when 240 teachers placed their resignations in the hands of the Union, 130 of which were duly passed on to the Authority. In February 1914, more than sixty schools were closed and the Authority was persuaded to settle the matter, after conciliation by the Bishop of Hereford.[36]

One other case should be mentioned before we leave this prewar

[34] C. and A. Daniels, still flourishing though now part of a large business group.
[35] Tropp, *op. cit.*, p. 204.
[36] *Ibid.*, pp. 205-6.

period: The British Medical Association versus Lloyd George. I have mentioned that the BMA was not legally a trade union, but when occasion arose it behaved just like one. One of the social security measures introduced by the Liberal government was the National Health Insurance Act. An overwhelming majority of BMA members resolved not to accept services under the scheme until the Association had approved the conditions. The doctors demanded 11s. per patient per year, and, in protracted negotiations, pushed the Government up to 9s. Until then, the doctors had acted as a united body; now their resolution began to waver. At a special conference held on December 21, 1912, 2,408 voted in favor of accepting the government's terms, 11,219 against. By January 2, Lloyd George was able to announce that ten thousand doctors throughout the country had signed on. The BMA was compelled to release the balance from their undertaking not to sign on until agreement had been reached. It had achieved a great deal, for the initial offer had been for 4s. 6d., but the membership drew back when faced with the logical conclusion of their decision—the breakdown of the scheme.[37]

THE WAR AND ITS AFTERMATH

Union activity had mounted after 1910; total membership of trade unions rose by 22 per cent in 1911, 9 per cent in 1912, 21 per cent in 1913. Membership of the National Union of Clerks rose from 3,608 in 1911 to 12,700 in 1914. Membership of clerical unions in the Civil Service was small but growing; 1,200 in 1908 and 2,837 in 1914, with an additional 2,000 in departmental unions. The Railway Clerks' Association had 10,000 members in 1910 and 42,000 in 1915; the National Joint Committee of Post Office Unions had 56,971 members in 1910 and 61,417 in 1914. The white-collar unions had completed their apprenticeship, but the main struggles lay ahead.

Between 1914 and 1920, the unions made rapid progress: profits were high, unemployment negligible, sentiment sympathetic. But it was probably the runaway inflation of those years that brought home to workers most strongly the value of trade unions. This was of particular moment in the Civil Service. In 1917, a Civil Service Arbitration Board was established to deal with pay claims. Organization was now forced upon civil servants, for each group now had to agree on a claim, enter into negotiations with the departmental heads and the

[37] The story of the BMA is told by Paul Vaughan in *Doctors' Commons* (London: Heinemann, 1959). See also Carr-Saunders and Wilson, *The Professions* (Oxford, 1933).

Treasury and, if agreements were not reached, nominate representatives and plead their case before the Board.[38] This had required a transformation of attitude on both sides, for previously it had been only as a very great concession that the Treasury had agreed even to speak to the representatives of a staff association, since all approaches were supposed to go through the departmental heads.

The spirit of the age is perhaps best shown in the reports of the Whitley Committee.[39] These gave powerful support to the extension of workers' control and envisaged the transformation of industrial relations in a syndicalist way. Whitley Councils were set up in a number of industries to consider matters of mutual interest to employers and employees.

The final years of the war and the two years that followed displayed symptoms of economic mania that, in this more phlegmatic age, we have almost forgotten. Hours of work of manual workers were drastically cut and their unions fought desperately to keep wages abreast of prices. White-collar unions developed rapidly. The Railway Clerks' Association had sixty thousand members out of a possible one hundred thousand but had to begin preparations for a strike before recognition could be wrung out of the companies. The idea that the strike was a weapon available to white-collar workers was gaining currency. "The strike idea was at first something wonderful, but fearful; a monster hideous and repulsive; impossible, undesirable, awful and unthinkable. Despite all this it was a grim necessity."[40] Since 1922, the railway clerks have had the same status, vis-à-vis their employers, as the civil servants, with formal negotiating machinery leading to arbitration tribunals (the Central and National Wages Boards).

The National Association of Local Government Officers also recruited heavily immediately after the war and, by 1920, had 36,500 members. But its task was much more formidable than that of the Civil Service unions, for each of some thousands of local authorities fixed its own scales of pay. It was not until after World War II that national machinery was established and rates and conditions standardized.

[38] Miss Humphreys describes these events in *Clerical Unions in the Civil Service, op. cit.*, chap. VI.

[39] Committee on the Relations betwen Employers and Employed, established October 1916 under the chairmanship of J. H. Whitley, Deputy Speaker of the House of Commons. In the socially unstable conditions of that time, their proposals appeared as an alternative to something much more drastic. Some of them were adopted, but much of the spirit was lost in the deflation and depression of the early twenties.

[40] *The Railway Service Journal*, February 1919. Quoted by Lockwood, *op. cit.*

But much tougher than any of these were the tasks of the clerks in business, banks, and insurance. The National Union of Clerks had also grown rapidly during the war, from 12,680 members in 1914 to 47,528 in 1920. At the latter date they had formal pay agreements with a number of firms and a general agreement for coal mines in South Wales and Monmouthshire.[41] But the economic collapse of 1921 was followed by a collapse of its influence and membership, which was down to 7,442 by 1924. The Union's journal, *The Clerk*, was out of existence between September 1921 and January 1923, then was revived by a band of faithful members who kept the union ticking over until its new lease on life in World War II. Pay agreements lapsed and were not renewed except for the chocolate firms[42] and some of the great companies in shipbuilding and steel.

The Bank Officers' Guild was formed early in 1918 to organize bank employees in England and Wales.[43] The most potent grievance of the staff had been the failure of the banks to pay adequate cost-of-living allowances. By mid-1919, the Guild had 10,000 members and 17 branches. By August 1920, it had 24,000 members and 128 branches and by the beginning of 1921, membership was up to 30,000—nearly half the eligible staff.

In Scotland, too, a union of bank clerks had been formed: the Scottish Bankers' Association. The major difficulty, almost surmounted in Scotland, was to get recognition from the banks. But this was refused, both in Scotland and the south and, as sometimes happens, refusal was accompanied by substantial concessions to the staff and the recognition of staff associations.

Likewise, in insurance, the Guild of Insurance Officials was formed in 1919 and made rapid progress—by the beginning of 1920 its membership was 15,000. Some companies negotiated pay revisions with the Guild, but the main obstacle again was nonrecognition and the rivalry of associations peculiar to the company concerned.

THROUGH THE DEPRESSION

The twenties and thirties were years of great difficulty, divided by the tragi-heroics of the General Strike. Total union membership reached a peak of 8,348,000 in 1920, then declined to not much more

[41] See Klingender, *op. cit.*, p. 51.
[42] Cadbury, Fry, and Rowntree, established by Quakers, took pride in being model employers.
[43] By contrast, the Irish Bank Officers' Association won recognition and access to arbitration by its strike call for December 20, 1919.

than half this number in 1933. Teachers, civil servants, railway and bank clerks were on the defensive; all suffered cuts in pay. Unemployment rose to 25 per cent and rarely fell below 10.[44] But by 1935 or 1936, cuts had been restored and membership was set on an upward path that has continued, with some ups and downs, ever since.

But the unions themselves, getting little change out of the employers, turned to their own organization. It was a period of consolidation and amalgamation. Unions of postmen, telephonists, telegraphists, and counter clerks amalgamated into the Union of Post Office Workers. A dozen unions, in 1922, formed the Civil Service Clerical Association. In 1936, the Inland Revenue Staff Federation emerged as a result of various amalgamations. After the war, the process continued: the Union of Shop, Distributive and Allied Workers was formed in 1947 by an amalgamation of the National Union of Distributive and Allied Workers and the National Amalgamated Union of Shop Assistants, Warehousemen and Clerks. In 1950, after nationalization, the Railway Clerks' Association changed its name to the Transport Salaried Staffs' Association, the better to embrace the clerks in road transport, docks, hotels, and catering who came within the scope of the British Transport Commission.

THE PRESENT STRUCTURE

The Civil Service

The official booklet, *Staff Relations in the Civil Service*,[45] states that "A civil servant is free to be a member of any association or trade union which will admit him under its rules of membership. Civil servants are, moreover, encouraged . . . to belong to associations, for the existence of fully representative associations not only promotes good staff relations but is essential to effective negotiations on conditions of service." Indeed, if unions did not exist in the Civil Service, it would be necessary to invent them, for they play an indispensable role in channeling grievances and aspirations and in ensuring that the complex staff regulations are carried out justly and impartially.

The Whitley Councils provide an elaborate machinery for ensuring proper consultation and coordination of policies, both between

[44] Some occupations are more susceptible to unemployment than others; in general, the rate for white-collar occupations is about half that for manual workers. But the loss of a white-collar job is a more serious matter than that of a manual job.

[45] Compiled by the Treasury (Her Majesty's Stationery Office, 1958).

the official and staff sides and between unions and groups of unions.[46] Below the National Whitley Council, with its subcommittees, are Departmental Councils concerned with affairs peculiar to the department in which they operate.

The National Council itself is a somewhat elusive body that does not often meet, but the Staff Side, which leads an independent existence, is a body of great importance—a coordinating body for all Civil Service unions, with premises, permanent officials, and a journal of its own.

It was through the Whitley machinery that the reorganization of the Civil Service was carried out in 1919 and that the cost-of-living sliding scale, 1920 to 1935, was agreed upon. More recently, it has negotiated a number of Service-wide increases to keep Service pay roughly in line with the increases effective outside the Service.

The Civil Service provides two of the seventeen unions in the United Kingdom with more than one hundred thousand members each —the Union of Post Office Workers and the Civil Service Clerical Association. Both these unions inhabit their own modern buildings, but, like most British unions, dues are much too low to enable them to build up adequate reserves. Dues brought in £282,000 to the UPW in 1961 and £245,043 to the CSCA in 1960, while the book value of their investments was £58,000 in the one case and £249,000 in the other.

Both these unions are affiliated to the TUC and the UPW is, in addition, affiliated to the Labour Party and sponsors and supports six parliamentary candidates.

The Civil Service Clerical Association is one of the four unions constituting the Civil Service Alliance[47] which represents clerical assistants, machine operators, and typists.

Of the other white-collar unions, the most important is the Institution of Professional Civil Servants, a flourishing organization that has recently built itself a fine new building in the heart of London. It is affiliated neither to the TUC nor the Labour Party; indeed, so

[46] The constitution states the object as follows: "To secure the greatest measure of co-operation between the State in its capacity as employer and the general body of Civil Servants in matters affecting the Civil Service with a view to increased efficiency in the Public Service combined with the well-being of those employed; to provide machinery for dealing with grievances and generally to bring together the experience and different points of view of representatives of the Administrative, Clerical and Manipulative Civil Service."

[47] The others are the Inland Revenue Staff Federation, the Ministry of Labour Staff Association, and the County Court Officers' Association.

particular did its members become that, by conference resolution, it severed its relations with the Federation of Professional Workers because the Federation in turn, was affiliated to the Conference of Unions Catering for Non-Manual Workers which is sponsored by the TUC. However, this decision was reversed in 1963. But the IPCS seems no nearer affiliation to the TUC, for a motion for affiliation was rejected by a three-to-one majority in a ballot of members in March 1964. But we shall return to this theme later.

The Civil Service Unions have a vast range of responsibilities to keep their officers busy. Each one is concerned with salary negotiations covering, perhaps, a dozen different grades. Apart from that, they are concerned with a mass of provisions regarding Civil Service staff—provincial pay differentiation, allowances, hours and overtime, holiday and sick leave, recruitment and duties, superannuation, promotion, civil rights, redundancy—and a mass of personal cases in which individual claims and complaints must be pursued.[48]

Since the acceptance of the recommendations of the Priestley Commission,[49] pay negotiation has become particularly onerous. There is a certain irony in this, for the Commission produced a doctrine relating to pay determination that, on the face of it, seemed to make the unions superfluous. Civil Service pay was to be adjusted on the basis of "fair comparison" with what was paid outside the Service to workers doing comparable work, allowance being made for advantages and disadvantages peculiar to the jobs compared. The facts necessary for this comparison were to be collected by an impartial body, in the light of whose findings adjustments would be made to Civil Service pay.

In the event, the interpretation of the facts collected by the Civil Service Pay Research Unit has involved both the official and the staff sides in labors of unexpected magnitude. In former days, the two sides came to the table with a few statistics from official publications, a few scraps of information produced by their own researches, and a general impression of the economic, social, and political climate. They listened to each other's views (the official side politely, the staff side with signs of impatience and incredulity), gauged each other's temper, and then struck a bargain.

Post-Priestley, they have to argue about what workers in what

[48] For an orderly exposition of the activities of a Civil Service union, see the *I.P.C.S. Handbook* (published by the Institution of Professional Civil Servants).
[49] Royal Commission on the Civil Service, 1953-55.

organizations should be investigated, wait while exhaustive investigations are made, then process and digest an enormous volume of data which greatly widens the area of possible disagreement! There has recently been an attempt to limit these general reassessments to once in five years, with something much more like the old bargaining system in between.

Local Authorities

We have noted the high density of trade-union membership in the local government service. This is the result of a number of circumstances including the very large number of authorities (1,959 at present) who employ a vast army of specialists in planning, health, social welfare, civil engineering, housing, parks, sanitation, libraries, and markets, and an army of clerks to serve them. But since most authorities employ each grade in small numbers, there is a strong impulse for them to seek the society of their co-occupants in other areas. Against this, there was (at least since World War I) no danger that joining an association would jeopardize one's job or chances of promotion.

Nowadays, union membership is actively encouraged and the National Joint Council for Local Authorities' Administrative, Professional, Technical and Clerical Services has adopted the following resolution:[50]

> The National Joint Council . . . is a joint organisation of employers and employed and constitutes the recognised machinery for the application of collective bargaining in the Local Government Service. Negotiations between individual local authorities and unorganised officers are impracticable. The National Council recommends local authorities to recognise all the organisations represented thereon. On both sides the National Council agrees that the interests of local authorities and their staffs are best served by individual officers joining their appropriate organisations, it being understood that the organisation he joins is a matter for the unfettered judgment of the individual officer.

Unions in the field are the National and Local Government Officers' Association (NALGO), the National Union of Public Employees (NUPE), the Clerical and Administrative Workers' Union, National Union of General and Municipal Workers, and a large number of specialist societies.

There are four national joint negotiating committees for town clerks or chief officers, a number for manual workers, and the one

[50] *Scheme of Conditions of Service* (National Joint Council, etc., March 1958), para. 44.

already mentioned for administrative, etc., workers, which was established in 1944, and, in 1946, adopted a scheme to standardize pay and conditions of service throughout the country.[51]

The activities of the local authorities have been greatly expanded under the welfare state, many of whose provisions they administer, and it is in this favorable environment that the local government unions, in particular NALGO and NUPE, have flourished.

Of the two, NALGO has grown the faster—at a rate that is a record for British unions since the war. In recent years, when the membership of most unions has hardly changed, it has been expanding by ten thousand members a year. Its membership has more than doubled since the end of the war. Since 1950, the increase has been nearly one hundred thousand. Part of this, as I have said, must be attributed to its favorable environment; but in part, too, it is due to the extraordinary degree of initiative shown by the union. It has not been afraid to pay for qualified staff, has a lawyer for General Secretary, and a professional journalist as public relations officer. By good briefing of the press, it has managed to get unusually favorable publicity. Apart from this, it runs a bright, well-written, and well-designed weekly newspaper that is actually entertaining to read—even for nonmembers.

NUPE organizes all and every sort of public employee and seems to hold effectively the most diverse elements, but its image is much more plebian than that of NALGO. It is affiliated to the Labour Party, the TUC, and the National Federation of Professional Workers and supports two Labour Members of Parliament. Also, its dues are lower: 1s. entrance fee and 1s. a week for men and 6d. a week for women.

NALGO's dues vary according to income: 2s. per month for those with annual salary up to £300; rising in five stages to 7s. per month for those at more than £1,500. NALGO has remained nonpolitical and, until October 1965, outside the TUC. In that month, in the sixth ballot since 1962, a majority was at last obtained for affiliation.[52] However, like the Institution of Professional Civil Servants, it affiliated to the Federation of Professional Workers in 1963.

National Health Service

Another thing that has boosted NALGO and NUPE has been the creation of the National Health Service. The Service took over

[51] See *A Survey of the Local Government Service* (N.J.C., 1950).
[52] Affiliation had been rejected, though by a narrow margin, in a ballot in 1962.

all hospitals in 1948 and brought the general medical and dental practitioners into the scheme. It established an elaborate administrative organization.

To regulate pay and staff conditions, there are a general and nine functional Whitley Councils.[53] One of these is the Administrative and Clerical Council that consists of 18 members representing the Ministry of Health and boards of managers and 30 staff representatives, drawn from the following organizations:

Association of Hospital Welfare Administrators	1
Association of Officers of Executive Councils	2
Confederation of Health Service Employees	4
Institute of Hospital Administrators	4
NALGO	12
National Union of General and Municipal Workers	1
NUPE	4
Society of Clerks to Executive Councils	1
Transport and General Workers' Union	1
	30

Education

The Education Act of 1944 requires County Councils to provide both primary and secondary education and makes provision for the regulation of teachers' pay by the Burnham Committees.[54] This it does in a peculiar (should one say peculiarly English?) way. The Minister of Education does not *appoint* the Burnham Committees, but must *secure* that they exist. The members must be appointed by bodies representing local education authorities (i.e., the County Councils) and the teachers, but the Minister must *approve* of the committees. The committees may submit salary scales to the Minister whenever they think fit (or when he asks them to) and he may, if he approves of the scales, require the education authorities to pay them, the Central Government meeting most of the bill.

In England and Wales, teachers' representatives are appointed by the National Union of Teachers (in which is incorporated the Association of Teachers in Technical Institutions) and four small and more specialized associations.

In Scotland, the same function is performed by The National

[53] The system is described in H. A. Clegg and T. E. Chester, *Wage Policy and and Health Service* (Oxford: Blackwell, 1957).

[54] Three were established in 1919, but there are now two—one for elementary and secondary schools, the other for technical colleges.

Joint Council to deal with Salaries of Teachers in Scotland, where the staff side is delegated by the Educational Institute of Scotland.

Nationalized Industries

The legislation imposes on boards of management similar duties with regard to staff relations as exist in the public service. The board of each industry must "enter into consultation with the workers' organisations as to the establishment and maintenance of joint machinery for the settlement of terms and conditions of employment, and for joint consultation on matters of common interest."

The staffs in all these industries are highly organized and support elaborate structures for negotiation and consultation.[55] NALGO and NUPE are active amongst them, but the largest indigenous white-collar union is the Transport Salaried Staffs' Association with its membership of 87,000. However, British Railways (like most other railways) have been having a thin time of it for many years and the size of its staff is on the decline, taking the TSSA membership with it. Thus the Association has never reachieved its high point of 91,514 members in 1952. It is unusually well off for a white-collar union, with an income of over £300,000 a year and a reserve fund of nearly £1½ million.

TSSA has a long tradition of support for the Labour Party, supports five Members of Parliament, and has a political fund to which nearly 90 per cent of its members contribute.[56] It was one of the few white-collar unions who "came out" in the General Strike of 1926. It is, of course, affiliated to the TUC.

The Private Sector

There are a number of Joint Industrial Councils in operation in the distributive trade, covering, *inter alia,* Wholesale Groceries and Provisions, the Retail Meat Trade, the Retail Multiple Grocery and Provision Trade and, of course, the Co-operative Societies. The Union of Shop, Distributive, and Allied Workers has succeeded in negotiating agreements with most of the big chain stores,[57] but for the other employees in the trade, all it is able to offer are the Wages

[55] See the Ministry of Labour's *Handbook of Industrial Relations* (London: H.M.S.O., 1961), chap. IV.
[56] Those who do not wish to contribute to the fund must "contract out," i.e. notify the union in writing that they do not wish to contribute to the fund.
[57] Multiple grocers, meat traders, tailors, and shoe retailers.

Council agreements—legally enforceable minima which are, as a rule, below the market rates.[58]

The difficulties of organizing shop assistants are well known—either they are isolated in comparatively small shops, under the boss's eye, or using up a few years in a chain store between leaving school and getting married, or in more permanent employment in a department store with pay and conditions in advance of what the union has been able to get in other shops by years of hard bargaining. Thus, since 1948, while the number of shop assistants has increased by more than 30 per cent, USDAW's membership has increased by less than 5 per cent. Recruitment has been substantial, but has been almost balanced by losses.

USDAW is a staunch supporter of the TUC and the Labour Party, and its exceptionally able General Secretary, Sir Alan Birch, who died in 1961, had been one of the most enterprising trade-union leaders in seeking new ways of tackling the problems both of the trade unions and of the country.

Outside the public sector and the distributive trade, the only major collective bargains affecting white-collar workers are with the Engineering Employers' Federation. It has procedural, salary, overtime, and leave agreements with the Clerical and Administrative Workers' Union, the Clerical Section of the National Union of General and Municipal Workers, the National Association of Clerical and Supervisory Staffs (Transport and General Workers' Union), the Draftsmen's and Allied Technicians' Association, the Association of Supervisory Staffs, Executives and Technicians (ASSET), and the Association of Scientific Workers.

The agreements go out of their way to specify that there shall be no closed shop and generally show the limited rights that these unions have been able to exact from the employers.[59] The procedural agreement with ASSET, for instance, specifies that it shall apply only when ASSET has majority membership of a particular grade. Even then, the agreement states that every effort must be made to settle differences without reference to ASSET. Where failure to agree has been registered, members of ASSET may refer the matter to their association, and the employer to the local Engineering Employers'

[58] See *Industrial Relations Handbook, op. cit.,* chap. X.

[59] See *Handbook of National Agreements* (Engineering Employers' National Federation, 1961), sec. 5.

Association, and the two associations try to settle the matter; if settlement cannot be reached by the district officers, it is referred to the respective executive authorities for further negotiation.

The white-collar unions have some agreements with individual firms, but in general they have been able to make little impact on the private sector of the economy and staff matters are still dealt with on an individual basis or by salary scales and procedures and lines of promotion determined by the employer unilaterally.

The National Union of Bank Employees is in a peculiarly frustrating position in this respect. Only two of the big banks recognize it, and then as representing only a part of their staff, while another section are members of the staff association attached to the bank concerned. There are no less than twelve of these staff associations. The General Secretary of NUBE in his annual report for 1960 quotes two cases where the Union, having obtained majority membership, approached the management for recognition. Various delays occurred, during which time the staff association in each case conducted a campaign for membership, as a result of which the bank concerned was able to report that membership of the staff association exceeded that of NUBE. The Union took the unusual step of complaining to the ILO that the attitude of the managements constituted "acts of interference" in breach of Clause 2, Article 2 of Convention 98.

However, the ILO mission that visited the United Kingdom in 1960, though mentioning complaints from NUBE and the insurance unions, remained noncommittal. "It was suggested to the Mission that the situation of the employees in banks and insurance companies indicated that their freedom of association is limited. On the other hand it was stated that these staffs are completely free to join any association or union if they wish. Be this as it may, it was frequently pointed out to the Mission—and not only by persons directly concerned—that the situation in banking and insurance was exceptional." What it was exceptional to, the Mission did not state.[60]

The dilemma of the bank clerk has been well put in a prize-winning essay in, surprisingly, the Barclays' Bank Staff Association magazine.[61] The problem in Barclays is particularly clear, because NUBE has twelve thousand members in the Bank, the Staff Association ten thousand, and both are recognized by the management,

[60] *The Trade Union Situation in the United Kingdom, Report of a Mission from the International Labour Office* (Geneva: I.L.O., 1961), pp. 24-25.
[61] *Essay* (Winter 1961), pp. 374-76.

though neither was consulted before the pay increases of 1961.[62] "Let us consider the blatant fact," Mr. B. H. Cummins writes,

> that after 40 years of struggle at times verging on fratricide, the Staffs of Banks are roughly divided between the two forms of representation, and due to the diversity of human nature and the economic, social and other influences at work it should be obvious that there will always be those staff who will be drawn to the ranks of N.U.B.E.—just as others will give support to the Staff Associations. The fact that Staff Associations draw subsidies from the Banks and are managed by employees of the Banks will always present insurmountable barriers to a vast number. On the other hand, N.U.B.E. has its obstacles as well. Its affiliation to the T.U.C. and that body's close affinity to the Labour Party as well as the irresponsible behavior of many so-called trade unionists will frighten away many from its ranks.

Since their aims are the same, the writer suggests that the chance of achieving them would be greatly strengthened if joint representations were made by a staff committee consisting of equal numbers of officials and members from each organization. Similar arrangements might be made in other banks from which national machinery might emerge.

Following on NUBE's complaint to the ILO, Lord Cameron, with three assessors, was appointed to hear evidence and report on the matters in dispute. He found that the banks were not in breach of the relevant ILO convention, but commented favorably on the extent of NUBE membership: "even with the disadvantages which NUBE has in comparison with the recognized Staff Associations, membership of it is attractive to many who are both independent minded and responsible in character and position on the staffs of the Banks." The banks concerned have declined to accept his recommendation that they agree to accept oral as well as written representations from the Union, but joint action by the Union and the Central Council of Bank Staff Associations seems to have been brought a little nearer.

There are a number of staff associations attached to insurance companies too, but the largest organization of employees is a federation of nine of these associations which is itself affiliated to the TUC. Negotiations are in progress for the Federation to combine with the National Amalgamated Union of Life Assurance Workers (which has 2,500 members) under the title of the National Union of Insurance Workers.

The Guild of Insurance Officials is organized on the same pattern

[62] "It is apparent from the circular that the recent scale increases were 'made known' to both staff bodies, after neither discussion nor negotiation." *Essay* (Summer 1961), p. 335.

as NUBE. Their representative at the last Trades Union Congress made a similar complaint—that though his union was growing rapidly, "Whenever we appear on the scene in any large insurance office, up comes a house union." [63]

TRIALS OF STRENGTH

The Civil Servants

In the House of Commons on July 25, 1961, the Chancellor of the Exchequer, Mr. Selwyn Lloyd, reviewed the economic situation. Salaries and wages had risen by 8 per cent between 1959-60 and 1960-61, other personal income by 6½ per cent. The real national product, in the same period, had risen by only 3 per cent. "In my view there must be a pause until productivity has caught up and there is room for further advances. . . . In those areas for which the Government have first responsibility we shall act in accordance with this policy, and the government ask that the same lines should be followed elsewhere. . . ."

The nine months following this statement, and the government policy that characterized them, became known as the pay pause. But whereas, in 1948, Sir Stafford Cripps, Labour Chancellor, had marshalled the trade unions in support of his wage freeze, the unions now were actively hostile to government policy. The problem was to overcome balance of payments difficulties: the government solution to hold down wages and other costs relative to foreign competitors even though this meant holding down production, the trade-union solution to raise productivity by increasing production and investment.

As always in these circumstances, it is those in the public sector who get the full impact of government economy; while national settlements in privately owned industry might be slowed down and moderated, at plant level competition for labor would go its own sweet way and earnings rise accordingly.

But it was no use for the Treasury to refuse to grant increases to civil servants if the Civil Service Arbitration Tribunal could reverse their decision, so the next step was an announcement by the Chancellor that the date of operation of awards would no longer be subject to arbitration. Not only would the Tribunal not be entitled to make retroactive awards, as it often does, but the implementation of any award that the government considered to be excessive would be postponed until some future date.

[63] *Trades Union Congress Report* (1961), p. 321.

The Civil Service Alliance had already had a major clash with the Treasury. In May 1957, they had submitted a claim for the Clerical Classes. But the Treasury had insisted on a full Pay Research Unit investigation, which was presented in April 1958. By October the Treasury was still unable to make an offer. *Red Tape* commented: "the delaying tactics of the administration seem to be designed to arouse the maximum distrust and suspicion." [64]

The answer was presented to the executive committee of the CSCA on November 26—modest increases along the scale, nothing at the top. The executives felt an unwonted urge to action.

> . . . the normally sober and sedate members . . . suddenly found themselves, rather to their surprise, pouring out into the street and forming up in ragged column in Upper Belgrave Street. Some of them carried hastily improvised placards. They bore slogans demanding "Justice"; "A Square Deal" and other such unattainable ideals. Their goal was the House of Commons and their object, to hand their written protest to the Chancellor. Then, led by ex-Sergeant Major, now President, Lillywhite, the protest march began. They shambled briskly past the raised eyebrows of Belgravia, down to the frankly astonished proletariat of Victoria. . . . That night the picture was "on the telly." Next day the story was in the national and provincial newspapers. The British public became aware that Civil Service clerks were aggrieved—very aggrieved indeed. "They must have felt very strongly to do that sort of thing." [65]

Seven thousand members of the Alliance, meeting a few weeks later, recorded "its bitter protest" and pledged support to the Alliance in its decision—to go to arbitration. This somewhat tame decision normally ends a resolution expressing the thundering indignation of civil servants. And as often as not, one must hasten to explain, it pays off. The Tribunal makes a handsome award and the Treasury breathes a sigh of relief that the matter has been satisfactorily settled without loss of its reputation for parsimony. In this case, the Tribunal more than doubled what the Treasury had offered and handed down an award worth £7½ million a year, compared with the Treasury offer of £3 million.

And at the 1959 Conference of the CSCA a motion calling upon the NEC to prepare a strike policy was heavily defeated.

But the pay pause, with its tampering with the inviolate right to arbitration, was a much more direct challenge to the unions. On August 14, 1961, the affiliates of the Civil Service National Whitley Council decided to launch a national protest campaign. White-collar

[64] *Red Tape,* December 1958, p. 77.
[65] *Ibid.,* January 1959, p. 99.

unions outside the Civil Service also sprang to action. But the government was unyielding: only part of an award was implemented for the Post Office Engineers, and a claim by the Union of Post Office Workers was flatly rejected. Mr. Ron Smith, UPW General Secretary, announced, "It gives me no joy to announce that the Union will resort to industrial action. It is the sheer stupidity of the Chancellor and his economic policies which make it necessary. He and his Government are responsible for the damage which will be done to the negotiating machinery I have spent 30 years of my life building up."[66]

The CSCA also prepared for action. "Civil Service unions have no tradition of militancy. Their loyalty to the public is reflected in their union's renunciation of the strike weapon. This leaves them helpless in dealing with a Government which has no scruples about dishonoring agreements or wrecking well-tried joint consultative machinery. . . . The National Executive Committee . . . has now recognised this hard reality. They are putting definite proposals to the membership for direct action in the offices throughout the country."[67]

The UPW, CSCA, and P.O. Engineering Union all decided on a work-to-rule campaign to begin early in 1962. The UPW was the first off the mark. The postal service, from being the finest in the world, became utterly unreliable. Sorters were called upon to work long hours of overtime to clear the accumulation of mail. The Postmaster-General complained that a letter addressed to "The Postmaster-General, London," had been returned to sender marked, "Insufficiently addressed—state name of firm." Generally, the Post Office workers were having fun.

On January 11, all inland parcel mail to and from London was suspended. On the same day, the UPW wrote to the Postmaster-General (the letter was sent by hand) suggesting that negotiations on their pay claim be resumed. In reply, the PMG repeated his conditions.

The CSCA had fixed January 17 for the commencement of their work-to-rule, but on the previous day the campaign was abruptly canceled. On February 1, the UPW work-to-rule was brought to an end. *Red Tape* explained the CSCA decision thus:

On the day before the C.S.C.A. was due to start "work to rule" leaders of the Civil Service unions met the Government spokesman, Mr. Henry Brooke. As a result the General Secretary announced to a mass rally of members in London that the Government had conceded the main principle for which

[66] *The Post,* December 16, 1961, p. 652.
[67] *Red Tape,* December 1961, editorial.

we fought—the independence of the Arbitration Tribunal; that from the end of the pay pause full independence would be restored. But—and it was a big "but"—there would be no question of retrospection on any claim made during the period of the pause. . . . And now the great debate goes on throughout the Association. Was this a victory?

Insofar as the principle of unfettered arbitration is concerned the answer is an emphatic "yes." The very existence of independent arbitration was in danger. . . . The undertaking to restore unfettered arbitration at the end of the pause is a triumph won by our members' determination to fight.[68]

Then why did the UPW prolong its action until February 1? The General Secretary wrote, "The Postmaster-General was informed on January 31 that his letter had been read against the background of his recent statements in the House, which included his expressed willingness to enter into free discussions with the Union and his reference to the fact that he could not negotiate while work-to-rule conditions continued." [69]

The pay pause ran its predetermined course to the end of March and was followed by the institution of a "Guiding Light" designed to lead pay negotiators not to exceed, in their agreements, the increase in the national product estimated to occur in the ensuing year. The government has attempted to keep the pay increases of civil servants down to this level and, where it has been too flagrantly exceeded in private industry has, as it were, attempted to pillory the parties by a public investigation of the agreement by the National Incomes Commission. But boycotted by the unions and regarded with suspicion by employers, the NIC has met with little success.

In April 1964, the Union of Post Office Workers elected to play a return match with the Post Office. The issue was a union demand for a far-reaching inquiry into the pay and conditions of postmen, with a view to bringing their earnings up to the level of earnings in manufacturing and industry. When the government rejected the demand for an inquiry, the union announced plans for a one-day strike, to be followed by a ban on overtime. It is remarkable after the collapse in 1962 that the union should have come up fighting again; what is still more remarkable is that this time the government's nerve broke first. One week before the day of the strike, the Chancellor, in consultation with the Postmaster-General, conceded the demand for a committee of inquiry, albeit with somewhat narrower terms of reference than the union wished.

[68] *Ibid.*, February 1962, p. 153.
[69] *The Post,* February 24, 1962, p. 149.

The Teachers

In July 1961, the Main Burnham Committee agreed on a rise in teachers' pay that would have cost £47 million a year. But when the agreement was submitted to the Minister, he declined to accept it unless the cost was reduced to £42 million and the increases redistributed so that the basic scale got relatively less and the graduate allowance was increased relatively more. The teachers' and local authority panels united in rejecting this as a piece of ministerial interference, to which the Minister riposted that he would then put legislation before Parliament to enforce his proposals from January 1, 1962.

No sooner had the schools opened after the summer holidays than the National Association of Schoolmasters called a one-day strike, for which they claimed 100 per cent response from their members.[70]

The National Union of Teachers consulted its members on various proposals: a national one-day strike on October 23, combined with a mass lobbying of Parliament; an extended strike in selected areas, financed by a levy on other areas; or a refusal of their salaries by teachers in selected areas, schools being kept open; a withdrawal of teachers from the supervision of the school midday meal.

At a special delegate conference it was announced that 43 per cent of the teachers in the selected areas supported strike action and 37 per cent of the general membership was prepared to pay the strike levy.

While the debate still raged, the Minister of Education notified the Burnham Committee of his intention of overriding their decision by introducing a bill on October 31. The only way of avoiding this would be for the Committee to accept the reduction. The National Executive Committee of NUT went into agonized session and, by a majority of one, approved acceptance, calling off even the one-day strike.

Violent criticisms came from many branches and strikes closed schools in various parts of the country. The North London Teachers' Association (a branch of NUT) took over the plan for a mass lobbying of M.P.'s and combined it with a protest march that called at Union headquarters on the way, a thousand strong. Fifteen hundred teachers gathered at Parliament to interview M.P's. The Teachers' Colleges Salary Campaign Committee, reported to have thirty thousand trainee teacher members, telegraphed the Union describing the

[70] The NAS has not been represented on the Burnham Committees, but has now been promised admission. It has only a tenth of the NUT membership, but claimed a thousand recruits of dissident NUT members as a result of its strike.

settlement as "despicable and cowardly." Mass meetings in various towns called for an emergency conference and the resignation of the NEC.[71]

But Sir Ronald Gould, the General Secretary, claimed that the teachers had lost nothing and gained something by the agreement. It avoided the legislation that would have imposed crippling handicaps on salary negotiations. A commitment had been made that fresh negotiations would begin in June 1962, with a new settlement to be implemented in April 1963.

Clerks, Bank Managers, Actors

The government proved unyielding before the numerically powerful Civil Service and Teachers' unions. By contrast, the Clerical and Administrative Workers' Union and the National Union of Bank Employees have gained some immediate benefit from direct action in the last few years. In 1960, clerks in the Birmingham office of the Automobile Association walked out in the course of a dispute after the A.A. had refused recognition for the Union. Union officials advised them to return pending a fresh attempt at negotiation, but when they did they were dismissed. The strike (which now was really a lockout) was declared official.

The strike excited a great deal of public interest, for although only 34 were on strike, the A.A. responded with declarations more reminiscent of the nineteenth century than of the twentieth. "The committee did not feel that it would be possible to reinstate the dismissed staff, but it was decided to consider the principles on which a limited form of recognition might be granted to the union with a view to further discussions with it." [72] A few days later, the formation of a staff association was announced.

But by this time, the TUC had brought its influence to bear and other unions began considering possible means of assistance. When the dispute had run for six weeks, a settlement was reached: the clerks would be reinstated without loss of status or seniority. Though the Union agreed not to claim national salary scales until it was agreed that their membership in the Association justified it, any staff member was free to join and Union officials would have access to the management.[73]

[71] *The Times,* October 20, 1961.
[72] *The Times,* September 2, 1960.
[73] *Seventieth Annual Report of the CSCA,* pp. 15-16.

In November 1960, the National Union of Bank Employees found themselves in dispute with the Derby Trustee Savings Bank over the pay of 14 branch managers. Their maximum was £931 a year; many had been paid no more than this for fifteen years and had no prospects for promotion. In a ballot, the 62 members in the Derby Savings Bank resolved to support a ban on overtime during the forthcoming bank balance period if a satisfactory offer was not made. A protest march was held through Derby on the afternoon of November 12 and received a great deal of publicity, for it was an odd spectacle to see the managers marching at the head of their staffs.

After the Employers' Council had failed in its efforts to have the overtime ban called off, a settlement was reached. The top of the scale was raised to £1,250, with possible merit increases above this, and it was agreed by the management to give favorable consideration to payment for overtime.[74]

The British Actors' Equity Association had a much tougher struggle against the commercial television companies. The companies hotly contested their claim for fees. From November 1961 to April 1962, the actors boycotted the commercial companies, many enduring great hardship as a result. Help from the technicians' unions, that might have brought the dispute to a rapid crisis, was not forthcoming and public reaction to the loss of their favorite shows was much less than had been expected. The strike was won by dogged determination and unity—characteristics that the companies had not expected the actors to display.

CHARACTERISTICS OF WHITE-COLLAR UNIONS

While the white-collar unions have shown themselves capable of winning in small-scale trials of strength, they have been singularly unsuccessful on the big issues, especially in their challenges to the government. In such a tussle, one of the main strengths of the unions is missing: loss of profit to the employer. Where principle is mixed with profit, common sense will often prevail. Where it is all principle, the problem becomes much more intractable.

The postal unions put up an impressive demonstration, but at the end of the month it seemed clear that the government was prepared to sit the dispute out: the country would simply have to make the best of things, just as London had had to make the best of the bus

[74] NUBE General Secretary's Report for 1960; *The Times,* November 11 and November 12, 1960.

strike two years before. To break the deadlock, the UPW would have had to take some more drastic form of action. Instead, their campaign was called off. The teachers and Civil Service clerks, by contrast, never got their actions off the ground. Whether there would have been an adequate response, one cannot say, though it is certain that a substantial proportion of the membership would not have joined in and instead might have resigned.

The union leaders face a serious dilemma. They are generals of an army that shows up well on the parade ground but about whose willingness or ability to shoot there is much doubt. In his negotiations with the enemy, the general must rely on appeals to equity or bluff. This by itself would not present any special difficulty, for the leadership would then be taken by men with a flair for diplomacy rather than for action who would be well adapted to getting the best out of their limited resources. The bulk of the membership may be very well satisfied with this; the union plays a small part in their lives, they rarely if ever attend their branch meetings, they do not take the trouble to vote. They have joined because someone has asked them to do so, it seems the thing to do, they can get a reduction at some shops by showing their membership card, they might need the union sometime and, since it negotiates their pay, it seems only right to support it. An eruption of the union into the member's life with the demand that he disrupt his personal arrangements by going on strike would be most unwelcome.

The trouble for the peace-loving General Secretary comes from that indispensable little band of branch officials who have made a hobby of their union work. Other members get on with their gardening, home-building, television, or evening courses and leave the running of the union to the paid officials. But there are always some who regard the union as their own and who use their spare time for doing its work. They tend to identify themselves with the Labour Movement, to believe in the Brotherhood of Man, and to feel that they more truly represent the aspirations of the rank and file than the cautious bureaucrats at the head of affairs. In a sense, these zealots represent a much greater menace to the career trade unionist than do the employers. In time of crisis, they are likely to press him to take extreme measures and to criticize him in the most savage terms if he declines. To them, it is all-important to demonstrate their faith, their solidarity, and their anger. But a strike is a terribly expensive thing and can swallow up the union's reserves in a few weeks; if the strike is accompanied by mass resignations, it may take the organization many years to recover.

The campaign of the Civil Service Clerical Association was called off by the General Secretary; the Executive Committee subsequently decided not to follow the usual practice of offering him an extension of his office beyond retiring age. The campaign of the National Union of Teachers was called off by a narrow majority of their Executive Committee and brought forth a storm of protest from the branches. In this latter case, we can examine further evidence of who was right and who was wrong, for the decision has been followed by a ballot for membership of the Executive Committee. First, it must be noted that there was a 40 per cent poll—heavy for British unions, but nonetheless indicative of the fact that the majority of members do not care. Second, the militants did not defeat the moderates.[75]

But the attitude to direct action is not the only test by which the quality of a union may be judged. There are also the questions of affiliation to the Trades Union Congress and to the Labour Party. The attitude of the members of the bank staff associations is typical of that of many white-collar workers. They distrust organizations that are affiliated to the TUC, in part because of the close relationship of the TUC to the Labour Party. This led to the formation of a committee representative of eighteen white-collar unions that were nonaffiliates of the TUC, including NUT, NALGO, the Institution of Professional Civil Servants, the Association of University Teachers, and the Central Council of Bank Staff Associations, with a combined membership of seven hundred thousand. They were met by the Chancellor on September 29, 1961, and told him, "the unions we represent generally repudiated striking and pinned their faith on collective bargaining and arbitration. The government's actions, we said, were destroying that faith, had gravely damaged staff-employer relations, and had dealt a shattering blow at public service morale. But we got nowhere on these issues. . . . We have so far avoided strikes. We told the Chancellor that we may not be able to hold our members back much longer."[76]

The Committee hoped to be given representation on the National Economic Development Council, on which the TUC has a monopoly

[75] Although the names were published in *The Schoolmaster* of N.E.C. members who had voted in favor of accepting the government offer and those who had voted against, the election showed no swing in favor of either group. The sitting Treasurer, who had voted for compromise, was re-elected with 57,000 votes against his opponent (who had voted against), who got 38,000 votes.
[76] *Public Service,* October 1961, p. 1.

of the workers' side, but after considering their request for a month, Mr. Selwyn Lloyd, the Chancellor of the Exchequer, replied, "I have come to the conclusion that it would not be appropriate to set up any formal machinery of consultation with the group of organisations participating in the conference, or to appoint a representative of the conference as a member of the National Economic Development Council. . . . I can, of course, assure you that if individual organisations or the conference collectively wanted to make representations at any time on any particular subject, I should be very ready to consider them."

This trims the white-collar unions down to size as far as the government is concerned. It is the unions of manual workers whose support the government is after and whose opposition they fear. It seems that they do not regard the white-collar unions as a threat and can face their protest meetings and poster parades with equanimity.

And yet, politically, the Conservative Party is heavily dependent on the middle class, white-collar vote for its parliamentry majority. Before the rise of the Labour Party, Gilbert wrote of how surprising it was

> That every boy and every gal
> That's born into the world alive
> Is either a little Liberal
> Or else a little Conservative.

In modern times, of course, the division has been between Labour and Conservative, with a loyalty to party that took no regard of candidate or program. But in recent years, the Liberals have made a remarkable comeback, a fact correlated by many with the discriminatory application of the pay pause. When, in a by-election at Orpington the Liberal candidate won by a handsome majority, *The Times* diagnosed it as "the revolt of the white-collar workers." This was followed by the resurgence of support for the Labour Party, powerful enough to more than compensate for the trend to conservatism inherent in the increase in white-collar employment.

This gives evidence of the progress of a mass rethinking, a general loosening up of the conditioned reflexes. The elimination of manual work may after all not convert us into a nation of obedient bureaucrats. Fifty years ago, it was a mark of distinction to be a clerk and Bernard Shaw wrote: [77] "the clerks have tall hats and hymnbooks and keep up the social tone by refusing to associate on equal terms with anybody." Times have changed and a clerk is now a very ordinary

[77] *Major Barbara,* Act III, Scene 1.

thing to be. The same, in due course, will apply to scientists and technologists. Their lead in pay over manual workers has already been much reduced and who can doubt that, when everyone has a university education, the lead will narrow still further, until, in the words of Wicksteed, the utopian ideal would be approached "of a higher payment for the more monotonous services rendered to society by the manual worker, than for the more varied and pleasant ones rendered by the exercise of the artistic and intellectual powers." [78]

However gradual the transition, it is likely to be painful for the white-collar workers and to drive them to unionize in self-defense as one can see them doing today in offices, banks, schools, and hospitals. Is it too sanguine to hope that the broad humanitarianism of British trade unionism will be continued, that as personal ambition is tempered with a consciousness of occupational solidarity something more admirable will result? Being of a cautious disposition, I shall not essay a reply.

[78] *The Common Sense of Political Economy* (first published 1910) (London: Routledge, 1935), p. 335.

VI

UNIONIZATION OF WHITE-COLLAR EMPLOYEES IN JAPAN

BY SOLOMON B. LEVINE*

White-collar unionization has been a key and integral aspect of the postwar Japanese labor movement. Today, not only do nonmanual workers comprise a significant proportion of the nearly ten million trade unionists in Japan, but also, without the white-collar element, the structure, functions, leadership, and ideology of organized labor in that country would be fundamentally altered. Perhaps in no other major industrialized nation has so intimate a relationship been achieved between the blue- and white-collar components of a trade-union movement.

The present chapter explains why the postwar labor movement in Japan has developed a major dependence upon its white-collar adherents for achieving the political and economic impact that organized labor thus far has made. Further, it probes the paradox of why a traditionally high-status group throughout the course of Japanese industrial development assumed strategic importance in a protest

* The author is indebted to Mr. Yoshitaka Fujita for his assistance in preparing this chapter. Thanks are also due to Dr. Bernard Karsh, Dr. Masumi Tsuda, and Dr. Ezra F. Vogel for their careful reading of the manuscript and critical comment, although the author alone assumes sole responsibility for the final product.

movement aimed at reforming a "traditional" society. Finally, it touches upon a number of problems that the white-blue collar alliance, viable as it seems for the time being, has created for Japanese trade unionism.

To approach these questions, the study first sketches the course of Japanese industrialization with particular reference to the emergence of a white-collar labor force and its status in the industrializing process. Next, it traces the history of white-collar unionization since its bare beginnings at the end of World War I. Much of this account centers on the four or five years immediately following Japan's surrender to the Allied Powers in 1945, for in that period the present extent and structure of Japanese trade unions were essentially established. The analysis then turns to the role of white-collar members in trade-union activity, particularly in providing leadership at the local and enterprise level and within government worker organizations. Finally, the chapter assesses the relationship of white-collar unionization to the general labor movement, especially in view of the rapid economic, technological, political, and social changes besetting Japan at present.

STRUCTURING OF THE WORKFORCE IN JAPAN'S INDUSTRIALIZATION [1]

The industrialization of Japan has been proceeding for almost a century. By World War I, Japan had become a predominantly industrial nation. Today, Japan ranks as the fourth or fifth most industrialized nation of the world. In the wake of this transformation, an entirely new labor force was created, but its structure aimed primarily at warding off threats (real or imagined) of Western invasion and colonialism and at assuring Japan's nationalistic destiny as the "land of the gods." Japan's rapid march into industrialism, beginning soon after the Meiji Restoration in 1868, was thus relatively specific in purpose, requiring a workforce deeply inculcated with a sense of diligence and devotion to the work demanded by an oligarchic leadership. A

[1] For the most thorough accounts in English on Japan's industrialization, see William W. Lockwood, *The Economic Development of Japan, Growth and Structural Change, 1863-1938* (Princeton: Princeton University Press, 1954); G. C. Allen, *A Short Economic History of Japan, 1867-1937* (London: Allen and Unwin, 1946); William W. Lockwood, ed., *The State and Economic Enterprise in Japan* (Princeton: Princeton University Press, 1965); and Thomas C. Smith, *Political Changes and Industrial Development in Japan; Government Enterprise, 1868-1880* (Stanford: Stanford University Press, 1955).

set of newly structured institutions—a centralized, bureaucratic state, a powerful military establishment, a few giant centers for capital accumulation, and a universal education system—were all launched to serve these aims. Despite the devastating military defeat of World War II and the demanding reforms of the Allied Occupation, these institutions left a lasting impress on the nature of Japanese industrialization and, in turn, on the Japanese industrial relations system.

The approach of the Meiji elite to the problem of industrializing was to superimpose modern industry without disturbing the existing agrarian society. This called for developing an industrial force which, only to a small degree and but gradually, would separate itself from its agricultural roots. The agrarian sector was not displaced, but, in fact, until recently expanded and intensified to support the burgeoning population of the industrial and commercial centers. Throughout the process, the industrial workers continued to draw their major behavioral cues from, and tenaciously clung to, the value systems of their farming cousins. For the most exacting tasks of industrial work, this relationship served to underpin needed industrial discipline. To achieve industrialization, Japan's leaders fully exploited the long-established values spawned by the land tenure system, landlord-tenant relations, village hamlet solidarity, family centrism, fealty to local lords, and so forth—all fortified by precepts of Buddhism, Confucianism, and Shintoism and capped by Emperor deification.

Despite a near doubling of the Japanese population from thirty-five to sixty million in the fifty years up to 1920, a distinct urbanized industrial wage earner class was slow to develop.[2] Only a comparatively small proportion of the labor force became permanently committed to industrial work in the earlier phases. A large segment of the workers moved back and forth between factory and farm. Given the relatively low wages of the time and the undesirable conditions of industrial work, for two or three generations the Japanese labor force to a considerable degree remained "half-proletariat, half-peasant." For decades after industrialization began, young females composed a major part of the industrial workforce—recruited to work only a few short years at unskilled tasks in the textile mills and other light industries that long characterized Japan's early industrializing effort.

[2] This theme is especially developed in Okochi Kazuo, "Rōdō" in *Gendai Nihon Shōshi*, Yanaihara Tadao, ed., II (Tokyo: Misuzu Shobo, 1953), 111-215, translated into English as *Labor in Modern Japan* (The Science Council of Japan, Division of Economic, Commerce, and Business Administration, Economic Series No. 18, Tokyo, 1958). In this chapter citations of authors of works in Japanese follow the Japanese style of name order.

The economic structure accompanying Japan's industrial development also contributed to the lack of a highly differentiated nonfarm workforce. Scarcity of capital and raw material supplies for industrial production required tightly dovetailed management of basic industries. As a result, a relatively few clusters of giant industrial complexes—vertically and horizontally integrated, each under the control of a *zaibatsu* family or a governmental agency—became the centers of this managing process. Alongside these relatively few huge enterprises grew a plethora of tiny shops and factories, backward in technology, relying mainly upon oversupplies of labor, centered in family units, and maintaining close ties to agrarian origins. Although these small firms were extremely important for Japanese economic growth,[3] they failed to provide an industrial milieu for a sharply distinctive nonagricultural wage earner class. Even today, a majority of the nonfarm workers remain attached to such petty enterprises. Thus, what industrial worker class came into being was concentrated mainly in the few large-scale enterprises. Even there, since turnover was rapid and there were constant labor market pressures on the supply side from the farm communities and the huge mass of small firms, its permanence was generally limited.[4] Only by the 1930's, after Japan's thrust into Manchuria and rapid shift to heavier industry, did the character of the industrial labor force begin to change toward a predominantly distinctive, permanent wage earner group. Indeed, with the onset of World War II, it became apparent in mounting labor shortages, especially of skilled workers, that earlier Japanese industrialization had succeeded in creating a fully committed industrial workforce on a limited scale.[5]

As might be expected, the dual economic structure that had emerged—with its agricultural base of six million farms intact and with as many as three to four million small enterprises coexisting alongside fewer than two thousand major firms—engendered considerable degrees of unemployment and underemployment. Even by the 1920's, when Japan had entered the full swing of industrialization, a majority of the workers performing industrial jobs were still only part-time—a condition continually worsened by population growth

[3] See Lockwood, *The Economic Development of Japan, op. cit.*, p. 578.
[4] See Koji Taira, "The Characteristics of Japanese Labor Markets," *Economic Development and Cultural Change*, Vol. X, No. 2, part I, January 1962, pp. 150-68.
[5] Jerome B. Cohen, *Japan's Economy in War and Reconstruction* (Minneapolis: University of Minnesota Press, 1949), especially chap. 5.

and the vicissitudes of business cycles that incessantly gripped Japan. One result of this use of the labor force was a startling proliferation of tertiary industry. Unable to secure full-time employment in factories and underemployed on the farms, large numbers of workers turned to performing personal services that required little or no capital. Tertiary industry soon outstripped secondary in the proportion of employment, most of which was in the form of self-employment and unpaid family work outside of agriculture and other primary industry. Today, the vestiges strongly remain. One-third of Japan's labor force of more than forty-five million is attached to the service industries. As many as one-half or more of the thirty million nonfarm workers are employed in enterprises with fewer than fifty employees, a majority of which have less than five workers.[6] One-fifth of the labor force is self-employed and about one-fourth is composed of unpaid family workers. More than one-third are females.

Until relatively recently, then, permanent wage employment was confined to a minor sector of the Japanese labor force—despite the rapid industrial development of that nation. However, those who did become permanent wage earners were the labor elite. By the 1920's it had become apparent that the industrial workers of major enterprises were dividing into two distinct cadres: those with permanent status and those with temporary status in an enterprise. Any enterprise of significant size (usually defined as more than five hundred workers) and durability built up a core of permanent regular workers who were induced to remain in the enterprise with guarantees of lifetime employment, higher wages (periodically increased), better working conditions (underpinned by some protective labor legislation), improved welfare benefits, paternalistic treatment, and so forth. Around this core were concentric layers of temporary workers, some indefinitely attached to the given plant, but most moving back and forth from field to factory or within a particular labor market. Perhaps only one-fourth or one-fifth of the total nonfarm labor force actually achieved permanent status.[7] For this labor elite, especially the permanent white-collar employees, social and cultural traditions were brought into full play to emphasize the mutual obligations of loyalty and protection between the employer and employee.[8] No doubt this structuring

[6] *Year Book of Labor Statistics, 1960* (Tokyo: Ministry of Labor, 1961); and *Rōdō Hakusho 1960* and *1961* (Tokyo: Ministry of Labor, 1961 and 1962).
[7] Taira, *op. cit.*, p. 167.
[8] For a full description in English of these relationships, see James C. Abegglen, *The Japanese Factory, Aspects of Its Social Organization* (Glencoe: The Free Press, 1958).

of the labor force had much to do with the failure of a substantial labor movement to make headway in the pre–World War II era.

ORIGINS AND HERITAGE OF THE WHITE-COLLAR GROUP

Against this brief sketch of labor force development in Japanese industrialization, the nature of the white-collar employee in Japan may be seen more clearly. Perhaps more than any other group, from the beginning the nonmanual worker became part of the permanent employee elite that was in the distinct minority. White-collar employment meant unusually high security in industry, where the common experience was instability and temporary attachment.

Along with this element of security was the high social status accorded the white-collar workers. From the outset of the march into industrialization, intellectual work was identified with a deep-felt responsibility for achieving national economic strength. Managers, technicians, clerks, teachers, engineers, and so forth, few in number at the beginning, were rapidly inculcated with the idea that in their hands and minds lay much of the task of planning and supervising the needed economic modernization. That the new Meiji government took the lead in training these employees and that there was a close association between government and basic private industry throughout Japanese industrialization certainly enhanced the status position of the white-collar workers. In a sense, the white-collar worker in private enterprise was a semi–civil servant and acquired the attitudes of the civil servants themselves. "Revere the official, despise the common people" (*"kanson mimpi"*) was a slogan that rubbed off on white-collar employees in and out of government.

The identification between the nonmanual worker and his enterprise was intense. In addition to receiving permanent status, he usually benefited from special welfare privileges. Once he entered a given firm, he rarely moved to another. Indeed, alternate employers would look with suspicion on mobile white-collar workers; they were considered disloyal employees who either could not be trusted or had been dismissed for incompetence.

Two labor market results flowed from these phenomena. First, competition for white-collar employees took place largely at the point of entry to the labor force. Since higher level training and education was, as a rule, necessary for white-collar employment, the educational system became a focal point for recruitment. This system in itself sharply differentiated the white-collar employee from the manual workers, many of whom in contrast came to an enterprise anonymously through the device of labor contractors. The increasingly narrow channels up through the educational system became closely associated with selected sources of white-collar employment (as for example the tight connection between the Tokyo Imperial University and the higher civil service).

Second, once having cleared the various educational hurdles, among which were a demonstration of unfaltering loyalty to one's group and unquestioning acceptance of the authority of one's superiors, the white-collar employee got wholly caught up in his enterprise, becoming a specialist within his own firm with little possibility of transferring his services to another enterprise. Usually leeway existed only within a given *zaibatsu* complex to transfer talents if necessary. Thus, while open markets existed for unskilled and skilled manual workers in the early stages of Japanese industrial development, in contrast there was relatively little evolution of distinct white-collar labor markets except for professionals such as medical doctors, writers, and artists. Even many of these became permanently wedded to enterprises. If there were distinctions among white-collar workers, it was less in terms of occupational skills and more in terms of enterprise identification. Early in Japanese industrial development, the white-collar worker was known as a *company man* (*shain*) or *staff employee* (*shokuin*). This title meant high social status and sharply demarcated his position from that of the manual worker (*kōin*) even when the latter had attained permanent employment status.

Origins of the white-collar employee group early fortified its high social status. To staff the new institutions established by the Meiji leaders—the new government bureaucracy, the modern military apparatus, the expanding *zaibatsu* complexes, the universal education system, etc.—several existing high status sources were initially drawn upon. First, the dispossessed lower samurai—long accustomed to elite social and political positions and by tradition identified with feudal fief administration (and disdainful of manual work)—were offered most of the managerial and administrative posts in the new bureaucracy (although some did take up farming, intellectual pursuits, and other occupations, and the least successful were soon lost among the laboring masses).[9] Perhaps nowhere in the history of industrialization was there so readily available an elite cadre as devoted to the idea of selfless service to organizations—steeped as it was in the military ethics of *bushidō*. When the early state-owned industrial

[9] See Tsuchiya Takao, *Nihon Shihonshugi No Keieishiteki Kenkyū* (Tokyo: Misuzu Shobo, 1954).

enterprises were transferred to private entrepreneurs, many of this group went with them. By that time (1880's), the commercial world had become legitimate enough for the former warrior class to embrace in larger numbers.

Second, the earlier Tokugawa period had produced a highly skilled and specialized merchant class in the great towns of that era. Although rated lowest on the traditional social scale (beneath the samurai, farmers, and artisans, in that order), the merchants had succeeded in legitimizing their functions by faithfully serving the interests of the ruling *daimyō* and avoiding any challenge to established value systems and feudal institutions.[10] With the turn to nationalism and industrialization, especially out of recognition of Japan's critical dependence upon foreign trade, the merchants were readily available to carry out the myriad of administrative and clerical tasks required in the handling of financial transactions, industrial operations, and commercial manipulation. The merchant houses, built as they were on stern Confucianist principles, supplied and recruited a steady stream of *company men*, steeped in loyalty to enterprise and nation, diligent in work habits, skilled in the art of management. Especially in alliance with the former samurai, the merchants almost overnight were vaulted into the highest positions of prestige that reflected upon their hired white-collar functionaries. They became administrative nuclei of the *zaibatsu* complexes, whose managers (*bantō*) and lesser white-collar staff (*shokuin*), although employed from outside the immediate circle of the controlling families, were fully identified with the owners.

Third, there had grown up in Japan during the Tokugawa era a class of well-to-do landlord-farmers, who had been important both in introducing considerable technological change in agriculture and also in successfully managing a highly complicated system of land tenure.[11] Some of these farmers had been casting about for additional outlets for their funds and energies, and soon after the Meiji Restoration they began to join in with the new entrepreneurial movement for industrialization. Again, they represented a group that embraced much of the traditional value system and thus readily fitted into the pattern of the new Japanese state.

Fourth, as one of the first steps toward economic development, the Meiji leaders by the early 1870's launched a system of universal

[10] See Robert N. Bellah, *Tokugawa Religion: The Values of Pre-Industrial Japan* (Glencoe: The Free Press, 1957).

[11] See Thomas C. Smith, *The Agrarian Origins of Modern Japan* (Stanford: Stanford University Press, 1959), especially chap. 13.

primary education not only to assure that all citizens would be adequately prepared to cope with the needs of the new society but also to dragnet the population for talents that could be utilized for the new managerial, administrative, clerical, and technical functions. On top of the basic six-year elementary schooling by the early 1900's were erected tracks of middle and higher schools and special technical colleges and general universities, most operated by the state. In making one's way up the educational ladder, which narrowed at each rung, the aspirant was subjected to the severest examinations of loyalty and self-denial as well as mastery of his subject matter. However, successful ascendance meant almost certain assurance of entry into the civil service, the military leadership cadre, *zaibatsu* management, the professions, or school teaching for life.

The epitome of white-collar status was to be found among the government bureaucrats. Overriding concern with the aims of the state thrust this group into elevated positions of privilege.[12] Civil servants felt little responsibility for serving the populace as such; rather they represented the ruling oligarchy in the name of the Emperor and in this capacity permeated almost every nook and cranny of the society as a huge network of civil, military, and economic operations spread. From the beginning, an enormous status gulf separated these functionaries from the ordinary citizenry.

The highly visible status distinction between white-collar workers and manualists no doubt contributed to the striving of the Japanese to develop their economy. Few families indeed failed to aspire for at least one of its members to enter the intellectual employee class. Not only did it offer the advantage of avoiding back-breaking work and the attractions of lifetime job security, welfare benefits, steady advancement of income with length of service—all of which were highly sought after especially in view of the general economic instability and employment insecurity; but also it was identified with the primary aims of the developing society.

White-collar prestige reached its peak by the 1920's heightened by increasing industrialization. More and more was it urgent to rationalize the managerial system through fuller utilization of the white-collar functionaries. For example, by this time white-collar staffs in the modern enterprises began to take control of personnel functions away from labor bosses who had commonly been relied upon to re-

[12] Kiyoaki Tsuji, "The Cabinet, Administrative Organization, and the Bureaucracy," in "Japan Since Recovery of Independence," *The Annals*, CCCVIII (November 1956), 10-17.

cruit, supply, and discipline industrial workers. The need for expanding and committing a nonfarm labor force had become especially critical during the rapid industrialization of World War I. This development coupled with the increasing range of functions assumed by managements no doubt strengthened the exclusiveness of the white-collar groups and produced even greater social distance between them and manual workers.

Within a modern enterprise a sharp distinction was made between the white-collar and blue-collar employees. The *shokuin,* who as already mentioned had to follow selective educational routes to attain their positions, were very much a part of the management cadre. They did not rise from among the blue-collar workers nor would they be demoted to manualists. The latter were recruited from the lower educational levels and remained manualists. A worker's status was determined early in life. The highest a blue-collar worker could rise was the position of shop or gang boss (commonly termed *hanchō*) who had very few managerial functions and mainly transmitted orders prepared by the white-collar staff. The *shokuin* rarely came into direct contact with the manual workers although they carried out the planning and coordination of their work. Little resembling foremanship of the first-line-of-management concept emerged. In all likelihood, this was a gap that could be tolerated because the tendency of workers to accept authority unquestioningly made unnecessary a large amount of direct managerial supervision. On the other hand, planning and control required large office staffs.

Among the white-collar staff members in an enterprise there developed a highly stratified ranking system based on levels of educational attainment and length of service in the enterprise. New recruits, gathered in annually after graduation from higher-level schools, first became apprentice clerks (*kakariin*), with almost no responsibilities or authority except to carry out faithfully biddings of superiors. Competition to rise from these lower positions to higher ones was intense and to a considerable degree depended upon one's demonstration of complete devotion to influential superiors. With great patience, a *kakariin* in time would rise in rank. Following historical models of family and village social structure, Japanese industrial enterprises have been characterized by cliques and ingroups (*habatsu*). The new recruit had to become entrenched within such a clique—a task best accomplished by exhibiting unswerving loyalty to one's boss (*oyabun*) and mastering the detail of work assignments. This cliquishness bound the individual to his group and in turn to the enterprise. It was not unusual for the white-collar employee to remain within a given section or division for his career. Particularly in the civil service did this "departmentalism" flourish—an organizational characteristic, incidentally, that later the Allied Occupation scarcely touched.[13] Under these circumstances, the white-collar worker was narrowly confined not only to his enterprise but also to his smaller subgroup and paid little heed to the possibilities of relating to white-collar workers outside his own narrow circle.

Furthermore, cliquishness no doubt led to empire building within the typical Japanese large enterprise. Department and section chiefs added to their staffs to increase their group's influence within the organization. The practice of lifetime attachment, advancement by length of service, and the high degree of identification of the individual with his unit supported this tendency. Such a trend grew stronger as Japan shifted to heavier industry in preparation for military adventurism. Whereas in the 1920's white-collar staff workers hardly grew in numbers (measured in terms of standard occupational groups), as Japanese management consolidated its position within the enterprises throughout the 1930's the number of white-collar employees more than doubled while that of manual workers rose by only 50 per cent. During the 1920's, white-collar employees had accounted for only slightly more than 10 per cent, but by 1944 had reached one-fourth of the nonfarm labor force.[14] It was during these years that the urbanization of Japan leapt ahead, with the increasing expansion of the concentrated government bureaucracy in Tokyo and the establishment of sprawling *zaibatsu* headquarters and branches in the capital city, Osaka, and other major metropolitan areas.

On the other hand, the white-collar groups historically were not equivalent to the urbanized middle class of the industrialized Western nations. Rather they proliferated to meet the needs of a highly bureaucratized industrializing nation, guided and controlled by a relative small oligarchy of state officials, political chieftains, business leaders, the military, and landlords. Throughout the process, white-collar work was not a way to escape the traditionally confining Japanese social structure and to achieve individual mobility and independence in identification with a free private enterprise system. In contrast, it was a way of gaining status within the established structure.

Outside the *shokuin* group of the major enterprises, it was not

[13] *Ibid.*

[14] Fujibayashi Keizo, ed., *Nihon Rōdō Undō Shiryō*, X (Tokyo: Chuo Koron Jigyo Shuppan, 1959), 78-79.

easy to identify an emerging white-collar occupational class, except perhaps for the independent professionals and intellectuals. The great number of nonmanual workers employed in the plethora of small and medium enterprises, especially in the sprawling service trades, were by background, training, status, and outlook far more a part of the laboring masses, rooted in their agrarian origins, rather than a new urban middle class. In short, neither the intellectual workers in the major enterprises nor in the small and medium firms until rather recently came to embrace middle class status in Japanese society. As will be later developed, this failure had much to do with the role of white-collar workers in the labor movement since World War II.

GROWTH OF THE WHITE-COLLAR LABOR FORCE

Until recently, Japanese labor force statistics have lacked reliability and consistency, especially with respect to breakdowns by occupational groups. For these reasons, it is not possible to trace in any detail the rise and changes in the white-collar component of the Japanese labor force, however it may be measured. Enough statistical sources, nonetheless, are available to indicate the general trends since about 1920. Table 1, compiled from a variety of sources, indicates this development in terms of the manual and nonmanual components of the nonfarm labor force.

By 1920, 46 per cent of the 27.3 million civilian labor force of Japan were nonfarm workers. In the nonfarm worker category almost 12 per cent were clearly white-collar employees, this being the proportion of *shokuin* of that time. In all likelihood, the white-collar labor force was larger than this. One estimate places the proportion of *shokuin* in Tokyo just prior to World War I at 5.6 per cent of the total workforce, and by 1920 at 21.4 per cent.[15] The 1920 census also counted almost 3.6 million self-employed, which no doubt included professionals and perhaps other white-collar types. However, it is probably reasonable to estimate that these were mainly manual workers or service industry members of the labor force, operating for the most part on their own account without paid employees.

During the 1920's there was only a slight growth in the white-collar group, for reasons indicated earlier. By 1930 *shokuin* accounted, in fact, for a slightly lower percentage of nonfarm workers than in 1920—a mere 10.1 per cent. While blue-collar workers in that decade

[15] Noda Masaho, "Senzen Ni Okeru Sarari Man No Kumiai Undō" (1), *Ginkō Rōdō Kenkyū* (April 1961), p. 22.

grew from 7.5 million to 9.4 million, *shokuin* increased fewer than twenty-five thousand. By 1930 nonagricultural workers had grown to just about 50 per cent of the total civilian labor force. The self-employed totaled slightly under four million.

Table 1. Estimates of Japanese Population and Labor Force Composition for Selected Years, 1920-63 (in Thousands)

Year	*1920*	*1930*	*1940*	*1944*	*1955*	*1963*
Total population	55,963	64,450	71,380	73,064	89,070	96,156
Total civilian labor force	27,261	29,619	32,482	31,796	40,860	46,130
Agricultural, forestry, and fishing labor force	14,686	14,686	14,191	12,071	17,260	12,960
Nonagricultural labor force	12,575[a]	14,933[b]	18,291	19,725	23,600	33,170
Nonmanual workers	1,496	1,517	3,524	4,842	6,100	9,090
Manual workers	7,502	9,442	14,767	14,883	17,500	24,080

[a] Includes self-employed, totaling 3,577,000, unclassified as to manual and nonmanual workers.
[b] Includes self-employed, totaling 3,974,000, unclassified as to manual and nonmanual workers.
Sources: 1920, 1930, 1940, and 1944 from Fujibayashi Keizo, ed., *Nihon Rōdō Undō Shiryō*, X (Tokyo: Chuo Koron Shuppan Jigyosha, 1959), 78-79. 1955 and 1959 from Bureau of Statistics, Office of the Prime Minister, *Japan Statistical Year Book 1960*, pp. 44-45. 1963 from *Japan Statistical Year Book 1964*, pp. 48-49.

The 1930's showed a great spurt in white-collar employment with the preparations for war and the shift to heavy industry in Japan. The census for 1940—using breakdowns for managerial, clerical, engineering, professional, governmental, and other office workers (rather than merely *shokuin*)—registered more than 3.5 million white-collar employees out of a total nonfarm labor force of 18.3 million, or close to 20 per cent. This was more than double the number in 1930, although the figures are probably inflated due to the changes in classifying methods. In all likelihood, the white-collar workers in that decade advanced at a faster pace than the nonfarm manual workers, who grew about 56 per cent to almost 14.8 million. By this time, more than 56 per cent of the total civilian labor force of 32.5 million were nonfarm workers.

Since the 1930's the above-average growth of the white-collar worker group has continued. Notable expansion occurred during the war years. The census of 1944 reported more than 4.8 million white-collar workers (using the same categories as the 1940 census), or 24.5 per cent of the total nonfarm labor force of close to twenty million (out of a total civilian labor force of nearly thirty-two million). This 37 per cent increase in white-collar workers was accompanied by a growth of fewer than 125,000 manual nonfarm workers, reflecting the proliferation of the wartime bureaucracies (private as well as public), the growing complexities of a wartime economy, the drainage of manual worker manpower into the military services, and similar factors. While the nonagricultural workforce grew to 19.7 million out of the total civilian labor force of less than thirty-two million, farm labor suffered a sharp decline from 14.2 million to less than 12.1 million.

In the turbulent decade following Japan's surrender, the Japanese economy passed through three major phases. From 1945 to 1947, the economy was barely permitted under Occupation policy to recover. This was a period of Allied retribution during which the intention was to permit Japan merely to exist at a subsistence level. With the repatriation of five million overseas Japanese and a sudden rise in the birth rate, agricultural population burgeoned while industrial activity virtually stood still. Occupation policy began to shift, however, after 1947, and the next five years saw a concerted effort to rebuild Japanese industry in the attempt to secure Japan as a major ally in the Cold War and to provide a powerful industrial base for the Western Powers in the Pacific. This was the second phase. The third, which followed the outbreak of the Korean War and continues to the present, saw Japan reattain its prewar industrial strength and go on into a period of unprecedented economic growth.

By 1955 Japan's population had reached more than eighty-nine million, and the civilian labor force had grown to almost forty-one million with about 55 per cent of the total engaged in nonagricultural work. Among the latter, white-collar employees continued their steady above-average advance. From 1944 to 1955 blue-collar workers added 2.7 million or about 18 per cent, but white-collar employees grew almost 1.3 million, or more than 25 per cent. By this time new organizational and technological methods were being introduced into the rapidly expanding Japanese industry, bringing about a steady change in the blue- and white-collar mix of the nonfarm labor force.

The shift to white-collar work has continued during the past ten years, accompanying the remarkable growth of the Japanese economy and its continual development of new industries, especially in shipbuilding, electronics, chemicals, steel, automotive products, machinery, and so forth. For virtually the first time under peacetime conditions, the farm population began to fall. In a 1963 survey nonagricultural employees reached over 70 per cent of the total labor force. Again from 1955 to 1963, while blue-collar nonfarm workers grew about 38 per cent, white-collar workers advanced almost 50 per cent. White-collar employees in 1963 numbered 9.1 million, or about 27 per cent of the total nonfarm labor force. Thus, in Japan of the 1960's, almost one out of every five members of the labor force was a white-collar worker, and at least one out of every four nonfarm workers was in this category—a remarkable shift from the prewar composition of the Japanese labor force. There is every reason to believe that, as Japan further industrializes, utilizing the newer technologies and administrative methods, this change will continue at a rapid pace.[16]

In Table 2 the shift in the occupational composition of the Japanese labor force may be seen in greater detail for the years 1930 and 1955. Because of differing methods of classification, the figures for the white-collar groups are higher than in the previous table, but the trend is equally clear. In this breakdown, all the categories of nonmanual labor force members are included, totaling more than 2.2 million of the entire labor force or less than 7.5 per cent in 1930. These groups had nearly tripled in number by 1955 to more than 6.2 million, or almost 16 per cent of the total labor force. Almost all these nonmanual labor force groups increased considerably more than the increase of 34 per cent for the entire workforce or the increase of 22 per cent for the manualists during this twenty-five-year period. The most notable jump was made in the categories of engineers and office clerks, who increased from about eight hundred thousand to 3.3 million. In 1955 office clerical workers alone numbered over 2.9 million, almost half of all the nonmanual labor force members. In addition, during the same period, civil servants nearly tripled, while private industry managers, medical workers, and teachers almost doubled.

[16] The figures cited above are confined to the Census categories of professional and technical workers, managers and officials, and clerical and related workers. They therefore represent minimum estimates of the white-collar workforce which should be expanded by including a portion of the 5.4 million sales workers and 3.0 million service workers in Japan in 1963.

Table 2. Japanese Labor Force Composition by Nonmanual and Manual Worker Categories, 1930 and 1955 (in Thousands)

Year	*1930* *Number*	*1930* *Per Cent*	*1955* *Number*	*1955* *Per Cent*	*Per Cent Change 1930 to 1955*
Total Labor Force	29,614	100.0	39,642	100.0	+133.9
Nonmanual Workers	2,218	7.4	6,256	15.8	+282.0
Managerial	324	1.1	629	1.6	+194.1
Civil service	375	1.3	1,020	2.6	+272.2
Engineering and technical }	809	2.7	360	0.9	+407.5
Clerical }			2,937	7.4	
Medical	133	0.4	299	0.8	+224.8
Educational	327	1.1	731	1.8	+223.5
Artists	44	0.1	30	0.1	− 68.0
Other professional	206	0.7	250	0.6	+121.3
Manual Workers	27,396	92.6	33,386	84.2	+121.9
Individual proprietors (including farmers)	9,066	30.6	9,104	23.0	+100.4
Self-employed craftsmen	223	0.8	270	0.7	+121.0
Production workers (including farm laborers)	14,757	49.8	19,603	49.4	+132.8
Commercial family workers	632	2.1	1,015	2.6	+160.6
Commercial wage employees	824	2.8	1,408	3.6	+170.9
Service workers	1,603	5.5	1,679	4.2	+104.7
Policemen, firemen, and others	291	1.0	307	0.7	+105.4

Source: Fukutake Tadashi, *Nihonjin No Shakai Ishiki* (Tokyo: San-Ichi Shobo, 1960), p. 22.

As indicated earlier, these figures have probably understated the number of white-collar workers in Japan, due to classifying the self-employed and certain categories of workers in commercial establishments as manual workers. For these groups, it has not been possible to separate the nonmanual elements because of the nature of the enterprises and the combination of manual and nonmanual aspects of work. However, it should be noted that commercial employees have been the fastest growing category of manual workers in the labor force, increasing by at least 70 per cent from 824,000 in 1930 to more than 1.4 million in 1955. In 1957, it was estimated that 1.3 million of these workers were engaged in sales work, but probably large proportions of these, especially those who work in extremely small retail and wholesale firms, also perform manual labor. Still another group difficult to identify are the clerks engaged in the transportation and communications industries, who usually have been classified as production workers. The estimate for 1957 placed these at about 300,000. If still other borderline groups, such as 430,000 police, defense force personnel, and the like, are added, Japan in 1957 had between 7.5 and 8 million white-collar labor force members, or close to one-fifth of the entire labor force of Japan and nearly one-third of the nonfarm labor force.[17]

Since 1955 white-collar groups have shown continuing growth during the rapid, almost phenomenal, expansion of the Japanese economy of the past seven years (with GNP per capita increasing 8 per cent a year on the average). From 1955 to 1959, professional and technical employees grew almost 14 per cent from 1.66 to 1.77 million, and managerial and clerical workers leapt ahead more than 20 per cent (from 4.34 to 5.24 million). Sales workers increased by a sixth (from 1.35 to 1.62 million) in the same period.[18] It is probably not too inaccurate to state that in the years since 1955, 40 to 50 per cent of the increment of the total labor force has flowed into nonmanual work, representing another 30 per cent increase in this category.[19] One survey in 1961 claimed that close to 9.5 million workers were white-collar, distributed as follows: 4.0 million in private manufacturing, 2.8 million in government operations, and 2.7 million in sales and service industries[20]—although this is probably an overestimate because of the last category.

It seems logical that in view of this disproportionate growth of white-collar groups during the postwar period, the sense of exclusiveness earlier identified with the *shokuin* has been giving way. Lower grades of *shain* (*company men*) have been created in the process, hardly distinguishable in status from manual workers, to meet the expanding needs for clerical, service, and technical work. Women,

[17] Fukutake Tadashi, *Nihonjin No Shakai Ishiki* (Tokyo: San-Ichi Shobo, 1960), p. 202.
[18] See *Shūgyō Kōzō Kihon Chōsa* for 1956 and 1959 (Tokyo: Ministry of Labor).
[19] *Warera Sarari Man* (Tokyo: Yomiuri Shimbunsha, 1961), p. 12.
[20] *Shukan Asahi,* July 7, 1961, p. 12.

in large numbers, have been recruited into these jobs (they still comprise more than one-third of the total workforce). With the raising of educational levels, moreover, more and more workers have become qualified for nonmanual work. In some cases, also, *kōin* are now permitted to rise into *shokuin* ranks, although the traditional separation of both groups has remained strong. And the fact that educational requirements for manual workers in large enterprises also have been generally on the rise has broken down status distinctions between *kōin* and *shokuin.*

To summarize, during the past thirty years an entirely new white-collar employee group came into being in Japan—inheriting at first status distinctions that sharply separated the white-collar workers from the manualists. Thus, trade unionism came to Japan on a wide scale at a point in time when the labor force composition was in the midst of transition. Whereas in 1920 there had been one *shokuin* for every sixteen *kōin,* by 1940 the proportion had dropped to one to ten, and by 1960 to about one to five.[21] These developments had important implications for the nature of the trade-union movement that emerged following 1945, as will be developed below.

EXTENT OF POSTWAR WHITE-COLLAR UNIONIZATION

Japan's prewar trade-union movement virtually ceased to exist during World War II and thus was organized from scratch once the Allied Occupation began in 1945.[22] The call for unionization of workers as a means for developing a democratic Japan received enthusiastic response especially where there were large concentrations of wage earners—among the major manufacturing enterprise, the utilities, mining, and government agencies. Unionization therefore occurred particularly in locales where white-collar employees were most prominent and distinctive.

In addition to the concentration of unionism in major enterprises, a leading structural characteristic of postwar Japanese unions was the formation of enterprise-wide units of organization, in which the basic

[21] Fukutake, *op. cit.,* p. 218. For an insightful sociological analysis of the Japanese white-collar employee's pattern of life in recent years, see Ezra F. Vogel, *Japan's New Middle Class: The Salary Man and His Family in a Tokyo Suburb* (Berkeley: University of California Press, 1963).

[22] For studies in English dealing with this development see Solomon B. Levine, *Industrial Relations in Postwar Japan* (Urbana: University of Illinois Press, 1958); and Kazuo Okochi, *Labor in Modern Japan, op. cit.*

union entity embraced all the regular workers of a firm, blue- and white-collar alike. These "combined" unions have accounted for at least 60 per cent of all the basic labor organizations in Japan.[23] While the reasons for these structures will be discussed later, their existence has assured a heavy white-collar representation in the membership of the postwar Japanese trade-union movement.

An exact count of white-collar unionists in Japan is not available, but various indirect estimates indicate that of the 9.3 million unionized workers in 1963 perhaps as many as 35 per cent or more were in the nonmanual work categories. It is believed that at least this proportion has obtained since the beginning of the postwar union movement, and, more likely, that the percentage of white-collar members has actually increased during the past decade due to shifts in the occupational composition of the nonfarm workforce.

Within about a year after the surrender in August 1945, Japanese trade-union membership rose from zero to more than five million. Another 1.5 million members were added by 1949, the total representing at that time close to 50 per cent of the organizable workforce. Although union membership suffered a decline between 1949 and 1951, falling below six million, as the result of economic retrenchment, purge of left-wing elements, and revisions of the labor laws, it resumed a gradual rise year by year. On the other hand, with the employment expansion of the nonagricultural sector, the proportion of unionizable workers steadily declined after 1949 to below 35 per cent, turning up slightly in 1961.[24] This was a reflection, at least until recently, of expanding employment opportunities mainly in small and medium enterprises, where union organization has been notably low. It also reflected a growing use throughout industry of temporary workers who for the most part have not been granted membership in established enterprise unions.[25] Where trade-union membership has expanded—either in new firms or in the growth of the workforces of established firms—the white-collar component has been preserved under the system of "combined" enterprise-wide organization.

For the most part, then, white-collar unionization has taken place

[23] Okochi Kazuo, *Nihon Rōdō Kumiai Ron* (Tokyo: Yuhikaku, 1953), p. 117.

[24] *Japan Labor Bulletin* (Issued by the Japan Institute of Labor) New Series, Vol. I, no. 2 (May 1962), p. 5.

[25] Only recently has there begun to be some notable success in organizing small- and medium-sized firms and temporary workers—these, too, usually on an enterprise basis.

where unionism in general has occurred. Three-fourths of Japanese union membership has been concentrated primarily in four major industrial sectors: 35 per cent in manufacturing, 19 per cent in transportation and communications, 13 per cent in the service trades, and 10 per cent among the government civil service. Other sectors provide relatively small percentages of the total membership: agriculture and forestry, 0.9 per cent; fishing and marine, 0.6 per cent; mining, 3.8 per cent; wholesale and retail trades, 2.8 per cent; real estate, 0.1 per cent; finance and insurance, 5.3 per cent; electricity, gas, and water, 2.3 per cent; and construction, 6.3 per cent.[26]

In other words, unionism has had its strongest hold where white-collar employment has been expanding most rapidly. In manufacturing about 23 per cent of the close to three million organized workers are estimated to be white-collar,[27] and in all likelihood at least as high proportions obtain among the 1.5 million members in transportation and communications and among the one million organized service workers. These sectors together probably have between one and 1.5 million white-collar unionists. And, of course, nearly all of the 1.2 million (probably 90 per cent) organized civil servants (including public school teachers) fall into the white-collar category.[28] The remainder of the white-collar unionists are drawn from finance, insurance, and real estate, which have 350,000 union members, predominantly white-collar; from the wholesale and retail trades, which have more than 200,000 members, many of whom are white-collar; and from the public utilities, which have 185,000 unionists, in part white-collar. Scatterings of white-collar members are spread throughout other sectors. The total approximates 2.75 to 3 million white-collar members.[29]

[26] *Japan Labor Bulletin, op. cit.,* p. 5.
[27] *Rōdō Hakusho, 1961, op. cit.,* p. 93.
[28] *Rōdō Kumiai Kihon Chōsa Hōkokusho, 1960* (Tokyo: Japan Ministry of Labor, 1961), pp. 58-63.
[29] Still another estimate of the proportion of white-collar members may be derived from the coverage of the various Japanese labor relations laws, of which there are five: (1) the Trade Union Law of 1949, applying generally to private industry; (2) the Public Corporation and National Enterprise Labor Relations Law of 1948, to the manufacturing, communications, and transportation corporations owned by the national government; (3) the Local Public Enterprise Labor Relations Law of 1952, to enterprises owned by prefectural, municipal, and other local government bodies; (4) the National Public Service Law of 1947, covering central government civil servants; and (5) the Local Public Service Law of 1950, prefectural, municipal, and other local government civil servants, including teach-

It is also notable that as many as half the white-collar unionists are employed by government either as civil servants, school teachers, or workers in publicly owned enterprises. As will be developed later, the organization of these workers in government has had much to do with the nature of the leadership and functioning of the Japanese labor movement.

On the other hand, important gaps exist in white-collar unionization. These, of course, obtain where unionism in general has failed to gain hold. For example, in construction, which abounds with small firms, merely 30 per cent of the 1.6 million workers are unionized. Only about one-third of the more than 7.8 million manufacturing employees are in unions; and only slightly more than one-fourth of the 3.6 million service workers are union members. No doubt all of these groups have sizable white-collar ratios. But the sectors with the greatest potential for white-collar unionization—wholesale and retail trades, finance, insurance, and real estate—have a mere 15 per cent of their 3.9 million workers in unions. Even in the government civil service other than teachers, especially in the local government levels, less than 60 per cent of the 1.3 million employees have joined unions.[30]

The failure to organize these white-collar workers does not appear to be due merely to a disinterest in unionism. Rather, it is pri-

ers. As of June 30, 1960, the number of trade-union members covered by these various acts and the estimated percentage of white-collar unionists believed to be included in these groups were:

Law	*Union Members Covered*	*Estimated Per Cent of White-Collar Members*
Trade Union	4,944,747	23
Public Corporation and National Enterprises	916,040	20
National Public Service	267,675	90
Local Public Service	1,255,987	90
Local Public Enterprise	131,867	20
TOTAL	7,516,316	36

These rough estimates indicate, then, that at least one-third or more of the organized workers are white-collar employees. See *Rōdō Kumiai Kihon Chōsa Hōkokusho, 1960, op. cit.*, pp. 54, 57-63; and Matsunari Yoshie, Tanuma Hajime, Izumitani Hajime, and Noda Masao, *Nihon No Sarari Man* (Tokyo: Aoki Shoten, 1957), pp. 166-67.

[30] *Rōdō Kumiai Kihon Chōsa Hōkokusho, 1960, op. cit.*, p. 29.

marily the result of the general confinement of unionism itself to limited sectors of the economy and of the organizational structure identified with enterprise unionism. Where unionism has succeeded, it usually occurs on an all-or-nothing basis with the white-collar workers, if present in the unit organized, joining up alongside the manual workers. Mutuality in organizing has been a chief characteristic of postwar unionism—for which there were few roots in the prewar union movement. The reasons for this will be explored after next reviewing the prewar experience with white-collar unionism.

PREWAR UNIONIZATION OF WHITE-COLLAR WORKERS

Even though white-collar unionization made little headway in the decades before the war, what organization came into being was of importance in developing an ideological heritage of considerable importance for the postwar movement. While the Japanese labor movement traces its origins to the closing years of the nineteenth century, unionism in general hardly flourished in the prewar years.[31] Only after World War I did it grow to any significant size. Throughout the 1920's and early 1930's, trade unionism grew fairly rapidly, reaching a membership peak of about 420,000 in 1936 and its highest organizing rate of about 8 per cent in 1931. Following the mid-thirties, it went into rapid decline with the takeover by the military in that decade. By the beginning of World War II mere vestiges of the movement remained. Its place had been taken over by the government-sponsored labor front (*Sangyō Hōkokukai,* or *Sampō*).

The early Japanese trade unions were exclusively manualist organizations, although significantly intellectuals were instrumental in launching them. With the *shain* tradition so strong among the *shokuin,* few white-collar workers had any interest in the labor movement. Only toward the end of World War I were there the first faint stirrings of white-collar unionism.[32] Throughout the interbellum period white-collar unionists comprised an extremely small fraction of the general labor union membership. The number of white-collar unionists in that period reached a peak about 1932, when it is estimated 4,500

[31] For a history of the prewar Japanese labor movement, see Robert A. Scalapino, "Japan," in Walter Galenson, ed., *Labor and Economic Development* (New York: John Wiley and Sons, Inc., 1959), chap. 3; and Okochi Kazuo, "Rōdō," *op. cit.*
[32] For a full review of early white-collar unionism in Japan, see Noda Masaho, *op. cit.;* and Nishioka Takao, *Nihon No Rōdō Kumiai Soshiki* (Tokyo: Japan Institute of Labor, 1960). The materials in this section are based largely on these sources.

white-collar workers were organized in 18 unions (out of 932 unions in all). Moreover, the prewar white-collar unions were almost entirely organized on a basis separate from the manualists. Combined unionism was to be a postsurrender phenomenon.

The first white-collar organizations that appeared in the closing year of World War I were prompted by inflation and shortages which especially threatened the living standards of office employees. In this movement the white-collar groups merely followed parallel manualist unionizing efforts. By that time, moreover, the Japanese government had begun to display a more liberal attitude toward trade unionism, in part to gain international respect from the Allied Powers and in part to gird for the need to commit a growing proportion of the labor force to industrial work.

The first white-collar groups known to organize were a union of manufacturing office employees (formed under the leadership of a newspaper reporter) and a public school teachers' union (called the *Nippon Kyōin Kumiai Keimeikai,* founded by a teacher later to become a leading journalist). Neither became significant and both disappeared by the middle of the 1920's. In February 1919, an organization known as the Osaka Young Men's Employee Association of Industry and Commerce recruited white-collar clerks mainly employed in small shops with the intention of modifying the apprentice system; it managed to attract 20 members and dissolved by 1921. White-collar unionists were active in such major companies as Mitsui Bussan, Jyugo Bank, Nippon Yusen, and the Nagasaki yards of the Mistubishi Shipbuilding. Other small unions—often formed secretly—appeared among civil servants, policemen, and motion picture operators. In 1919, for the first time, white-collar workers went on strike at the Yokohama Silk Exchange, while another group engaged in a slowdown at the Osaka Electric Company.[33]

Perhaps the first sizable organization was the Salaried Men's Union (*Hōkyūsha Kumiai*), begun in September 1919 under the leadership of a Tokyo University professor and advised by such leading intellectuals as Abe Isoo (then professor at Waseda University) and Kanbe Masao (of Kyoto University). This union managed to enlist white-collar clerks from manufacturing companies and banks, and from among government workers, reaching a total membership of 850 by the end of 1920. In the following year it added groups of typists and communications workers, but went out of existence as a union by 1923, succumbing to the idea of employer-employee cooperation urged

[33] Noda, *op. cit.,* pp. 23-24.

at that time by the Harmonization Society (*Kyōchōkai*). Actually, the *Hōkyūsha Kumiai* hardly got off the ground. Little more than a mutual benefit association, it failed to withstand large-scale dismissals among major companies during the 1921-23 depression, which affected the membership and repelled others who might have been interested in joining. Its chief accomplishments were the establishment of cooperative hospitals in Tokyo in 1922 and 1923 and the conduct of research on *shokuin* employment conditions at major *zaibatsu* companies. These reports, however, revealed some of the degrading treatment lesser white-collar office members often received, and, it is alleged, led some companies to re-examine their employment policies and to order changes in various practices.[34]

On the other hand, with the upturn of business conditions in 1923 white-collar unionists in other quarters began to show increasing aggressiveness. In 1923, a union of white-collar day workers was formed in the Tokyo plants of the Nippon Electric Company, a major manufacturer of electrical equipment, and worked in cooperation with the newly established manualist union of that company, actually joining in a strike for higher wages in 1924. Around this time, it should be noted, the trade-union movement as a whole began a major upsurge, giving encouragement to white-collar workers to join its ranks. White-collar workers were known to have participated in fifteen labor disputes in 1924, seventeen in 1925, and fourteen in 1926. In 1925 and 1926, white-collar unions appeared among salaried office workers in Kobe, the clerks of the Electric Bureau of the Tokyo Municipal Office, and general white-collar workers in the Kanto Region, Yokohama, Kyoto, Osaka, and Kawasaki. Still others developed, for example, as a general nonmanual workers' union in Kobe and among the *shokuin* employed in the Tokyo streetcar industry.

An exceptional instance of the viability of early white-collar unionism in Japan was seen in the activities of the Japan Maritime Officers' Association (*Nihon Kaiin Kyōkai*). The membership of this organization was made up of ship officers, including captains, pilots, engineers, radio operators, chief clerks, and doctors, and, when first organized in 1896, was a mutual benefit and a professional society. However, beginning in 1919, it began to turn its attentions to job security problems and wage demands. In 1925, the Association, probably comprising more than ten thousand members by that time, actually reconstituted itself as a union in order to gain official participation in the ILO. By the mid-twenties, moreover, it had devel-

[34] *Ibid.*, pp. 24-25.

oped, along with the Japan Seamen's Union (*Nihon Kaiin Kumiai*—formed in 1921 and embracing eighty thousand members by 1928), machinery for bargaining with the major shipowners, perhaps as a forerunner of "combined" unionism. This was one of the very few examples in prewar Japan in which the right to collective bargaining was explicitly recognized. Negotiations established agreements on minimum wage rates, employment exchanges, shipboard working conditions, dispute procedures, crew recruitment, and management of seamen's homes. No doubt the acceptance of collective bargaining—so exceptional for Japan at that time—was due mainly to widespread recognition of the strategic importance of the shipping industry and to international influences upon the maritime trades generated, for example, by the ILO.[35]

In December 1926, the first nationwide federation of white-collar unions was established under the name of the Japan Salary Men's Union Federation (*Nippon Hōkyū Seikatsusha Kumiai Remmei*—a year later changed to the *Nippon Hōkyū Seikatsusha Kumiai Hyōgikai*). At its height it reportedly enlisted more than four thousand members. The federation also affiliated with the most radical of the three major labor centers of that time, the communist-inclined Japanese Council of Labor Unions (*Nippon Rōdō Kumiai Hyōgikai*). Its life, however, was to prove to be a short one (see below, p. 231).

At no time, however, did the white-collar unionists achieve any meaningful degree of unity in the prewar period. The units that were formed were extremely small, thinly spread, and ideologically divided. They were not action groups in any real sense but for the main part served as debating societies, drawing in as members intelligentsia principally among the lower *shokuin* and technicians in factory offices, banks, trading companies, municipal agencies, and among writers, actors, lawyers, and so forth. They were concerned chiefly with ideological and political issues, although they sporadically attempted to set up mutual assistance plans, employment referral systems, and consumer cooperatives. They rarely bargained and almost as rarely engaged in labor disputes. In 1930 there were twelve identifiable local organizations, none with more than 750 members. Some of these included all types of white-collar workers; others confined themselves to technicians such as moving picture operators. Some were based only in a local area such as Tokyo, Osaka, Kobe, or Nagoya, while others attempted to achieve nationwide organization.

[35] See Nihon Rōdō Kyōkai Chōsa Kenkyū Bu, *Senin No Dantaikōshō No Jisshoteki Kenkyū,* Chōsa Kenkyū Shiryō No. 38 (Tokyo, 1961).

It took several years after the first organizational stirrings among white-collar workers before the manualist unions welcomed them to trade-union ranks. White-collar workers were suspect. Despite a large increase in *shokuin* during World War I, bringing to them for the first time considerable economic insecurity and harsh working conditions, they were still perceived as *company men*—with little identification with the working class, still a part of management, and favored by employee paternalism. The government itself, in joining the ILO in 1920, reinforced this perception by explicitly refusing to consider unions that included *shokuin* for the selection of worker delegates to be sent to Geneva.[36] In the early 1920's, the only major labor federation at that time, the moderate socialist Japan Federation of Labor (*Sōdōmei*), turned down applications of white-collar groups for admission as affiliates. At *Sōdōmei*'s 1924 convention, the matter was actually brought to a formal vote and was defeated. After 1924, however, this attitude was reversed, and in 1925 white-collar unions were admitted to *Sōdōmei*. By this time, various white-collar groups had displayed their solid support of manualists' unions, as in the case of the Nippon Electric strike; and the organized blue-collar workers became less suspicious of their white-collar colleagues.

But of even greater importance was the ideological struggle that had begun to grip the Japanese labor movement itself. By the mid-twenties a three-cornered rivalry had set in among the social democrats, the communists, and the anarcho-syndicalists, splitting *Sōdōmei* into three factions; each was attempting to cultivate support from every possible group. For ideological purposes alone each needed, especially after universal male suffrage was established in 1925, the white-collar intelligentsia. Throughout the remainder of the 1920's, the white-collar organizations in turn divided in varying proportions among the various ideological groups.

Within this context, the white-collar unions were converted from fairly ineffectual mutual aid societies to political wings of rival left-wing parties. In 1926 the three largest white-collar unions, with a total membership of 1,950, came out in support of the newly established Social Democrat Party (*Shakai Minshutō*); while five smaller ones, with hardly more than 600 members in all, rallied behind the

[36] In 1926, a proposed law (which failed to pass the Diet) to grant limited trade-union rights stipulated that labor organizations be limited to manual workers. This limitation was one reason for the formation of white-collar unions which sought a broadening of the bill. Also, in the May Day Parade of 1927, the police banned participation of *shokuin* on the grounds they were not workers. See Nishioka, *op. cit.*, p. 126.

middle-left that later became the National Mass Party (*Zenkoku Taishūtō*), and two others joined in the activity of the communist-inclined Labor Farmer Party (*Rōnōtō*). Although the white-collar groups were almost insignificant in size within these parties, they were important for providing some of the more articulate political leaders of the left.

Government repression of left-wing activity soon led to the disintegration of the white-collar groups. The one national white-collar union federation, the *Nippon Hōkyū Seikatsusha Kumiai Remmei,* which through the *Nippon Rōdō Kumiai Hyōgikai* supported the Labor Farmer Party, fell apart when the government ordered this party dissolved in 1928. Faced with arrests and other forms of police repression, the federation eventually went out of existence in 1931. Both the Social Democrats and the National Mass Party made further attempts to organize white-collar federations in 1928 and 1929, but gained only token memberships and then went into oblivion by 1931. When two new white-collar unions were established in 1931 in Tokyo —one for unemployed intellectuals and the other for *shokuin* in the Tokyo Electric Company (merely 243 and 600 members each)—neither was known to establish political connections.[37] With the Manchurian Incident, the attempts at a national movement among these workers virtually ceased—bludgeoned by government repression, lack of appeal for white-collar workers, and ideological fractionalism. What white-collar activity took place after 1931 was minimal and largely underground.

Perhaps the most that may be said of the extremely small white-collar unionism of the 1920's is that it provided a continuing base for the intellectual leadership of Japan's prewar labor movement. Organized labor in its formative stage had been strongly influenced by men such as Katayama Sen, Takano Fusataro, Abe Isoo, Kotoku Shosui, Sakai Toshihiko, Osugi Sakae, and Suzuki Bunji, none of whom arose from the working class but came from intellectual backgrounds and usually learned about trade unionism in foreign countries such as the United States. Typically, the leaders had been university professors, politicians, social workers, Christian ministers, writers, artists, actors, and lawyers. Many of this group were tossed into jail in the late 1920's and the 1930's and later emerged as leaders of the postwar movement, this time with the blessing of the Allied Occupation. Japan's labor movement, always struggling for existence in the prewar period, had

[37] Shortly after its formation, the Tokyo Electric Company union was ordered to disband by the management, and its leaders were discharged.

little opportunity to become disaffected with intellectual leadership, but in fact saw these leaders as its martyrs.

With the sweep of democratic idealism in the period immediately following World War II workers once again were to turn to white-collar leadership, especially as the conveyors of the earlier intellectual tradition. What was not realized was the divisiveness for the movement that this type of leadership could produce. The prewar divisions had left a heritage around which to rally: the democrats promised a gradualistic way out from tight traditional social controls to individual freedom; the anarcho-syndicalists supported mass action by white- and blue-collar alike as a way of replacing the hierarchial compartmentalism of Japanese society; the Marx-Leninists offered a simple formula to rid Japan both of Western imperialism and Japanese ultranationalism. All three ideological strands, developed during the inter-war period and reflected particularly by the white-collar intellectuals, were seen as means of implementing the call by the Allied Occupation for new institutions, particularly among labor, to prevent the re-emergence of oligarchical political, social, and economic controls. While during the prewar period the rank-and-file worker, merely a "half-step" from peasantry and accustomed as he was to narrowly tight social structures and to paternalistic treatment by the boss, had been fairly remote from the intellectuals, the shock of surrender and occupation for the first time in Japanese history drew the manualist close to the intellectual in the attempt to understand how his particularistic position fitted into the broader national economic and political structure.

THE POSTWAR EMERGENCE OF WHITE- AND BLUE-COLLAR UNITY

It has been stressed that a unique feature of the postwar labor movement in Japan has been the unity achieved between blue-collar and white-collar workers in union organizational structure. One reason for this has already been suggested from the earlier prewar history of white-collar unionization: the role of the intellectuals in providing an ideological base for the general postwar movement. Still other factors were at work. Wartime experience produced a high degree of mutual identification of both the manual and nonmanual workers with the enterprise in which they were employed together. The organization of the patriotic labor associations (the *Sampō*) deliberately had stressed the unity of the two groups and their common dependence upon the employing unit. These strong bonds were fed by patriotic appeals that relied heavily upon traditional Japanese cultural factors such as close family association and social compartmentalization. Undoubtedly these factors played an important role in generating enterprise-wide unions after the surrender. Further, when the Occupation gave the signal to unionize rapidly, the intellectual leaders, now released from jail, played upon the need for unity between the two groups within an enterprise—both to fulfill ideological goals and to achieve a ready base of organization.

As it was the white-collar employees who could best articulate the new philosophies of egalitarianism and democracy, they became vital links in the process of organizing unions. No doubt the fact that they still retained high prestige inherited from *shokuin* status helped to catapult them into positions of leadership at the enterprise level. Many were university trained and some were experienced in the prewar ideological and political struggles even though inexperienced in unionism. In a sense, the white-collar employees in the large enterprises were akin to the lower samurai of eighty years earlier who felt it was their responsibility to erect a new order and to prevent the resurgence of the old—but now, with the approval of the Supreme Commander of the Allied Powers (SCAP).

An economic factor, too, accounted for the prominence of the white-collar role in the immediate postwar period—in contrast to the prewar period. The near collapse of Japanese industry threatened to depress the social status of the white-collar employee—especially in view of their proliferating numbers and the then narrowing of *shokuin-kōin* wage differentials. To maintain their positions it was important to exercise leadership within the enterprise. This was facilitated by the common enterprise identification (rather than separate job consciousness) of white- and blue-collar groups, fortified by tightly knit social substructures within which *kōin* depended heavily upon *shokuin* guidance. Also, that the *shokuin* had ready access to management information and better understanding of the firm's total operations supported their prominence in union organizations. After all, in this period of chaos and depression, all members of an enterprise workforce shared the same loss of income and threats to their employment security. White-collar employees were hardly any more secure than the blue-collar workers—and this was mutually recognized.

In the months following the surrender, unionism spread like wildfire. By 1948, almost half of Japan's wage earners were organized. But the unionists were gathered together into singularly uniform structures that have come to be known as enterprise-wide unions. In the great majority of cases, union organization followed the plant or, in the case of multiplant firms, the entire enterprise. Regardless of job performed in the company, the employee, blue- or white-collar, was called upon to join this basic unit, and join he did. Few craft, regional, industrial, general, or other patterns of organization sprang up.

Today, of the more than 45,000 basic units of organization, close to 90 per cent are enterprise unions or parts of enterprise unions. Of these, as noted earlier, 60 per cent have combined memberships, and probably 40 per cent of all the white-collar unionists are in combined unions. Since at least 60 per cent of all unionists are in combined unions, as many as one-fifth are white-collar members. Only in a few exceptional cases is there a separation of the two groups, a major example being coal mining. Elsewhere they are usually together. The "pure" white-collar unions which exist (as a rule where white-collar workers alone are employed) account for little more than 20 per cent of the total union membership. Similarly, only 15 per cent of the total membership is found in pure blue-collar unions.[38]

In effect, the establishment of combined unions in Japan has welded the permanently employed blue- and white-collar members together, for it is characteristic of these organizations to exclude those wage earners not permanently on the enterprise payrolls. Another way to put this idea is that the permanent manual workers have through the union movement joined the white-collar employees in receiving lifetime commitments for their working careers. The determination of the permanent worker cadre has been a cardinal point in postwar Japanese collective bargaining, and the inclusion of manualists as permanent workers was formalized through unionism, including the device of the union shop and check-off, thus cementing the relationship between the two groups. In 1961, 77 per cent of the total union membership were in enterprise unions composed only of permanent workers. Unions that admitted both temporary and regular employees accounted for only 10 per cent of all the basic organizational units and but 12 per cent of the total union membership.[39] It should be noted further that until recently temporary workers usually did not achieve permanent status; those who did typically were

[38] *Japan Labor Bulletin, op. cit.*, p. 7.

[39] There is no exact estimate of the number of nonfarm temporary workers in Japan, although it is believed to range as high as 10 per cent or more of the workforce. In 1961, there were 367 union units whose members were exclusively temporary or casual employees, with a total membership of 35,000, although their numbers have been growing. See *Japan Labor Bulletin, op. cit.*, p. 7.

only the new young recruits entering industry for the first time, while older temporary workers rarely qualified because of the seniority practices in most Japanese companies. Exclusion of temporary workers from the enterprise unions has no doubt heightened the "enterprise" consciousness of a large majority of trade-union members in Japan.[40]

ENTERPRISE UNIONISM

The reasons for the emergence of enterprise unions in Japan have been fully explored elsewhere and may be quickly summarized here.[41] Economic, political, cultural, and ideological factors all contributed to their development. As mentioned, in the immediate postwar years, enterprise employees, blue- and white-collar alike, were threatened equally by the ravages of rampant inflation and dire shortages. Their economic interests suddenly merged. Since open labor markets did not exist, the greatest assurance of economic security for a worker lay in gaining recognition of permanent attachment to his enterprise. By pooling their bargaining strength together, white- and blue-collar workers could extract employment guarantees from management, weak as the latter were in this period of economic chaos and mindful of Occupation directives. For economic reasons alone, the manualists depended on their alliance with the white-collar workers, and vice versa.

In addition, the white-collar workers were in key positions to know about and understand the technical operations and financial conditions of their enterprise. With management sorely harassed by the Occupation and in peril of being purged, the manual workers in many cases looked to the white-collar members for leadership in presenting bargaining demands, organizing the union, and oftentimes actually administering the company. In a sense, white-collar leadership replaced management in looking out for the welfare of the firm's employees. A chief motivating force was to preserve the enterprise as a source of livelihood for all the permanently attached.

Enterprise organization was a highly convenient basis for rapid unionization. Communications were quick and easy. As a result, not only was this structure vital for achieving economic security, but also for providing a base for the new reform political parties, mainly of the left, whose establishment the Occupation urged in order to coun-

[40] See Levine, *op. cit.*, pp. 104-5.
[41] *Ibid.*, pp. 101-7.

teract a possible resurgence of the ultranationalistic right. The prewar opposition parties had been obliterated and were in need of a ready means of organizing such as provided by the enterprise units. Inasmuch as enterprise unionism could be reconciled, so it appeared, with the idea of industrial unionism and harked back to earlier anarcho-syndicalist themes, the new parties used these appeals to encourage organization on an enterprise base. Enterprise unions provided visible working class solidarity and were readily mobilized for demonstrations, rallies, parades, strikes, and so forth.

Alongside these motivations were deep-seated cultural and social elements. Particularism, as noted, sharply characterized Japanese social structures—a factor that had been capitalized upon by the wartime *Sampō*. Management paternalism and the ethic of harmony wedded the worker to his organizational entity, which was sociologically similar to the solidarity of traditional family and village society. The system of employment, promotion, and compensation was based on length of permanent attachment to the firm. Welfare programs were built around the enterprise rather than the community or through the state. With little history of individualism in Japanese culture, workers were immersed in groups, so that, when the postwar chaos threatened the existence of their enterprises, white-collar and blue-collar employees felt a close psychological affinity to one another.

The enterprise structures therefore served economic, political, and social needs at a time of greatest stress. But paradoxically, while they were basically compartmentalized and particularistic, they became the umbrella for a wide range of egalitarian ideological appeals. Whether democratic socialists, syndicalists, or Marx-Leninists, the intelligentsia leadership of Japan had from prewar days stressed a cosmic approach, group solidarity, and working class unity. Added to this was the sweep of democratic idealism that came with the Allied victory. All were now alike—blue- and white-collar status distinctions were seemingly swept away. Although the Occupation authorities stressed the need to develop "business unionism" of the American type, in the context of the time this suggestion fell flat; it served none of the political, economic, and social impulses of most of the organized working class.

Enterprise union structure, on the other hand, was accompanied by two distinct levels of activity in the newborn Japanese labor movement. At the enterprise level, particularistic activities prevailed with almost exclusive attention given by the enterprise union to problems immediately affecting the enterprise. At the national level, the primary preoccupation of the union leaders was with ideological and political issues (a point to be developed more fully later in the chapter).

Particularism at the local level was fortified by the strong alliance of the white- and blue-collar workers within enterprises. With management suffering a great loss in prestige and the very existence of many enterprises threatened by Occupation policies, white-collar leaders essentially took over the administration of the workforce and in some cases the entire operations of plants. They made up the bulk of the union organizers in this period. Until the Trade Union Law, initially adopted in 1946 (providing the right to organize, bargain, and strike to virtually all workers), was amended in 1949, enterprise union membership reached in many instances into the ranks of department heads, section chiefs, station masters, school principals, and similar supervisory posts.[42] It was often a mark of prestige for the white-collar employee to be elected to an enterprise union office—a recognition of leadership among all the workers within the enterprise. Also, because of *jōshi-buka* and *oyabun-kobun* traditions (literally, "superior-subordinate" and "parent-child" relationships) blue-collar workers tended to support white-collar leaders to insure their own permanent tenure in the organization.

But for the most part, this meant that the enterprise unions would be primarily concerned with problems at the local level and would give little heed to the needs for integrating and developing the labor movement at the national level. A vigorous but narrowly confined collective bargaining system developed, centering mainly on the career guarantees for permanent workers and wage advances geared to length of service within the particular enterprise. The enterprise union usually secured union shop and dues check-off guarantees for its members, provision of office space on company premises, and some share in the management-sponsored welfare program. Only in a few instances—such as in shipping and to some degree in coal mining, textiles, and private railways—did multiple-enterprise bargaining emerge. Moreover, negotiations were handled strictly by the enterprise union's officers; neither they nor management particularly welcomed participation of "outsiders" from national union organizations to which the enterprise unit affiliated. Finally, the bargains made usually applied to the entire regular work group, white- and blue-collar alike, in the form of blanket wage increases and bonus payments. The stake of the white-collar employee thus was tied to the blue-collar worker. In some agreements the distinction between *shokuin* and *kōin* was

[42] Okochi Kazuo, *et al.*, *Sengō Rōdō Kumiai No Jittai* (Tokyo: Nihon Hyoronsha, 1950), pp. 169-80.

formally abolished, and in the early years there was a noticeable closing of the wage differential between the groups. Little attention was given to job evaluation and classification plans, the bargainers preferring to rely mainly upon factors of age, education upon entry, length of service, family size, and other nonproduction related elements. In a sense, all the permanent employees had become *shain*—egalitarian except in the distinction with the temporary workers and the millions who could not achieve permanent status at all among the myriad of small- and medium-sized shops that were unorganized.

White-collar leadership in the enterprise unions remained prominent until fairly recently. A survey in 1950 indicated that as many as 50 per cent of all elected union officers came from white-collar groups, and as many as 20 per cent of these held supervisory or management titles.[43] In the typical combined enterprise union, the offices are usually systematically divided among white- and blue-collar employees and rotated from one group to the other year by year.[44] Only after the decline of unionism in the 1949-52 period did white-collar leadership begin to lose its hold, as management regained prestige with the reversal of American economic, political, and military policy toward Japan, and as white-collar workers were again awarded higher status in companies, especially with the boom of the Japanese economy.

Decisions within the enterprise union are usually based upon felt consensus and unanimity, as is often the case in traditional Japanese social structures, rather than upon open debate, parliamentary procedure, and voting majorities. Union policy-making therefore is likely to be highly centralized within the inner council of top officers. In this process, the white-collar official is certain to play a role disproportionately large compared to white-collar membership strength in the union because of his traditional higher status and his knowledge about the conditions of the enterprise, particularly if he should be elected from the union branch of headquarters personnel.

Under these arrangements, there has been no decline in white-collar membership within the enterprise unions and there have been relatively few instances of permanent breakaways (with the exceptions to be noted) of the white-collar elements from them. Management, it may be added, probably has not been wholly displeased with the combined union structure, since, if unionism there must be, the enterprise form serves to strengthen the ties of the workers to the

[43] *Ibid.*
[44] See case examples in Okochi Kazuo, *et al.*, *Rōdō Kumiai no Kōzō to Kinō* (Tokyo: Tokyo Daigaku Shuppansha, 1959).

enterprise, and enterprise-union white-collar leadership often moderates union demands upon the management (who often consider such experience for white-collar employees as good training for promotion up managerial ranks).

Widespread development of enterprise unions almost immediately raised questions of employer interference and company-dominated unionism, primarily because of the prominent leadership role exercised by white-collar members. Both the new Trade Union Law of 1946 and the Constitution of 1947 guaranteed workers the right to organize unions on virtually whatever base they chose. The problem, of course, was how to draw the line between worker and manager in organizations where the distinctions between the two were highly blurred because of Japanese methods of administration, allocation of authority, and decision-making. While the Trade Union Law was finally amended in 1949 to eliminate management representatives from union jurisdictions, many of the unions opposed the changes partly out of fear that their leadership would be weakened and bargaining strength reduced at the enterprise level. Some of the most active organizers of the new unions had been white-collar employees. For example, a survey in 1947 found that in the metal industry close to half the active organizers had been drawn from *shokuin* positions, and of these half had come from the ranks of *kakarichō* (subsection chiefs). It was also found that 60 per cent of the *kōin* organizers actually were senior first-line work leaders who were likely to be the closest subordinates of *kakarichō*.[45]

The revised law now excluded from the protection of the labor relations legislation any worker organizations "which admit to membership officers, workers at the supervisory post having direct authority to hire, fire, promote or transfer, workers at the supervisory post having access to confidential information relating to the employer's labor relations plans and policies so that their official duties and obligations directly conflict with their loyalties and obligations as members of the trade union concerned and other persons who represent the interest of the employer" (*sic*).[46] The administrative task of drawing the line between those eligible and not eligible to become unionists

[45] Okochi, *Sengō Rōdō Kumiai No Jittai, op. cit.*, p. 62; and Nishioka, *op. cit.*, pp. 156-65.

[46] The amended law also provided for democratic procedures in internal union affairs. Failure to have these procedures disqualifies a union from using the Labor Relations Commissions in their functions of dispute adjustment and unfair labor practice proceedings, from obtaining certification as a juridicial person, and from nominating commission members. See Japan Ministry of Labor, *Japan Labor Legislation 1959* (Tokyo: Institute of Labor Policy, 1959).

was left to the tripartite Labor Relations Commissions established by the act, through a set of provisions for examining trade-union qualifications. At least 60 per cent of all unions before the 1949 amendments had permitted higher management functionaries to serve as officers.[47] As a general rule, the commissions now drew the line to include *kakarichō* provided they were not engaged in labor relations or personnel functions. This has meant that most of the new recruits into the unionized enterprise or organization, even though destined to rise into management ranks, still almost inevitably become union members. Some of these, young university graduates imbued with a sense of reformism or even radicalism, keep alive the white-collar militancy originally exhibited among the enterprise unions. Those who do rise into management ranks usually can boast of earlier trade-union ties and are often able to continue in close contact with the enterprise union leadership.

In all likelihood, had the commissions insisted upon a stricter definition of union member eligibility, the enterprise unions might have fallen apart rapidly because of the tendency of rank-and-file workers to remain close to their superiors in the tradition of Japanese *oyabun-kobun* relationships. As it was, the trade-union movement suffered a serious decline in membership from 1949 to 1952, in part because of the organizational disruption produced by revision of the law.[48]

The autonomy and independence from management of the enterprise unions in many cases, however, remains in serious doubt. As evidence, collective bargaining issues have remained narrowly confined in scope and area. Unions only seldom take advantage of unfair labor practice provisions (virtually the same as those of the Wagner Act), especially regarding employer refusal to bargain and employer dominations or interference.[49] Moreover, there have been increasingly frequent instances of union splits over challenging management—a point further developed below.

"FIRST" AND "SECOND" UNIONS

As the Japanese economy has diversified and grown in the past decade, it appears that increasing divergence has been developing

[47] Okochi, *Sengō Rōdō Kumiai No Jittai, op. cit.*, p. 105.
[48] See Isoda Susumu, *Rōdō Hō* (Tokyo: Iwanami Shoten, 1954), pp. 129-38. Other reasons, of course, were also at work to explain the decline: tougher government and management attitudes toward unionization, disinflation resulting from the Dodge Plan, and the "red purge" ordered by the Occupation.
[49] See Solomon B. Levine, "Japan's Tripartite Labor Relations Commission," *Labor Law Journal* (July 1955), pp. 462-82, 590.

among the various groups embraced by the enterprise union. Most notable has been dissatisfaction on the part of white-collar groups, although other tensions exist, for example, between the older and younger workers and between skilled and unskilled manualists. Under the prevailing length-of-service pay system, management has attempted to reinstitute greater differentials between white-collar and blue-collar workers as well as to favor the former with increased welfare benefits, special wage allowances, and promotion privileges.

At the same time, enterprise unions find it difficult to cater to individual or subgroup grievances because of their chief concern with treating the membership as a unitary group. It is well known that American-type grievance procedures have failed to develop in practice in Japan despite the earlier urgings of the Occupation officers and the actual writing of these procedures into many contracts. This failure has permitted grievances to accumulate, which, while having certain advantages for union activity as described below, also permits divisiveness within the enterprise union. Under these conditions, the enterprise union is at once strong and fragile: strong in the ability to mobilize the entire workforce over a common issue, weak when subgroups find their own particular interests neglected.

Splits of enterprise unions—the so-called "first" and "second" union phenomenon—usually first develop around ideological issues. It should be noted here that enterprise unions exist within the context of competing national labor centers that are essentially separated from one another in terms of basic trade-union philosophy. The period 1945-50 was marked by bitter rivalry between the communist-dominated National Congress of Industrial Unions, or *Sanbetsu* (*Zen Nihon Sangyōbetsu Rōdō Kumiai Kaigi*) and the Fabian-socialist Japanese Federation of Labor, or *Sōdōmei* (*Nihon Rōdō Kumiai Sōdōmei*). The period 1949-53, during which the moderate unionists emerged predominant, saw the formation of the General Council of Trade Unions of Japan, or *Sōhyō* (*Nihon Rōdō Kumiai Sōhyōgikai*). But in 1954, internal ideological issues led to the breaking off of the leading constituents on the right end of *Sōhyō*'s spectrum, chiefly the textile workers and seamen. They joined with elements of *Sōdōmei* that had earlier refused to enter *Sōhyō* to form the Japanese Trade Union Congress, or *Zenrō Kaigi* (*Zen Nihon Rōdō Kumiai Kaigi*).[50] A smaller left-wing federation known as the National Federation of Industrial Organizations, or *Shinsanbetsu* (*Zenkoku Sangyōbetsu Rōdō*

[50] In April 1962, *Zenrō Kaigi* reorganized itself and formed a new central federation called the Japanese Confederation of Labor, or *Dōmei Kaigi* (*Nihon Rōdō Kumiai Dōmei Kaigi*) formally inaugurated in November 1964, and called *Dōmei*.

Kumiai Rengō) has existed since 1949, while a set of national unions that have spurned involvement in the ideological disputes recently formed a loose confederation known as the Federation of Independent Unions, or *Chūritsu Sōren.* A number of other national unions and enterprise units, moreover, have refused to affiliate with any outside bodies. This division of the labor movement has resulted in competition for the allegiance of the fairly autonomous enterprise unions, especially since neither the central federations nor the constituent national unions have been able to exert significant discipline over them. The enterprise unions are seen as important prizes because, once they do affiliate, the internal nature of these units greatly assures solidarity of support—especially in carrying out political activities.

But at the same time the ideological rivalry often brings out the restiveness within the enterprise union over its failure to deal with problems other than those common to the general membership. Since the union is likely to be organized informally along *oyabun-kobun* lines, personal rivalries tend to develop among the leaders. Thus, in a growing number of strike cases, the white-collar workers often lead a back-to-work movement and proclaim the establishment of a new "second" union which, under law, management must recognize and bargain with.[51] It should be noted, however, that usually these breakaways do not aim at establishing a separate union for the white-collar group, but rather as securing the entire membership of the original enterprise union. Prominent instances of breakaways have been seen in the cases of the Nissan Automobile Union and the Nikko Muroran Factory Workers Union in 1953, the National Railways Workers Union in 1957, the Oji Pulp and Paper Workers Union in 1958, and the Mitsui Miike Coal Miners Union in 1960.

For example, in the Oji Company Tomakomai plant strike in 1959, three-fourths of the 446 white-collar unionists withdrew all at once from the established or "first" union and formed a "second" union. Again, in 1960, at the Ube Kosan Company in the chemical industry (especially significant because it was the home union of Ohta Kaoru, chairman of *Sōhyō*), 16 white-collar members began a "second" union during a labor dispute in 1961. Within a few days fifteen hundred of the firm's twenty-five hundred employees had joined this group, adding three hundred more over the following three months. By that time virtually all of the white-collar members had switched.[52]

[51] See Fujita Wakao, *Daini Kumiai* (Tokyo: Nippon Hyoron Shinsha, 1960), revised edition.

[52] Of the 101 university graduates who were union members only 3 remained in the "first" union; of the 550 supervisors, foremen, and work leaders only 60 failed to join the "second" union. See *Warera Sarari Man, op. cit.*, pp. 198-99, 202.

Union splits such as these usually are fomented in secret and are carried out quickly because of cultural distaste for direct confrontation and lack of well-developed parliamentary procedure for debate and contests within the unions.[53] Once top-level white-collar workers form a "second" union, heavy pressure falls upon their subordinates to join, largely because of *oyabun-kobun* relationships. In a typical case, the "second" union is composed of the office employees or staff departments, long-service manual workers, the more skilled and higher educated, and other principal "core" employees; while the "first" union retains the white-collar workers in the production shops, the less skilled and educated, the younger workers, and general employees. Once the "second" union gets into motion, management commonly gives it encouragement through dispensing welfare benefits and promotions in favor of its members.

These incidents, although relatively small in number, reveal a growing stratification within the white-collar group itself in terms of a differential identification with management. However, the majority of white-collar employees still appear to remain close to the blue-collar workers in economic status because only few who aspire to management positions actually attain them. Despite the increasing employment of white-collar workers, it is likely that on the whole the white- and blue-collar alliance will remain firm.

On the other hand, in the last four or five years, especially since Japan first experienced labor shortages in the categories of young skilled workers and technical and professional white-collar employees, the pressures toward union splits have increased because of growing diversity of economic interests within the enterprise union. The "second" union phenomenon highlights a major problem facing the Japanese labor movement as the result of its basic structural form of enterprise unionism. While this structure originally served a highly useful function for establishing quickly a wide and unified base of trade unionism, nonetheless it has generated a problem of disunity that may worsen.

GOVERNMENT WORKERS' UNIONS

While "combined unions" provide a dominant theme, more organized white-collar workers belong to unions that are made up exclusively or heavily of white-collar workers. This is largely the

[53] See Kichiemon Ishikawa, "The Regulation of the Employer-Employee Relationship: Japanese Labor Relations Law," in Arthur Taylor von Mehren, ed., *Law in Japan: The Legal Order in a Changing Society* (Cambridge: Harvard University Press, 1963), pp. 460-62.

result of the highly successful organization of civil service employees at the national and local governmental levels, especially among the public school teachers. Other largely white-collar unions, of course, are found in the retail and wholesale trades, in insurance and banking fields, and in real estate—although minor in strength compared to the government workers' unions. Nonetheless, it is to be stressed that almost all of these unions, too, follow the enterprise or agency base, and there are no white-collar federations that have been formed exclusively on the basis of occupational characteristics.

In the great organizing drives that followed Japan's surrender, government workers were among the first to form unions.[54] Labor organizations sprang up overnight in virtually all the central government ministries and agencies as well as among various local government groups. As in the standard enterprise-union pattern in private industry, organization followed governmental structure. A single ministry or public corporation became the basic union unit, and branch offices and plants became subunits of the overall union. Because of the scale of these units, most central government worker unions were organized from the beginning on a nationwide basis.[55] (The local government units, except for the teachers, took longer to federate among themselves and were far more diverse.) Unions in government-owned corporations have been among the largest in Japan: the national railways, the postal service, the telegraph and telephone corporation, the national monopolies (tobacco, salt, camphor), etc. Government employee unions have also been highly coordinated, dealing as they do with a common employer.

Organization of the civil servants and public workers represented a sharp break from the past. It was these groups that had been among the most elite and "departmentalist" in Japanese society. Numerous factors contributed to unionization once it was clear that all workers were encouraged to organize. There was great fear among government employees that their units would be dismantled or considerably reduced in size under the Occupation. (Actually, except for the abolishment of the military and home ministries, the structure of the

[54] The materials in this section are based largely on Nakayama Ichiro, ed., *Kankōrō No Sōgi* (Tokyo: Rōdō Sōgi Chosakai, 1959).

[55] For example, national unions are formed for each of the various ministries (Agriculture, Forestry, Construction, Labor, Commerce and Industry, Justice, Welfare, Finance, Education, and Transportation) and for such groups and agencies as the tax collectors, medical service, the National Personnel Authority, the Economic Planning Agency, the Prime Minister's Office Pension Bureau, Customs, Mint, National Procurement Agency, and the Garrison Forces units.

bureaucracy was left virtually untouched.) Government workers suffered severely in the rampant postwar inflation; they received almost no wage increases to keep abreast of price rises. The lower civil servants also found for the first time an opportunity to challenge the traditional arbitrariness of the higher civil servants. Ideological expression was strongest among the government workers, especially university graduates who were exposed to Western economic and political philosophies and yet protected by permanent tenure. Perhaps, as will be developed later, no group was so affected in this respect as the teachers.

The public workers took the initiative in the most militant union activities of the immediate postwar period. The government at first did little to restrict them, but on the other hand neither could it readily provide wage increases and job guarantees. Throughout 1946, the public service unions engaged in a series of harrassing campaigns against the government, culminating in a call for a general nationwide strike of all workers for February 1, 1947. Only upon the prohibition of General MacArthur was this strike averted, and as a result of the agitation SCAP required the Japanese Government to adopt a series of measures to limit the activities of public worker unions.

In the fall of 1947 the Diet legislated the National Public Service Law, which denied the right to bargain and strike to national government civil servants and placed them under the jurisdiction of a newly constituted and autonomous National Personnel Authority, similar to the American Civil Service Commission. These workers still were permitted to organize but their unions were eligible for recognition only if confined to members of given jurisdictions (usually an agency or ministry) and if officers were elected only from within their respective memberships. In the next year, the Public Corporation and National Enterprise Labor Relations Law was adopted, permitting employees in the industrial operations owned by the central government to organize and bargain but not to strike. They were also subject to special mediation and arbitration procedures in cases of disputes, and, in order to gain recognition, to restrictions in their jurisdictions and selection of officers. In 1950 and 1952 similar acts were passed applying to employees in local government offices and corporations. By 1958 the restrictions in these laws were to become the basis for complaints lodged with the ILO by Japanese government workers' unions against the Japanese government as infringements on trade union rights, under ILO Convention 87. Only by 1965, following considerable investigation by the ILO itself, did the government, by adopting the Convention, begin to take steps to remove these restrictions.

Despite these restrictions (and perhaps because of them) the government workers' unions continued to give major emphasis to ideological issues and to engage mainly in political activity. Their prominence within the Japanese labor movement in general, especially in dealing directly with government, no doubt heightened the political involvement of organized labor in Japan. Usually secure in their job tenure, the leaders of these unions have been among the most vociferous in demanding social, political, and economic reform.

The various government unions early moved to federate among themselves to deal with the government *en bloc.* Among their first demands was the "democratization" of the government services, particularly the abolition of the then existing highly stratified civil service status system. In part, they have been successful in achieving this reform.

By January 1946, the union that had formed in the Agricultural and Forestry Ministry (one of the largest ministries in the central government and with major political influence) initiated the organization of an all-ministry union conference. Two months later, there was established a preparatory committee for a nationwide confederation of all central and local government civil servants, or the *Zenkankōrōkyō* (*Zenkoku Kankō Shokuin Rōdō Kumiai Kyōgikai*) with the avowed purpose of taking the lead in the entire labor movement and of cooperating with peasant groups (this was before land reform, and tenant-peasants also were forming unions) in building a "democratic" Japan. Included in the group were the postal workers, the national railway workers, and the civil servants in Agricultural and Forestry, Finance, Education, and Welfare Ministries and in the Audit Bureau, the Tokyo Municipal Government, the Central Weather Observatory, and the municipalities of Saitama Prefecture. Their demands partly reflected the failure of the Occupation to undertake the sweeping reforms of the government bureaucracy as it had of the military, *zaibatsu,* education system, and landlords. It was the *Zenkankōrōkyō,* adding demands for wage increases and price controls, that led a number of demonstrations as well as a one-day strike in the summer of 1946—a prelude to the general strike call of February 1, 1947.[56]

[56] The protests at that time were also directed at a proposal to include in the Labor Relations Adjustment Bill, then being considered by the Diet, a restriction of strikes among government workers and in vital industries.

Despite widespread affiliations, the response was far short of the goal of a complete federation of the public workers' unions. It became apparent that large sectors of these workers were unwilling to run the risk of defying superiors or upsetting traditional organizational arrangements in government operations. The *Zenkankōrōkyō* actually dissolved in September 1946 (after the Labor Relations Adjustment Law was passed) upon the withdrawal of the postal workers' union. However, a coordinating committee was retained with representatives participating from the national railways, postal workers, local government workers, and teachers as well as central government civil servants.

The next effort was to achieve federation only among the civil servants of the central government. In the fall of 1946, the *Zenkankō* (*Zenkankōchō Shokuin Rōdō Kumiai Renraku Kyōgikai*) was established, but the unions it attracted had only about eighty thousand in total membership. Now the emphasis was shifted to demands mainly of an economic nature: special wage bonuses, minimum wage guarantees, cash payment of wages, abolishment of income taxes, end of discrimination in government personnel administration, and the conclusion of written labor agreements. Combining political protest with these economic and trade-union demands, the *Zenkankō* spearheaded the formation of a general struggle committee for all union groups in the government. It was this committee that SCAP ordered dissolved as the fomenter of the general strike call of February 1, 1947.

Following the passage of the National Public Service Law in the fall of that year, the *Zenkankō* turned increasingly to the political objective of overthrowing the Cabinet. When the socialist-led government of Prime Minister Katayama refused to yield to embarrassing demands of this federation, the *Zenkankō* staged a demonstration on March 1, 1948, essentially in defiance of the law. SCAP promptly issued a warning of reprisal, only to provoke the *Zenkankō* leadership to further action. On July 23, 1948, General MacArthur ordered a ban upon the announced summer "struggle" of the *Zenkankō*. Actually, during these months, the rank-and-file support for *Zenkankō*'s agitation proved lukewarm. In the summer of 1948, defections began in protest against communist domination of the federation, and in December right and center groups began to form a new organization, launched in 1949 as the *Kankōrō* (*Nihon Kankōchō Rōdō Kumiai*), embracing the national railway workers' union, the teachers' union, and the postal workers along with the civil servants. It claimed 1.6 million members. The *Zenkankō* then began to wither, dissolving finally in June 1950, and its remnants, purged of communists in part by government and SCAP action, joined the *Kankōrō* in 1952.

Rejecting revolutionary ideology, the *Kankōrō* at first concentrated primarily upon improving the economic status of its members within the legal restrictions imposed upon the government workers' unions. At the same time, it resolved to combat the influence of both the extreme left and right. It was partly to protect themselves against the extremism of the *Zenkankō* that the *Kankōrō* unions accepted the limitation of selecting officers only from among employees within the government units that they organized. Nonetheless, the more moderate elements of the civil servant unions felt that *Kankōrō* was still too far to the left and formed their own federation, the *Nikkanrō* (*Nihon Kanchō Rōdō Kumiai Kyōgikai*), in January 1951 as a rival of *Kankōrō*.

By this time, in 1950, the newly formed *Sōhyō* resolved to combat totalitarianism of the right and left (also declaring its intention of joining the newly established International Confederation of Free Trade Unions). The *Kankōrō* unions individually joined *Sōhyō*, but the *Nikkanrō* held off partly because *Sōhyō* promoted industrial unionism exclusively and therefore hesitated to grant admission to the *Nikkanrō* as long as it remained a loose confederation of ministry and agency unions. However, resolution of this issue was reached in June 1953, with *Nikkanrō* entering *Kankōrō,* which now had been reorganized into three divisions: central government civil servants, local government civil servants, and public enterprise workers. Within this structure, it should be noted, the national railways union and the postal workers' union remained predominant.

Nonetheless, *Kankōrō,* although not affiliated as a body, was still an anomaly alongside the *Sōhyō* structure. As an intermediate body between the national unions and the central federation, it appeared to violate the concept of industrial unionism and labor movement solidarity. Also, the power of *Kankōrō* as a group overshadowed the private industry unions in the latter's influence within *Sōhyō*. *Kankōrō* had come to embrace about 2.5 million members, close to two-thirds of the entire *Sōhyō* membership. Its dominant position was apparent in the formation of *Sōhyō* policies and programs.[57] From about 1955

[57] The preponderant influence of the government workers' unions partly explains the withdrawal of the textile and seamen's unions from *Sōhyō* in 1954 to join with *Sōdōmei* in forming the *Zenrō Kaigi*. Later, *Dōmei* also furnished a home for dissident government workers' groups that had split off from the *Sōhyō* postal workers, national railway employees, and public school teachers.

on, *Sōhyō* leaders began to urge the dissolution of *Kankōrō* as a formal body and succeeded in having a resolution adopted to this effect at its convention in August 1957. Shortly thereafter, due to these pressures, the *Kankōrō* dissolved itself and urged its constituents to strengthen their direct affiliation with *Sōhyō*. Coordinating councils for central and local government workers' unions, however, have been continued within *Sōhyō*. (The most prominent for central government employers is the *Kōrōkyō*, made up of nine major public corporations and national enterprise unions.)

In contrast to the enterprise unions in private industry, many of which are weakly linked to national labor organizations, the government workers have provided greatest support for unity at the national level of the labor movement. But one result is that political and ideological emphasis of the movement—particularly through *Sōhyō*—remains intense. That this large group must deal with government agencies, of course, is a large factor in the situation. Demands for wage and benefit increases for government workers in most instances have had to be referred to the Diet and the Cabinet even though they have proceeded through the administrative machinery provided in the law. Unable to resort to strikes, the government unions employ a variety of harrassing tactics such as mass absenteeism, refusal of overtime, and even "law abiding" work stoppages, as well as participating in political demonstrations and campaigns for favored political candidates. Frequent retaliation by the conservative government has often intensified political counteraction by the unions. A notable example of this is found in the case of the public school teachers' union, or *Nikkyōso* (*Nihon Kyōshokuin Kumiai*), to which we now turn.

THE TEACHERS' UNION

Nikkyōso is the largest national white-collar union in Japan. With a membership of approximately six hundred thousand members, it is composed of public school instructors and is affiliated to *Sōhyō*. *Nikkyōso* virtually embraces all public school teachers except for some small splinter groups, primarily higher school teachers, some of which now are affiliated to *Dōmei*. In structure, *Nikkyōso* is a descendant of a ministry union in the sense that all public teachers were once civil servants under the Ministry of Education, although its formal organization is by prefecture. On the other hand, as a distinct professional group, the teachers' union is perhaps the closest equivalent in Japan to an occupational union.[58] The evolution of *Nikkyōso* is instructive because it epitomizes the role of the white-collar employee in the Japanese labor movement generally and in the public workers' unions in particular.[59]

It should be remembered that in launching Japan down the road of industrialization, the Meiji leaders gave universal primary education (along with universal military prescription) a vital and prominent role almost from the beginning. In 1872 the new government proclaimed the establishment of such an educational system, which within a decade was well on its way to fulfillment. The process of developing this educational system called for training large numbers of teachers who were especially subjected to government scrutiny as key conveyors of the values sought in Japan's modernization. As early as 1880, teachers were prohibited from engaging in any political activity and in 1893 were denied any right to speak publicly or have relationships with political parties except in regard to purely educational matters. The Ministry of Education exercised tight centralized control over the teachers, who were subject to all the rules of the central government bureaucracy. As civil servants, teachers were ranked at the lowest levels of the bureaucracy, subject to directives about their personal living habits as well as the subject matter and methods of instruction. As one author has pointed out, teachers were "on the first line of Japanese nationalism."

As noted earlier, in the pre–World War II labor movement, Japanese teachers, like other white-collar workers and civil servants, played a feeble role except to furnish some of the more prominent ideologists. At the end of World War I, some teachers protested to the government for an improvement of their economic status and an increase in their personal freedom—no doubt a reflection of both the inflation and the introduction of the new foreign ideologies at that time. In 1919 a teachers' union was organized among the elementary school teachers of Saitama Prefecture (near Tokyo) and actually participated in Japan's first May Day parade in 1920. However, it met with fierce government opposition, and, as salary improvements were granted, the union withered away, disappearing by 1928. There is evidence of further unionizing activity among teachers following

[58] Unionization of professional workers spread rapidly after the surrender in 1945. Important unions have been formed including journalists, radio and theater actors, doctors, and nurses as well as teachers.

[59] Materials in this section are based mainly on Nakayama, *op. cit.;* and *Nikkyōso Jūnenshi,* 1947-57 (Tokyo: Nihon Kyōshokuin Kumiai, 1958).

1930—mainly protests against lowered living standards in the Great Depression as the result of government pay cuts at the time. These were informal and often secret groups about which little is known. Following the Shanghai Incident in 1938, the government sternly prohibited organizing and agitating activity among teachers. Perhaps all that may be said of this period is that the goal of self-organization became firmly implanted among some teachers.

Teacher unionization surged immediately after the surrender. With the official blessings of SCAP (especially following the recommendation of the advisory American Education Commission in March 1946 that the organization of teachers was desirable), teachers' unions appeared everywhere. If the teachers had earlier been the "first line of Japanese nationalism," they had now become the first line of defense against the resurgence of totalitarianism.

During 1946 two national teacher union federations were formed. In February of that year, the communist-dominated *Zenkyō* (*Zen Nihon Kyōin Kumiai*) was established with prewar unionists as leaders. In December appeared the *Nikkyō* (*Nihon Kyōiku Kumiai*), socialist in orientation. Although *Zenkyō* urged a merger of the two, *Nikkyō* refused to have any communist connections, setting the stage for an ideological quarrel that has continued to plague the teachers' union to the present.

Changing its name to *Nikkyōrō* (*Zen Nihon Kyōin Rōdō Kumiai*) in May 1946, *Zenkyō* presented a set of demands to the Ministry of Education for immediate implementation: wage increases, menstrual leaves, school lunch programs, school building reconstruction, use of obsolete war factories for schools, recognition of teacher control of school administration, elimination of Education Ministry control over school curriculum, dissolution of wartime patriotic educational organizations, expulsion of "war criminals" from the education field, and establishment of a national education board on which teachers would have representation. Teacher control of schools was the key demand, and the union began to form committees to take over local school administration.

The Ministry of Education immediately condemned *Nikkyōrō* as failing to conform to the definition of a union under the new Trade Union Law because of its emphasis on a "political" program. Nonetheless, during 1946, school "control" was achieved in a number of communities—Ibaraki, Kanagawa, Tochigi, and Tokyo—even to the point of the union taking over the administration of entrance examinations and graduation exercises. The Tokyo union of *Nikkyōrō* at that time openly resolved to refuse any orders handed down by the Education Ministry or the Tokyo Municipal Education Bureau, to ignore supervision by the officially appointed school superintendents and inspectors, to compile the textbooks to be used, to administer a school lunch program, and to invite parents to join the union in carrying out school administration. Although none of these resolutions were actually carried out, the role which the teachers' unions believed they should assume in the reform of Japan was clear.

By 1947, SCAP, now increasingly concerned with the Cold War, withdrew its encouragement of teacher union activity. When at the end of 1946 *Nikkyōrō* established a centralizing coordinating body for teachers known as the *Zenkyōkyō* (*Zen Nihon Kyōin Kumiai Kyōgikai*) to carry out full-scale political campaigns in cooperation with other government workers, this body joined in with the central struggle committee to organize the call for the general strike of February 1, 1947. *Nikkyō*, in order to counteract the activity of *Nikkyōrō*, in March 1947 similarly formed *Kyōzenren* (*Kyōin Kumiai Zenkoku Remmei*), which particularly attracted middle school teachers and some elementary and vocational school teachers, who had become dissatisfied with the political aims of the *Zenkyōkyō*.

The general strike was called off; nonetheless, the Ministry of Education granted recognition to both the *Zenkyōkyō* and the *Kyōzenren* in the hope that orderly collective bargaining would restore stability to the education system. (This was prior to General MacArthur's order on July 22, 1948, forbidding civil servants to engage in collective bargaining or to strike—later written into law.) A number of agreements were made at both national and local levels. Their significance was of great importance because for the first time agreed-upon provisions were laid down governing minimum working conditions for teachers in public schools. Many of these provisions have remained in effect to the present despite the prohibition of collective bargaining by law after 1948.[60]

[60] Among these provisions were a 42-hour workweek; 20 paid free days for independent study; maternity leaves; three-year leaves of absence for tuberculosis recovery; joint teacher-supervisor administrative committees to consider transfers, promotion, discharge, salary adjustments, injury compensation, welfare benefits, and other personnel items; and freedom for the teacher to engage in political activity. Similar contracts were also made at the prefectural level, for by this time SCAP had forced reforms in the education system to provide for decentralization of control and administration. Still another provision of importance was assurance that full-time union officers would be retained with full pay in their respective civil service statuses, the number to be decided by joint consultation between union and administrators. Union representatives were also to be consulted on appointment, discharge, and transfer of superintendents and principals.

These contracts along with the decentralization of education required by the Occupation, marked a revolution in the running of the public schools of Japan, and as such were a tremendous victory for the teachers' unions. Not only had they gained full recognition and the right to participate in administration, but also they gained a considerable measure of influence over education policy. Moreover, despite their internal ideological differences, the agreements served to draw the two major federations, *Zenkyōkyō* and *Kyōzenren,* together. Their amalgamation on June 8, 1947, was further hastened with the enactment of the new legislation restricting the trade-union rights of the public workers. (They were joined also by a union of university professors.) Now not only did the teachers' unions feel it necessary to protect these contract gains but also they saw themselves as spokesmen in the effort to prevent any "reverse course" in the postwar reforms generally.

As early as June 1947, however, the central government began to hedge on living up to the terms of the agreements when the Deputy Minister of Education unilaterally ordered "retraining" courses for teachers without consulting the unions, who claimed that the order was a violation of the agreements. Then, in August, the Cabinet at that time declared it would refuse to maintain full-time union officers on civil service rolls with pay. It also asked for a decrease in the number of union officials. On a number of occasions also, the unions in Tokyo alleged that they were being ignored in the process of selecting school principals, despite an understanding in their case that the teachers themselves in these schools would "elect" these officials.[61]

Nikkyōso, the present-day Japan Teachers Union, was the result of the June 1947 merger. The objectives of *Nikkyōso* as stated in its inaugural meeting may be summarized as follows: the building of a New Japan through a system of democratic education; the installation of a system of six years of primary school and three years of secondary school as free education; guarantee of academic freedom and democracy; provision of a subsistence wage for teachers; price stabilization; observance of labor contracts; school construction; emancipation of the youth and women; guarantee of a "bright, healthy" culture; affiliation with the WFTU (this was prior to 1949); purge of war criminals and expulsion of fascists from education; and unity with all

[61] In the years immediately following Japan's surrender, school principals and superintendents often joined the new unions to assure their own status. It was not uncommon for the rank and file to "elect" them to positions they already held.

other workers and the ordinary citizenry. In this declaration, *Nikkyōso* primarily emphasized the social and political role of the new organization as the guardians of education, peace and democracy, academic freedom, and economic security.[62]

The Teachers Union has from the beginning been a thorn in the side of the conservative governments of Japan. Since 1948 it has been involved in a series of battles with the government.[63] When in July of that year General MacArthur issued a memorandum canceling the right of civil servants to bargain collectively (followed by a government ordinance to that effect), the Ministry of Education notified *Nikkyōso* that not only would collective bargaining cease but also union officers would no longer be retained on government payrolls and that strikers would be severely punished. All existing contracts were declared null and void. This meant in effect that *Nikkyōso* lost access to bargaining not only at the national level but also in prefectural and local jurisdictions.

While the communist-dominated *Sanbetsu* lodged a bitter protest against this action, the right-wing democratization groups (*Mindō*) now in control of *Nikkyōso,* along with the railway workers', the coal miners', and seamen's unions, issued a joint declaration indicating a willingness to accept the restrictions (although strongly expressing dissatisfaction) in order to preserve law and order.

Nonetheless, *Nikkyōso* was continually impelled to expend its energies on political activities. By 1948, after a series of expert studies, SCAP had prepared its plan to overhaul the public education system.

[62] As the union made up of white-collar intellectuals, who had had a highly specialized role in Japan's modernization, it has felt especially obliged to be the most outspoken labor organization on all aspects of the reform of Japan. *Nikkyōso's* role in *Sōhyō,* from this point of view, is a critical one. It has been of considerable importance for formulating the basic political position of *Sōhyō,* including the latter's stand on international affairs. Espousal of neutralism for Japan—including the end of American military bases on Japanese soil, abrogation of the United States–Japan security agreement, opposition to Japanese rearmament and amendment of the Peace Constitution, and conclusion of an over-all peace treaty with Russia and the United States (as well as a host of other issues such as recognition of Red China, return of Okinawa and the Bonins to Japan, cessation of atomic bomb tests, return of southern Sakhalin, etc.)—has been the keystone of this position.

[63] SCAP, too, had found some *Nikkyōso* activities undesirable, especially after the shift of American policy toward Japan. In April 1948, for example, SCAP officials forbade the Saitama prefectural branch of *Nikkyōso* to renew its labor contract with regard to salaries, work rules, and welfare and recreational activities, and gave notice that union officer salaries were to be paid out of union dues. When the union refused to comply, SCAP officials ordered an election of new officers at this union branch.

In July 1948, the Board of Education Act was adopted providing for local autonomy in the schools, the end of Education Ministry control, and the local election of school boards—to mention only the most relevant items. The original proposal sought to prohibit teachers from being elected to these boards, but *Nikkyōso* pressure on the Diet succeeded in changing the proposal to permit teachers to resign from their posts as teachers upon becoming candidates for school board officers. The first local board elections were held throughout the nation in October 1948, and *Nikkyōso* mustered all its resources to elect its own candidates. Out of a total of 1,566 office seekers, about 25 per cent were former teachers, and a majority of them were elected. Elections such as this have given considerable leverage to *Nikkyōso* for continuing to influence the educational system, as well as for maintaining the conditions of employment for teachers earlier agreed upon.

Since 1948 there has been a concerted effort by the government to reduce or eliminate *Nikkyōso's* influence in the operation of the school system. A concerted campaign to root out communists in 1949-50 (which came close to matching the earlier purge of ultranationalists) has already been mentioned—a primary target was (and continues to be) the teachers' unions. Government, as well as SCAP, officials also insisted that there be a minimum of "teaching" of ideologies such as socialism and communism—a problem complicated by the introduction of a new social studies curriculum to replace the teaching of traditional Japanese ethics. But of greater long-run importance has been the incessant campaign by the government, especially the Ministry of Education, to discredit *Nikkyōso* as subversive of cherished Japanese traditions. In self-defense, *Nikkyōso* sought allies, joining the *Kankōrō* in 1948 and *Sōhyō* in 1950 and affiliating with the new ICFTU (only to withdraw a few years later).

Throughout the 1950's government education policy stimulated the teachers' unions to greater and greater political involvement. A series of bills introduced at the Diet culminated in 1954 in a proposal to restrict teacher political activity by changing their status from local to central government civil servants. In protest, *Nikkyōso* sponsored a series of hunger strikes and school closings as well as petitioning demonstrations at the Diet (these were to become familiar tactics in all of the skirmishes between *Nikkyōso* and the government). The bill in question failed to pass, although the campaign had its divisive effects within the union. Also, in 1954 the government established a committee for "neutralism in education," following a highly publicized incident in which a school child's diary revealed that his teacher had been instructing him and his classmates to treat the Americans and South Koreans as the aggressors in the Korean War. *Nikkyōso*'s response to this committee was to invite parents to the schools, organize protest meetings, and conduct one-day school closings. Still another bill in the same year forbade teachers to run for school boards in the localities in which they taught and provided a clearer prohibition against teachers engaging in political activity and offering "political" education. This legislation was adopted in the face of widespread *Nikkyōso*-sponsored protests, although the union was successful in reducing the proposed punishment for offenses to a very minimum.

Then in 1956, a battle ensued when the government proposed a revision of the Education Board Law to eliminate local school board elections entirely and to provide for appointment of local school board members by the elected prefectural governors. This move, aimed so clearly at reversing the earlier reform principle of decentralization, led to an agonizing series of reprisals and counter-reprisals between government and union. Stormy Diet sessions, street protests, and the like fanned the issue. The bill, however, was adopted, forcing *Nikkyōso* to emphasize other means to influence educational and political policy, such as the direct election of Diet candidates and increased support for the opposition parties. Among the most major recent items of controversy has been the enactment of a law subjecting public school teachers to merit rating under the supervision of the Ministry of Education—an attempt, in essence, to wrest control of teacher personnel administration completely away from the *Nikkyōso* unions. Such a merit-rating system was finally adopted in 1960 after considerable controversy with incidents bordering on violence.[64]

Until Japan's ratification of ILO Convention 87, the government refused to accord recognition to *Nikkyōso* or its constituent units on the grounds that they did not constitute legitimate trade-union bodies but were in fact political instruments. Much of the trade-union movement—especially *Sōhyō*—had perceived this attitude as general antiunionism on the part of the government. The example of *Nikkyōso* impels other *Sōhyō* affiliates and other unions to emphasize political activity—at least as a matter of self-defense. The Teachers Union encapsulates a basic issue in Japan's postwar trade unionism: whether or not the labor movement is to be permitted to assume a major role in the reformation of traditional Japanese society.

[64] Still other issues have concerned Ministry of Education actions to supervise textbook revisions and to control school curricula.

WHITE-COLLAR UNIONISTS AND THE GENERAL LABOR MOVEMENT

It is clear from the foregoing materials that white-collar unionization has had a pervasive effect upon the postwar labor movement of Japan in general. At two levels, the white-collar unionists have become an integral part of the labor movement: in the role they play within the combined enterprise unions, and in the influence of the pure white-collar national unions, such as that of the teachers, upon the major national labor federations. In *Sōhyō,* particularly, the prominent role of the *Kankōrō* group provided a heavy impress of white-collar leadership.

Nonetheless, certain sizable organized white-collar groups have wavered in their support for or have refused to become part of the general labor movement. The bank employees, with more than 140,000 members, for example, in the early 1950's joined *Sōhyō,* but internal divisions centering on differences between city and rural banks led to a split within this union in the middle 1950's. The two unions that emerged disaffiliated with the national center and have remained "neutral." Similarly, there has been little success in gaining the affiliation of the department store workers' union with more than forty thousand members (although the private railway union, affiliated to *Sōhyō,* claims twenty thousand department store clerks in its membership), of the fifty-thousand-member federation of life insurance workers' union, or the one hundred thirty-five-thousand-member life insurance brokers' union. A number of other smaller national white-collar unions in banking, insurance, broadcasting, movie and theatre fields have continued to remain neutral—accounting for as many as 85,000 members in all.[65] The total white-collar membership in all the unaffiliated unions probably exceeds 420,000. While there has been some attempt to coordinate the activity of many of these unions through the independent *Chūritsu Sōren,* the unions have by and large remained tied to their enterprise bases. *Sōhyō* and *Dōmei,* of course, have maintained a continuous rivalry to attract these groups as affiliates. Moreover, the threat of affiliation to a national center by a neutral union is often used as a bargaining weapon at the enterprise level.

Despite restlessness among white-collar unionists who are attached to combined enterprise unions or to the national federations, the factors binding the bulk of the white-collar unionists to the gen-

[65] *Year Book of Labor Statistics 1963* (Tokyo: Ministry of Labor, 1965).

eral labor movement remain strong. First, much of the leadership at both enterprise and national levels has been drawn from white-collar ranks. Second, the union movement has provided for the first time in Japanese history a legitimate outlet for political expression by the intellectual white-collar workers, who also become spokesmen for manualists. Unions have been the stepping stone for many leaders directly into politics. Third, paradoxically, the presence of white-collar unionists, especially in the combined enterprise unions, has helped to preserve the compartmentalization of Japanese industrial society whereby traditional identifications with one's employing entity may be maintained along with the movement for social reform. This has no doubt preserved the elite quality long associated with white-collar employment.

Under these conditions in the Japanese context, it is not likely that a distinct and separate white-collar union movement of large proportions will emerge in the foreseeable future. On the other hand, the problems that the present position of the white-collar unionists create for the general labor movement are many. With the present organizational structure, the movement is easily torn by divisions. In turn, there is likely to be an absorption of energies in futile political activity led by white-collar government workers' unions, while collective bargaining and economic activity remain narrowly confined to the enterprise base, unable to solve satisfactorily many of the white-collar workers' problems. Also, as the economic development of Japan continues to unfold, surely white-collar groups will expand and become increasingly torn between middle class aspirations and loyalty to trade unionism.

Yet, the prospects for a continued alliance between white-collar and blue-collar unionists in Japan seems strong, although it may be predicted that years of turmoil and realignment lie ahead. The present alignment has been a singular product of Japanese economic and political history. On the one hand, the integration of the white- and blue-collar membership has taken place within the conservative context of enterprise unionism—an integration that could be achieved because of the very loose and divided structure of the whole labor movement itself. On the other hand, integration is also the product of the demand for radical reform of Japanese society—led by the white-collar unionists especially in government employ. Japan's modern history has been just such a delicate blend of conservatism and radicalism.

GLOSSARY

bantō—Aministrative head, manager, or chief clerk.

Chūritsu Sōren—Federation of Independent Unions (post–World War II).

Dōmei—*See* Dōmei Kaigi.
Dōmei Kaigi, or Nihon Rōdō Kumiai Dōmei Kaigi—Japanese Confederation of Labor (post–World War II). *See* Zenrō Kaigi.

habatsu—Cliques or ingroups.
hanchō—Shop or gang boss.
Hōkyūsha Kumiai—Salaried Men's Union (1919-23).

jōshi-buka—Superior-subordinate relationship.

kakarichō—Subsection chief in a company.
kakariin—Assistant or apprentice clerk.
Kankōrō, or Nihon Kankōchō Rōdō Kumiai—Unions of public corporation employees and civil servants (1949-57).
"kanson mimpi"—"Revere the official, despise the common people"—a traditional Japanese slogan.
kōin—Manual or factory worker.
Kōrōkyō—Coordinating council of central government employees in public corporation and national enterprise unions.
Kyōchōkai—Harmonization Society (pre–World War II).
Kyōin Kumiai Zenkoku Remmei—*See* Kyōzenren.
Kyōzenren, or Kyōin Kumiai Zenkoku Remmei—Association of socialist-oriented teachers' unions (1947). *See* Nikkyō.

Mindō—Democratization movements within communist-dominated Sanbetsu and affiliated and other leftist unions (late 1940's).

Nihon Kaiin Kumiai—Japan Seamen's Union (1921——).
Nihon Kaiin Kyōkai—Japan Maritime Officers' Association (founded 1896).
Nihon Kanchō Rōdō Kumiai Kyōgikai—*See* Nikkanrō.
Nihon Kankōchō Rōdō Kumiai—*See Kankōrō.*
Nihon Kyōiku Kumiai—*See* Nikkyō.
Nihon Kyōshokuin Kumiai—*See* Nikkyōso.
Nihon Rōdō Kumiai Dōmei Kaigi—*See* Dōmei Kaigi.
Nihon Rōdō Kumiai Sōdōmei—*See* Sōdōmei.
Nihon Rōdō Kumiai Sōhyōgikai—*See* Sōhyō.
Nikkanrō, or Nihon Kanchō Rōdō Kumiai Kyōgikai—Federation of Japanese civil servants' unions (1951-53).
Nikkyō, or Nihon Kyōiku Kumiai—Socialist-inclined teachers' union (1946-47).
Nikkyōrō, or Zen Nihon Kyōin Rōdō Kumiai—Communist-dominated teachers' union (1946-47).
Nikkyōso, or Nihon Kyōshokuin Kumiai—Japan Teachers Union (1947——).
Nippon Hōkyū Seikatsusha Kumiai Hyōgikai—Japan Salary Men's Union Federation (1926-28).

Nippon Hōkyū Seikatsusha Kumiai Remmei—*See* Nippon Hōkyū Seikatsusha Kumiai Hyōgikai.
Nippon Kyōin Kumiai Keimeikai—First-known union of Japanese public school teachers (World War I).
Nippon Rōdō Kumiai Hyōgikai—Communist-inclined Japanese Council of Labor Unions (1920's).

oyabun—Boss or father-role. *See* oyabun-kobun.
oyabun-kobun—Parent-child relationship.

Rōnōtō—Communist-inclined Labor Farmer Party (1920's).

Sampō, or Sangyō Hōkokukai—Government-sponsored wartime labor front.
Sanbetsu, or Zen Nihon Sangyōbetsu Rōdō Kumiai Kaigi—Communist-dominated National Congress of Industrial Unions (post–World War II).
Sangyō Hōkokukai—*See* Sampō.
shain—Company man or member.
Shakai Minshutō—Social Democrat Party (1920's).
Shinsanbetsu, or Zenkoku Sangyōbetsu Rōdō Kumiai Rengō—National Federation of Industrial Organizations (post–World War II).
shokuin—Staff member or white-collar employee.
Sōdōmei, or Nihon Rōdō Kumiai Sōdōmei—Moderate socialist Japan Federation of Labor (founded World War I).
Sōhyō, or Nihon Rōdō Kumiai Sōhyōgikai—General Council of Trade Unions of Japan (post–World War II).

zaibatsu—Commercial, financial, and industrial cliques originally organized around family groupings.
Zenkankōrōkyō, or Zenkoku Kankō Shokuin Rōdō Kumiai Kyōgikai—National confederation of local and central government civil servants' unions (early postwar).
Zenkankō, or Zenkankōchō Shokuin Rōdō Kumiai Renkaku Kyōgikai—Federation of central government civil servants (early postwar, dissolved 1950).
Zenkankōchō Shokuin Rōdō Kumiai Renkaku Kyōgikai—*See* Zenkankō.
Zenkoku Kankō Shokuin Rōdō Kumiai Kyōgikai—*See* Zenkankōrōkyō.
Zenkoku Sangyōbetsu Rōdō Kumiai Rengō—*See* Shinsanbetsu.
Zenkoku Taishūtō—Moderate leftist National Mass Party (1920's).
Zenkyō, or Zen Nihon Kyōin Kumiai—Communist-dominated teachers' union (1946). *See* Nikkyōrō.
Zenkyōkyō, or Zen Nihon Kyōin Kumiai Kyōgikai—Communist-dominated coordinating council for teachers' unions (1946-47). *See* Nikkyōrō.
Zen Nihon Kyōin Kumiai Kyōgikai—*See* Zenkyōkyō.
Zen Nihon Kyōin Rōdō Kumiai—*See* Nikkyōrō.
Zen Nihon Kyōin Kumiai—*See* Zenkyō.
Zen Nihon Rōdō Kumiai Kaigi—*See* Zenrō Kaigi.
Zen Nihon Sangyōbetsu Rōdō Kumiai Kaigi—*See* Sanbetsu.
Zenrō Kaigi, or Zen Nihon Rōdō Kumiai Kaigi—Japanese Trade Union Congress (post–World War II). *See* Dōmei Kaigi.

VII

WHITE-COLLAR UNIONISM IN SWEDEN

BY ARNE H. NILSTEIN *

INTRODUCTION

Sweden, with a population of about 7.5 million people, has a labor force of 3.6 million of which close to 20 per cent are employers and upwards of 80 per cent employees. Five-eighths of the employees are blue-collar workers and three-eighths have white-collar jobs. Although the dividing line between blue- and white-collar workers is difficult to identify, tradition and practice has planted it deep in popular consciousness and it does mark the separation of the groups into different unions. Traditionally, white-collar workers enjoyed greater job security, more favorable working conditions, and far better fringe benefits, but social legislation enacted after World War II diminished some of these differences by introducing statutory three-weeks' vacations for all workers, general compulsory health insurance, and comprehensive social security.

The percentage of organization among blue-collar workers is more than 80 per cent; in mining and manufacturing the percentage is above 90. Among white-collar workers, not counting those in managerial positions, it is close to 70 per cent.

Sweden's blue-collar workers are organized in the Trade Union

* The author expresses his thanks to Sylvia von Eltz for her assistance in editing this essay.

Federation (LO), which has 1.5 million members in 42 affiliates. Some central and local government white-collar workers in lower income brackets belong to LO affiliates, and other white-collar groups in retail trade are also affiliated with LO.

The Central Organization of Salaried Employees (TCO) with 410,000 members in 36 affiliates is Sweden's largest white-collar federation. Thirty-one per cent of its 410,000 members are employed in the central government, 14 per cent in local government, and 55 per cent in private employment. Most of its affiliates are organized "by industry," so that one union representing white-collar workers in all positions and wage brackets confronts one employer or organization of employers. There are, however, some important "craft" unions within the federation.

The Swedish Professional Association (SACO) organizes college graduates and persons with a similar professional standing "by crafts." In addition to forty thousand employees, its membership includes fifteen thousand self-employed persons and students. Sixty per cent of the members are in central government service, 21 per cent in local government, and 19 per cent in private employment.

Jurisdictional disputes between affiliates of the same federation are rare, and settlements reached with the cooperation of the federation or established by its decision are respected. Raiding is unknown.

Relations between LO, established in 1898, and TCO, established in 1944 through a merger of an organization of public employees and one of private employees, are basically cordial and friendly. LO favored the organization of white-collar workers in a separate federation. The white-collar unions are politically neutral while LO supports the Social Democratic Party. A joint LO-TCO committee settles jurisdictional disputes between affiliates; such disputes have been limited in number and scope.

SACO, established in 1947, claims that it champions the special interests of college graduates. TCO, however, felt that these groups should join TCO rather than isolating themselves, and after about ten years of friction, TCO-SACO relations are now fairly cordial though cool.

Industrial relations in Sweden are peaceful in blue- and white-collar fields alike. Employers have accepted the unions as necessary and respected partners, and, as a result, labor and management regulate their mutual relations themselves, with the government observing a hands-off policy demanded by both.

Who Is a White-Collar Worker?

The concept "white-collar worker" or "salaried employee" has been under discussion ever since the first national white-collar worker unions were established in Sweden. Sometimes the dividing line between white- and blue-collar workers has been identified with the nature of the work: intellectual work of white-collar workers, manual work of blue-collar workers. Others saw a fundamental difference in the nature and terms of employment, drawing general conclusions from the fact that the majority of white-collar workers held preponderantly intellectual jobs, traditionally received monthly salaries, and were entitled to certain fringe benefits such as pay during periods of sickness, often some kind of pension, and observance of termination periods in case of discharge. Blue-collar workers rarely enjoyed similar terms. However, large groups of white-collar workers do routine work, and, on the other hand, some blue-collar workers have markedly intellectual job assignments. Also, there are wage earners who, though working under the same terms of employment as white-collar workers, are generally not regarded as white-collar workers. These criteria have proved as useless in formulating a definition as the requirement of a certain amount of education for a job.

Sociological analysis of the historical origins of white-collar jobs aided in the formulation of another definition. This approach led to the conclusion that the social position and work function of white-collar workers had their origins in the managerial functions of earlier times. The entrepreneur, originally a craftsman, then performed all work functions himself. The function he first ceded to others was that of production (working or shaping the material, transporting it). The entrepreneur directed and supervised this work; he planned and experimented, received orders, and sold the finished products. However, later on these functions also were performed by other persons, frequently members of the entrepreneur's family, and they became positions of trust. When these functions were transferred to hired personnel, the employees performing them held responsible positions which brought them into close contact with the entrepreneur and his family, frequently as members of his household, but above all identified with his way of thinking. As the enterprise grew in size, the white-collar staff increased and the functions originally performed by these employees—who were members of the entrepreneur's family, as it were—were divided among an ever larger group of employees whose social position was still characterized by the fact that they were performing managerial functions. These people felt that they belonged to the same class as their employer; in addition they had a chance for careers through gradual promotion to positions requiring increased qualifications.

In the popular view, the groups of employees performing second-level managerial work—supervisory and technical industrial work, administrative work and accounting, commercial and distributive work inside and outside shops and warehouses—came to hold an intermediate position between the entrepreneur and the production workers.

A similar explanation applied to the white-collar workers in central and local government service, whose special responsibility as compared with that of other groups of employees in public service gave them a special position of trust in relation to the public employer.

Croner developed and systematized the theory that white-collar workers are employees who perform certain functions—supervisory, constructive (or analyzing), administrative, and mercantile—which were originally delegated to them by the employer,[1] and he declares that as a social class they hold a special position in society. Trade unionism among white-collar workers in Sweden is not, however, founded on any definition of this kind. Rather, the unions have found it useful for their statistics and other purposes to establish an occupational classification system defining the different groups within the organizations.

Any attempt at illustrating the development and size of the white-collar worker group must be based on official statistics, although the statistics, in turn, are based on a classification system which has been undergoing change and which differs in some respects from a classification based on systematic theoretical principles as well as from one conforming with popular notions. In the historical description of the development of the white-collar worker group we are using census statistics, adjusted in some respects to changes in the system of classification which have been introduced. The classification used in the census of 1950 has been adopted as standard for the purpose of the present description. This means that in distinguishing between entrepreneurs and white-collar workers, persons are considered white-collar workers who in their capacity as employees in executive posi-

[1] F. Croner, *Tjänstemannakåren i det moderna samhället* (*The White-Collar Workers in Modern Society*) (Uppsala, 1951). Also the same author's "Salaried Employers in Modern Industry," *International Labour Review*, XLIV (February 1954), 97-110.

tions administer an enterprise (managers). In establishing a distinction between white-collar workers and blue-collar workers, the nature of the work performed is decisive. In addition, consideration has been given to education, whether the work involves the right to give orders to other employees, and to the affiliation of the occupational group concerned with a white- or blue-collar trade union.

The following groups of employees are among those classified as white-collar workers:

- office workers
- receptionists, telephone operators
- technical personnel
- foremen and supervisors in all industries (including transportation, commerce, etc.) as well as in government service
- retail clerks
- bank and insurance employees
- civil servants
- police and firemen
- commissioned, warrant, and noncommissioned officers in the armed forces
- doctors, dentists, and nurses
- teachers of all categories

The Numerical Growth of White-Collar Workers

The volume of work functions commonly attributed to white-collar workers has continuously increased in modern society. This increase has been a precondition and a consequence of technical, economic, and social progress. Four different processes form its component parts: industrialization, rationalization, commercialization, and socialization, and all four are significant in an analysis of the growth of the white-collar worker group.

Industrialization involved a structural change of the national economy, which caused agriculture to recede in favor of the various city trades in which the number and scope of white-collar worker functions are great. The development can be illustrated by a study of the distribution of the population among the main fields of economic activity.

Table 1 shows the relative growth of the city trades, to begin with in the field of industry and crafts and later with increasing speed in commerce, communications-transportation, public administration, and professions, which reflects commercialization and socialization. Commercialization is a result of the growing demands on the distribution, communication, and transportation systems, inherent in the higher production of an industrialized society; the need for services—banking and insurance, forwarding of goods, etc.—increases because of the rising demand for services in connection with production and, in part, because of the increased purchasing power of the population. Socialization in this context is the process by which society claims a greater

Table 1. Distribution of Population According to Economic Activities, in Per Cent of Total Population

Year	*Total Population in 1,000*	*Agriculture Horticulture Forestry Fishing*	*Industry Crafts*	*Commerce Communications Transportation*	*Public Administration Professions*
1870	4.169	72	15	5	8
1880	4.566	68	18	7	7
1890	4.785	62	22	9	7
1900	5.136	55	28	10	7
1910	5.522	49	32	13	6
1920	5.904	44	35	15	6
1930	6.142	39	36	18	7
1940	6.371	34	38	20	8
1945	6.674	30	40	21	9
1950	7.042	24	43	23	10
1960 [a]	7.495	19	45	25	11

[a] The percentages for 1960 are estimates.

share of the total resources for the satisfaction of certain collective needs, many of which belong to the service area. These public services include, for instance, the expansion of education, social insurance, and public welfare.

In the city trades, the percentage of white-collar functions is considerably higher than in agriculture and other rural occupations. (See Table 2.)

The table also shows that the percentage of white-collar workers is higher in commerce and communications than in industry and crafts, and higher still in public administration and professions. Furthermore, it indicates that the percentage of white-collar workers in all fields of economic activity has gradually increased. This rationalization which has taken place in all fields of activity implies the gradual introduction of increasingly efficient methods of production and work—a systematization and standardization of work processes which has caused the workers' functions in production to be replaced by machine operation and white-collar functions.

The figures indicating the growth of the proportion of white-collar workers in the different fields are concurrently a measure of the structural changes which occurred within them. Activities have shifted

Table 2. White-Collar Workers as a Proportion of the Labor Force, in Per Cent

Year	*Agriculture Horticulture Forestry Fishing*	*Industry Crafts*	*Commerce Communications Transportation*	*Public Administration Professions*	*Total*
1930	2	9	36	29	13
1940	3	11	41	42	20
1950	4	15	48	59	27
1960	5	23	59	58	35

from fields with low percentages of white-collar workers to fields with high percentages and from small to large enterprises, in which the percentage of white-collar workers is usually greater.

The aggregate effect of these processes is an increase in the total number of white-collar workers, as shown in Table 3.

Table 3. Number of White-Collar Workers, 1920-60

	In 1,000					*Percentages of the Gainfully Occupied*		
Year	*Agriculture Horticulture Forestry Fishing*	*Industry Crafts*	*Commerce Communications Transportation*	*Public Administration Professions*	*Total*	*Self-employed*	*White-Collar Workers*	*Blue-Collar Workers*
1920	11	50	138	87	286	19	11	70
1930	15	79	184	114	392	21	13	66
1940	23	112	267	201	603	20	20	60
1950	25	192	360	269	843	19	27	54
1960	23	333	401	377	1134	14	35	51

THE HISTORY OF WHITE-COLLAR ORGANIZATION

Union of White-Collar Workers

In Sweden, as in other countries, the advent of industrialism in the nineteenth century brought forth a working class which was highly dependent on the employers. Conditions and terms of work were poor, reflecting a conflict of interests between the employers and their employees in which the latter were the weaker party. By organizing into trade unions, the different groups of workers sought to achieve a more favorable balance of power in relation to the employers in order to improve their terms of employment. Responding to the establishment of trade unions, the employers set up employer organizations in order to strengthen their position in relation to the organized workers. This process occurred in Sweden at the end of the nineteenth and the beginning of the twentieth centuries. A trend toward cooperation among the different trade unions resulted in the creation of the Confederation of Swedish Trade Unions (LO) in 1898. The Swedish Employers' Confederation (SAF) was established in 1902.

Unlike the LO and SAF, the white-collar workers' central organization came into being rather late, although the white-collar workers' movement toward organization has its roots in a remote past. Several existing white-collar unions can trace their origin back to occupational associations which were related to the guilds. As early as 1848 the Governor of Stockholm authorized the constitution of the Marine Engineers' Society. Later, several similar associations were formed by other groups: bank clerks, railroad employees, foremen, ship captains and mates, and office clerks.

These associations dealt with occupational interests and engaged in social relief activities—relief funds, health insurance, and the like—to aid members and their families in emergencies. To a large extent they merely promoted social intercourse. In the beginning, the associations did not concern themselves with their members' interests in relation to employers. It was a natural development, however, that discussions at the meetings arranged by the associations eventually turned to problems of this kind. The more homogeneous an association was, the greater was its inclination to include employer-employee relations in its program. The organizations strictly limited to employees with specific qualifications thus were the first to engage in trade-union activities. This was done in the first decade of the twentieth century. The Swedish Marine Engineer Officers' Union was established in 1906, and in the same year its right to organize and to negotiate was recognized in a collective agreement by the employers. The Union of Swedish Pharmacists had been established earlier, in 1903, but achieved recognition of collective bargaining rights only in 1918 after threatening a walkout. The Swedish Ship Officers' Association was formed in 1907, but obtained collective bargaining rights only in 1914 after resorting to a strike.

The journalists were another homogeneous group that engaged early in trade unionism. The Swedish Federation of Journalists was formed in 1901, but had to wait until 1916 to conclude its first collective agreement which laid down rules for the individual employment contracts. One of the leaders of the Journalists' Association, who was editor of the Confederation of Trade Unions' periodical, advanced a proposal for the establishment of a central organization of white-collar unions in the early 1920's. The proposal failed, but the proponent continued to work for his idea in various ways and took an active part in efforts at the end of the 1920's which resulted in a white-collar federation.

The Swedish Bank Employees Union of 1887 was quite successful in dealing with the serious after-effects of World War I on the bank employees; its actions brought it to the forefront among the white-collar unions in the early 1920's. The proposal failed, but the pro-white-collar workers' unions emanated to a large extent from this union.

Foremen had witnessed the blue-collar workers' drive for organization at close quarters, but a national foremen's organization was not established until 1928.

Other categories of white-collar workers, such as the various groups in commerce and industry, lacked specific professional features. Therefore, the idea of unionization took time to mature. The precursor of today's Swedish Union of Clerical and Technical Employees in Industry was established at the end of the 1920's. One reason for the initial slowness of organization in industry was the dispersion of the white-collar workers among a relatively large number of enterprises and localities, and the considerable differences in terms of employment, particularly of salaries and fringe benefits, among enterprises.

Similar conditions prevailed in other fields, for example, in commerce. Retail clerks and warehouse workers, it is true, formed a union affiliated with LO in 1907. Although certain groups of office workers joined this organization, many kept aloof from it and formed clerks' societies of a social nature. These societies established a white-collar union, the Swedish Union of Commercial Employees, as late as 1937.

Federation of White-Collar Unions

As previously mentioned, a proposal for a federation of white-collar unions was made in the early 1920's, but no action was taken at that time. Subsequently, in the middle of the decade, unemployment stimulated the formation of a committee—the White-Collar Unions' Committee on Unemployment—to handle questions of common interest. Next, the White-Collar Unions' Pensions Committee was established to seek an acceptable solution to the problems created by postwar inflation, which had greatly reduced the value of the assets of the old pension funds.

It is characteristic that cooperation focused on various problems of job and income security rather than on salaries. This cooperation proved fruitful in making clear to the various groups of white-collar workers that they had important interests in common, and in 1929, a committee was appointed to examine the possibility of establishing a central organization (or federation). Such an organization, *De anställdas central-organisation* (DACO), i.e., the Salaried Employees' Central Organization, was formed in 1931. Originally, DACO comprised nine employee unions with a total membership of about twenty thousand, including bank employees, foremen, and white-collar workers in industry and in commerce. In many respects DACO was modeled on LO. The editor of the LO periodical, a man prominent in its leadership, took an active part in the establishment of DACO in his capacity as member and president of the Journalists' Association. His activities implied some guarantee of LO's taking a favorable view of DACO.

DACO's primary task was to create favorable conditions for an effective organization drive. The central organization energetically promoted unionization in fields where the employees were not yet organized or where they were divided among several organizations which were unable to champion their members' interests effectively. Several new unions were formed under DACO's auspices.

Another task for DACO was to obtain statutory rights of organization and collective bargaining for white-collar workers. Certain white-collar groups had been able to secure recognition of these rights by collective contract, as the blue-collar workers had done before them, but for other groups legislation bestowing these rights was a prerequisite for organization. In 1936 a law on the Right of Association and Collective Bargaining was enacted, which was the starting point for a consolidation of the white-collar unions. The law broke employers' resistance to organization among white-collar workers and at the same time provided psychological impetus for the enlistment of new members in the unions.

DACO concurrently shouldered the task of public relations with the government and the general public, spreading propaganda and disseminating information about the white-collar workers' aims and interests.

Through a collateral organization—the Salaried Employees' Educational Association (TBV), sponsored jointly by DACO and its affiliates—white-collar workers were enabled and encouraged to study subjects related to trade unionism, for example, economics and law, as well as liberal arts, in order to improve their general education and, in addition, their qualifications for union leadership.

DACO's affiliates organized privately employed white-collar workers only (*anställda,* i.e., private employees as distinct from public employees). Certain groups of publicly employed white-collar workers (*tjänstemän*) belonged to societies and associations which bore some resemblance to unions, and some of these associations were approached at an early stage with proposals for the establishment of a central organization which would comprise privately employed white-collar workers as well as public employees. The plan had to be abandoned because the public employees were not interested.

The 1936 Act on the Right of Association and Collective Bargaining did not apply to public employees. In 1937, a special decree extended similar rights to employees of the central government. This greatly facilitated efforts to organize them, and in the same year a central organization of unions of white-collar workers in central and local government service was established. A law ensuring municipal workers the right to negotiate was enacted in 1940.

The new central organization, founded in 1937, was called the Public Employees' Central Organization (TCO). It consisted originally of eight unions which organized elementary school teachers, municipal employees, warrant officers and noncommissioned officers, civil employees in the defense establishment, police, and employees of the social welfare local administration, with a total membership of forty thousand.

Even while the TCO was being formed, hope was expressed that the two central organizations would cooperate, and as early as 1937 a joint cooperation committee was established. Its task was to settle jurisdictional disputes, to discuss questions of common interest, and to examine possibilities of closer organizational ties between the two organizations.

The committee limited its activities to *ad hoc* cooperation and did not consider a possible merger of DACO and TCO. However, the idea of a merger was under review in the early 1940's in anticipation of the problems which could be expected to arise in the labor market as a result of World War II. Eventually, DACO and TCO merged in 1944 to form a new central organization, *Tjänstemännens Central Organisation* (TCO), which is usually translated "The Central Organization of Salaried Employees." After the merger, TCO had 36 affiliates with a total of 175,000 members.

It is interesting to note that the Swedish word *tjänstemän* which earlier was used only for white-collar workers in government service (and in banking) now applies to white-collar workers in public as well as in private employment; the latter were previously called *anställda.* This change in terminology results from the merger of DACO and the earlier TCO.

In addition to the organizations which affiliated with DACO and TCO, other categories of white-collar workers are organized according to different principles. Before TCO was formed, large groups of white-collar workers in certain central and local governmental services, who performed work requiring fewer qualifications, joined unions affiliated with LO; their successors still cooperate with blue-collar workers. These groups include white-collar workers in government-owned and -operated utilities and enterprises, e.g., railroads, telecommunication, the postal service. The employees of each of these utilities formed separate unions, which cooperate within a special "cartel" inside LO. Retail clerks and office clerks of warehouses and other branches in commerce also formed a union affiliated with LO. White-collar workers in the retail section of the cooperative movement belong to this union. Those in the cooperatively owned industries, however, belong to TCO. Musicians are affiliated with LO but actors are in TCO. Certain groups of high-ranking civil servants did not join TCO, but have a separate central organization of their own called *Statstjänstemännens Riksförbund* (SR—National Federation of Civil Servants). Some minor groups of white-collar workers are entirely independent.

During the 1930's and 1940's, college graduates faced difficulties in finding jobs, and in the early 1940's a number of associations were established to champion the interests of young college graduates entering gainful occupation. These associations established a cooperation committee, which in 1947 was transformed into a central organization with affiliates organizing different groups of professionals. *Sveriges*

Akademikers Central Organisation (SACO), the Swedish Confederation of Professional Associations, consisted at the outset of 15 unions with fifteen thousand members.

PRESENT STATUS OF UNIONIZATION OF WHITE-COLLAR WORKERS

The Statistical Picture of Sweden's Organized White-Collar Workers

Sweden's white-collar workers are organized mainly in the four federations previously described.

TCO comprised in 1961 about 410,000 white-collar workers organized in 36 affiliates. Table 4 shows the affiliates and their members by classes of employers. (By 1964 TCO membership had risen to 489,000.)

Table 4. White-Collar Unions in TCO According to Types of Employers [a]

Employers	*Number of TCO Affiliates*	*With Members (Male and Female) in 1,000*	*in Per Cent*	*Female Members in 1,000*	*in Per Cent*
Central government	17	116	28	52	33
Local government	4	74	18	45	28
Private employers	15	220	54	63	39
All employers	36	410	100	160	100

[a] The unions are here classified according to the field in which the majority of their members are employed. For instance, some of the unions here classified as organizing white-collar workers in private employment also have members employed by central and local government. This is true also of the data in the following pages. Of the total members in the TCO unions, 31 per cent were in central government service, 14 per cent in local government service, and 55 per cent in private service.

Some TCO affiliates are "vertical," i.e., they organize all white-collar workers, from the lowest to the highest salary brackets, who work for the same employer or employers represented in negotiations by the same employer association. Examples of vertical organizations are, in private employment: the Swedish Union of Clerical and Technical Employees in Industry, the Swedish Union of Commercial Employees, the Swedish Union of Insurance Employees, and the Swedish Bank Employees Union; in municipal (local government) employment: the Swedish Union of Municipal Employees; and in central government employment: the Federation of Civil Servants, the Union of Civilian Employees in the Defense Forces.

There are also "horizontal" unions organizing all white-collar workers performing a certain kind of work or having the same education, and possibly (though not always) confronting more than one employer association. Examples of horizontal TCO affiliates are the Swedish Union of Supervisors and Foremen, the Swedish Union of Policemen, the Swedish Nurses' Association, the Swedish Union of Warrant Officers, and the Union of Non-Commissioned Officers in the Defense Forces.

***Table* 5.** White-Collar Unions (in LO and SACO) According to Types of Employers[a]

Employers	*Number of LO Members (Men and Women)*		*Number of SACO Members (Men and Women)*	
	in 1,000	*in Per Cent*	*in 1,000*	*in Per Cent*
Central government	90	53	25	60
Local government	15	9	9	21
Private employers	65	38	8	19
All employers	170	100	42	100

[a] Some of these figures are estimates.

Most LO affiliates are vertical, while SACO applies the principle of horizontal organization based on graduation from the same type of school of higher education: law, medicine, the humanities (i.e., secondary school teachers), etc. Out of the LO affiliates' total membership of 1,486,000 [2] in 1960, only 170,000 were white-collar workers. In 1960, SACO had 57,000 [3] members, of whom 15,000, however, were self-employed or students. White-collar workers organized in LO and SACO, respectively, are shown in Tables 5 and 6; the total number of organized white-collar workers compared with the total number of white-collar workers according to the 1960 census is also shown in Table 6.

The increase in the percentage of organized white-collar workers indicated below suggests that the unions have been successful in their attempts to enlist the growing white-collar population.

Between 1950 and 1960 the increase in white-collar union mem-

[2] The membership of LO in 1964 was 1,563,000.
[3] The membership of SACO in 1964 was 74,000.

bership and in total number of white-collar workers was about the same, implying an increase in the percentage of organization. In comparison the total membership of LO, not counting white-collar workers, is about 80 per cent of the total number of blue-collar workers

Table 6. Degree of Unionization of White-Collar Workers [a]

Fields of Employment	*Total Number of White-Collar Workers in 1,000*	*White-Collar Workers Organized in 1,000*				
		TCO	*LO*	*SACO*	*Other*	*Totals*
Agriculture, Horticulture, Forestry, Fishing	23	7	5	2	—	14
Industry and Crafts	333	163	8	7	—	178
Commerce, Communications, Transportation	401	40	137	2	6	185
Public administration and Professions	377	200	20	31	14	265
Totals	1134	410	170	42	20	642
Percentage		64	26	7	3	100

[a] Some of these figures are estimates.

in Sweden. In comparing these percentages it should be remembered that the white-collar workers counted in the census include executives of joint-stock companies and other managerial employees who are not

Table 7. Growth of White-Collar Union Membership, 1950-60

	1950	*1960*
White-collar workers (in 1,000)	843	1134
Total union membership (in 1,000)	443	642
Percentage	53	57

eligible for union membership. If allowance is made for them, the adjusted percentage of white-collar organization is about 70 per cent.

The distribution by fields of employment shows that organization is lowest in commerce, presumably because numerous enterprises are small and it is very difficult for the unions to make contacts with employees working there. An additional reason may be that more of the old patriarchal relationship between the employer and his employees survives in enterprises with only a few white-collar workers who are more inclined to identify with employer interests than are employees in large enterprises, where employer-employee relations are less personal.

The percentage of organization in public and private employment compares as follows:

Table 8. Degree of Organization in Public and Private Employment

	Estimated percentage
Private employment	about 50
Central government	about 80
Local government	about 75

The average percentages in these three sectors conceal great differences among various groups. In central government, for instance, the percentage of organization of employees in national defense approximates one hundred, while it is less in other government sectors. In private employment, the following figures exemplify variations in percentages of organization:

Table 9. Degree of Organization in Private Employment

	Estimated percentage
Banking	about 75
Insurance	about 60
Manufacturing	about 75
Retail and Wholesale Trade	about 20

The Constitutional Structure of the White-Collar Worker Movement

As previously mentioned, Sweden's white-collar workers are organized in a number of separate unions, affiliated with various federations. It may be useful to set out briefly the constitutional structure of TCO, the largest of these federations.

The TCO Congress, which meets every three years and consists of about two hundred delegates elected by the affiliates, is the highest authority in TCO. At least once a year, the TCO General Council, consisting of one hundred members elected by the unions, meets to discuss various problems, primarily those pertaining to annual wage negotiations, and to examine a report on the activities of the TCO Executive Board. This Board, which consists of ten members elected by the Congress, convenes once a week for current policy decisions. The preparatory work and the administrative execution of its policies are performed by a Secretariat, the head of which is concurrently President of the Board.

The Secretariat is subdivided into divisions, e.g., a legal division, a research division, an information and press division, a division for negotiations, and a secretariat. In addition, there is a special section in charge of matters pertaining to "collective bargaining" in the field of public employment (central and local government); this section serves as secretariat to a special board, which consists of representatives of unions organizing central government employees. The board negotiates on behalf of these unions with the Civil Service Minister—a cabinet post created for this purpose—on salaries and such other terms of employment as can be the subject of negotiations.

There are also two separate committees, one of them in charge of matters of common interest to all municipal employees and the other performing the same function with regard to private employees.

Three advisory bodies within TCO deal with specific professional problems: one for technicians, one for foremen, and one for teachers. In cities where several TCO affiliates have local organizations, contacts and cooperation among the locals are maintained through TCO local committees engaging in propaganda and information on questions of common interest. These committees do not take any action in regard to wage negotiations, however.

Regarding the structure of white-collar unions—TCO affiliates as well as unions outside TCO—the usual pattern is a union consisting of locals, which comprise either all union members within a certain geographic area (a city, a rural district) or at a certain enterprise. Some of the unions promote cooperation among locals within the same region through county or regional bodies. A few unions are national associations of employees in certain professional categories.

The TCO's organization is shown in Chart 1.

TRADE-UNION ACTIVITY

The Right to Organize and to Negotiate

According to their constitutions, the various white-collar organizations have the task of asserting the common economic and social

CHART 1

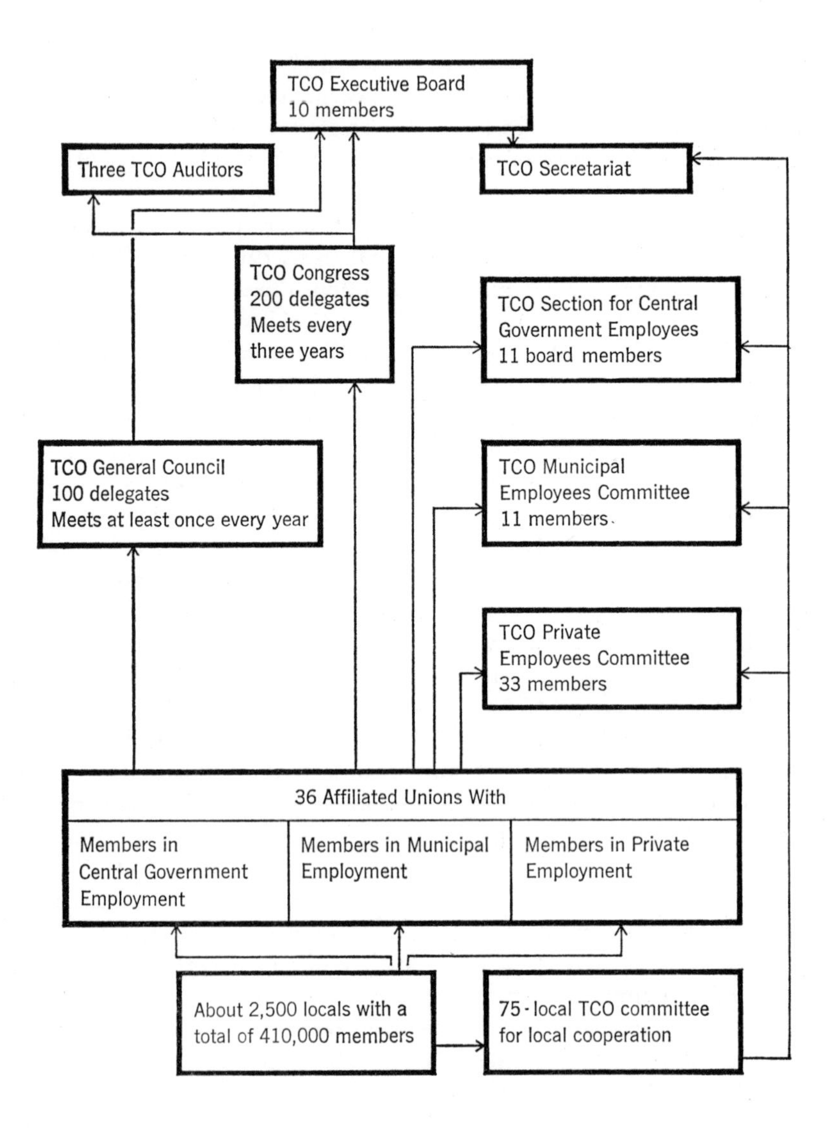

interests of the affiliated groups. The central organization has the additional task of leading Sweden's white-collar worker movement. A primary responsibility in this context is the protection of the statutory foundations of trade-union activities. It has been mentioned in a preceding section that it was one of DACO's foremost goals to achieve a statutory right of negotiation. Under the Act on the Right of Association and of Collective Bargaining in 1936, only organizations of wage earners may negotiate with employers on terms of employment, whereas individual employers as well as employer associations may be a party to negotiations. On either side of the table, the negotiating party can be a federation of organizations. The Act bases the right to negotiate on the right to belong to an organization, and further upon the right for the unions to negotiate. The employer is obligated to respect the right of organization and to enter into negotiations. The Act bans attempts to induce a person to refrain from membership or from work for the organization. Provisions to this effect in a private contract would be invalid. The employer can, however, demand that supervisors and foremen should not join blue-collar unions. Many collective agreements stipulate that employees in certain executive positions may not be union members.

The Act of 1936 does not apply to white-collar employees of central and local governments. The legal provisions of 1937 and 1940 applying to these groups are of a different nature. Under present legislation, the two negotiating parties in public employment—government and the employees—do not have equal status as they do in private employment. The procedural rules applying to negotiations with public employees reserve for the employer the right to make decisions but impose on him the obligation to inform the white-collar workers of his basic decisions concerning salaries and other terms of employment before the decisions become final, and early enough to enable the employees to propose negotiations. As in private employment, the right to negotiate is reserved for unions or federations of unions. In practice, the system of negotiations for public employees has developed an ever closer resemblance to the private system, even though this development lacks support in present legislation. The Civil Service Minister negotiates on behalf of the central government with the organizations representing government employees, but the resulting agreement is not legally binding on the government. In other words, it is not a collective agreement in the legal sense. To become valid, the provisions of the agreement must be embodied in a bill and enacted by Parliament. Parliament has never failed so far to enact the terms of the agreement without change, and parliamentary approval has thus become a mere formality. The Civil Service Minister and the organizations of white-collar workers are discussing the establishment of the same kind of collective bargaining rights for salaried public employees as those applying to private employees. This matter is closely related to another fundamental problem, a resort to direct action—the kind of measures salaried public employees should be entitled to take in a conflict.

Under the Act of 1936 on the Right of Association and Collective Bargaining, white-collar workers in private employment can resort to the same direct action in a conflict as blue-collar workers. Salaried employees of central or local government on the other hand cannot call a strike or take other direct action. However, their organizations have been able to produce a similar effect by tendering resignations en masse on behalf of their members, after obtaining individual authorization from each member concerned. Such resignations have been tendered only on behalf of nonpermanent public employees, because the permanent (in Swedish *ordinairie*) employees pose a special problem. Salaried public employees enjoying permanent status cannot be discharged by the public employer unless found guilty, in due process of law, of criminal abuse or gross neglect of duty. Therefore, the public employer is deemed to have the right not to accept their resignation —a course which would not be adopted normally, e.g., when an employee wishes to enter private employment, but which might be taken in case of mass resignations. Another weapon which public salaried employees may wield is the "blocking" of vacancies: a union may issue a public warning to members and nonmembers alike that they should not apply for jobs of a certain type offered by a certain employer. Such a "blockade" is a highly effective weapon—whether used by white- or blue-collar workers, public or private employees—because of the general respect which the unions enjoy. Next to full bargaining rights, the right to resort to effective measures in a conflict has first priority in the organized white-collar workers' efforts to establish legal foundations for the effective defense of their members' interests.[4]

Conflicts Among White-Collar Workers

Thus far, white-collar workers have been involved in relatively few and limited conflicts, in public as well as in private employment. Some of these conflicts are worth mentioning, however. The Swedish

[4] In 1966 salaried employees of central and local governments obtain the same legal rights for collective bargaining as private employees, including the right to strike.

Marine Engineer Officers' Union was involved in a protracted conflict in the early 1920's, which ended in defeat. The Navigation Officers had several conflicts at different periods. Twice in the postwar period (1948 and 1955) they resorted to individual resignations by members enrolled on board ships. Both conflicts were rapidly settled, the first under a threat of legislation imposing compulsory service—which might have been passed because of the difficult supply situation prevailing in the country at that time—and the second under a threat of legislation on compulsory arbitration. Things had gone so far in 1955 that the government introduced a bill on compulsory arbitration over TCO protests that the pending conflict was not more damaging to the national interest than other conflicts and that legislative interference was unjustified and an undue encroachment on the freedom and right of labor and management to settle their differences themselves. Since the parties were able to settle the conflict, the bill never reached the floor of Parliament for final action.

In 1948, members of the Swedish Union of Clerical and Technical Employees in Industry were involved in a five-week strike against the government-owned and -operated Tobacco Monopoly, while members of another TCO affiliate—the Swedish Foremen's and Supervisors' Association—working at the same plants kept aloof from the conflict.

One of the more noteworthy conflicts occurred in 1946 when the Swedish Bank Employees Union demanded the conclusion of a collective contract on salaries and general terms of employment for bank clerks, which had previously not been subject to contractual settlement. Protracted negotiations failed to yield results, and the Bank Employees Union issued a strike warning. A last-minute settlement was reached, and the strike never was called. The support of the TCO and its affiliates, who placed considerable funds at the disposal of the bank employees, no doubt had a propitious effect on the results which the bank union was able to achieve through negotiations. This experience assumed great importance for the entire white-collar movement because it changed the attitude of white-collar workers toward strikes. Other lessons learned were the need for union funds of sufficient size and the significance of mutual support and solidarity among white-collar organizations.

In 1955, the Commercial Employees' Union resorted to rotating localized strikes at ironware shops, which lasted for about three weeks. This action, too, was supported by TCO and the other white-collar groups. A compromise settlement was reached.

At the same time the Swedish Metal Trades Employers' Association, affiliated to the Swedish Employers Federation, was discussing the possibility of a lockout involving 35,000 members of the Union of Clerical and Technical Employees in Industry employed by members of the Association as a reprisal for a strike warning issued by the Union on behalf of the employees of a single machine plant. The conflict never broke out.

In public employment there are several interesting instances of white-collar workers' resorting to action in conflicts. In 1947, the Swedish Union of Policemen and the Association of Swedish Towns (a body created for the purpose of bargaining with employees) were engaged in negotiations concerning a central agreement on salaries and general terms of employment, applicable in all cities. No agreement was forthcoming, and the Union of Swedish Policemen secured authorization by its members to tender their resignations. In this situation Parliament enacted a law on compulsory service for policemen, stipulating that policemen who had been serving on the police force as of a certain date could be called upon to resume their duties in case of a shortage of policemen arising in their former district, with their salaries being set by the central government. The act, which would have become operative only by governmental decision, was never put into force, the Swedish Union of Policemen having been able to reach separate local agreements with the different cities.

A similar situation arose in 1950-51 after a failure of negotiations between the Swedish Nurses' Association and two municipal employer associations. The issue was nurses' wages and general terms of employment. At a fairly early stage, the government issued a warning that in case of a failure of the negotiations, it would introduce a bill on compulsory service for nurses and compulsory arbitration concerning their wages. In the final stage of the negotiations, Parliament was reconvened for an extra session during summer recess and the bill was introduced. Before Parliament had time to act on the bill, the parties settled the pending issues. The settlement was a compromise, but must be considered a success from the point of view of the white-collar workers. In part it was a result of the pressure of public opinion on both parties to reach a settlement without government interference based on an Act of Parliament; this pressure was felt most strongly by the employers.

Generally speaking, the white-collar workers, however, have been relatively more reluctant to resort to strikes than the blue-collar workers. The reason may be that it is a delicate question for white-collar workers—at least for certain groups among them—whether or not to resort to a method of settling a conflict which would entail the danger of blue-collar workers being laid off at the enterprises concerned. If blue-collar workers strike, there is no danger of lay-offs for white-collar workers. For a long time the white-collar workers in industry have had a clause in their collective agreements to the effect that they are entitled to remain neutral in labor conflicts. This neutrality implies that, in case of blue-collar workers being involved in a lawful strike, the white-collar workers must not perform work other than that normally performed by employees belonging to the white-collar category, or work which renders possible or facilitates the resumption of operations after the conflict has ended. In certain cases, white-collar workers are under an obligation to participate in so-called protective work, i.e., work which is necessary to protect lives and property from danger and damage. The employer, on the other hand, cannot terminate the employment of white-collar workers but must pay them their full salaries during three months, and thereafter reduced salaries, the reduction amounting to 10 per cent each month (i.e., 90 per cent of the salary is paid in the fourth month, 80 per cent in the fifth month, etc.) until the salary is down to 60 per cent, which continues indefinitely. There is only one exception to the rule that the employer cannot terminate a job of a white-collar worker during a strike: he can do so if he is able to prove that changed conditions will make it impossible for him to keep a certain worker in his employment after operations have resumed. These provisions, of course, have been very important for white-collar workers in private industry. There is no corresponding protection for white-collar workers in public employment who might find themselves in a similar situation, e.g., those employed at publicly operated plants and utilities.

In the 1930's, labor conflicts occurred with alarming frequency in Sweden, and as a result legislation circumscribing industrial warfare and protecting the rights of third parties was proposed and debated in Parliament for several years but was not enacted. Labor and management, while at odds on other issues, were agreed that labor legislation should be restricted to a minimum and that to the greatest extent possible labor issues should be settled by the parties in negotiations. In order to prevent legislation limiting strikes and lockouts by rendering it superfluous, LO and SAF concluded the Basic Agreement on Industrial Peace (*Huvudavtalet*) in 1938. The agreement, which was partly amended in 1947, specifies unified procedural rules for negotiations on wages, grievances, and dismissals, provided some protection from unjustified discharge, and created machinery for the settlement of disputes by conciliation. However, it does not curtail the rights of unions and management to resort to strikes, lockouts, and other direct action in a dispute arising in negotiations for a new collective agreement when they have exhausted the negotiation procedures. The letter of the *Huvudavtalet* was of subordinate significance compared to the spirit of conciliation and fair play from which it sprang and which has prevailed since then. The willingness to talk things over and seek a reasonable compromise instead of engaging in a fight pervades Swedish management and organized labor from top to bottom and enables the government to observe a hands-off policy.

Nineteen years after the conclusion of *Huvudavtalet,* the two TCO affiliates representing white-collar workers in industry (the Union of Technical and Clerical Employees in Industry, abbreviated SIF, and the Union of Supervisors and Foremen, abbreviated SALF) reached a similar peace agreement with SAF. As under the LO-SAF agreement, negotiations are first conducted locally, and if they are unsuccessful, the issue is referred to negotiations between the union (SIF or SALF) and the branch organization of the industry concerned. As a third step, the issue can be referred to an Industrial Disputes Council (*förtroenderåd*) established for this purpose in each branch of industry. These councils take up only disputes which the union and the employer association concerned submit for decision by common consent, and their rulings are binding on both parties.

To provide additional machinery for peaceful settlement in cases where the parties—for reasons of principle or for economic reasons—do not wish to refer the dispute to the Industrial Disputes Council of their branch of industry for final settlement, the SAF, SIF, and SALF formed a permanent board to which either party, without the consent of its opposite number, has the right to refer questions pertaining to salaries and termination of employment. Other disputes can be referred to this permanent board by common consent. Both parties are under an obligation to refrain from direct action (strikes, lockouts, etc.) as long as an issue is being handled or can be handled on any of the levels foreseen in the procedural rules of the peace agreement. In order to expand collaboration on matters of common interest and to promote mutual understanding, the organizations have also established a central committee for discussion and exchange of information.[5]

[5] In 1965 a similar agreement was reached by the union of commercial employees. Also, the salaried employees in central and local governments reached a *Huvudavtal.*

Improving the Financial Resources of the White-Collar Movement

Under its constitution, the TCO has the function of promoting the establishment and maintenance of effective white-collar unions. To accomplish this task, it must have sizable financial resources. Ever since the present TCO was established in 1944, it has consistently pursued a policy of sound economic foundations for its affiliates, in part because the possibility of a strike must be a real enough threat in negotiations and in part because effective administration and negotiation require economic strength.

Average members' dues in TCO affiliates are shown in the following table, which presents dues in private and public service in absolute figures and in percentages of average salaries.

TCO	*Members' Dues (in kroner per year)*	*Percentage of Average Salary*
Private employment	136 (roughly $27)	0.9
Public employment	109 (roughly $21)	0.7

The unions pay 9 kroner a year per member to TCO.[6] For certain groups the dues also include contributions to unemployment insurance.

The total strike funds of TCO affiliates, plus a TCO fund for subsidizing affiliates involved in a conflict, amount to 149 million kroner ($30 million). This amount would provide an allowance of 60 per cent of salaries for 16 days of strike for all members.

	Assets in Strike Funds	
TCO	*Totals (in million kroner)*	*Kroner per Member*
Unions in private employment	944	435
Unions in public employment	479	271

The total strike fund in TCO amounts to 345 kroner per capita (1959). It is worth mentioning for comparison that for LO the corresponding amount is 347 kroner. The strike funds of TCO affiliates organizing public employees have increased by 610 per cent during the 1950's as against 129 per cent for the unions of private employees.

A natural expectation is that white-collar workers in public employment will obtain the same full right of negotiation and of resorting to strikes which private employees enjoy. In addition, TCO affiliates organizing public employees have created a joint supporting fund comprising 100 kroner per member in the unions concerned, on which any of these affiliates can draw if it becomes involved in conflict.

[6] A kroner is worth slightly less than 20 U.S. cents at the official rate.

Streamlining the Structure of the Organization

In order to enhance the efficiency of white-collar organizations by streamlining their organizational structure, TCO has established a plan of organization outlining a desirable delimitation of the jurisdictions of its affiliates. The historical survey indicated that, as a result of these efforts, the number of affiliates has declined while the TCO's total membership increased. The present plan of organization postulates that only one white-collar worker organization should confront the same employer organization or employer. The principle is, however, modified if existing organizations do not represent the same category of white-collar workers, if the terms of employment differ, or if the terms applying to different groups are not markedly interdependent.

For employees of the central government, the purpose which this principle serves has been attained through cooperation of the TCO affiliates within a special section (the TCO Section of White-Collar Workers in Civil Service).

The plan of organization provides in addition that an affiliate representing a specialized professional group, the bulk of which is employed in a limited field, may be authorized to organize white-collar workers of the same profession who are employed in another similar field, provided that salaries and other terms of employment are closely related. To create a separate affiliate, the membership must be sufficient for effective activity and close cooperation must be established in negotiations with neighboring affiliates. Under the TCO constitution, the right to settle jurisdictional disputes among affiliates rests with TCO.

Although the structure of TCO affiliates has been streamlined to some extent, it does not yet meet the demands of maximum efficiency. Among the problems to be solved, jurisdictional issues have a high rank.

Demarcation Lines in Other Central Organizations

Regarding the separation of the jurisdictions of TCO affiliates from those of unions affiliated with other federations, the situation prevailing in relation to LO affiliates is different from that which exists in relation to SACO affiliates. In 1949 LO and TCO, both of which took part in the founding of the International Confederation of Free Trade Unions, established a joint committee to deal with problems of common interest. This committee took over the tasks of a special body in charge of jurisdictional disputes between TCO- and LO-affiliated unions. Since the creation of this committee, several LO and TCO affiliates have worked out agreements on jurisdictions, notably unions organizing municipal white- and blue-collar workers, respectively; those organizing certain groups of employees of the central government; and those in commerce. In certain fields of public administration—postal service, telecommunications, and railroads—however, disputes between the TCO and LO unions still occur.

When SACO was established in 1947, TCO and the organizations of college graduates discussed the possibility of cooperation and of merger. These negotiations failed, primarily because TCO and the SACO groups held different views on the principles of organization of white-collar workers. TCO affirmed that employees who were college graduates, should, in principle, join the same unions as other groups of white-collar workers while SACO felt that the graduates should form separate unions—differences which to some degree reflected differences of opinion on goals and means, especially concerning wage policy. During the 1950's there was considerable tension between the two federations and their affiliates. In recent years some cooperation on specific questions has been established. TCO has declared its goal to be one central organization in which groups now divided between TCO and SACO should join.

The Wage Policy of the White-Collar Organizations

The function of the white-collar unions and the TCO is to champion the members' economic and social interests. In fulfilling this task, they concentrate on influencing wage developments and general terms of employment. In a modern society it has, however, proved necessary for the trade unions to engage in activities outside of fields which are directly subject to contracts or agreements between the employees and management. Social legislation, for instance, is of basic importance for the members' economic and social well-being. Union concern with social legislation brings taxation into the picture as it is the instrument for procuring the means for governmental action. Tax policies also receive the unions' attention, because taxes are one of the factors which, together with wage and price levels, determine the members' standard of living. Price developments must be watched by themselves as well as with regard to the interrelationship between wages and prices. However, it must be borne in mind that this relationship—wage costs influencing prices—is not absolute, but contingent in part on the degree of efficiency achieved in the use of productive capacity. The unions' task of defending their members' interests necessitates their cooperation in measures which are aimed at a full use of productive capacity and at increasing productivity as a basis for economic growth. The unions must decide what they consider a desirable balance between investment and consumption. In order to be able to influence the distribution of the nation's aggregate resources, the unions must thus develop policies of their own concerning the various aspects of the national economic policy.

This bird's-eye view shows that the activities of the white-collar worker organizations comprise or, at any rate, touch upon an extremely large number of national policies.

The cardinal task of a union being the improvement of the members' economic conditions, it follows in the view of Swedish white-collar union leaders that the unions' goal must be economic growth and an increase in the share of total wages in the rising national income. Furthermore, an organization comprising more than one category of wage earners must include in its wage policy some principles concerning the distribution of the total payroll among various groups and individuals.

The white-collar unions consistently encourage measures to improve productivity, since its growth is a prerequisite for a rising prosperity in a full employment economy, quite apart from its effects on the terms of trade. The white-collar movement supports measures to improve the use of productive capacity in order to achieve a higher degree of satisfaction of the needs of the wage earners–consumers. The term "improved use of productive capacity" covers a wide range of measures in various fields, primarily technological progress and structural changes in industry, i.e., the elimination or curtailment of unprofitable plants or entire industries and the transfer of manpower and capital from them to expanding and competitive industries. It supports similar measures with regard to governmental enterprise, which in Sweden traditionally comprises the operation of numerous utilities (e.g., railroads, telecommunications) and a few industrial plants. Sweden's participation in projects promoting some degree of international integration, which will speed up structural changes, is in harmony with this policy.

In pursuing these policies, the unions realize the importance of avoiding undesirable economic and social consequences for the workers. Such consequences can be avoided or alleviated through an active and selective labor market policy—based on efficient public employment agencies, retraining facilities, and relocation benefits for displaced workers—and a comprehensive social insurance system. Another basic requirement is adequate facilities in general education as well as in vocational training and vocational guidance. Forecasts of the expected demand and supply of various kinds of trained manpower are prerequisites of an active labor market policy.

The unions also are aware that in order to enhance productivity, plant and equipment must be improved and increased, requiring investments that will encroach temporarily on the resources available for consumption. This encroachment creates a problem which reflects the difficulty of achieving balanced economic development under full employment.

The white-collar worker organizations reject the maintenance of full employment through inflationary excess demand for goods and services and are equally opposed to fighting inflation through restraint in wage policy. They feel that other ways and means must be found to achieve full employment without inflation. National economic policy, the organizations affirm, should, as far as possible, be pursued through resort to financial and monetary measures whose over-all effects must be supplemented by an effective labor market policy. The goal should be full employment in an economic climate of a degree of austerity just sufficient to keep wage increases resulting from free labor-management negotiations from attaining inflationary size. Labor and management, they say, have the prime responsibility for establishing a wage structure which is considered "just and fair."

That aspect of wage policy which is concerned with the national product and the nation's total payroll determines the organized white-collar workers' policies in regard to national economic issues. Another aspect of wage policy is concerned with problems of distribution which, from the point of view of the individual worker or a specific group, appear primary.

The basic principles guiding the white-collar worker organizations when it comes to distributing the total national payroll among groups and individuals are "justice" in wage relations and a manner of wage-setting appropriate to stimulate work performance. The point of departure is "equal pay for equal work," a principle which has, however, been interpreted in different ways in different fields. Common to all groups is an effort to base wage relations on an evaluation of the difficulty of the various jobs, so that equally difficult jobs are rewarded with equal pay. Each job is deemed to make certain demands on the worker performing it, and the total of these demands constitutes the "job difficulty." The equal pay principle can be defined as "equal pay for equal job difficulty," which means, inversely, "unequal pay for unequal job difficulty."

In certain fields, the application of the principle to the wage system is modified by consideration of the manner in which the individual meets the demands of his job, i.e., individual efficiency. In other fields, individual performance in meeting job demands influences wages only indirectly. In private employment, wage systems usually enable the employer to consider individual work performance and ability in each position. In public employment, however, wages are established for certain jobs and job performance is not a factor. Differences in ability and performance result, however, in different prospects of promotion to higher positions and higher salaries.

A characteristic of the wage policy of organized white-collar workers is that it gives prominence to the element of wage differentiation within the equal pay principle. This emphasis springs from the white-collar unions' resistance to the trend toward wage equalization promoted by LO, and the fact that this resistance became a rallying point for their organizations. It should, however, be noted that the white-collar wage policy contains elements of solidarity: to the extent job difficulty and efficiency are equal, wages should be equal, regardless of other circumstances such as the wage-paying capacity of the enterprise or the industry. Horizontal wage comparisons between individuals performing the same work within the same enterprise, or in different enterprises within the same industrial branch or in different branches, are a traditional feature in their negotiations. From their viewpoint, the very existence of unions and, above all, of wage statistics entails solidarity in wage policy.

In accordance with the basic principles of the wage policy of white-collar workers, length of service is deemed to increase efficiency in both private and public employment, and therefore the white-collar unions insist on inclusion in wage systems of seniority and/or "qualification" increments based on length of service.

In fields where most jobs have the same content, employees have few prospects of promotion and salaries tend to remain static. Therefore, the unions seek differentiation of job content through negotiations in order to prepare the way for wage differentiation and ultimately for promotion opportunities for the employees.

Wage differentiation also is a subject of negotiation, the parties (management or the association of employers and the unions of white-collar workers) seeking a compromise between their divergent views. The outcome frequently depends to some extent on the relations between the supply of and demand for employees with certain skills. Consequently, the resulting wage relations have often been thought to be at variance with the equal pay principle, and wage increases in some jurisdictions have often caused other wage earners to invoke the equal pay principle and to raise demands for immediate negotiations on improvements in their salaries. In a full employment economy, wage policy can thus stimulate the trend toward inflation.

If the union policy is to avoid inflationary pressures, it is essential to achieve wage relations corresponding to a fair evaluation of different job difficulties and individual merit. The goal is to create long-term equilibrium in wage determination; its attainment is facilitated by mobility of manpower. This is why the white-collar organizations, in their endeavor to pursue an effective wage policy, have come to consider well-planned and energetic action in the fields of forecasting of manpower needs, vocational guidance, vocational training, retraining, advanced training, and the like as fundamental prerequisites for their wage policy, or, more accurately, as part of their wage policy.

Meaningful Statistics Are Important

No objective norm exists for the evaluation of the relative difficulty of all existing types of jobs. Systematic job and merit evaluation has not been used in the white-collar field thus far, but for many years wage statistics have been compiled for use in negotiations. These statistics must be highly refined to be meaningful in the context of wage policy objectives.

Within TCO there is a committee which assists the affiliates in efforts to shape their wage statistics according to certain norms. TCO statisticians then coordinate the material so that comparisons can be made among individual white-collar workers, as well as among groups of positions with the same or similar tasks. Comparisons are also made of salaries received at different times by employees or groups of employees who performed the same kind of work. Such comparisons are essential for the application of the principle of equal pay for equal work. For comparisons of wage levels between employees or groups of employees performing different jobs and therefore entitled to different salaries, wage statistics are only part of the gauge. Another part is the evaluation of an adequate wage differential matching the differences in job content. As there is no system of job or individual merit evaluation in general use by the white-collar organizations, this evaluation is intuitive.

TCO's job classification system is based on a systematic survey of the functions constituting the content of each job, the kinds of objectives at which the work task is aimed, and the degree of difficulty, complexity, or scope of the objectives of the work task. Functions are grouped according to their similarity. Thirteen groups are distinguished:

Administrative work in general, public administrative work, and related tasks
Experimentation, statistical, and theoretical analytical work
Medical care and nursing
Design and manufacture of products
Transportation and communication
Plant safety
Maintenance
Artistic and other creative work
Teaching
Commercial work—purchasing, selling, advertising
Economic administration—budgeting, disbursing, accounting, auditing
Correspondence and recording of other oral or written statements in shorthand and/or typing
Data processing with punch cards and/or electronic equipment

Each main group comprises subgroups representing specified functions. Each subgroup consists of a number of types of jobs which are arranged vertically according to the degree of difficulty and responsibility within the respective class. The classification of the different jobs according to this system is then based on a very detailed description of the work tasks performed by each individual employee.

In Diagram 1 we have plotted for each of ten age groups median and quartile monthly salaries of three occupational subgroups (1103, 1104, 1105) within the major occupational group of "Managing and supervising of production" (code number 110). The quartile values are connected so as to define an area, in which exactly half of the individuals within each unit occupational group are to be found. The medians are marked by horizontal lines. An interpretation of the codes of the unit groups belonging to the major group 110 follows:

110 *Managing and Supervision of Production*

1102 *Factory (Plant) Manager*

Is responsible for production work in two to four large production sections, including maintenance departments, if any. (For a single large production section, see Factory (Plant) Superintendent in 1103.)

1103 *Factory (Plant) Superintendent*

Is responsible for production work in a large production section, including maintenance departments, if any.

DIAGRAM 1 **Median and Quartile Salaries of Three Occupational Groups of Managing Personnel in Private Industry (Men)**

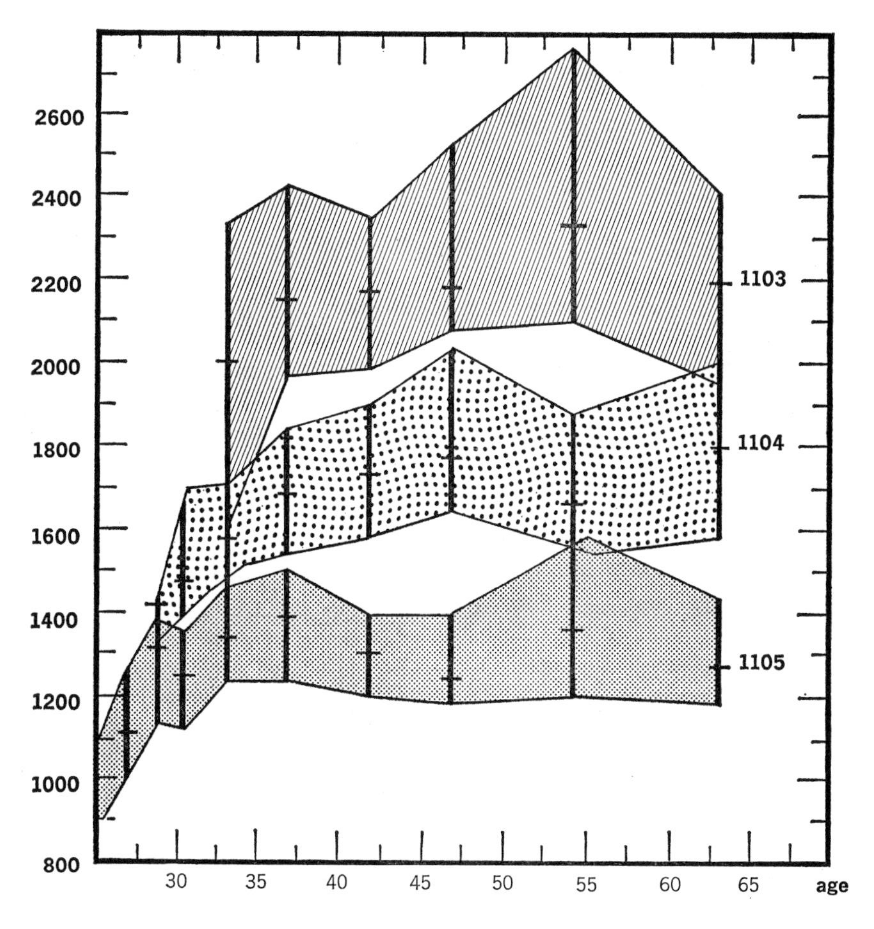

Provided that the production is approximately of the average degree of complexity and rationalization existing in the industry, a large production section means:

in the mining industry, iron and other metal works, engineering works, and in the electrotechnical industry, a section with, as a rule, about 150-300 workers;

in the chemical industry, a section with, as a rule, about 75-150 workers;

in other industries, a section where the Factory (Plant) Superintendent is expected to perform similar duties.

1104 *First Factory (Plant) Engineer*

Is responsible for production work in a medium-sized production section, including maintenance departments, if any.

Provided that the production is approximately of the average degree of complexity and rationalization existing in the industry, a medium-sized section means:

in the mining industry, iron and other metal works, engineering works, and in the electrotechnical industry, a section with, as a rule, about 75-150 workers;

in the chemical industry, a section with, as a rule, about 35-75 workers;

in other industries, a section where the First Factory (Plant) Engineer is expected to perform similar duties.

1105 *Factory (Plant) Engineer*

Is responsible for production work in a small production section, including maintenance departments, if any.

Provided that the production is approximately of the average degree of complexity and rationalization existing in the industry, a small production section means:

in the mining industry, iron and other metal works, engineering works, and in the electrotechnical industry, a section with as a rule, up to 75 workers;

in the chemical industry, a section with, as a rule, up to 35 workers;

in other industries, a section where the production engineer is expected to perform similar duties.

An analysis of the results of the white-collar organizations' activities in the field of wage policy would be beyond the scope of this survey. Diagrams 2 and 3, however, show figures reflecting the development of average annual salaries of certain groups of white- and blue-collar workers on a semilogarithmic scale. They suggest that the evolution of white-collar wages by and large has kept abreast of blue-collar wages since the end of the 1940's, whereas earlier, i.e., during and immediately after World War II, wages of white-collar workers were lagging behind.

It should be noted that the data in the diagrams are based on statistics compiled according to different principles. For government employees (local and central), the data refer to salaries set in wage schedules, and consideration was given to changes in the composition of the groups concerned. The data for white-collar workers in industry indicate average annual salaries, while data for blue-collar workers are based on hourly earnings and estimates of annual hours worked by full-time workers.

White-Collar Unions and Social and Tax Policy

As suggested in preceding sections, white-collar workers used to enjoy more favorable general terms of employment than blue-collar workers, partly as a result of their consistent efforts to improve these general terms even at the price of lower gains in cash salaries, and partly as a result of tradition. For example, the white-collar groups usually had guarantees of pay during periods of sickness, either under collective agreements or, in the case of public employees, under governmental regulations; they had vacations longer than the statutory minimum; their daily work hours were shorter than those of blue-collar workers; in most fields, the employer provided pensions, which frequently proved inadequate, however, as a result of inflation. During the 1940's and 1950's social legislation in Sweden was vastly expanded: general compulsory health insurance was enacted in the middle of the 1950's, statutory vacations were increased from two to three weeks a year, and a change in the legislation on hours of work brought about a three-step reduction of the average work week from 48 to 45 hours at the end of the 1950's. Even though these reforms improved the general employment terms of white-collar workers in some respects, they mainly benefited blue-collar workers. The social reforms established only minimum standards. In other words, the law does not preclude higher or supplemental benefits, longer vacations, etc., being granted under negotiated contracts, and allows for coordination of the statutory minimum with corresponding contractual provisions more favorable to the employee. The white-collar organizations played an active part both in influencing the legislation and in implementing the coordination of statutory and contractual provisions. This coordination entailed major problems only in regard to general health insurance, and, above all, general supplemental pensions insurance, which became operative in 1960. It is not possible to explain in detail how previous contractual health insurance, sick pay, and pension benefits were coordinated with and adjusted to the new general social insurance system, but it should be stated that in jurisdictions where previous contractual pension levels were more favorable to the white-collar employees than the new statutory pensions alone would have been, the old level was maintained and in some cases even improved, and that the white-collar workers as a group gained by the reform. They obtained, in addition to other benefits, cash wage increases offsetting the lower cost to the employer of that part of the

DIAGRAM 2 **Real Salaries Per Annum 1939-60 for Six Groups of Male Employees Evaluated at 1961 Prices**

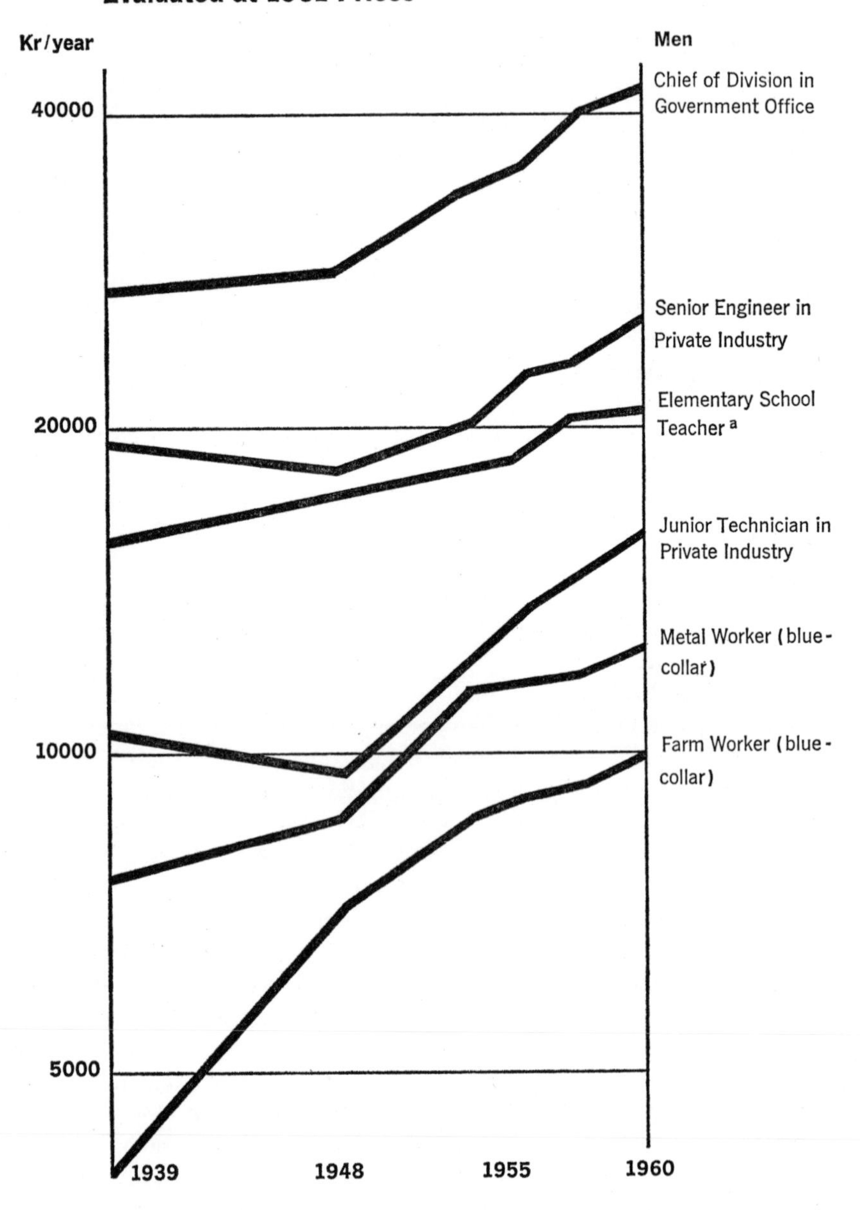

[a] Elementary school teachers are paid by the Central Government.

DIAGRAM 3 **Real Salaries Per Annum 1939-60 for Five Groups of Female Employees Evaluated at 1961 Prices**

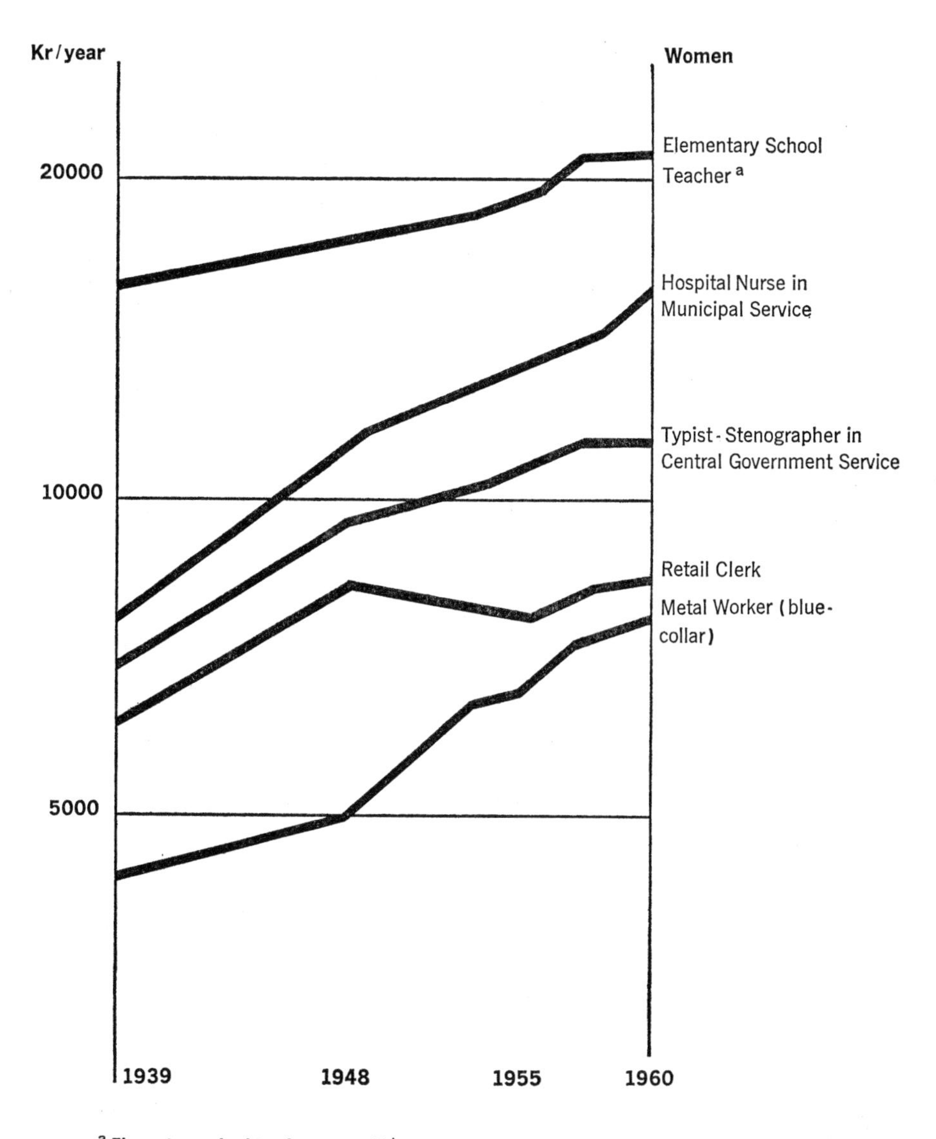

[a] Elementary school teachers are paid by the Central Government.

benefits which are now covered by social insurance, and are retaining in addition the premiums they themselves formerly paid toward private pension systems.[7]

In exerting their influence in behalf of the new social legislation, the white-collar organizations worked for general coverage to the widest extent possible and for the abolition of means tests. At the same time, they favored the development of the social welfare system in the direction of social insurance, the benefits being financed by specific contributions (or premiums) paid by the employees and/or the employers, and with only a minor part of certain benefits covered from general tax revenue.[8]

The white-collar workers' preference for the financing of social benefits by specific premiums instead of general tax revenue and their great interest in this matter can be understood in the light of the high relative wage levels of large groups of white-collar workers. The central government's income tax is sharply progressive, and the white-collar workers are therefore interested in forestalling a further increase in progressivism, and if possible, reducing it. Their promotion of premium-financed social insurance instead of improvements in tax-financed social benefits was one way of working toward this goal. Another approach, favored by the white-collar organizations and to some extent adopted in recent years, is supporting a shift from direct toward increased indirect taxation. Such a shift would be in keeping with the white-collar worker's desire to bring about a more equitable distribution of the tax burden between wage earners and other groups: while the wage earners' full income is automatically reported and taxed, other groups have opportunities of concealing part of their income. Indirect taxes cannot be evaded. In short, the white-collar organizations can be said to have been highly active in the fields of social legislation and tax policy, especially since the late 1940's.

White-Collar Organization and Society

The development of the white-collar federation has reached a stage which allows it to obtain representation (together with the

[7] The new wage related supplemental pensions are financed entirely by the employers, but premiums are lower than under former private systems, which were financed by employer and employee premiums.

[8] For example, roughly half of the expense of general health insurance is covered by beneficiary premiums, one-fourth by employer contributions, and the remaining fourth by the Treasury. While basic national pensions, payable to all Swedish citizens, are tax-financed, the new wage-related supplemental pensions are financed exclusively by employers and those self-employed who wish to secure a pension, without any subsidies from general tax revenue.

federation of blue-collar workers, various farmer organizations, and other important groups) on committees preparing new legislation which affects the interests of its members. When an important piece of legislation or a major amendment is contemplated, the government usually appoints a fact-finding committee, consisting of some members of Parliament, representatives of the major organizations concerned, and some experts, to gather all available background information and formulate the principles of the new legislation. The committee's report is submitted to all authorities and organizations concerned (including those who were represented on the committee) for statements of opinion; then, bearing in mind the criticisms and suggestions, the Ministry in charge of the matter drafts a bill and introduces it in Parliament. If a report arouses strong objections, it can be scrapped and a new fact-finding committee appointed. Thus, the white-collar organizations are able to assert their influence before a bill is written—through their representatives on the fact-finding committee and through their statements of opinion concerning the report. During subsequent stages of the legislative process, they continue to publicize their views, seeking to influence the legislators.

Apart from participation in the legislative process, the position which the white-collar organizations have achieved is marked by their representation on a large number of public boards and committees in charge of the administration or supervision of public policies pertaining to conditions in the labor market. The most important of these are the Labor Court, the Labor Market Board (which directs the administration of labor market policies) with its regional offices, the National Social Insurance Agency, the court and investigating bodies on antitrust matters and price supervision, different bodies representing consumer interests, the board administering public pension funds, boards for international aid, the committee responsible for the cost-of-living index and wage statistics, the European Free Trade Association (EFTA) advisory committee, fact-finding and advisory committees on matters pertaining to European economic integration, and advisory committees on agricultural policy.

Political Neutrality

Although taking an active part in the shaping of policies on social welfare, taxation, employment, and the national economy in general, which are finally settled by political decisions in Parliament, the TCO and its affiliates have always adhered to the principle of political neutrality. When the TCO was reconstituted in 1944, this question was thoroughly discussed. The principle was laid down that the TCO and its affiliates must not support any political party in elections or on other occasions. However, it was agreed that these organizations should support the democratic forces in the national community, these forces being the foundation for the action of free employee and employer organizations. Furthermore, it was established that the organized white-collar workers had an obligation to state their views on political questions of interest to them and to seek to influence the political parties in favor of a course compatible with their interests. In addition, it was stated that the political neutrality of the white-collar organizations did not imply a ban on political activity by their officers and board members. On the contrary, the statement emphasized the importance and desirability of individual political activity. It should be borne in mind that the political neutrality characteristic of the white-collar organizations distinguishes them from the Confederation of Swedish Trade Unions (LO) and its affiliates, many of whose local organizations have in their collective capacity joined the Social Democratic Party.

The question of the position of the white-collar organizations in relation to the political parties has been repeatedly under discussion during recent years. There were proponents of the view that political neutrality is a precondition for maintaining a united white-collar movement, since the white-collar workers are divided in their political allegiance. Among blue-collar workers there is a considerable degree of political agreement. Other spokesmen averred that it is a weakness for the white-collar groups not to be represented by a political party, and some of them recommended the establishment of a white-collar workers' party. At the same time, the question has been occasionally raised as to whether the political neutrality professed by the white-collar organizations was really observed. That this question should be raised is rather natural. Representatives of political parties who found that the views expressed by white-collar organizations on specific problems were at variance with the position their parties had adopted were sometimes inclined to call the white-collar organizations to account in the name of political neutrality. They can be expected to do so again in the future, the more so, the larger and stronger the white-collar organizations become and the more often these organizations take a stand on controversial political questions.

The Educational Activities of the White-Collar Organizations

Educational activities are a vital part of the organized white-collar workers' program. The training of members in trade unionism was the first educational task to receive attention, and it was mainly to give such training that the TCO affiliates in 1935 established *Tjänstemännens Bildningsverksamhet* (TBV), the White-Collar Workers Educational Association, a separate organization of which nearly all TCO affiliates now are members. Subsequently, educational activities have been vastly expanded to include studies of political and social science and certain kinds of vocational training as well.

At present, educational activities are being conducted by TBV, the various TCO affiliates, and TCO itself. For courses and conferences on the national level, two residential colleges—situated in the immediate vicinity of Stockholm—are run by TCO.

TBV arranges courses and conferences on both national and local levels for the purpose of imparting general information on issues of fundamental importance to the unions and their members. Weekend conferences are frequent. The TCO affiliates give specialized education on matters of particular interest in their respective jurisdictions. TCO sponsors courses dealing with a variety of matters significant for trade-union activities in a more thorough and effective manner than is otherwise possible. The subjects include legislation, taxation, social policies, national economy, and the like, as well as policies and goals of the white-collar worker organizations in these fields. In general, these educational activities are aimed not only at educating the members, but also at maintaining and strengthening democracy within the organization. In this respect, the organizations play an important part in the national community as well.

In recent years, educational activities have been extended to subjects beyond those that have a direct bearing on trade-union activities. By offering their members courses of advanced training to improve their professional skills, or, in some fields, by reaching agreements with employers or employer organizations on facilities for advanced training, the unions are enabling members to improve their standard of living through self-improvement. Educational activities of this type are thus part of the union's general policy of seeking to raise the members' standard of living. The retraining of displaced employees for new jobs was previously cited as an integral part of the active labor market policy, which, in turn, is a complement to the national economic policy seeking to achieve and maintain full employment and monetary stability. Retraining is one of the responsibilities of the labor market board.

The entire public school system in Sweden, from elementary schools to universities and including vocational training, has been under lively discussion for almost two decades, and a process of incisive reorganization is under way. This development is being followed with intense interest by the white-collar organizations, which have made some important contributions toward the shaping of the new school system.

SUMMARY AND OUTLOOK

Sweden is a thoroughly organized society. Organizations representing the specific interests of the various professional and occupational groups—wage earners, employers, big industry, small industry and crafts, commerce, professionals, farmers—play a dominant part in public life. Side by side with organizations representing business in its capacity as employer and therefore in charge of wage negotiations and other matters relative to industrial relations are separate business organizations promoting its other interests. In mining and manufacturing, for instance, business is represented by one organization in its capacity as employer and by another in regard to other matters. The most powerful interest groups are those representing labor and management. There are several employer organizations: the Employers' Federation (SAF) representing the bulk of mining and manufacturing, and corresponding organizations for commerce, banking and insurance, shipping, agriculture, newspaper publishing. There are also the labor federations: LO representing the blue-collar workers, and three federations—one of them very small—representing white-collar workers.

White-collar organizations in Sweden have achieved a strong position in the national community. They have proved able to accomplish essential tasks in the interests of their members and of the community. However, their position in both these respects is not yet quite equal to that of the blue-collar organizations, a fact which is reflected, for instance, in the white-collar workers' somewhat lower percentage of organization. Broadly speaking, however, unionization among white-collar workers has been rather successful, mainly as a result of the following circumstances:

1. All other groups in society were organized to assert their own interests, and there was a strong feeling among the white-collar workers that they should do the same.

2. The white-collar workers formed unions, the statutes of which stipulated that they must be politically neutral, that is, that they must not support any political party in elections or in other ways.

3. Legislation, collective agreements, and practice have laid a foundation for employer-union relations which has made them fair and "clean," and each side considers the other an equal.

4. The white-collar workers have developed their own goals on wage policy and related matters, which reflect the special interests, of their members.

5. Since the law establishing the right of negotiation and collective bargaining was enacted (1936), employer resistance against unionization among white-collar workers has on the whole disappeared. Only a very small category of employees with managerial responsibility form an exception and are precluded from organizing.

6. The blue-collar workers' federation, LO, took a favorable view of the white-collar workers' efforts to form unions of their own.

Relations between the organized white-collar workers and the organized blue-collar workers are good; jurisdictional disputes are few and are settled in an orderly manner. The machinery for settling such disputes is a joint committee of TCO, the largest white-collar federation, and LO, the blue-collar workers' federation, which promotes jurisdictional agreements between affiliates of the two federations. Several such agreements are in force. At present, jurisdictional disputes occur only regarding certain segments of government-operated enterprises. In comparison to LO, TCO exercises less central control over the activities of its affiliates, i.e., the TCO affiliates can pursue their activities with far less interference from their federation than can LO affiliates. First and foremost, TCO has conducted central wage negotiations covering its entire field of organization only in rare and exceptional instances, whereas central coordination has become the rule with LO during the past decade.

Future developments in Swedish white-collar unionism are difficult to forecast. It is obvious that the percentage of white-collar workers in the gainfully employed population will continue to increase, and that this increase will make new and perhaps greater demands on the white-collar organizations than they have had to face in the past. An improvement in the effectiveness of their activities will be required and can be achieved only if they join forces in a united white-collar worker movement. The question then arises whether in the future the white-collar organizations will continue their existence separate from the blue-collar movement. It is hard to provide an answer. The difference in political attitudes must be taken into consideration: the white-collar organizations are politically neutral, while the blue-collar organizations have links with the Social Democratic Party. In addition, there are important differences in wage policy. It is an open question as to whether these and other differences will be maintained or will gradually disappear. Judging the future by the present situation, however, the assumption appears to be justified that a merging of all wage earner groups into a single trade-union movement is not likely to occur in the foreseeable future.

February 1962

VIII

WHITE-COLLAR UNIONISM IN THE UNITED STATES

BY EVERETT M. KASSALOW

The United States is the first country in the world in which manual or blue-collar workers have ceased to be the largest single occupational groups of the labor force. They have been displaced in recent years by white-collar workers.

Unionization among white-collar workers has, however, as yet made only limited progress. In a few industries, including entertainment, the railways and some other parts of transport, and the federal postal service, white-collar unions are well established. Elsewhere in the economy, although a fair number of unions exist and some have been established for many years, the degree of unionization among white-collar workers continues to be only moderate or slight.

Developments in recent years suggest that the relatively weak state of white-collar unionism may be in the process of change. A series of social, economic, and technological shifts are tending to create a more favorable environment for unionizing efforts among white-collar workers.

THE UNITED STATES LABOR FORCE

Changing Employment Patterns

Among the developments which have great significance for the prospects of white-collar unionism are the changes which have been occurring in the nation's labor force. In 1957 the number of white-collar workers exceeded corresponding figures for manual workers for the first time. By 1960 the white-collar sector constituted 43.3 per cent of the labor force. The proportion of manual workers had fallen to 38.6 per cent with service workers making up 11.7 per cent and farm workers accounting for 6.4 per cent. (See Table 1.)

While the growth in nonmanual employment has been rather widely noted only in recent years, the change has been under way for many decades. One student of the conditions of the American workers in the twenties has commented, for example, that especially "dramatic" in that decade "was the marked movement from blue-collar to white-collar work, from physically productive to overhead employment. . . . During the twenties, that is, the American worker on an increasing scale took off his overalls and put on a white shirt and necktie." [1]

Yet, one must note that while the percentage of white-collar workers in the labor force has increased steadily for decades, the nature or source of this increase has changed in the past ten years. Until 1950, gains in the white-collar sector reflected declines in extractive employment such as agriculture and mining; other manual percentages were still advancing slightly or holding even. Between 1900 and 1930, for example, the farm work force declined from 37.5 per cent to 21.2 per cent as a percentage of the total civilian labor force. Correspondingly, white-collar workers advanced from 17.6 per cent to 29.4 per cent of the total; manual workers also increased moderately as a relative share of the labor force, rising from 35.8 per cent to 39.6 per cent. Between 1930 and 1950, the share of manual workers in total employment continued to rise slightly, and the percentage of farm workers fell once more. The number of white-collar employees once again increased on a relative as well as an absolute basis.[2]

The trend in the 1950-60 decade, however, was of a different nature. Farm employment continued to decline, but so did manual or blue-collar employment. The upsurge of white-collar workers in the 1950's was a result of a relative decline in the number of both farm and manual workers. Employment in the service industries also showed an important relative increase in the 1950-60 period.

[1] Irving Bernstein, *The Lean Years* (Boston: Houghton, Mifflin, 1960), p. 55.
[2] David L. Kaplan and M. Claire Casey, *Occupational Trends in the United States 1900 to 1950* (Washington: Bureau of the Census Working Paper No. 5, U.S. Dept. of Commerce, 1958).

Table 1. Selected Occupations, Employed Civilian Workers, United States, 1940-60 [a]

Occupational Group	*1960* Number	*1960* Per Cent	*1950* Number	*1950* Per Cent	*1940* Number	*1940* Per Cent	*Per Cent Increase* 1940–50	*Per Cent Increase* 1950–60
White-Collar Workers	26,587,834	*43.3*	20,819,314	*37.4*	14,676,255	*32.9*	41.9	27.7
Professional, technical, and kindred workers	7,232,410	11.8	4,921,272	8.8	3,579,585	8.0	37.5	47.0
Clerical and kindred workers	9,306,896	15.1	6,954,440	12.5	4,382,300	9.8	58.7	33.8
Sales workers	4,638,985	7.5	3,906,794	7.0	3,080,714	6.9	26.8	18.7
Managerial, officials, and proprietors, except farm	5,409,543	8.8	5,036,808	9.0	3,633,656	8.1	38.6	7.4
Manual Workers	23,746,463	*38.6*	22,437,059	*40.3*	16,394,204	*36.7*	36.9	5.8
Craftsmen, foremen, and kindred workers	8,741,292	14.2	7,820,634	14.0	5,171,394	11.6	51.2	11.8
Operatives and kindred workers	11,897,636	19.4	11,180,315	20.1	8,079,922	18.1	38.4	6.4
Laborers, except farm and mine	3,107,535	5.1	3,436,110	6.2	3,142,888	7.0	9.3	−9.6
Service Workers, Including Private Household	7,170,784	*11.7*	5,708,178	*10.2*	5,291,594	*11.9*	7.9	25.6
Agricultural Workers	3,950,491	*6.4*	6,727,789	*12.1*	8,289,911	*18.5*	−18.8	−41.3

[a] While this table and some of the subsequent discussion is based upon the decennial census material, elsewhere I have used the various Monthly Reports, on the Labor Force of the U.S. Department of Labor as well as material drawn from monthly employer payroll reports to the U.S. Department of Labor. The Monthly Report on the Labor Force is based upon a sample, 35,000 household surveys, and is perhaps not quite as reliable as the Census data which is based upon a total population report, from which is drawn a 1 per cent sample. The differences are not very great, however, when laid side by side, and moreover, the trends within the different series are similar.

Source: U.S. Census of Population, 1960, summary table in U.S. Dept. of Labor, Bureau of Labor Statistics, *Monthly Labor Review* (November 1962), p. 1211.

Projections of labor force evolution into the 1960's and 1970's indicate a further development of these trends. The Bureau of Labor Statistics points to the great increases in the labor force which will take place in the 1960's and early 1970's, but BLS studies also note that these increases will be led by heavy additions of professional, technical, and clerical workers, with only modest absolute increases in the number of manual employees. (See Table 2.)

Table 2. Employment by Occupational Groups, 1960 Actual and 1975 Projected (Millions of Persons)

	1960	*1975*	*Per Cent Change 1960–75*
Total employment	66.7	87.6	31
Professional, technical, and kindred	7.5	12.4	65
Managers, officials, and proprietors, excluding farm	7.1	9.4	32
Clerical and kindred	9.8	14.2	45
Sales workers	4.4	5.9	34
Craftsmen, foremen, and kindred	8.6	11.2	30
Operatives and kindred	12.0	14.2	18
Service workers	8.3	12.5	51
Laborers	3.7	3.7	0
Farmers, farm managers, farm laborers, and foremen	5.4	3.9	−28

Source: *Manpower Report of the President* and *A Report on Manpower Requirements, Resources, Utilization, and Training*, U.S. Dept. of Labor (1963), p. 100.

These changes in the composition of the workforce are a result of the fact that American consumers are demanding relatively more and more services—more education, entertainment, medical treatment, and travel, to name a few—and relatively fewer commodities. As Table 3 shows, the trend to white-collar employment certainly reflects this relative shift from goods-producing to service-producing industries. The service industries as a whole, including government which has been its fastest growing component, tend to employ a higher proportion of nonmanual workers than do the goods-producing industries. This trend insures further relative gains for nonmanual workers. As we shall indicate below, moreover, in manufacturing, the core of goods-producing employment, internal forces are also shifting the labor force increasingly into nonmanual channels.

Equally important from a labor relations and unionization viewpoint are the great changes taking place in the nation's industrial processes. There is a steady shift to automated equipment, automatic processes, and flows, with a corresponding increased demand for engineers and technicians. Both developments are producing a sharp growth in white-collar work measured either in absolute or relative standards.

Table 3. Per Cent Distribution of Employment by Industry Division and Selected Subdivisions, 1947, 1957, 1962

Industry Division	*1947*	*1957*	*1962*
Total [a]	100.0	100.0	100.0
Goods-producing industries	51.3	45.9	41.8
Manufacturing	29.8	29.0	27.7
Service-producing industries	48.7	54.1	58.2
Government	10.5	12.9	15.2

[a] Represents wage and salary employment in nonfarm industries based on employers' payroll data, plus total employment in agriculture based on household survey data.

Source: *Manpower Report of the President* and *A Report on Manpower Requirements, Resources, Utilization, and Training,* U.S. Dept. of Labor (1963), p. 17.

One further broad aspect of the shift to white-collar work is worth noting: it opens up new, wide employment opportunities for women. In 1960, females constituted better than 50 per cent of total white-collar employment (not including managers and supervisors); they account for only 15 per cent of the blue-collar force.

Notable in the labor force trends for its influence on white-collar employment has been the substantial growth in public employment reflecting the widening role of government in American society. Government employment of 3.2 million in 1930 accounted for 10.8 per cent of total nonagricultural employment; by 1960 government employment totaled 8.5 million or 16 per cent of total nonagricultural employment.

Contrary to popular misconception about the supposedly constant growth in federal employment, an analysis by Daniel H. Kruger shows that federal employment in 1960 was actually one-third below its

1945 peak, while state and especially local government employment showed the greatest gains in the past decade. (See Table 4.)

Of the nearly 4.8 million employees in local government, it should be added that about half are employed in education. Approximately two-thirds of the 2.4 million who are in education are teachers, the rest being counsellors, administrators, clerks, janitors, and the like.

Aside from the increase in public employment, some growth in

Table 4. Summary of Public Employment, by Level of Government[a] (in Thousands)

Year	*All Government*	*Federal*	*State and Local*	*State*	*Local*
1930	3202	580	2622	433	2189
1945	6556	3375	3181	n.a.	n.a.
1955	7432	2378	5054	1250	3904
1960	8808	2421	6387	1592	4795

(1945, 1955, and 1960 are for month of October; 1930 is annual data.)

[a] See Daniel A. Kruger, "Trends in Public Employment," paper presented to *Annual Meeting of Industrial Relations Research Association* (New York City, December 29, 1961).

service and trade also helps to account for the relative gains in white-collar employment. Service employment, which made up 11.5 per cent of total nonagricultural employment in 1930, was up to 13.5 per cent by 1960. Trade employment grew from 19.7 per cent of the total in 1930 to 21 per cent in 1960.[3]

Occupational Groupings

The various categories of white-collar, manual, and service workers, of course, have their own special definitions under occupational nomenclature in the United States. Broadly speaking, the Census Bureau recognizes three main occupational categories in the economically active civilian population: white-collar workers, manual and service workers, and farm workers. Beyond this, for most purposes, the service workers are generally broken out of the second category to make a separate group, leaving four major occupational groups in all.

[3] *Employment and Earnings,* U.S. Bureau of Labor Statistics, Bulletin No. 1312-1 (1963).

For a clearer understanding of what is included under white-collar occupations, it is essential to set forth at least a minimum tabulation of the other major labor force groups.

Manual workers

Craftsmen, foremen, and kindred workers
- Carpenters
- Construction craftsmen, except carpenters
- Mechanics and repairmen
- Metal craftsmen, except mechanics
- Other craftsmen and kindred workers
- Foremen, not elsewhere classified

Operatives and kindred workers
- Drivers and deliverymen
- Other operatives and kindred workers

Laborers, except farm and mine
- Construction
- Manufacturing
- Other industries

Service Workers

Private household workers

Service workers, except private household
- Protective service workers
- Waiters, cooks, and bartenders
- Other service workers

Farm Workers

Farm laborers and foremen
- Paid workers
- Unpaid family workers

Since there may be some confusion about certain marginal groups, let it be noted that such occupations as hospital attendants, plant guards, watchmen and doorkeepers, all types of policemen and marshals, counter and fountain workers, ushers, practical nurses, barbers and beauticians, elevator operators, firemen and janitors, among others, are included under the category, "Service Workers."

White-Collar Workers: Professional, Managerial, Clerical, and Sales

The white-collar occupational group is broken into four main sections: professional, technical, and kindred workers; managers, officials, and proprietors, except farm; clerical and kindred workers; and sales workers. Each of these four main categories of white-collar workers has its own subgroups and these are listed below in Table 5, along with employment for each of the groups and largest subgroups in 1960.

Table 5. White-Collar Workers, Selected Occupational Distribution, 1960 (in Thousands)

Occupational Group	*1960*
Professional, technical, and kindred workers	7,232
Medical and other health workers	1,306
Teachers, elementary and secondary schools	1,522
Engineers	854
Other professional, technical, and kindred workers	3,350
Managers, officials, and proprietors, except farm	5,410
Salaried workers	3,388
Self-employed workers in retail trade	2,022
Clerical and kindred workers	9,306
Stenographers, typists, and secretaries	2,179
Other clerical and kindred workers	7,127
Sales workers	7,334
Retail trade	4,639
Other sales workers	2,695

Source: U.S. Census of Population, 1960, summary table in U.S. Dept. of Labor, Bureau of Labor Statistics, *Monthly Labor Review* (November 1962), p. 1211.

Returning to Table 1, we can see that the category of professional, technical, and kindred workers has been the fastest growing part of the labor force in the decade of the 1950's. In 1960 the group comprised over 7,232,000 persons. In addition to the rather obvious professional types, such as lawyers, engineers, doctors, and teachers, it includes technicians such as draftsmen, engineering aides and laboratory testers in factories, airline pilots, professional nurses (but not practical nurses), and those employed as entertainers. According to the 1960 Census the following were the six leading groups in the professional, technical, and kindred category: teachers, 1,522,000; engineers, 854,000; professional nurses (including student nurses), 640,000; auditors and accountants, 471,000; physicians and surgeons 229,000; lawyers and judges, 212,000.

These six categories accounted for well over half the employment in the professional and technical group of more than 50 listed occupations (as well as a large miscellaneous group of not otherwise classified professionals). Indeed, the first three—teachers, engineers, and nurses—totaled over 3 million in 1960. This latter group is particularly significant since most of them more closely resemble employees in the traditional sense than do, for example, doctors and lawyers, who are generally self-employed or in partnerships.

The clerical and kindred category, as Table 5 shows, breaks down broadly into the two classes of stenographers, typists, and secretaries on the one hand, and clerical and kindred workers on the other hand. Aside from stenographers, typists, and secretaries, the largest groups among the clerical category are bookkeepers and cashiers as well as telephone operators, shipping and receiving clerks, office machine operators, bank tellers, and mail carriers.

In addition to the usual shop clerks, the sales worker white-collar category includes the following important occupations: insurance agents and brokers, real-estate agents and brokers, and newsboys.

Putting aside the managerial employees, the following Table 6 shows the distribution of various categories of white-collar workers by industry in the United States as of April 1963 (a stable month, from the standpoint of seasonal employment fluctuations).

As indicated in this table, the services account for the largest number of white-collar workers, totaling over 7 million. Trade, both wholesale and retail, accounts for over 5 million white-collar employees. These two areas are popularly associated with white-collar employment; but, surprisingly, manufacturing accounts for the employment of almost 4.5 million white-collar workers of all types.

The nearly 4.5 million white-collar employees in manufacturing are worthy of special attention in any study of white-collar unionism in the United States. The very rise of mass unionism in America, which dates back only a little more than 25 years, was triggered by the upsurge of unionization in the mass-production industries. While many individual unions can point to proud histories which predated the mid-1930's by 50 years or more, it has only been in the past 25 years or so that unionism has operated as a continuing mass force in American life. Indeed, the latest available count still shows that unionized manufacturing workers make up some 45.8 per cent of all union membership, and 48.4 per cent of the membership of the AFL-CIO.[4] Considering that manufacturing accounts for only a little over 30 per cent of total nonagricultural employment in the United States, the importance of manufacturing unionism is obvious.

In a very immediate sense, then, what happens to manufacturing employment and unionism sharply affects the state of organized labor

[4] *Union Membership, 1962, Summary Release,* U.S. Dept. of Labor (January 1964).

Table 6. Distribution of White-Collar Workers by Industry, April 1963 (in Thousands)

	Professional, Technical, and Kindred	*Sales*	*Clerical and Kindred*	*Total*
Agriculture	43	5	19	67
Forestry and Fisheries	42	—	10	52
Mining	41	4	50	95
Construction	175	4	197	376
Manufacturing	1,663	597	2,190	4,450
Durable	1,142	184	1,280	2,606
Nondurable	521	413	910	1,844
Transportation and Public Utilities	248	22	1,064	1,334
Railroads	18	—	152	170
Other transportation	45	9	307	361
Other utilities	185	13	605	803
Trade	237	3,117	1,814	5,168
Wholesale	53	432	519	1,004
Retail	184	2,686	1,295	4,165
Finance, Insurance, and Real Estate	123	552	1,387	2,062
Service	5,120	96	2,039	7,255
Business and repair	195	49	377	621
Private household	7	—	14	21
Other personal	94	17	204	315
Entertainment	106	10	87	203
Education	2,629	7	445	3,081
Other professional	2,089	13	912	3,014
Public Administration	621	4	1,387	2,012
	8,313[a]	4,401[a]	10,157[a]	22,871[a]

[a] Columns not always additive due to rounding.
Source: Unpublished data of U.S. Dept. of Labor, Bureau of Labor Statistics.

in the United States. On the whole, manufacturing employment as such has held up reasonably well (32.5 per cent in 1930 and 29.7 per cent in 1964 of all nonagricultural employment); but the percentage shift in the past few decades toward white-collar work within manufacturing has been very significant. Union strength in manufacturing, of course, remains highly concentrated in the blue-collar or manual sector, while more and more of the employment in manufacturing tends to be white-collar.

The relative decline of the manual worker and with it the relative union strength in manufacturing has particular significance for the whole of American labor. Much of what is new in collective bargaining in the United States in the past 25 years has stemmed from the activities of the unions in manufacturing, especially in the mass-production industries. To assess the shift from manual to nonmanual work, it is helpful to look at some other labor force data drawn from key manufacturing industries. In the postwar period (1947-64) employment of production and related workers in manufacturing as a percentage of total employment fell 9.5 per cent. (For our purposes here, production and related workers are equated with manual workers in manufacturing, though this definition does not precisely accord with the Census classification which has been used above.) But this trend was by no means an even one, as shown by Table 7. In aircraft, the drop is over 18 per cent since 1947 and nonmanual workers now constitute 45 per cent of the workforce in this industry. In motor vehicles, the decline of production and maintenance employment was less than 5 per cent, and in steel the percentage trend has been a little less than the general manufacturing shift since 1947. In chemicals and petroleum the switch to nonmanual labor has been nearly as spectacular as in aircraft, and blue-collar workers are well below two-thirds of the workforce in these industries.

Part of the relative decline of blue-collar employment in manufacturing (and elsewhere in the economy) in the late fifties and early sixties may have been the result of the near stagnation of the American economy in those years. As the economy strengthened and employment advanced more briskly between 1962 and 1964, blue-collar employment also grew notably, and between those years the relative decline in blue-collar or production worker employment was almost negligible. In several industries earlier downtrends were actually reversed to a degree.[5]

Continued strength in the economy may act as a brake on blue- to white-collar trends in the years ahead; but given the nature of

[5] For the economy as a whole, blue-collar workers, whose number had declined almost steadily for a decade to 35.7 per cent of the labor force by 1961, crept up again to 36.3 per cent by 1964. During the same years white-collar employment rose only from 43.6 per cent to 44.2 per cent (at the expense of farm employment). See the *Manpower Report of the President, March, 1965,* Table A-10, U.S. Dept. of Labor (1965), pp. 202-3.

technological change, and the likelihood of further shifts in consumer tastes from goods to services, it is probable that the long-run relative decline of blue-collar workers will go on.

Table 7. Production and Related Workers [a] as a Per Cent of Employment in Selected Industries, 1947-64

	1947	*1951*	*1955*	*1959*	*1962*	*1964*
All Manufacturing	83.6	79.2	78.7	75.6	74.1	74.0
Lumber and wood products (except furniture)	92.7	91.8	90.8	88.9	89.6	89.4
Stone, clay, and glass products	87.7	86.4	84.4	82.1	80.2	80.6
Basic steel	87.7	86.8	85.5	80.2	80.3	81.9
Machinery	73.4	77.6	73.8	70.7	69.6	69.6
Electrical equipment and supplies	78.3	77.7	74.5	69.5	67.8	67.1
Motor vehicles and equipment	81.5	81.9	80.6	77.7	77.2	76.9
Aircraft and parts	73.8	74.5	69.0	61.2	55.0	55.9
Ship and boat building and repairing	88.6	87.4	86.4	83.3	83.8	83.5
Food and kindred products	77.5	73.4	70.8	68.3	66.5	66.1
Textile mill products	93.9	92.6	91.6	90.7	90.0	89.4
Apparel and related products	90.7	89.6	89.1	89.0	88.9	88.9
Paper and allied products	87.3	85.1	82.5	80.4	79.2	78.2
Chemicals and allied products	75.2	71.1	67.0	62.5	61.1	60.3
Petroleum refining and related industries	76.9	74.9	68.8	64.9	64.3	62.1
Rubber and miscellaneous plastic products	81.4	81.1	79.3	77.7	77.4	77.2

[a] Production and related workers include maintenance workers, working foremen, and various service workers such as janitors, warehousing employees, etc., who are closely associated with the above production operations.

Source: U.S. Dept. of Labor, Bureau of Labor Statistics.

The differences between these rates of change from blue- to white-collar workers will, to some extent, explain the interest building up on the issue of white-collar unionism in some unions as opposed to others. These trends are, however, becoming so broad and generalized that many of these differential rates may blur in the next decade. Moreover, as Hill and Harbison have suggested, it is usually the expanding and dynamic companies in any industry which show the most rapid increases in nonmanual employment.[6] American unionism has usually had an eye for the "lead company" in its collective bargaining tactics and objectives. The necessity for maintaining strength in these lead sectors may turn the labor movement increasingly toward the problem of unionizing white-collar workers in manufacturing.

In manufacturing the most rapidly growing employment segment has been the professional and technical group, reflecting the rapid increase in engineering and related occupations. The clerical force in manufacturing has not grown in the past few years, though it did expand in the early fifties. The manual force in manufacturing, including semiskilled operatives and laborers as well as craftsmen, has been fairly stable (with laborers declining and semiskilled operatives and craftsmen increasing moderately). Relatively speaking, the proportion of manual workers as a percentage of total employment in manufacturing has declined. (See Table 8.)

Beginnings of White-Collar Unionism in the United States *

Although the American labor movement has always been a predominantly manual workers' organization, one can find important instances of the organization of white-collar workers early in the history of each of the main labor federations which developed in the past seventy or eighty years. On the other hand, there has never been what one might call an over-all concerted white-collar union movement as such in the United States. This is, of course, in contrast to most other Western labor movements which have produced either separate white-collar federations or separate councils, departments, or coordinating committees for white-collar workers within the main labor federations.[7]

In the early years of American labor history, and reference here

[6] Samuel E. Hill and Frederick Harbison, *Manpower and Innovation in American Industry* (Princeton: Princeton University Press, 1959), pp. 53-56.
* For reasons of space it is impossible to sketch even briefly the beginnings of more than a few of the white-collar unions. We have generally chosen the largest or those that tend to illustrate some special aspect of white-collar work in American society as well as those which have organized a substantial section of key jurisdictions. Another factor in the selection has been that many unions still lack a good written history. Unions whose importance seems to date exclusively or primarily from the period of World War II and later are treated below under "The Current Status of White-Collar Unionism."
[7] Interestingly enough, the Canadian Labour Congress has announced its launching of an over-all concerted white-collar organizing drive on behalf of 20 unions in the CLC. *AFL-CIO News*, March 9, 1962.

Table 8. Persons Employed in Manufacturing by Major Occupational Groups (in Thousands), 1952, 1960, 1963, April of Each Year

	1952	*1960*	*1963*	*Per Cent Change 1952–63*
Total Employed	16,270	17,400	17,952	+10.3
Professional, technical, and kindred	858	1,415	1,663	+93.8
Managers, officials, and proprietors	858	1,076	1,147	+33.7
Clerical and kindred	1,922	2,180	2,190	+13.9
Sales	462	575	597	+29.2
Craftsmen, foremen	3,226	3,318	3,353	+ 3.9
Operatives	7,304	7,331	7,763	+ 6.3
Service	330	366	303	− 8.2
Laborers	1,304	1,144	935	−28.3

Selected White-Collar Occupations as a Per Cent of Total Manufacturing Employment, 1952, 1960, and 1963

	1952	*1960*	*1963*
Professional and technical	5.3	8.1	9.3
Clerical and kindred	11.8	12.5	12.2
Sales	2.8	3.3	3.3

Source: Unpublished data of U.S. Dept. of Labor, Bureau of Labor Statistics.

is made primarily to the pre–New Deal and pre–Wagner or National Labor Relations Act era, white-collar unions were subject to many of the same pressures and attacks as were unions of the manual workers. Yellow-dog contracts were used against them in private industry on occasion, and in government so-called gag rules and dismissals without hearing were employed to combat their efforts to organize.

Notable among the early white-collar organizations at the end of the nineteenth and in the early twentieth century were those of the government postal employees, the retail clerks, and the railway clerks.

Early AFL White-Collar Affiliates

Retail Clerks. The present Retail Clerks International Association [8] was formally chartered by the American Federation of Labor in 1890. Its roots, however, seem to go back as far as 1865 when local efforts at organizing retail clerks were undertaken in Cleveland, Ohio. In succeeding years similar organizing beginnings can be traced to Providence, New Orleans, and Indianapolis. The Knights of Labor, the principal central labor federation in the decades after the American Civil War, established several locals of clerical employees in the 1870's and 1880's.[9]

The incredibly long work day required of retail clerks was a prime factor in inducing some of them to form "early closing societies" in those years. These early groups were caught up in the great campaign being conducted for the eight-hour day by the Knights of Labor. By 1890 the early closing societies among clerical employees felt the need for an organization that could meet their own problems more directly. The American Federation of Labor had issued individual charters to units of retail clerks in Muskegon, Michigan, and Indianapolis, Indiana, in 1888 and 1889. In 1890, 18 additional charters were granted to clerks' units and later that year the Retail Clerks Union was chartered as a national body. The union virtually from its origin, incidentally, voted to admit women to membership.

In its first years the union had considerable growth, from a membership of three thousand in 1897 to twenty thousand in 1900, and in 1904 it was paying per capita tax to the AFL on the basis of fifty thousand members. (This was, however, possibly some overstatement of actual membership.)

Reflecting in part the relative importance of the clerks in those years, Max Morris, Secretary-Treasurer of the Clerks, was also a vice-president of the American Federation of Labor until his death in 1909. It was not until 1957 that another official of the Retail Clerks was to reach the top council of the Federation.

The onset of the depression in 1907 and the entrance into the trade field of new and large groups of employers who were deter-

[8] The name of the union which has been used here is the present one. In a number of cases a union's present title represents an evolution from an older title. In this case, for example, the union was formerly named the International Protective Retail Clerks Association. It should be also noted that in some instances the name officially accepted by the AFL, and later the AFL-CIO, differs from the title assumed by the union itself.

[9] I am indebted to Mr. Ben Seligman, Research Director of the Retail Clerks International Association, for his unpublished "Notes Toward History of the Retail Clerks Movement" for this sketch of the beginnings of retail unionism in the United States.

minedly anti-union also placed great obstacles before the union. By World War I its membership was down to fifteen thousand. The impact of chain stores and department stores in the 1920's as well as the great depression further weakened the Clerks and by 1933 membership was down to five thousand. The coming of the New Deal as well as more favorable social and legal conditions led to a renaissance of this union in the forties and fifties. (Trends in the Clerks Union in this latter period are sketched below.)

Postal Workers. The first important stirrings of organization among white-collar workers in the government service seem to have taken place among postal workers and particularly among letter carriers in the 1880's. As a result of an order by the Post Office Department, these workers found themselves deprived of the protection of the eight-hour day which had been accorded to others employed by the United States Government as "laborers, workmen, or mechanics" in 1868. The employees turned to the Knights of Labor and the eight-hour movement being led by that body.

The Knights supported federal legislation to establish the eight-hour day for carriers and were successful in pushing this through Congress in 1888. In several cities the earlier informal groupings of letter carriers burgeoned into locals of the Knights of Labor affiliated to the central city bodies of the Knights of Labor. Other groups of letter carriers were developing and remained on an independent basis.

These different local groups felt the need for a more national basis of organization (generally labor groupings within the Knights were limited to a city-type of affiliation) and in 1889 and 1890 the National Association of Letter Carriers was established. Unsuccessful efforts were made by some of the locals of the Knights (which locals, however, were also part of the National Association) to bring the entire group within the Knights of Labor. Some early efforts were also made to affiliate the carriers with the AFL, but the necessary votes failed to carry and it was not until 1917 that the formal affiliation of the Letter Carriers to the AFL took place. By 1900 the National Association of Letter Carriers had organized its jurisdiction of city letter carriers almost completely.[10]

The postal clerks' organizing efforts paralleled those of the letter carriers of the 1880's but were less successful. The clerks did not

[10] Sterling D. Spero, *The Labor Movement in a Government Industry* (New York: Doran, 1924). Has an outstanding account of the early efforts of postal employees to unionize.

enjoy the natural advantages of the letter carriers who were operating in the large cities. Moreover, the clerks covered a more varied series of occupations and did not enjoy the special occupational identity that characterized the city letter carriers.

The postal clerks were also involved with the Knights of Labor in efforts to obtain favorable legislation on working hours. Early organization efforts resulted in the formation of a National Association of Post Office Clerks in 1890 and a split-off of this union, the United National Association of Post Office Clerks, in 1899. The former was shortly to be plagued with corruption involving promotion scandals in the postal service. UNAPOC admitted supervisors to membership and these supervisors tended to dominate its policies to the dissatisfaction of many rank-and-file postal clerks.[11]

The AFL had also, during this period, chartered a few locals of postal clerks and notably one in Chicago. Relationships between the AFL and UNAPOC were fairly sympathetic. The Chicago AFL local worked for some time, but without success, to bring about the affiliation of the UNAPOC with the AFL.

Additional friction occurred in the UNAPOC. Finally, under the leadership of the Chicago postal clerks in 1906, the National Federation of Post Office Clerks was formed, and shortly thereafter the union was officially chartered by the AFL. In a relatively short time the NFPOC became the leading postal clerks' organization.

In the years 1900-1910, the postal unions of carriers, clerks, and railway mail clerks (the Railway Mail Association, which later became the National Postal Transport Association, merged in 1961 with the Postal Clerks) operated in the face of severe difficulties. Irritated by pressure from the postal organizations who were clamoring for improvements in their unsatisfactory working conditions, President Theodore Roosevelt in 1902 issued the first of the famous "gag" orders which made it illegal for federal employees "either directly or indirectly, individually or through associations, to solicit an increase of pay or to influence or attempt to influence any legislation whatsoever either before Congress or its committees, or in any way save through the heads of the Departments in or under which they serve, on penalty of dismissal from the Government Service."

Membership in postal unions as such was permissible but no direct lobbying could be undertaken legally with Congress. When the president of the Letter Carriers violated the order to lobby for a

[11] See Spero, *op. cit.*, pp. 79-95; and Karl Baarslag, *History of the National Federation of Post Office Clerks* (Washington, D.C., 1945).

reclassification act in 1907, the Postmaster General successfully demanded that he not stand for re-election in the union on penalty of being suspended from the postal service.[12]

In issuing the gag rule, Roosevelt was also echoing the sentiments of Representative Loud of California, Chairman of the Post Office and Post Roads Committee of the House of Representatives. Loud aroused the opposition of all the postal unions who endorsed his successful Democratic opponent in the 1902 election. The House Committee continued, however, under the control of forces unfriendly to the postal unions.

The gag rule was not always strictly enforced in its first years, but President Roosevelt and after him President Taft emphasized and strengthened it.

During these years many groups in the postal service, with much personal heroism, continued to fight against the gag rule. They also campaigned against the atrocious working conditions under which many railway mail and postal clerks were employed. "In one year 27 railway clerks had been burned or crushed to death in railroad accidents, 98 had been seriously injured or maimed for life, and 617 had suffered 'minor injuries.' This heavy toll of human life and injury was largely due to the use of obsolete, rickety, wooden mail coaches between the locomotive and heavy steel cars. . . . In wreck after wreck the wooden mail cars were crushed to splinters while the heavy locomotives and steel coaches suffered little damage or even remained upright on the tracks. When railway clerks pleaded with the railroads to carry these death traps at the end of the train, they were curtly told that this was impossible. . . ." Indeed, the gag rule was extended by a special order in 1906 which "forbade giving out any publicity or information involving the service of the railroads." [13]

Very heavy workloads in some post offices were intensified as a result of a speed-up order issued in 1910 by the Postmaster General in President Taft's Cabinet. Postal clerks were subject to fines up to $25 for shortcomings or rules infractions until the union successfully sued for the recovery of these fines and put an end to the system.[14]

The physical working conditions of the postal clerks were also miserable in a number of cities. In 1909 NFPOC President Oscar Nelson smuggled four members of the State Commission on Occupa-

[12] Spero, *op. cit.*, pp. 115-17.
[13] Baarslag, *op. cit.*, p. 56.
[14] *Blazing a Trail Thru NFPOC Headquarters, 33 Years of Service,* National Federation of Post Office Clerks (1939), p. 9.

tional Diseases in to examine the working conditions of Chicago postal clerks on the night force. The inspectors were horrified with the conditions and publicly condemned them. Under the gag rule which was still in effect, Nelson was dismissed from the service for having publicly exposed the conditions and for bringing them directly to the attention of Congress.[15]

Unlawful strikes began to erupt in the postal service; in a number of instances the leaders of the insurgents were dismissed. The AFL and its leaders in key cities, and President Gompers at the national level, argued the case of the clerks and their organizations but to little avail. The Chief Inspector of the Postmaster General, indeed, sought to portray the AFL as some sort of secret, seditious type of organization.

Congress was drawn into the struggle and Congressman Lloyd in the House and Senator La Follette of Wisconsin took the lead in investigating working conditions in the postal service. La Follette claimed that postal authorities were secretly opening his mail in an effort to sabotage his inquiries.[16]

The postal authorities now rushed to withdraw the old gag rule, but Congress pushed ahead and on August 24, 1912, the Lloyd–La Follette Act was passed, guaranteeing the rights of federal employees to join unions to bring about improvements "in the conditions of labor of its members" by handling grievances, petitioning Congress and the like. (The Lloyd–La Follette Act is discussed in more detail below on pp. 330-37, "Legal Framework of White Collar Unionism Today.")

A long struggle for recognition by postal carriers and clerks had come to fruition. Until the passage of this legislation, some of the unions in the postal service tended to be under the influence of the Post Office Department. This situation began to disappear after 1912, especially in the case of unions affiliated with the American Federation of Labor.

In the debates which took place during these years over the various federal acts regulating the rights of federal employees and their unions, one critical issue which was settled concerned the propriety of federal employees' unions affiliating with the AFL. While some objections were first made to such affiliation, by the end of World War I this right of affiliation was well established.

[15] Baarslag, *op. cit.*, pp. 59-60.
[16] This was the father of the late Senator La Follette whose investigation in the thirties helped to destroy the labor spy and company union systems in private industry.

Railway Clerks. The present union of Railway Clerks had its formal beginnings in 1899, but "clubs" for these workers existed in Cincinnati, St. Louis, Cleveland, Sedalia, and New Orleans for some years before 1899. These were largely fraternal organizations but they were the nucleus out of which true unionism was to develop. An American Association of Railway Clerks attempted to federate these clubs, and while there is no evidence it had any relationship with the railway carriers, it did attempt to set up a national insurance fund for clerks. Such insurance funds had already been established by railway unions operating on behalf of engineers, conductors, and firemen.

Some discussions about the necessity for serious unionism among railway clerks seem to have gone on in 1888 and 1889, but when employers got word of it, they warned that continuation of this activity would lead to discharges.[17]

Finally on December 29, 1899, railway clerks employed on the Missouri-Pacific and Missouri-Kansas-Texas lines convened in Sedalia to found a national organization. By the time of the first convention in 1901, 20 lodges were functioning and the union was well on its way. The Order of Railroad Clerks of America, as it was first called, affiliated briefly with the AFL but quickly withdrew, apparently for financial reasons. The union went through its first lockout in 1902 and its first strike in 1906.[18]

In 1908 the Clerks applied for readmission to AFL and were readmitted. A jurisdictional dispute with the Brotherhood of Teamsters led to a suspension of the Clerks in 1926, but they returned in 1928 and have remained since then.

In the first decade of its existence the Clerks made slow progress and by World War I had a membership of only fifteen thousand. Along about that time the successes of other railway unions on both the collective bargaining and national legislative fronts (the famous Adamson Act providing an eight-hour day for railway employees was passed during this period) began to have an impact on railway clerks. These factors, the opportunities for organization presented by World War I, and more vigorous leadership moved the union along swiftly in the next few years, and by 1920 the Clerks' membership was up

[17] Most of this sketch of unionism among railway clerks is drawn from Harry Henig, *The Brotherhood of Railway Clerks* (New York: Columbia University Press, 1937), pp. 3-37.

[18] *Manual of Brotherhood of Railway and Steamship Clerks, Freight Handlers, Express and Station Employees,* Part IV, History of the Brotherhood (1946), p. 1.

to 186,000. From that period on, despite some fluctuations, it was to remain a leader in the white-collar field and, indeed, in the Federation generally.

Teachers. The roots of the American Federation of Teachers go back to 1897 with the formation of the Independent Chicago Teachers Federation. Salaries of Chicago teachers had been practically stationary for about twenty years in the latter part of the nineteenth century. Progress continued to be slow, however, and in succeeding years the Chicago teachers looked increasingly to the Chicago labor movement in their struggle for improved schools and teachers' conditions. By 1902 the Chicago Teachers Federation joined the local central Federation of Labor and was also chartered by the AFL. Attacks on education appropriations were common in those years, and teachers' salaries before and during World War I lagged behind those of other workers.

The Chicago teachers' group continued to lead in exposing shabby school conditions and starved educational appropriations. In retaliation the Chairman of the Chicago Board of Education issued the so-called Loeb rule "which placed all teachers under a 'yellow dog' contract prohibiting membership in labor unions." Only strong action by the teachers and the Chicago Federation of Labor prevented the authorities from enforcing this rule.[19]

Groups of teachers in other parts of the country were also banding together in these years, as in New York City, Butte, Montana, Gary, Indiana, Washington, D.C., and Scranton, Pennsylvania. Locals of teachers from these cities became charter members of the American Federation of Teachers which was formally launched in response to a call by the Chicago local on April 15, 1916.

During this same period, important independent groups of teachers were begun in Atlanta, Georgia, and St. Paul, Minnesota. These and other groups eventually joined the newly formed AFT. While the teachers made some fair progress at first and had a membership of 9,300 in 1921, by 1929 the union's membership had shrunk to 4,200 according to per capita membership reports of the AFL. Its greatest growth was to come in the post–World War II period.

Musicians. White-collar unions in the entertainment field have a long history in the American labor movement. The American Feder-

[19] *Organizing the Teaching Profession, the Story of the American Federation of Teachers,* by the Commission on Educational Reconstruction of the American Federation of Teachers (Glencoe, Illinois: The Free Press, 1955), p. 25.

ation of Musicians, which formally dates back to its founding convention in Indianapolis, Indiana, in 1896, had its roots deep into the nineteenth century. There are references to local groupings of musicians in Baltimore and Chicago as early as 1857. A clear-cut union beginning was made by a group in New York City in 1863. In succeeding years, additional locals sprang up in the Midwest and the East.

At the initiative of a Philadelphia local in 1871, the National Musical Association was established "to deal with matters of common interest" and "to tackle the problems of competition" raised by different locals for traveling musicians and road shows. The organization was never very effective, never covered more than seventeen locals, and lasted only ten years.[20]

By 1855 a new organizing effort was launched by a Cincinnati local and a meeting of representatives from seven large cities established the National League of Musicians of the United States. This organization grew rapidly to nine thousand members by 1896. Much debated in the conventions of the NLM were questions of whether musicians were "laborers in the field of music" or "professionals," and whether or not they belonged in the AFL.

By the early 1890's a majority of the locals were in favor of affiliation with the AFL, but the group in New York and a few other eastern metropolitan areas continued to stress their "professional" character. This group was successful in holding up affiliation. The eastern groups were also concerned about penetration by musicians from other cities.

The AFL at this point began to charter locals of musicians directly affiliated to itself. By 1895 a large majority of the locals of the NLM were also affiliated with the AFL. When in 1896 the NLM by a tie vote once again turned down affiliation, the AFL issued a call and at a convention on November 6, 1896, chartered the American Federation of Musicians. In the next few years the NLM began to disintegrate and its remaining parts were gradually absorbed by the AFM.

The failure of the NLM seems to have been due in part to the political struggle between the eastern groups and the rest of the organized musicians, and in part to its failure to develop sufficient central authority to meet such needs as a national death benefit fund and

[20] This sketch of the early beginnings of unionism among musicians is drawn from Robert D. Leiter, *The Musicians and Petrillo* (New York: Bookman Associates, 1953), esp. pp. 13-25.

the regulation of "competition" between home city and touring musicians.

For a few years some of the largest metropolitan locals remained out of the AFM for fear of an invasion from other areas. Gradually, however, the AFM evolved the system under which musicians could transfer from one local to another when in search of employment, under conditions laid down by the AFM. As a result, the AFM began to extend its own strength and authority. The large locals soon came into the AFM. Indeed, in time locals like that in New York found they could unionize the large theater houses such as Loew, Fox, and Proctor only with the help of the national AFM which kept potential strike breakers out of New York City during the critical periods of negotiations.[21]

Actors. Unions among vaudeville actors go back into the nineteenth century. One such group, chartered as the Actors Protective Union No. 6453, eventually grew into the Actors National Protective Union, chartered in 1896. In 1900 the AFL chartered a second organization of vaudeville actors, the White Rats Actors Union of America, and in 1910 the two unions were amalgamated under the name of the latter organization.[22]

So far as the so-called legitimate stage actors are concerned, they were part of a rather informal industry for most of the nineteenth century. Toward the end of the century, however, a powerful Theater Syndicate appeared on the scene and actors increasingly found themselves under severe economic pressure. In 1896, the first efforts at organization were made and the Actors Society was founded. The Society, however, made very little progress in the face of the Theater Syndicate which was later joined by the famous Shubert Syndicate.

Finally in December 1912, recognizing their own failures, members of the Actors Society dissolved the organization. Some of the members, however, were still determined to build a new organization and a few months later Actors Equity Association was born with 112 members. Several efforts at affiliation with the AFL were made, but not until a disastrous strike practically destroyed the White Rats did the AFL accept the Actors Equity who absorbed the White Rats under the name "Associated Actors and Artistes of America." Eventually this union extended itself to the other theatrical trades, including screen and radio artists, writers, and so forth.

[21] Leiter, *op. cit.*, p. 23.

[22] *Handbook of American Trade Unions,* 1936 edition, *U.S. Bureau of Labor Statistics Bulletin No. 618,* by Ethelbert M. Stewart, Section E.

CIO White-Collar Unionism

White-collar unionism played a very modest role during the upsurge of the Congress of Industrial Organizations in the mid and late 1930's. Unions were, however, formed among office workers, engineers, architects and draftsmen, public service employees, and newspaper editorial employees.

Newspaper Editorial Employees. Efforts to organize a union of newspaper men had been made by the AFL in the 1920's. Several federal locals were chartered and some of these later joined the American Newspaper Guild when it was established.

Wages of editorial employees declined sharply in the early thirties and were accompanied in many instances by heavy layoffs. Taking advantage of the government encouragement of unionism contained in President Roosevelt's National Industrial Recovery Act (NIRA), one of the most widely known and respected columnists of his day, Heywood Broun, and a group of representatives from twenty-one local bodies met and established the Guild as an independent union in Washington, D.C., on December 15, 1933. The organization was a very loose one with little treasury and no full-time officers.

Publishers with long collective bargaining experience involving the various printing unions did not look upon unionism with as much fear as employers in other industries. On the other hand, in the minds of many publishers, unionization of the editorial and news writers was incompatible with professionalism and with the freedom which they wanted to maintain in controlling the editorial policy of their papers. The Guild nevertheless made good progress in the next few years and also took in some newspaper commercial employees. The Guild's greatest strength lay in the newspapers in the nation's large cities.

After some hesitation, the Guild voted to affiliate with the AFL in its 1936 convention. Heywood Broun soon, however, took the lead in moving the Guild out of the AFL into the CIO. The Guild remained with the CIO right down to the 1955 AFL-CIO merger.

For several years the Guild had difficulties arising from the fact that a good part of its top leadership was under communist influence. Intense factionalism weakened the union's collective bargaining efforts until a sweep of the top officers was made by the anti-communist forces in 1941. Thereafter the Guild made substantial gains.

The union's activities have demonstrated that a white-collar professional group could organize without "loss of dignity, and that unionization of newsmen for collective bargaining purposes would not hamper freedom of the press . . . the Guild was and continued to be an important precendent in white-collar unionism."[23]

Public Employees. Other CIO operations in the white-collar field included the establishment of trade unions in the public employment field: State, County, and Municipal Employees in local public service and the United Federal Workers of America in the federal service. These unions were later merged into the United Public Workers of America. The leadership of both these unions tended to be very much under Communist Party influence. Eventually, the Public Workers was among those unions expelled from the CIO in 1950 because of Communist domination. The union disappeared some time thereafter although some of its locals eventually drifted into other unions.

Office Workers. The United Office and Professional Workers was set up by the CIO to organize general white-collar office workers. "To safeguard its principle of industrial unionism," the CIO, however, reserved "the right to delimit the jurisdiction so that automobile, steel, and other office workers might eventually join the industrial unions in their respective industries."[24]

The United Office and Professional Workers of America made some gains in the next few years but suffered from the fact that its leadership tended to be communist-oriented. The union was expelled from the CIO on charges of Communist domination in 1950.

Retail and Wholesale Workers. During these years the CIO also granted a charter to a group of retail clerks' locals who seceded from the AFL Retail Clerks Union, which was at a low point of effectiveness in the early thirties. The United Retail, Wholesale, and Department Store Employees Union, as it became known, made some impressive gains. It had, for example, some notable success in organizing department stores and warehouses in the New York City area. The union today is a member of the AFL-CIO and over the years has expanded its jurisdiction to take in employees in a number of industries.

Generalizations Concerning Early Phases of White-Collar Unionism

A few generalizations suggest themselves from the foregoing sketches of earlier white-collar union efforts in the United States. In

[23] Walter Galenson, *The CIO Challenge to the AFL* (Cambridge: Harvard University Press, 1960), pp. 548-65, for an interesting sketch of the rise of newspaper unionism.

[24] Edward Levinson, *Labor on the March* (New York: Harper & Brothers, 1938), p. 250.

the first place the almost exceptional success of the Railway Clerks indicates that where the work situation of a white-collar group places them in close and constant relationship to unionized related manual workers and where formal governmental procedures almost dictate the necessity of organization (the various Railway Labor Acts), it is not surprising that a certain group of nonmanual workers will unionize as extensively as manual workers in the same industry.

Second, the early and fairly successful efforts at unionization among the postal workers suggest that where, as in the case of a large bureaucratic structure like the federal government, white-collar work tends to lose some of its individuality, and uniform job classification develops, the prospects for unionism are enhanced. It should be noted that by the 1930's unionism was also making some headway among nonpostal employees, but the real breakthroughs in this area are only occurring today, and we have discussed these unions below under the heading, "The Current Status of White-Collar Unionism."

The beginnings of unionism in the entertainment and newspaper fields are also of interest. As we shall indicate below, they relate to the whole problem of infringement of professional status and the way in which this may affect unionization. It might be added here, however, that in the case of these two unions, as well as in the Air Line Pilots Association, referred to below, the union actually has served as a key professionalizing force for the occupation. Unlike teachers or engineers, for example, whose professional "badges" come from special college degrees, these three groups had to use unionism to help achieve full professional recognition. This no doubt helps account for the earlier emergence of successful unionism among musicians (and other entertainers), newspapermen, and pilots, as opposed to other professionals in the United States.

The experiences of the retail clerks are of more historical than substantive interest. It was not until the great revolution in retailing had its impact in food and other stores, that unionism would make serious advances here. Even this might not have proven a sufficient stimulus without the more favorable environment which was provided by the New Deal and the National Labor Relations Act of 1935.

LEGAL FRAMEWORK OF WHITE-COLLAR UNIONISM TODAY

In many other Western countries white-collar workers are treated as a special category in the labor force. Frequently they are covered by special social security systems. In some countries they are not subject to the same general laws with regard to unionism and collective bargaining.

With a notable exception here and there, this is not true in the United States. White-collar workers come under the regular Social Security laws. They are subject to the same labor relations and union regulatory legislation as other workers.

The National Labor Relations Act

The National Labor Relations Act of 1935, as later amended, is the basic law governing labor relations in all firms whose activities affect interstate commerce in the United States, except the railroads and some other branches of transportation. This Act covers all types of employees, blue- or white-collar. The law does not extend to public employment or to nonprofit charitable organizations, such as hospitals.

White-collar workers, like blue-collar workers, who wish to form a union must normally follow the procedures of the NLRA. Thus, they go about seeking exclusive bargaining rights from their employer and this leads to a petition for an election conducted by the National Labor Relations Board to determine whether or not they do have majority status among the given appropriate unit of white-collar workers. If they win this election, the NLRB will certify them to represent all employees in the given unit. They would normally proceed to negotiate a written agreement covering the wages, hours, and working conditions of all employees in that stipulated unit.[25]

Of special importance here is the nature of the unit which is found to be appropriate by the National Labor Relations Board. The NLRB itself has much discretion in determining what unit is appropriate. There are, however, in the statute itself two notable areas, so far as white-collar workers are concerned, where the law stipulates what is or is not an appropriate unit.

The unionization rights and status of foremen and supervisors were never entirely clear in the early years of the National Labor Relations Act. In 1943 after a number of cases were pressed to the Board, the latter decided that foremen were entitled to the protection of the NLRA in their efforts to organize. By 1945 the Board ruled that foremen were also entitled to use its election and certification procedures.

This policy was quickly reversed, however, by the Taft-Hartley amendments to the NLRA which were passed in 1947. These amend-

[25] A general survey of NLRB machinery and procedures, the history of coverage, Taft-Hartley amendments, etc., is contained in Nicholas S. Falcone, *Labor Law* (New York: John Wiley and Sons, Inc., 1962), chaps. 9-10.

ments provided among other things that no bargaining unit including higher foremen or supervisors could be set up by the Board. In effect, foremen and supervisors were taken out from under the NLRA and its protection.

This barrier to the unionization of foremen and supervisors may have some serious long-run repercussions on the general prospects of unionizing white-collar employees. In a few of the European countries where white-collar unionism has made notable progress, the example set by supervisors who have been unionized often has a considerable influence in stimulating organization among nonsupervisory white-collar employees.[26]

As regards other white-collar employees (if they are, for example, clerks employed in a retail store, professional people employed in a purely professional laboratory which has no manufacturing connections, or clerical workers employed in an unattached general office), the problem of unit determination for election and certification is simple. Such white-collar employees form their own appropriate unit and vote for or against unionization.[27]

Where the white-collar workers are part of a large company taking in blue-collar workers and/or taking in a number of different groups of white-collar workers, such as professional, technical, and clerical employees, the appropriate unit for a given election is up to the National Labor Relations Board to determine. There is one important exception here and this is the second of the instances in which the Taft-Hartley amendments to the NLRA deal with the white-collar unit problem explicitly. Under pressure from a number of professional societies and a few small independent engineering union groups, the law was amended to provide that the National Labor Relations Board could not order elections in units which combined professional employees with other employees "unless a majority of such [professional] employees vote for inclusion in such a unit." In practice this has meant that professional employees tend to have separate units for unionizing and bargaining purposes where they seek organization.[28]

[26] For more extensive discussion of the role of supervisors in white-collar organizing, see Everett M. Kassalow, "White-Collar Unionism in Western Europe," *Monthly Labor Review*, U.S. Bureau of Labor Statistics (July 1963), pp. 770-71.

[27] For a summary of current NLRB doctrine on unit determination for various white-collar groups, see *Labor Relations Reporter, Labor Relations Expediter*, Bureau of National Affairs (1963), pp. LRX 40 b, c, 41.

[28] The law defines professional employees as follows: "(a) any employee engaged in work (i) predominantly intellectual and varied in character as opposed to routine mental, mechanical, or physical work; (ii) involving the consistent exer-

In practice too this has meant professional employees are kept separate from such related groups as technical employees like engineering aides or laboratory assistants, except where the professionals decide a joint unit is appropriate.

While the NLRA is generally silent on what other units are appropriate, the Board itself over the years has tended to develop broad policy guidelines for setting up elections among other white-collar employees. Plant clerical workers (as distinguished from office clerical employees) are frequently included in the units covering the production workers in a given plant. Office workers are virtually never put in the same unit with plant production workers in the same company for election purposes, but they are sometimes linked with plant clerical workers.

The status of technical workers under NLRB policy has been somewhat fluid. For some time the Board tended to treat the technical workers separately, as the statute provides that professional employees be treated. The result was that if any party in a given case so desired, elections for technical workers were conducted entirely separate from those of other groups. More recently the Board seems to be moving to the position that technical employees should be related either to the professional group, the plant group, or the office group for unit election purposes, depending upon the nature of their work relationships to these other groups. In other words, if they have a "community of interest" with production employees, they should be part of a combined production-technician unit; if their "community of interest" lies with the office staff, they can be best placed in a combined office-technical unit.[29]

---

cise of discretion and judgment in its performance; (iii) of such a character that the output produced or the result accomplished cannot be standardized in relation to a given period of time; (iv) requiring knowledge of an advanced type in a field of science or learning customarily acquired by a prolonged course of specialized intellectual instruction and study in an institution of higher learning or a hospital, as distinguished from a general academic education or from an apprenticeship or from training in the performance of routine mental, manual, or physical processes; or

"(b) any employee, who (i) has completed the courses of specialized intellectual instruction and study described in clause (iv) of paragraph (a) and (ii) is performing related work under the supervision of a professional person to qualify himself to become a professional employee as defined in paragraph (a)." For full texts of the National Labor Relations Act as amended as well as the Railway Labor Act which is referred to below, see Falcone, *op. cit.*, Appendix.

[29] See, for example, the so-called Sheffield Corp. decision by the Board, *White-Collar Report,* Bureau of National Affairs (December 14, 1961), C1-C4.

The Railway Labor Act

The regulation of labor relations on America's railways is covered by special legislation, the Railway Labor Act, originally passed in 1926 but subsequently amended. This act leans heavily in the direction of establishing employee representation through the majority determination "of any craft or class of employees." This standard has resulted in the development of a systematic pattern of representation by craft groups, and where railway white-collar groups are organized, the units follow fairly narrowly defined occupational lines as compared, for example, with units normally determined under the National Labor Relations Act.

Regulations Affecting State and Local Government Workers

The legal status of unionism and collective bargaining among government white-collar employees is part and parcel of the general status of unionism in public employment. The rights and obligations of public employees so far as forming unions and conducting collective bargaining are concerned naturally vary from one level of government to another, from one state to another, and from one municipality to another. In many cases state and local governments lack specific legislation either protecting or prohibiting unionism among public employees. One expert report with special reference to local government employment concludes, "It is now taken as *datum* that government employees generally, including those serving municipalities, may, even in the absence of express statutory authorization, band together for purposes of their mutual aid and protection." As one New York court has affirmed, "They have the same right to mutual help and assistance that other citizens have, and to group themselves together for that purpose." Or in the words of a Connecticut court, ". . . In the absence of prohibitory statute or regulation, no good reason appears why public employees should not organize as a labor union."[30]

The right of government employees to organize has been explicitly prohibited by very few important state or local governments; but even where the liberty to organize is granted, it usually carries some restrictions not ordinarily found in the private sector of society. Notable among these has been the denial, either outright or by indirection, in most jurisdictions of the right of public employees to strike. Indeed,

[30] *The Right of Public Employees to Organize in Theory and in Practice,* City of New York (March 1955), Serial No. L.R. 1, pp. 2-3.

I am indebted to this study for a number of illuminating observations on the legal status of unions in government as well as to other studies in the same series prepared for New York City under the direction of Miss Ida Klaus, former Counsel for the New York City Department of Labor.

so established has this tradition become that a study of constitutions of twenty government employee unions covering all levels of government reveals that "in none was resort to the strike weapon advocated as a means of achieving stated objectives of the organization. Eleven . . . specifically banned strikes. The remainder contained no references to strikes. . . ."[31]

The acceptance of unions' right to negotiate collective agreements in state and local governments is also less well established than in private industry.[32] Here too, however, the evolution in recent years has been in the direction of the acceptance of collective agreements as a normal instrument in public employment.

Regulations Affecting Federal Employees

Under the terms of the Lloyd–La Follette Act of 1912 the explicit right of federal postal employees, including white-collar employees, to form unions was recognized so long as the organizations did not impose "an obligation or duty on them to engage in any strike or propose to assist them in any strike against the United States. . . ." The Act guaranteed the right of such organizations to seek improvements in wages, hours, and working conditions and also insured the same right to individual employees.[33]

This legislation was long looked upon as the Magna Carta of unions operating in the federal service, and in effect, its protections were also extended to other than postal employees. It has recently been augmented and in many important ways superseded by a Presidential Order issued January 17, 1962, on the subject of *Employee-Management Cooperation in the Public Service.*

The new Executive Order marks an important change from the Lloyd–La Follette Act in that it shifts the government's position from one of tolerance to encouragement of unions and of collective bargaining as the normal way of handling employer-employee relations. In this sense it puts employer-employee relations on a par with the same relations in private industry where collective bargaining is encouraged as a matter of national policy under the National Labor Relations Act.[34]

[31] *Ibid.*, pp. 7-8.
[32] *The Collective Agreement in Public Employment,* City of New York (November 1955), Serial No. L.R. 8.
[33] See above for the early struggle of federal workers' unions.
[34] See Wilson R. Hart, "The U.S. Civil Service Learns to Live with Executive Order 10,988," *Industrial and Labor Relations Review* (January 1964), pp. 203-20.

The new Executive Order affirmed the right of employees to join or refrain from joining unions without fear of reprisal—again, so long as a given union does not assert the right to strike.[35] The order also precludes unions which "advocate the overthrow of the U.S. Government as well as unions which discriminate with regard to membership because of race, color, creed or national origin." This new order marks an important step forward in that it provides for more substantial recognition of unions in the federal service. This recognition takes three forms:

(1) *Informal recognition,* which can be rather freely granted. This form of recognition guarantees a union access to present its views to appropriate public officials in the given unit of government in which it has been informally recognized. These officials, however, need not "consult with an employee organization so recognized in the formulation of personnel or other policies with respect to such matters."

(2) *Formal recognition* is accorded to employee organizations which have a stable and substantial membership of no less than 10 per cent of the employees in an appropriate unit of government. Formal recognition carries greater rights for consultation with officials in the formulation of policies. Formal recognition cannot be granted, however, if any organization is granted exclusive recognition described below, though informal and exclusive recognition for different unions can exist side by side.

(3) *Exclusive recognition* for a union to represent all the employees in a given unit is granted after the union "has been designated or selected by a majority of the employees" of a given administrative unit. Following the practices of the NLRA to some extent, the order states no unit for exclusive recognition is to include supervisory employees, personnel employees, or any professional employees unless such professional employees vote for inclusion in a given unit.

Each major agency of government is to issue orders for the determination of appropriate employee units. The assistance to the Secretary of Labor can be sought in the determination of what is an appropriate unit.

Of major importance is the provision that unions with exclusive recognition status have the right to negotiate written agreements.

[35] The Taft-Hartley Act of 1947 specifically prohibited "any individual employed by the United States, or any agency thereof, including wholly-owned Government corporations, to participate in any strike." Individuals who do so participate are to be immediately discharged, forfeit their Civil Service status, and are not eligible for re-employment by any U.S. Government agency for three years.

It is generally anticipated that the organization of federal employees, blue- and white-collar, will be considerably enhanced in the years to come as the result of this far-reaching Executive Order.

Indeed, with the federal government setting such a new and forward-looking policy with regard to union recognition and the right to negotiate written agreements, this is likely to have an impact upon state and local governments as well.

The Current Status of White-Collar Unionism

As part of its biennial survey of union membership, the United States Department of Labor addresses a questionnaire to all national unions which includes a question seeking information on the approximate "percentage of membership who are 'white-collar' workers (include professional, technical, and office workers). . . ." Based upon replies to this question and some of its own judgments, the Department of Labor estimates that approximately 2.6 million union members were in white-collar occupations in 1964.[36]

For several reasons this estimate is probably on the low side. In the first place the very question is rather limited. There are, for example, a number of industrial unions who have within their ranks some thousands of so-called plant clerical workers, such as blueprint clerks, expediters, and the like. In replying to a questionnaire of this sort, the typical industrial union ignores these plant clerical workers and thereby understates white-collar membership.

In addition to this understatement, one must note that several professional-type associations, as for example many of the state branches of the American Nurses Association, have evolved to a point where they engage in genuine collective bargaining, employ collective agreements, and in many ways, have taken on the characteristics of unions. There are several other such groups in the population who have taken on many of the characteristics which one usually ascribes to unions, but who also retain certain occupational professional functions which are not normally associated with unionism. Eventually it would seem that in any full and comprehensive survey of white-collar unionism at least some of these groups will have to be included.

In spite of some limitations, however, the Labor Department survey is a useful one and is certainly a reasonably good measure of trends of white-collar unionism in the United States. In its 1964 survey the Department of Labor also notes that there was a modest gain of around 190,000 from the 1962 total of reported white-collar union

[36] Letter to the author from U.S. Dept. of Labor, dated November 12, 1965.

membership. White-collar workers account for about 14 per cent of all union members. Inasmuch as there were around 23 million white-collar employees in 1964, who might broadly be considered as union potential (this excludes managerial, official, and proprietary white-collar workers), unionization seems to stand at about 11 per cent of white-collar employment.[37] In contrast, in 1964 the 14 million or so manual and service worker union members constitute between 50 and 60 per cent of the union potential among these occupational categories.

The Department of Labor also estimates that 45.8 per cent of all union members work in manufacturing, 47.2 per cent in nonmanufacturing, and about 7 per cent of total union membership in government. Relating white-collar union figures to these totals, we find that close to two-thirds of all white-collar union members are to be found in nonmanufacturing industries with the remainder more concentrated in government than in manufacturing. On the government side it is estimated that about two-fifths of the better than one million government union members are from the white-collar ranks. In manufacturing less than 5 per cent of all union members come from white-collar occupations.[38]

AFL-CIO White-Collar Unions

A number of unions with important white-collar membership also have substantial membership in blue-collar occupations. For this reason, it is often difficult to estimate precisely the white-collar membership of individual unions. Some idea of where the important points of concentration are, however, can be gleaned from a study of Table 9, which lists the membership of AFL-CIO unions who are known to have at least a very significant white-collar component. (We are dealing first with the AFL-CIO and here we use reported membership per capita payments which each union makes to the AFL-CIO. It is known these figures understate true membership in some cases since some unions do not pay on their total membership.[39] This series of

[37] For an early effort to estimate U.S. white-collar union membership, see C. Wright Mills, *White Collar* (New York: Oxford University Press, 1951), p. 302.

[38] These estimates are taken from the U.S. Bureau of Labor Statistics survey, *Directory of National and International Labor Unions, 1963* (Washington: U.S. Dept. of Labor, Bulletin No. 1395, 1964). The detailed tabulations from the 1963-64 survey were not available when this chapter was completed.

[39] For another estimate of white-collar membership, as such, in various American trade unions, see Benjamin Solomon and Robert K. Burns, "Unionization of White Collar Employees, Extent, Potential, and Implications," *Reprint Series No. 110* (Industrial Relations Center, The University of Chicago, 1963), Table 4, p. 146. Several of the estimates in this table seem too high to me, judged from other data, but the table is an interesting one.

figures, however, seems to be most consistent and objective and is being used for this reason. It should also be noted that these figures cover only the American membership of these listed unions, many of whom have substantial membership in Canada.)

Retail Clerks Association. The largest white-collar union in the AFL-CIO is the Retail Clerks International Association with a paid-up membership to the AFL-CIO of 410,000 in 1965. This union covers the whole range of retail trade so far as unionizing sales clerks is concerned, but it generally does not organize the blue-collar and office workers in retail establishments. It has an exceptionally heavy concentration of membership in the large food chain stores. Geographically the union's greatest center of concentration is the West Coast of the United States and particularly the southern California area. This union has been growing steadily, but for it and the Retail, Wholesale and Department Store Union, another important organization in the trade field, a great challenge seems to lie in the still largely unorganized department stores of the nation.

In accounting for the relatively rapid progress of unionization among the Retail Clerks mention should be made of the fact that with the development of giant food supermarkets and the mechanization of many other large retail establishments, large numbers of the employees in these stores have come to resemble operatives rather than traditional white-collar types.

Some of the most important gains of the Retail Clerks were made during the late 1930's in southern California. At that time the union took in store managers as well as clerks. Frequently it was the managers who took the lead in organizing a given store. This is no longer possible, since the Taft-Hartley amendments in 1947 specifically excluded foremen and supervisors from any bargaining unit which could be set up by the National Labor Relations Board.

An important obstacle to unionization in much of the trade field is the high proportion of women employees, many of whom lack a full career commitment to their jobs which they often regard as "temporary." The heavy employment of part-time help in retail trade, especially in the larger stores, also makes organization more difficult.

While the Department of Labor estimates union membership in the trade field—retail and wholesale—at an impressive 1,129,000 figure (not all white-collar, of course), this compares with total employment, including blue- and white-collar and service workers, of 8.8 million nonsupervisory employees in trade in the same year, 1962.

Brotherhood of Railway Clerks. For years the leading white-collar

Table 9. Trends in Selected AFL-CIO Unions with Substantial White-Collar Membership, 1955-65 (in Thousands)

	1955	*1957*	*1959*	*1961*	*1963*	*1965*
Actors and Artistes of America, Associated	34	43	51	58	57	61
Air Line Dispatchers Association	1	1	1	1	1	1
Air Line Pilots Association	9	14	18	18	17	18
Broadcast Employees and Technicians, National Association	4	4	4	4	4	4
Clerks, Brotherhood of Railway	264	267	250	215	196	186
Clerks, International Association, Retail	259	291	315	340	364	410
Communications Workers of America	249	250	261	255	273	288
Engineers, American Federation of Technical	10	12	13	13	11	11
Flight Engineers' International Association	1	2	3	3	1	1
Government Employees, American Federation of	47	56	56	68	97	132
Insurance Workers International Union			22[a]	22	21	21
Letter Carriers, National Association of	100	100	100	108	128	130
Marine Engineers' Beneficial Association, National	9	8	8	8	8	9
Masters, Mates and Pilots, International Association of	9	9	9	9	9	9
Musicians, American Federation of	250	255	255	247	233	225
Newspaper Guild, American	21	22	24	24	23	23
Office Employees International Union	44	45	46	48	50	52
Postal Clerks, United Federation of [b]				95	115	117
Radio Association, American	2	2	2	2	2	2
Railway Supervisors Association, American	—	1	6	6	6	6
Retail, Wholesale and Department Store Union	97	105	107	110	111	114
State, County and Municipal Employees, American Federation	99	147[c]	173	188	212	237
Teachers, American Federation of	40	48	50	57	65	97
Telegraphers, The Order of Railroad	30	30	30	30	30	29
Telegraphers' Union, The Commercial	29	29	29	26	22	22
Train Dispatchers Association, American	—	1	4	4	4	3
Yardmasters of America, Railroad	4	4	4	4	4	4

[a] This union was formed by merger of Insurance Agents International Union (13,000 in 1955; 12,000 in 1957) and Insurance Workers of America (9,000 in 1955 and 9,000 in 1957).

[b] This union was formed by a merger of the National Federation of Post Office Clerks and the National Postal Transport Association in December 1961. The Clerks reported their own membership in 1961, prior to merger, at 80,000.

[c] This union absorbed the Government and Civic Organizing Committee which showed a membership of 27,000 in 1955.

Source: Figures based on per capita payments to AFL-CIO as published in *AFL-CIO Convention Executive Council Report* (1963 and 1965).

union in the labor movement was the Brotherhood of Railway Clerks. While its membership goes beyond clerical employees and extends to some non–white-collar groups, it continues to center on railway clerical employees. Its decline since 1955 is largely attributable to the general decline in railway employment. The railway clerks have organized virtually all of their major occupational potential on the railroads. The same union has had some success in unionizing clerical employees on the airlines, but the percentage of unionization in this industry is lower than on the railroads.

The superior unionization of railway clerks reflects a number of factors including their close relationship to other manual railway employees who were strongly unionized at a relatively early date. Railway employees, moreover, for a long time in the United States, have enjoyed the advantages (so far as organizational facilities are concerned) of special railway governmental collective bargaining machinery. Again, railway clerks wherever employed tend to have a special kind of occupational identity as opposed, say, to file clerks or general clerks employed in other branches of American industry.

Entertainment Unions. Unionization in the entertainment field is also impressive. The American Federation of Musicians accounts for 225,000 members while the Associated Actors and Artistes (which takes in the screen, legitimate theatre, and television) includes some 61,000 members.

It is interesting to observe that creative artists in so many countries appear to unionize at a more rapid rate than do white-collar workers generally. One might expect a group like this which is so individualistically oriented to be less prone to accept unionism. The infringement which commercial employment makes upon the character and creativity of artistic work probably helps account for this greater propensity to join unions. Here too one must call attention to the high sense of occupational identity which no doubt makes organization easier among artists than some other white-collar groups.

Writing about the reactions of artists as well as journalists (the history of the American Newspaper Guild has been sketched above) and noting their higher propensity to join unions, S. M. Lipset comments,

> Members of these occupations hold standards of creative accomplishment clearly at odds with market demand. Since in modern capitalistic society rewards for cultural products increasingly depend on a market organized around business norms, the views of the employers are bound to diverge from those of the creative artist. . . . Musicians tend to react the same way. Within the occupational group great stress is placed upon preserving the

integrity of their art. Economic success, unfortunately, depends on pleasing popular taste, and since popular taste is low, economic success is at cross purposes with artistic success. . . . [Lipset concludes] This hostility towards business and the public seems to be reflected in the propensity of creative artists to support left or liberal politics and trade unions.[40]

Telephone Unions. Another major union in the white-collar field is the Communications Workers of America. First organized by skilled craftsmen employed in installing and servicing telephones as well as by some leaders in a few of the manufacturing units of the Bell Telephone Company, today this union is estimated to have 70 per cent of its membership among white-collar workers. With the exception of a small number of professional and technical employees, the membership is largely drawn from telephone operators and clerical workers.

The Communications Workers of America is actually the end product of the evolution of a number of independent unions in the telephone industry.[41] Some of these dated back to post–World War I and in many instances they were company sponsored. Following the passage of the Wagner Act, these employee representation plans ripened into a number of independent locals and groups of local unions; many of them joined together to form the National Federation of Telephone Workers in 1937-38. The organization continued as a very loose federation for another ten years when a more centralized structure was finally accepted and the name of the union was changed to the Communications Workers of America. CWA affiliated with CIO in 1950.

While this union has at times been stalled in its organizing efforts, in the past few years it has begun to make some progress in the still unorganized or independent union–organized parts of the industry.

AFL-CIO Supervisory Groups. Not very large but relatively well organized are several AFL-CIO unions which take in "managerial" white-collar employees, or at least employees so classified under the Census Bureau occupational system. These include the Organization of Masters, Mates and Pilots, and the Marine Engineers Beneficial Association, both of which organize officer personnel in the nation's Merchant Marine. In addition, there are several small unions covering different classes of railway supervisors.

[40] S. M. Lipset, "The Future of Non-Manual Unionism," December 1961, Institute of Industrial Relations, University of California, Berkeley, California. This is quoted from a preliminary, still unpublished paper which was first presented to a special seminar on white-collar problems conducted by the Industrial Union Department, AFL-CIO, at Santa Barbara, California, October 1961.

[41] Jack Barbash, *Unions and Telephones* (New York: Harper & Bros., 1952); and the same author's *The Practice of Unionism* (New York: Harper & Bros., 1956), pp. 395-96.

White-Collar Workers in Industry

Unionization is relatively slight among most of the office, technical, and professional employees in the private economy, including manufacturing.

Office Employees Union. The Office Employees International Union was chartered by the AFL in 1945 after functioning for three years as a Council in the Federation. Within the old AFL it was granted jurisdiction over all "persons engaged in office work excluding" those under the jurisdiction of the American Federation of State, County, and Municipal Employees, the Teachers Union, the Railway Clerks, the Retail Clerks, the Post Office Clerks, the American Federation of Government Employees, the Commercial Telegraphers, the Hotel and Teamsters unions.[42]

The OEIU, according to AFL-CIO per capita membership count, now has some 52,000 members in the United States, scattered among a whole series of industries, general office establishments, union offices, and so forth.

Technical Engineers. Although the American Federation of Technical Engineers only dates back officially to 1918, there had been efforts made to organize draftsmen in private and government shipyards in the East long before that. Indeed, in 1913-14, a short-lived National Association of Marine Draftsmen was organized, but it tended to be under the domination of supervisors in the industry and soon disappeared.

The continuation of the difficult working conditions and new pressures arising out of wartime conditions impelled a locally chartered AFL union of draftsmen in Portsmouth, Virginia, to call a national convention of marine draftsmen in Philadelphia in 1917.[43]

The union itself was more formally launched in 1918 at a meeting in Washington, D.C. Curiously enough, among the organization's first important business items taken up at the convention was the arrangement of a meeting to call upon the Assistant Secretary of the Navy, Franklin Delano Roosevelt, in order to review some pending grievances.[44]

[42] *Proceedings, First Constitutional Convention of the Office Employees International Union,* AFL, January 8-11, 1945, Cincinnati, Ohio, p. 12.

[43] *Silver Anniversary, 1918-1943, American Federation of Technical Engineers, Architects and Draftsmen* (Washington, D.C., 1943). (This program was originally prepared for the 1943 convention which was postponed and finally held in 1944.)

[44] *International Federation of Draftsmen's Unions, Report of Convention Held in Washington, D.C., May 19-22, 1918.*

Franklin Delano Roosevelt, as President, was later to send a congratulatory message to the American Federation of Technical Engineers on the occasion of its twenty-fifth anniversary convention.

Today the union numbers some eleven thousand members and has extended its jurisdiction beyond draftsmen to include some other technicians and engineers. Its greatest success, however, continues to be among draftsmen who have been organized in some manufacturing as well as shipyard and ordnance establishments.

Air Line Pilots Association. One of the more interesting professional-type unions in the white-collar field is the AFL-CIO's Air Line Pilots Association. First organized in the 1930's with the help of the NIRA and later the Railway Labor Act, this union has now organized its jurisdiction to a very high degree. Its wage scales and working conditions compare favorably with those of other professional employees. While it has been a firm adherent to the AFL, and then the AFL-CIO, it is not seriously involved in too many of the labor movement's general social and political efforts.[45]

Industrial Unions and White-Collar Workers

Additional tens of thousands of white-collar workers in industry, especially manufacturing, are organized by the industrial unions who claim jurisdiction over the office, technical, and professional employees, as well as the manual workers within their respective industrial jurisdictions.

In metal manufacturing it is estimated that approximately 150,000 nonmanual workers are organized within the four leading metal-manufacturing unions: the United Automobile, Aircraft and Agricultural Implement Workers of America, the United Steelworkers of America, the International Association of Machinists, and the International Union of Electrical, Radio, and Machine Workers.[46] While this is an impressive figure, it probably represents only a little more than 10 per cent of the organizing potential here, and this is in contrast with the degree of organization among the manual workers in these industries which is probably four or five times as great, and in some sectors approaches 100 per cent.

The Automobile Workers, the Electrical and Radio Workers, and the United Steelworkers have each set up a special department to organize white-collar workers in their jurisdictions. Special locals have been set up to group white-collar workers who have been organized

[45] *The ALPA Story,* Air Line Pilots Association International, Second Revised Printing (1957), *passim.*

[46] Figures based upon conversations with officials of these unions.

at the same plant as the blue-collar workers, and these white-collar workers often negotiate their own separate contracts. In the IUE frequently there is established a separate local for production and maintenance workers, another for office employees, another for professionals and technicals—in those companies where all three are unionized by the IUE.

In their organizing efforts, of course, these unions try to take advantage of such contacts as they can make through their production and maintenance workers who may have relatives working in the office or laboratory. The production and maintenance units are, in most cases, organized before white-collar organization is undertaken.

The United Steelworkers, for example, report that among the very first office workers unionized in basic steel at the Ellwood City, Pennsylvania, plant, at least half of the thirteen founders of the local office union had a father, son, or brother with a production job in the Ellwood City plant of U.S. Steel's National Tube Division.[47]

These four metal-working unions have exhibited only sporadic interest in the white-collar workers within their jurisdictions in recent years. Most recently the United Automobile Workers has undertaken a series of important efforts to unionize groups of white-collar workers within its jurisdiction. It has reorganized its white-collar organizing staff and started a special publication for white-collar members and prospective members. The UAW has also opened a Technical Training Center in Detroit, where in cooperation with the U.S. Department of Labor it is offering technical training in drafting, graphic illustration, and related skills.[48] The UAW seems to be taking a leaf out of the books of some of the unions of technical workers in Western Europe who have long concerned themselves with the technical training of their members.

The International Brotherhood of Electrical Workers with a wide jurisdiction, including construction, manufacturing, and utilities, also has a substantial white-collar membership.

Chemical, rubber, and a few other industrial unions have also organized some office and technical workers in their respective jurisdictions. The Teamsters Union has also extended its organization to take in some of the office employees in warehousing and trucking companies where they have the manual and chauffeur employees unionized.

[47] *Office and Technical Workers Move Ahead with the United Steelworkers of America* (1960), p. 13.
[48] *White-Collar Report,* Bureau of National Affairs (March 28, 1963, and January 9, 1964).

In a few campaigns for union recognition among white-collar workers in industry there have been occasional conflicts between the Office Employees and the Technical Engineers on the one hand, as opposed to some industrial unions who also sought to represent white-collar workers in the same plants where they already represented blue-collar workers. In other cases, however, industrial unions who represent blue-collar workers at a given plant have supported the effort of OEIU or AFTE to win bargaining rights for white-collar workers in the same plant. What is most striking, however, is the relatively small number of these elections being requested, and the small number of workers involved. In the four-year period, 1957-60, for example, the National Labor Relations Board, according to one survey, conducted some 691 elections in white-collar units, involving 16,265 workers. While this survey excludes telephone workers and some other groups, the small number of people involved is nevertheless striking when measured against the unorganized millions.[49]

Government White-Collar Unions

Postal Unions. The early struggles of government white-collar unions, especially in the postal service, have been described above. Today several of these unions are among the largest in the white-collar field. The National Association of Letter Carriers has 130,000 members while the United Federation of Postal Clerks has some 117,000 members, according to reports to the AFL-CIO in 1963. The Letter Carriers and the Post Office Clerks have had notable success in their lobbying activities with Congress on behalf of postal employees and, indeed, on behalf of all government employees. The very substantial gains of both the Letter Carriers and the Postal Clerks in the past two years (see Table 9) appears to be attributable in large part to the operation of the 1962 Executive Order governing labor relations in the federal service.

Government Employees Union. The American Federation of Government Employees was chartered in 1932 following withdrawal of the National Federation of Federal Employees from the AFL (described in the next section). While its growth has been modest in comparison to its potential, the AFGE has made striking progress in the past few years and reported a membership of 132,000 to the AFL-CIO convention in 1965.

The AFGE is not limited to white-collar employees, but it has a

[49] *White-Collar Report,* Bureau of National Affairs (February 6, 1961), p. B-4.

large part of its membership in the classified civil service. Its jurisdiction is, in a sense, industrial across the entire federal service, but it does not include the postal service or industrial workers (primarily skilled craft workers) eligible for membership in previously established AFL unions.

The new Executive Order governing union activities within the federal service has provided a great opportunity for new organization by the AFGE. To some extent, however, the AFGE has become bogged down in jurisdictional struggles with the other AFL-CIO unions, notably the affiliates of the Metal Trades Department. This stems from the fact that AFGE claims jurisdiction over manual as well as non-manual employees in government service; the unions affiliated with the Metal Trades Department generally assert jurisdiction over manual workers in government.

Teachers Union. The American Federation of Teachers, one of the older white-collar unions in the movement, has also shown some fair growth. Its last report to the AFL-CIO showed membership of 97,000 in 1965, a gain of 40,000 over 1961.[50]

There are important signs that the unionization possibilities among teachers are changing rapidly. The AFT local affiliate in New York City in December 1961 won an election giving them bargaining rights on behalf of some 44,000 teachers in the city; these bargaining rights include a voluntary check-off, exclusive representation, and the right to negotiate a written contract. AFL-CIO leaders hoped that this single largest union election victory in twenty years might be the harbinger of the organization of teachers in a number of other important cities. Beyond this, American labor as a whole was encouraged by the decision of so large a group of teachers to choose the labor movement for representation purposes; this was also looked to for its effects on the unionization of white-collar workers generally. (On teacher unionism developments, see also pp. 352-54.)

State and Local Employees Organizations. One of the most rapidly growing AFL-CIO unions in recent years has been the American Federation of State, County and Municipal Employees which has greatly increased its membership since 1955. The AFSCME claims an industrial jurisdiction over all employees in state and county government. It has on some occasions collided with the craft unions who claim jurisdiction over skilled mechanics employed by state and local

[50] By the end of 1965, as large numbers of teachers were recruited into membership in New York City and elsewhere, AFT officials indicated the union had reached the 115,000 mark.

governments. About one-third of AFSCME membership is white-collar; the remainder are blue-collar workers of widely varied occupational skills.

AFSCME's origin dates back to the activities of a Wisconsin State Employees Association which was established in 1932. This group joined the AFL in 1935 and in 1936 the national union was chartered, taking in the Wisconsin group along with several others.

It must be added that there are a large number of civil service associations operating at both the state and local levels, in many parts of the United States. Some of these organizations are quite large, and in a few instances, they have been evolving into something approaching bargaining associations.[51]

The evolution of these and other professional associations in the years to come, as collective bargaining is increasingly accepted in white-collar and public employment, will be interesting to observe. It may well represent a significant challenge to the AFL-CIO.

White-Collar Unions Outside the AFL-CIO

There is a substantial number of white-collar unions outside of the AFL-CIO. Most of them, however, are confined to one company—so-called independent unions. The Department of Labor directory of unions for 1961 also lists a handful of independent white-collar unions, with membership not confined to one company or establishment. These include the National Federation of Federal Employees as well as a number of smaller independent unions in the postal service.

Federal Employees. The National Federation of Federal Employees was created in 1917 when the AFL issued a charter to a group of local unions. The organization's jurisdiction was roughly the same as described above for the American Federation of Government Employees. NFFE has concentrated most of its efforts in the legislative field. It has been what one writer has described as a "corporate" type of body, a sort of conservative " 'business' union with a strong admixture of 'uplift' elements. Its program is devoted to a rather narrow preoccupation with the unique problems of a particular group of employees to the exclusion of broader social issues which confront labor classes in general. . . ."[52]

[51] Joseph Krislov has estimated that there are approximately 392,000 members in such independent associations (not all white-collar, of course). See his "The Independent Public Employee Association: Characteristics and Functions," *Industrial and Labor Relations Review* (July 1962), pp. 510-20.

[52] Morton R. Godine, *The Labor Problem in the Public Service* (Cambridge: Harvard University Press, 1951), p. 108.

In its early years the NFFE played an important role on behalf of white-collar and all classified workers in the federal service. It carried on a long struggle to improve the general classification scheme covering all federal employees, an activity which often brought it into collision with the craft unions, representing mechanics, helpers, and apprentices in the federal service. The craft unions tended to oppose any federal reclassification plans on the grounds that they would interfere with their own traditional descriptions of their jobs, their work, and rules. (The reader will recall from above that the AFL-CIO's current affiliate in the federal government field, the American Federation of Government Employees, is having friction with the Metal Trades Department unions of the Federation, roughly the same unions which battled the NFFE in the early 1930's.)

In 1932 a major classification program (for both white- and blue-collar workers) which the NFFE had helped to sponsor was rejected by the AFL convention in spite of NFFE's plea that it be accepted at least for white-collar employees. At this point the NFFE withdrew from the Federation and later extended its jurisdiction to the entire federal service. The NFFE has continued as an independent organization. Its claimed membership, in 1961, was 53,000. (This claim was made in its reply to the United States Department of Labor membership questionnaire. For other unions we have generally used AFL-CIO per capita membership payments which tend to be below, in most cases, those reported in response to the biennial questionnaire of the Department of Labor.)

Engineers

Some interesting efforts have been made to unionize engineers and scientists in the American economy. The Federation of Architects, Engineers, Chemists, and Technicians was organized in 1934, largely through the efforts of a group of engineers and technical workers employed on the WPA (a federal government emergency work project organized as an anti-depression measure) in New York. The organization spread its membership to include some skilled professionals in private industry in the next few years, and in 1937 it affiliated with the CIO.[53] The AFECT never became a large organization and was eventually merged with the United Office and Professional Workers of the CIO in January 1946.

It was really only after the revolution in the employment condi-

[53] Levinson, *op. cit.*, p. 249.

tions of engineers and scientists in American industry ushered in by World War II that unionism had much of a chance to expand in these professions. In aircraft, instrument, and electronic companies for the first time literally thousands of engineers and related professional and technical workers were employed together, a sharp contrast with the earlier period when these same types of workers worked in very small, informal groups, often in close relationship to middle and top management. It was in response to these changed working conditions that engineering unionism began to emerge towards the end of World War II. During the postwar period large numbers of engineers continued to be employed under defense contracts, and in electronic and development work, and these conditions continued to be relatively more favorable for organizing.

In a number of companies independent engineering unions with bargaining rights began to develop. Several of these unions joined together to form an independent engineering federation under the name of the Engineers and Scientists of America (ESA). Notable among the important units in this union was the Western Electric Division of the Bell Telephone Company, the Minneapolis-Honeywell engineers group in Minneapolis, as well as groups at RCA Victor, in Camden, New Jersey, in several electronic and instrument companies in Long Island, and at a few of the West Coast air frame plants.

The ESA early encountered difficulties arising out of the attitudes of those engineers who in no way wanted to have a joint organization which included technical employees, even high-level ones, along with professional engineers. This and other problems led to a split in the organization. When on top of this two important units were lost—the Minneapolis-Honeywell group which sought to switch to the United Automobile Workers but instead eventually lost all bargaining rights at the company, and the Western Electric employees which lost their bargaining rights as the result of a new NLRB election—the ESA voted to dissolve itself in 1960.

Two key units of ESA, incidentally, gradually evolved into an affiliation with AFL-CIO's International Union of Electrical, Radio, and Machine Workers. These were the Engineers Association of the Arma Engineering plant in Long Island (1956)[54] and the Sperry Engineers Association at the Long Island Sperry plant (1960). In 1962, however, IUE Sperry Engineers lost out in a decertification election

[54] For an interesting history of the Arma Engineering local, see *10th Anniversary* (Engineers Association of Arma, IUE, 1961).

conducted by the NLRB; Sperry technicians, however, voted to continue their affiliation and representation by IUE.[55]

Several independent engineering unions continue to hold bargaining rights in some of the West Coast aircraft companies, notably at Lockheed, Boeing, and Convair. These unions are, however, under great pressure from the companies, and a few of these West Coast unions lost decertification elections in 1963. Their future seems clouded, at best.

By 1960, 332,000 of the 648,900 engineers employed in U.S. industry were in companies employing 5,000 or more workers. There are approximately 500 such companies, making an average of 660 engineers per company. Actually, of course, the distribution of engineers is not so even, but this does give some idea of the heavy concentration of engineering employment.[56] The precise future of engineering unionism is still much of an open question, but as one studies the changed employment conditions that most engineers have come to work under in the past two decades, the increased emergence of some form of unionism or group representation seems probable.

Other Professional Groups

Aside from organizations listed in the Labor Department directory, mention should also be made of several other types of professional employee associations which seem to be evolving towards a form of unionism.

Nurses. A leading example among these organizations is the American Nurses Association, the professional association for American nurses. During the 1930's when there was a general upsurge of labor organization, the American Nurses Association continued its opposition to unionization of nurses and, indeed, recommended that nurses not become union members. World War II placed substantial economic pressure on nurses, as well as on a number of other professional groups who found their wages frozen under government wage administration. The ANA's California section petitioned the National War Labor Board for wage relief and was successful in establishing a new wage schedule in 1943. The California Nurses Association became the collective bargaining agent for its members in this process and negotiated its first collective agreement in 1946. Shortly thereafter

[55] *White-Collar Report,* Bureau of National Affairs (May 31, 1962), A-1.

[56] *Scientific and Technical Personnel in U.S. Industry, 1960,* National Science Foundation, NSF 67-75, p. 23.

the ANA itself, as an organization, accepted the necessity for "collective bargaining."

To be sure, the American Nurses Association tries to suggest that "collective bargaining is not to be confused with labor unionism. Collective bargaining is used by many organizations other than labor unions." The distinction seems rather thin, however. A study, for example, of the agreements negotiated by different state units of the ANA reveals that they resemble quite closely collective agreements generally. Thus, the agreements cover wages, holidays, sick leave, vacation, and so forth, and in addition some of them provide for a form of union shop and/or the check-off.[57]

Even more to the point is a relatively recent action of the American Nurses Association's New Jersey affiliate in seeking to sever, via an NLRB election, seven registered nurses from a unit of clerical and laboratory employees currently represented by the Independent Petroleum Workers of New Jersey at a plant of the Humble Oil and Refining Company in Linden, New Jersey.[58] ANA's status as a labor organization under the National Labor Relations Act was challenged by the Independent Petroleum Workers union but the NLRB regional director upheld the labor-organization status of the ANA.

Teachers. The National Education Association, the leading teachers' professional association, for many years resisted and opposed unionization and collective bargaining efforts on behalf of teachers. As pressures have built up, however, the NEA has finally been led to modify its policies somewhat, and in its 1961 convention it set forth a new policy which states: "The National Education Association believes, therefore that professional education associations should be accorded the right, through democratically selected representatives using appropriate professional channels, to participate in the determination of policies of common concern including salary and other conditions for professional service." [59]

In an election in December 1961 to determine who would represent the teachers in New York City, the NEA was active in supporting one of the groups on the ballot which was opposing the AFL-CIO's American Federation of Teachers. It remains unclear whether the NEA has genuinely come to accept collective bargaining or whether this is merely a defensive move against the American Federation of

[57] Daniel H. Kruger, "Bargaining and the Nursing Profession," *Monthly Labor Review* (July 1961).
[58] *White-Collar Report*, Bureau of National Affairs (March 1, 1962).
[59] *NEA Handbook, 1961-1962*, p. 62.

Teachers. Articles in the *NEA Journal* continue to draw a sharp distinction between unionism and teachers' professionalism; it insists on identifying unionism with "coercion" and raises the old issues that the NEA has employed against unionism in the past.[60]

On the other hand, in a dispute with the public education authorities in the State of Utah in 1963, while eschewing words like strike or boycott, the NEA advised its members to avoid taking up employment in the state until the dispute (which was primarily on salaries) was resolved. It set up a reserve fund to make loans to tide over Utah teachers who refused to accept employment under conditions rejected by the NEA's Utah affiliate. This dispute in Utah provoked a new examination of the entire bargaining and "sanctions" policy of the NEA.[61]

In February 1964, the NEA affiliate in Milwaukee, Wisconsin, went on the ballot against the affiliate of the American Federation of Teachers in an election requested by the latter from the Wisconsin Employment Relations Board. The NEA affiliate defeated the AFT by a vote of 2,249 to 1,645 and was certified to exclusive representation of teachers in Milwaukee.[62]

NEA affiliates took the lead in petitioning authorities in Philadelphia and in Yonkers, N.Y., to conduct elections for exclusive bargaining rights. In Philadelphia this was done in spite of the fact that the AFL-CIO's affiliate, the American Federation of Teachers, had been actively organizing for over a year.[63] Eventually the AFT won elections in both Philadelphia and Yonkers.

In Detroit, both the AFT and a local NEA affiliate competed in a major bargaining election covering over ten thousand teachers, in May 1964. Here the AFT was most aggressive in arguing for an election to determine who should have exclusive bargaining rights, but the NEA affiliate also supported the plea for such a type of an election —over the wishes of the Detroit School authorities who sought to avoid any exclusive bargaining right grants.[64] The AFT was the winner

[60] "A Matter of Philosophy and Program," *NEA Journal* (March 1962).
[61] *White-Collar Report,* Bureau of National Affairs (July 4, 11, 1963). The NEA invoked sanctions against the Oklahoma public school system in the spring of 1965 in protest against "subminimal" salary conditions. *New York Times,* May, 1965.
[62] *Ibid.* (Feb. 13, 1964), A10-11; NEA affiliates also defeated the AFT in elections in West Allis, Wisconsin, and New Rochelle, N.Y., in March and April 1964.
[63] *Ibid.* (April 9, 1964), A8-9.
[64] *Ibid.* (April 23, 1964), A2-3.

in this election. Subsequent AFT victories in Chicago and Boston seemed to indicate that this organization would probably outstrip the NEA in most large urban centers where AFL-CIO unionism in general was well established and accepted.

These and other scattered developments also suggest that one can expect NEA affiliates in different parts of the country more and more to be petitioning for exclusive bargaining rights. How much of this represents national NEA policy or just regional pressure is not yet clear. What does seem clear is that important segments of the NEA are likely to be caught up in the bargaining process in the next few years.

Professionalism and Bargaining. Unions seeking to organize professional employees, such as engineers, teachers, and nurses, must overcome some special hurdles. Among these is the often claimed or charged incompatibility between unionism and professionalism.

Actually it would seem that if unionism is to make substantial progress among professionals, it will be, in part, because these very professionals feel that their professional status is being infringed by the employment situation. One student of engineering unionism in the United States suggests that the infringement of professional status in industry has been one of the sources of dissatisfaction leading to the emergence of unionism among some engineers in the postwar period.[65]

The research of Professor S. M. Miller of Syracuse on professionalism and unionism among nurses similarly indicates that one reason why nurses unionize is the necessity to protect their professional status. Thus, nurses may otherwise be compelled to perform many menial non-nursing tasks, nontrained nurses may be assigned to what should be the exclusive, professional tasks of nurses in hospitals, etc.[66]

In the 1962 dispute between the unionized New York City teachers and the City Board of Education, those issues which seemed to arouse the most heat were the assignment of such nonprofessional tasks as bus patrol and cafeteria watch.

It is quite likely that the progress of unionism among clearly identifiable professional groups may require of their unions that *they* become *guardians* of their members' professional status. (In a sense this will be in the tradition of many of the older craft unions which

[65] Richard E. Walton, *The Impact of the Professional Engineering Union: A Study of Collective Bargaining Among Engineers and Scientists and Its Significance for Management* (Cambridge: Harvard University Press, 1961), pp. 21-22.

[66] S. M. Miller, "Professionalization, Organization, and Economic Advance in the Nursing Profession," *New York State Nurse* (March 1961), pp. 10-12, and 15.

took upon themselves the task of "protecting" the standards of the occupation.) The Air Line Pilots, a small but effective professional union in the AFL-CIO, also plays an important role in defending the interests of the profession, setting standards on accident investigation, safety, training, etc.[67]

The American Nurses Association, as it goes about promoting collective bargaining for its members, seems to be hammering on this theme of extending professionalism by organizing. In its newest "Leader's Discussion Guide in Economics," the ANA notes: [68] "Perhaps we need to think about whether we can really apply and practice our professional ethics *without* collective bargaining. How does collective bargaining offer nurses an avenue to promote their devotion to the ideals of nursing and professional ethics?"

One of the few successful union movements among professional employees has been established in Sweden. The Swedish Confederation of Professional Associations—SACO—is a result, for the most part, of situations in which Swedish professional associations have also taken on union and collective bargaining functions. Experience in that country seems to suggest that at least in some professions the union's road to successful organization will involve its assumption of defense of the profession as such.[69]

WHITE-COLLAR UNIONISM: PROBLEMS AND PROSPECTS

Many social and economic factors have doubtless tended to retard or restrict unionism among white-collar workers in the United States. In some instances these factors are in the process of change and as this occurs, the opportunities for unionization among white-collar workers should increase. This is not to say that certain differences between white-collar and manual workers, so far as their very work and their values and attitudes are concerned, may not continue to exist, but these should be viewed as differences and not necessarily as obstacles.

In the past, for example, the special nature and conditions of white-collar work have often stood as an obstacle to unionism. Typically, physical working conditions have been easier in white-collar work than in manual work; time clock pressures have been much less

[67] *The ALPA Story, op. cit.*, pp. 12-13.

[68] Quoted in *White-Collar Report,* Bureau of National Affairs (November 14, 1963), p. A-3.

[69] *Swedish Professional Associations as Trade Unions,* Swedish Confederation of Professional Associations (Trelleborg, Sweden, 1959), *passim.*

in evidence; work pace has been easier; paid vacations and holidays were granted at a much earlier date for white-collar workers; job security has been much higher.

Rightly or wrongly, too, white-collar workers have tended to identify themselves with management. This was often possible under conditions of white-collar work where an employee was in a small group and had direct contact and association with his supervisor.

As previously noted, a little over 50 per cent of all white-collar workers are women. This large number of women in white-collar work also has tended to pose some obstacles for unionism. Women workers are frequently much less oriented to their jobs in a career sense and often look upon their work status as "temporary." At the same time the disproportionately high number of women in white-collar work made (and still makes, for that matter) the promotion possibilities of the more "stable" male white-collar workers much greater, thereby reducing the appeal of unionism for the latter.

As suggested, however, many of these factors are changing over a wide range of white-collar work. The sheer growth in numbers inevitably eliminates some of the unique status of large groups of white-collar workers.

We have already alluded to the strains and tensions developing in certain branches of professional work. Some of the individuality of white-collar clerical work is also disappearing in many firms, and one now finds large batteries of cardpunch operators, comptometer operators, and the like employed in the same establishment. Under these conditions the special individual characteristics of white-collar work tend to disappear and more of it becomes routinized and bureaucratized.

White-Collar Workers and Automation

In one important white-collar area, office work, great technological changes are occurring in large firms. The automation of office work in these firms—the introduction of mechanization and electronic data processing systems—almost always has a highly disruptive effect upon traditional office organization and jobs. Even when unemployment is not directly a threat to the automated office worker, a new social "set" is often created in the wake of office automation.

One study of the impact of electronic machines on office work concludes that most office workers find their jobs less interesting than before. Indeed, "not only was there more intrinsic interest [before automation] since the employees might have been filing, checking, posting, typing, but the former occupations involved a certain amount of moving about the office and contact with other employees or customers. The workers now complain of 'being chained to the machines.' "[70]

This study did find some new highly skilled jobs created by the introduction of office automation, namely the positions of programmers and analysts, but they were relatively few.

In an exaggerated way, one can say that the traditional office is almost cut into two when major mechanical rationalization and automation are introduced. Traditionally, one has thought of office work as a kind of continuum; there were grades, of course, but these tended to be grades in a continuous hierarchy through which one could, theoretically, at least, advance by promotion. The work of both Ida Hoos and Claudine Marenco tends to stress the development of a deep split in the office.[71]

Large numbers of machine-operator types of jobs are created in the wake of automation (there is an important increase in the number of punchcard operators), while the middle office grades tend to disappear. Mrs. Marenco notes:

> The division between managerial duties, reserved to top and middle management, and the tasks performed by the employees is becoming constantly sharper. Whereas the employee could formerly hope to rise gradually in the hierarchy through a number of intermediate stages, he now finds himself confined to the role of mere operator, which not only fails to prepare him for more highly qualified posts, but makes it more and more difficult for him to adjust to situations requiring initiative. . . . The dividing line which is already being drawn in the rationalized establishment between machine operators (particularly in the punched-card-machine offices) and the rest of the clerical staff will become the more sharply defined as the qualifications and duties of certain technicians enable them to rise above supervisors who nevertheless, outrank them in the hierarchy. . . .

Mrs. Marenco does distinguish between those office-related jobs which continue to involve contacts with the public as opposed to those which are purely internal in the office. Automation obviously moves much more swiftly with the latter than the former and the sense of anomie and isolation from management and the firm can become

[70] Ida R. Hoos, "When the Computer Takes Over the Office," *Harvard Business Review* (July-August 1960), pp. 102-12.

[71] Mrs. Hoos's work has already been referred to in the preceding footnote. An English summary of Mrs. Marenco's study, "Psychosociological Incidences of Office Work Rationalization of Employee Status," appeared in *Trade Union Information*, No. 35 (early 1962), published by the Organization for Economic Cooperation and Development, Paris, France.

quite great for the inside mechanized clerk as compared to the clerk who continues to have contact with the customer.

In the cases we have just been describing—and they are by no means typical of all office automation—the automated clerical employee often finds great changes in his job. He no longer has the possibility of a certain freedom of movement that he used to enjoy. He cannot wander about from time to time, talking with fellow employees; he must be in at a set hour in the morning. He is almost like a blue-collar employee in that he is tending an important, costly machine. Indeed, so mechanized may his new job become that one begins to find companies experimenting with the introduction of workload requirements and piece rates for office workers who never before were confronted with these conditions.

The machines in operation are not only producing much data rapidly, they are also very expensive. As a result they must be constantly attended; often it becomes economically necessary to keep the office running two or even three shifts per day to defray the great expense involved in purchasing and installing these machines. (Where this occurs some clerical employees may, for the first time, be confronted with nightwork assignments.)

While layoffs are not common among office workers, the mere introduction of computers and other high-speed equipment tends to disrupt existing job structures and breed insecurity and unrest in the office. Certainly the sense of job security which many workers enjoyed before mechanization is shaken. Unlike the blue-collar worker, especially in industry, who has been "living" with technological change most of his working life, the white-collar worker is unprepared for it, and its psychological impact upon him (or her) may be considerable.[72]

As the white-collar force grows in many industries, it may be also more difficult in the future for companies to treat it as fixed overhead costs with few or no layoffs among white-collar workers, even in the face of the usual short business cycle. It is one thing to treat such workers as set costs when they constitute 10 or 15 per cent of total payroll, but possibly quite another when they reach 25 or 30 per cent or more.

[72] For a more extensive discussion of the impact of automation upon white-collar work and its implication for unionism, see Everett M. Kassalow, "Automation and Technological Progress, Its Impact upon White Collar Workers in the United States," paper presented to the German Metalworkers Union Conference (Frankfurt, Germany, July 1963), mimeographed, especially pp. 15-35 (published in German, in *Automation und Technischer Fortschritt in Deutschland und Der U.S.A.*, G. Friedrichs, ed., Europaische Verlagsanstalt, Frankfurt, 1963).

But for these new white-collar workers, working conditions may not appear more onerous (or even as onerous) as those under which their blue-collar fathers and mothers worked—and continue to work. These are the comparisons that will probably be the most relevant to the new white-collar workers, and not the superior conditions that may have been enjoyed by other white-collar workers in the past.

One must also note that management's traditional paternalism toward its white-collar workers still seems to be quite strong. Many firms still make very careful studies, plans, and procedures to safeguard their office staffs from automation unemployment. Two such plans in nonunionized firms, for example, are reported by the Department of Labor in its survey of office automation.[73] The firms are frequently aided in this adjustment process by the fact that many young women who take lower level clerical jobs generally have high turnover rates; management can, therefore, depend upon voluntary quits and attrition to carry off workers rendered surplus by office automation.

Some of the techniques and methods used to ease the impact of automation here are things for which manual worker unions have been battling for years—with successes only coming in recent union contracts.

Of course, not all firms treat their office staffs this well, and in any event the great insecurity attendant to office automation may provide an opening to unions which have been shut out in the past.

White- and Blue-Collar Workers: Status and Income Phases

While working conditions may change, and with them some traditional attitudes, there is, however, some good ground for believing that many white-collar workers will continue to cherish certain occupational attitudes which are not common among manual workers. Some sociologists have summarized these differences by noting that the manual worker has no less a drive for economic well-being and a higher material standard of living than the white-collar worker; but unlike the middle class–aspiring white-collar worker, whose occupational aspirations often take the form of a desire of "getting ahead," the manual worker is more often likely to be content with "getting by."[74] Keeping open fair channels of promotion, for example, will probably be an important union task among some white-collar groups.

[73] *Adjustments to the Introduction of Office Automation,* Bulletin No. 1276, U.S. Dept. of Labor (1960), especially Appendices E and H.
[74] See S. M. Miller and Frank Riessman, "The Working Class Subculture: A New View," *Social Problems* (Summer 1961).

More generally the "upward orientation" of white-collar occupational groups will be one of the factors union organizations must take into account when they frame their organizing appeals and campaigns.

In the area of politics and political issues, there appears to be some significant difference in attitude between blue- and white-collar workers. Many groups of white-collar workers seem to incline toward a more conservative political posture than do blue-collar workers. As more white-collar workers enter the union ranks, this conceivably could lead to some changes and reconsideration of traditional union political programs which are strongly liberal.

It is somewhat difficult to estimate whether or not economic pressures of a more purely income nature will be favorable or unfavorable so far as the unionization of white-collar workers is concerned. Certainly if one were to judge the period 1939-50—the period of the great upsurge of mass unionization in the United States—the better organized blue-collar workers made much greater gains relatively than the less organized white-collar groups. The traditional wage differentials between these two types of work were narrowed. Since 1950 the narrowing of differentials among major occupational groups appears to have halted, and there is some evidence that the earlier trend may even have been reversed. As Table 10 shows, in the past thirteen years the income of laborers has certainly lagged behind that of white-collar workers, reflecting in part much less steady employment and in part lower rates of wage increase. Semiskilled workers and operatives have done better than laborers but their median annual incomes have also advanced much less rapidly than those of professional employees. To some extent the slower progress on the part of blue-collar workers may also reflect the impact of temporary layoffs and shorter work weeks. This is especially true in the case of laborers.

Of course there are also many situations in which unorganized white-collar workers still tend to be lower paid compared to organized blue-collar workers. Moreover, in many large firms most wage increases for white-collar workers are an after-product of the union-negotiated increases for manual workers. It has become commonplace for employers to pass comparable benefits along to white-collar workers for a number of reasons, among which is the desire to forestall efforts at unionization.

Unionism and Collective Bargaining

Aside from changes in working conditions and job relationships, there is another force which may have even greater importance in

Table 10. Wage and Salary Movements, 1939-63

	Median Annual or Salary Income—Men			*Per Cent Increase in Annual Wage or Salary Income*	
Occupational Group	*1963*	*1950*	*1939*	*1950–63*	*1939–50*
White-Collar:					
Professional, technical, and kindred workers	$7182	$3874	$1809	88	114
Clerical and kindred workers	5318	3002	1421	71	111
Blue-Collar:					
Operatives and kindred workers	4830	2736	1007	76	172
Laborers, except farm and mine	2869	1850	673	55	175

Source: U.S. Dept. of Commerce, Bureau of the Census, Series P-60.

encouraging the unionization of white-collar workers. This is the very growth and acceptance of unionism and collective bargaining as basic institutions in American society, and, indeed, in all Western-type democratic societies.

There is an ever widening area of public and private policy which is being influenced by unionism in the United States. The encouragement being given directly to unionism in federal employment is one example. One student of employee relations in the federal government only recently wrote that as a result of Executive Order 10,988 (which he is certain will not be basically reversed by any new administration): "Government management people will tend to discard the traditional notion that their ability to resist employee organization and to reduce such organizations as do exist to a chronic state of impotence is an indication of management effectiveness. . . . The time will come when more prestige will accrue to the personnel director who demonstrates his ability to lead effectively with large and powerful organizations of his employees than to the one whose main claim to fame as a practitioner in the labor relations field is that his employees have not exercised their right to organize." [75]

The growth of unionism and collective bargaining among teachers is another case in point. This too should serve to legitimatize white-collar unionism in other areas.

[75] Hart, *op. cit.*, p. 215.

It is, however, more than collective bargaining which feels the widening impact of unionism in American society. One can cite the President's Labor Management Policy Committee which serves at the highest level of government and is consulted on matters ranging from fiscal policy (it was used as a sounding board and support builder for the Administration's tax-cut campaign in 1962-63), as a good case in point. Advisory committees of a similar nature exist for the Department of Labor's manpower policy agencies and the Area Redevelopment Administration; union-nominated advisers have been appointed to the State Department, the Interior Department, and others. All reflect an acceptance of interest group representation which is likely to have subtle pressure effects on large masses of unorganized white-collar groups. For until these groups do become more effectively organized, it is the presently organized labor unions which will hold the lion's share of the representation role in government and elsewhere on behalf of all workers in the society.

Special Issues of White-Collar Bargaining

It is hard to foresee all the issues which may distinguish an increasing and emerging white-collar union movement, but there is enough current experience to indicate some of the collective bargaining areas of special concern to white-collar workers. These include: better vacations and sick leave plans than have normally been bargained for by blue-collar worker unions; less interest in such things as supplementary unemployment benefit funds and more interest in insurance and stock-sharing programs.[76] These items are mentioned merely to suggest the kinds of new emphases that may be found in white-collar bargaining. On the other hand, it is easy to exaggerate the differences between blue-collar and white-collar groups. Once organized, white-collar groups seem to negotiate agreements that show more similarities than differences when compared to manual workers' agreements.

One cannot generalize about what the attitude toward strikes will be among white-collar workers. There is some evidence to indicate that there may be less militancy and less willingness to strike. Goldstein contends that among unionized engineers, for example, the

[76] It comes as a somewhat jarring note to traditional union literature to have the United Automobile Workers hail their victory in a newly organized Chrysler office by compelling management to preserve "the right of office employees to incorporate stock option programs into their contracts. . . ." See *TOP*, Technical Office Reporter, Monthly Publication of the Technical, Office, and Professional Department, UAW (December 1963).

very handling of grievances is looked upon as something that should "not come to be a matter of conflict between engineers and management." Goldstein also adds that among engineers there are "strong feelings against the use of a strike weapon." [77]

The American Nurses Association strongly advocates collective bargaining for its members but at the same time it maintains a no-strike policy. In abandoning the right to strike, however, the nurses propose some form of terminal arbitration machinery, either through collective agreement or legislation.[78]

Perhaps it was a similar view of white-collar workers and their attitudes toward strikes which motivated the Steelworkers to say in an organizing brochure directed at office and technical workers that "the United Steelworkers of America deplore strikes" and do not sanction them until "every possible means" of a reasonable settlement has been tried. In the same brochure the Steelworkers emphasized their close relationships with management and suggested that many times in conference company officials have indicated, "If I were in the mill or office or laboratory, I would be in the union." [79]

Once again, however, excessive generalization may have to give way to more cautious judgments even in this area of white-collar militancy. One can recall, for example, that certain telephone groups including women operators have revealed a sense of militancy and solidarity in the midst of past strikes that would compare favorably with that of any manual union group. The strong pro-strike attitude of the New York City teachers in 1962 and 1963 is a further example of militancy on the part of a white-collar group.

The Forms of Emerging White-Collar Unionism

As our sketch of existing white-collar unionism has shown, one cannot make any simple judgments of the forms this unionism is likely to take. Both craft and industrial types of unions have enjoyed some fair measure of success but neither has made sufficient progress in the still large, unorganized sectors of white-collar employment to suggest for sure what, if any, might be the ideal form.

One major over-all problem which is beginning to stand before the labor movement as a whole is whether or not the job of organiza-

[77] Bernard Goldstein, "The Perspective of Unionized Professionals," *Social Forces* (May 1959), p. 325.
[78] *White-Collar Report*, Bureau of National Affairs (March 28, 1963), p. A-6.
[79] *Office and Technical Workers, Your Key to a Better Future*, United Steelworkers of America, Pamphlet No. PR-105 (August 1960).

tion can and will proceed within the framework of the AFL-CIO. Unlike the central labor federations of most Western countries, the AFL-CIO does have the advantage of not being a clearly "class" marked organization. It is not encumbered with a purely "proletarian" past which in turn means that given the will and intelligence, it should be able to develop a fair appeal for white-collar workers.

On the other hand, because of its overwhelmingly predominant manual numbers and because of much of its tradition, the AFL-CIO continues to be regarded primarily as a manual workers' movement. This suggests the need for bringing more white-collar union officials into high posts of the Federation, the need to develop special appeals and structures for the growing number of women workers in the labor force, and the need to establish some sort of a separate division or department in the top structure of the labor movement itself to look after the special interests of white-collar workers.

Similar adjustments in terms of personnel (such as the recruitment of more organizers with professional and white-collar work experience), departments, and policies must also be made by most AFL-CIO affiliated unions, if they are to broaden their appeal to white-collar workers.

These "proposals" are merely suggestive of what probably needs to be done if the AFL-CIO itself is to become a great center for white-collar organizing.

Simply to pose the problem as one of "adjustment" may, however, miss the point. What will be called for over the next decade, if the AFL-CIO as a movement is to be successful in organizing white-collar workers on a large scale, is a major transformation of much of the institution itself. If the AFL-CIO and its constituent unions approach this challenge only by doing the minimum necessary to persuade the white-collar workers to join the "house of labor," these workers for the most part may never accept the invitation in very large numbers.

In any event, the signs of recent years suggest that while new approaches and strategy may be called for, there is apt to be substantial progress in the unionization of white-collar workers in the years ahead. What forms this unionism may take and its relationship to the older, already established unions, is more difficult to foresee.

WHITE-COLLAR UNIONS -- A COMPARATIVE ESSAY

BY ADOLF STURMTHAL

On the pages that follow I shall summarize some of the information presented in the various essays contained in this volume and attempt to draw some general conclusions from the data. This summary is not a report on a large-scale comparative research project such as might befit the subject of these essays, but simply an attempt to use this readily available information for analysis as far as the information will take one. Lack of data and, as shall be shown, lack of uniformity of data form the main barriers for a systematic comparative study.

The main question to which we shall address ourselves is the future of white-collar unionism in this country. Is there anything in international experience that would help us answer that question or at least assist us in finding out how we should go about obtaining an answer to the question? Are there sufficient regularities, at least in the highly industrialized nations, to permit generalization? A brief survey of some of the salient facts brought out in the reports included in this volume is thus necessary.

The fundamental importance of the issue for the future of the American labor movement is obvious. It affects United States unionism in terms of membership, but also in many other ways, including the nature of its leadership, its organizational structure, methods of operation, and ideological outlook.

Since the main growth of the labor force in recent years has been outside the blue-collar field, the current and future possibilities of expansion of American unionism depend largely on its ability to recruit members among the white-collar workers. During the fifties, American unions had only a small increase of blue-collar members, corresponding to the low growth rate of blue-collar workers in the labor force. Only a small fraction of the rapidly growing union membership potential among white-collar workers was, in fact, enrolled in unions. As a consequence, union membership is representing a decreasing proportion of the dependently employed labor force. If this trend were to continue, American unionism in its traditional form would become—numerically—a less and less significant factor in the economic, social, and political life of the nation. More important perhaps, it might become a marginal factor in the economy—playing an insignificant role in those sectors employing increasing numbers of white-collar workers of all kinds.

To meet this danger, observers and some participants have discussed changes in the system of organization of American labor, allowing for instance for a special role to be played by white-collar workers within the framework of industrial unions, or for the formation of special white-collar organizations in certain fields that would depart significantly and in many ways from the traditions of even the most recent forms of American unionism. New forms of collective bargaining and new types of bargaining objectives have been advocated as appropriate for at least some of the white-collar groups. Changes in leadership personnel and in ideology have been recommended as necessary if unionism is to succeed among professional workers, etc. In other words, many people feel that the rapid rise of the white-collar worker has introduced a new era in the history of American labor.

The basic underlying fact is the rapid change in technology characteristic of modern industrial societies. This seems to be accompanied everywhere by substantial changes in the structure of the labor force. The share of the labor force devoted to agriculture shrinks. While in pre-industrial societies up to 80 per cent—more or less—of the labor force work is in agriculture, this proportion drops in modern industrial societies to 10 per cent and less. This shift is so characteristic of advanced industrialization that the movement of labor out of agriculture is one of the essential aspects of economic development. The percentage of labor engaged in agriculture has been used as a first approximation in measuring the degree of industrialization of a given country.

CHANGES IN THE STRUCTURE OF THE LABOR FORCE

Another change in the structure of the labor force that seems to occur regularly is the emergence of a large white-collar group. In the United States, where this development appears to have advanced far, relative to other industrial nations, white-collar workers now (1960) appear to outnumber blue-collar workers, as indicated in Table 1 of Kassalow's article. More than 42 per cent of the labor force—excluding the employees of the service industries—consists of white-collar workers; less than 40 per cent are manual workers; the remainder are service workers, many of whom share the characteristics of white-collar workers. Some 6 per cent are agricultural laborers or farmers. If we follow the Census classification, the white-collar group consists of the following three major occupational groups: clerical and kindred workers; professional, technical, and kindred workers; and sales workers. First-line supervisors are included in these groups. As a proportion of the total labor force these three groups combined represented 5.7 per cent of the total in 1870, 15 per cent in 1910, 28 per cent in 1950, and 34.6 per cent in 1960.[1] Managerial personnel, officials, and proprietors make up the remainder of the white-collar labor force.

In the West German Federal Republic more than 36 per cent of the labor force were white-collar employees and government officials (1960). For the United Kingdom, the latest available figures go back to 1951; they indicate that at that time the various white-collar groups amounted to some 35 per cent of those gainfully employed. In Sweden, 35 per cent of the labor force in 1960 was white-collar. More than a quarter of the nonagricultural labor force in Japan in 1963 was white-collar.

Such comparisons, unfortunately, are of limited value. Occupational classifications vary from country to country. In particular, the American concept of the "white-collar worker" has few counterparts

[1] Census data as presented in Benjamin Solomon and Robert K. Burns, "Unionization of White-Collar Employees. Extent, Potential and Implications," *The Journal of Business*, Vol. XXXVI, No. 2 (April 1963).

in other countries.[2] United States subclassifications are similarly unknown elsewhere. German, French, and Austrian concepts have no equivalents in this country, etc. Available figures thus do not enable us to make rigorous comparisons from country to country.

The figures do permit, however, making some reasonably accurate statements about the trend. Most available statistics indicate that in the industrial nations the rise of the white-collar groups is under way. Even in manufacturing, an increasing portion of all work is carried on in the office.

In the United States, as Kassalow has shown, the proportion of white-collar workers has risen from less than 18 per cent at the turn of the century to 42 per cent in 1960. In the narrower terms of the Census classifications, the percentage of the three major categories referred to above (clerical, professional, and sales workers) has risen from 15 to close to 35 per cent. In Sweden the proportion of white-collar workers within the labor force has risen from 11 to 35 per cent during the period between 1920 and 1960. In England the share of manual labor has dropped from 75 per cent of the labor force in 1911 to less than 65 per cent in 1951. Similar trends seem to exist in Germany and Austria. For example, the proportion of white-collar workers and civil servants in the labor force of West Germany has risen from 2.5 per cent in 1882 to 20 per cent in 1950.

Even the non-Western industrial area seems to share in this development. For Japan, we are told that white-collar groups have shown continuing growth during the rapid, almost phenomenal, expansion of the Japanese economy since 1955. The share of white-collar workers in the total labor force has been steadily advancing since 1944. Thus, while blue-collar employment grew by 2.7 million or about 18 per cent between 1944 and 1955, white-collar employment rose by close to 1.3 million or more than 25 per cent. Presently almost one out of every five members of the labor force is a white-collar worker.

The trend thus seems universal in the industrial nations of the West and the great majority of observers forecast continued absolute and relative growth of the white-collar sector in the labor force for

[2] For instance, the category "professional, technical, and related workers" does not exist in most occupational statistics outside the United States. The United States classification "managers, officials, and proprietors, excluding farmers" is a mixture for which few countries, if any, have a counterpart. The category "administrative, executive, and managerial workers" cannot be distinguished in France from the category of proprietors and managers. The German and Austrian concept of "Beamte" often extends beyond the groups of civil servants, etc.

the foreseeable future. Inevitably, however, the rate of growth must decrease at some stage and may indeed have started to do so in one or the other Western country.

Michel Crozier sees a "leveling off" in the relative growth of the white-collar groups in France. "The ratio of white-collar workers to blue-collar workers in the private sector of industry has remained quite stable in the last ten years," he says, "progressing only from 22.9 per cent to 23.1 per cent between 1955 and 1960." This refers, however, only to clerical and sales workers. In their case, Crozier believes, the introduction of automatic equipment will offset the needs created by expansion. As to supervisors, technicians, and professional salaried workers, "both the numbers and the percentage in the total population . . . have increased tremendously" in France. As this group is included in the American concept of white-collar worker, the apparent decline in the white-collar growth rate refers to a subgroup rather than the total white-collar sector of the labor force.

Perhaps more to the point—though covering a very short period—is a decline in the growth rate of white-collar jobs in the United States during the years of 1962 and 1963. Thus, while the number of white-collar workers in the period from 1950 to 1960 increased by a yearly average of 2.8 per cent, the rate of increase in 1962 was down to 2.6 per cent and in 1963 to 0.9 per cent. Professional and technical workers on one hand, and clerical personnel on the other, shared in this slowing down of the growth rate.[3]

Of possible significance is the fact that a rise of white-collar employment by only 0.9 per cent in 1963 coincided with an increase of nonfarm employment of 2.3 per cent (from 55,840,000 to 57,170,000, while white-collar employment rose from 29,900,000 to 30,180,000). It is far too early, however, to draw major conclusions from these figures, especially as the period concerned is just two years.[4]

To some extent, the growth of the white-collar share in the total labor force corresponds to shifts in the distribution of employment among the various sectors of the economy. One such shift—from agriculture into other branches of economic activity—has been noted at the outset of this essay. This change is a fundamental expression of the process of progressive industrialization in an economy. Another

[3] *Wall Street Journal,* May 5, 1964, p. 1.

[4] White-collar employment may show smaller cyclical fluctuations than employment in general. The revival of the 1962-63 period may thus have been accompanied by less than proportionate expansion of white-collar employment. I owe this point to my colleague Melvin Rothbaum.

aspect of this process, manifesting itself perhaps at a later stage of industrial development, is the growth of the tertiary sectors of the economy, trade, transportation, services in general. Significant in our context is the fact that employment in these sectors contains on the average a larger proportion of white-collar jobs than the primary and secondary sectors. The shift from the latter to the tertiary sector is thus normally accompanied by a rise in the proportion of white-collar employment in the total labor force. Such a shift appears to occur regularly in industrial societies that have reached a relatively high standard of living. One particular aspect is the growth of public employment which reflects the growing importance of the government —in the United States, especially at the local and state levels—in society.[5] In the United States, the shift in aggregate employment and the employment shares of different industries since World War II is quite impressive in this respect. Table 1 presents a summary of these trends. Between 1957 and 1962 all shifts in both absolute and relative terms have been into the tertiary sector. To some extent this period may, however, have been influenced by cyclical factors, but the general trend is nevertheless unmistakable.[6]

Even within the secondary sector, moreover, employment has moved toward a greater share of white-collar jobs. This is particularly so in the United States where the share of production workers in manufacturing has been declining significantly for a number of years. In France, the proportion of white-collar employees in the metal-producing industries increased from 7.5 per cent in 1955 to 13.2 per cent in 1960.

For Germany, Tables 2 and 3 illustrate the change in the distribution of employment among the three sectors of the economy and the shift in the occupational distribution.

[5] Walter Galenson, "Economic Development and the Sectoral Expansion of Employment," *International Labor Review*, Vol. LXXXVII, No. 6 (June 1963). His study shows that in five out of eleven countries with high per capita incomes tertiary employment grew faster than secondary employment (manufacturing) during varying periods in the fifties up to 1962. In seven out of eight countries at the other end of the income scale the shift occurred in the opposite direction, i.e., manufacturing employment grew at a faster rate than that in tertiary activities.

[6] The inclusion (or exclusion) of the employees of certain service industries in the white-collar category is purely conventional and varies from country to country. The 1940 Census category "Amusement, recreation, and related services" (in the 1960 Census "Entertainment and Recreation Services") is a good example of such an industry. Are actors or musicians white-collar workers? Yet even if we exclude these doubtful cases, the shift into tertiary industries involves a considerable increase in the share of white-collar employment.

Table 1. Industrial Composition of Increases in Numbers of Wage and Salary Earners, U.S., 1947-62[a]

Industrial Sector	*Net Increase in Employment*			
	1947–57		*1957–62*	
	Total, 1,000	*Per Cent*	*Total, 1,000*	*Per Cent*
Total increase in nonagricultural wage and salary workers	9,023	100.00	2,421	100.00
Manufacturing	1,629	18.05	−424	−17.51
Mining	−127	−1.41	−181	−7.48
Contract construction	941	10.43	−227	−9.38
Transportation and public utilities	75	.83	−316	−13.05
Wholesale and retail trade	1,931	21.40	685	28.29
Finance, insurance, and real estate	723	8.01	316	13.05
Services and miscellaneous	1,699	18.83	1,008	41.64
Government (federal, state, and local)	2,152	23.85	1,559	64.39

[a] From *Economic Report of the President* (January 1963), p. 201; as computed and quoted in R. A. Gordon, "Twenty Years of Economic and Industrial Change." Reprint No. 222 (University of California, Berkeley, California, 1964), p. 58.

Table 2. Changes in Distribution of Employment Among Broad Sectors in Germany, in Percentages[a]

Year	*Sectors*		
	1	*2*	*3*
1882	42	36	22
1895	36	39	25
1907	34	40	26
1925	30	42	28
1933	29	41	30
1939	27	41	32
1950	23	45	32
1958	16	48	36

[a] Sector 1—primary industries (agriculture, forestry, fishing); Sector 2—manufacturing, handicrafts; Sector 3—services.

Source: Fritz Croner, *Soziologie der Angestellten* (Köln-Berlin, 1962), p. 197.

While Sector 2 is thus still growing, the service sector has been showing, since the beginning of the century, a growth rate exceeding that of manufacturing and handicrafts.

Even if we were to assume that the entire increase of employment in the tertiary sector since the beginning of the century or since 1939 consisted of white-collar employees—which is highly unlikely—it would not be sufficient to explain the rise of the share of white-collar employment. A shift in the nature of employment in the other sectors—most probably in the secondary sector—must thus have occurred to produce the full increase of white-collar jobs.

Table 3. Changes in the Occupational Distribution of Employment in Germany, in Percentages

Occupational Group	*1882*	*1895*	*1907*	*1925*	*1933*	*1939*	*1950*	*1958*
Independent	38	35	27	21	20	18	18	13
Collaborating family members	4	4	8	10	11	11	9	11
White-collar, including civil servants	8	11	14	19	18	20	22	26
Blue-collar workers	50	50	51	50	52	51	52	50

Source: Croner, *ibid.*

CHANGES WITHIN THE WHITE-COLLAR GROUP

Within the white-collar group itself significant changes have been occurring, which may have considerable bearing upon the social situation of these groups in general and their unionization in particular. First, female labor force participation has been increasing in general, in the white-collar occupations in particular. Second, the share of technical and professional workers in the labor force and among the white-collar workers has been rising. Third, employment in services, especially in government and education, has been increasing rapidly. To some extent—e.g., by way of the large female employment in education—these three trends are interrelated.

The change in the sex ratio of the white-collar workers in favor of females has been conspicuous. In the United States, females in 1960 constituted slightly more than half of the white-collar total. Female labor force participation has tended to increase in most Western countries and in many cases the most significant outlet for this has been in the white-collar group. Within that group itself, clerical and sales jobs seem to have offered the relatively largest number of job opportunities for female labor. In France, "the clerical and sales group, hundred years ago an almost exclusively male group, is now shifting more and more rapidly . . . to a predominantly female one. . . . Women have already outnumbered men significantly in the private sector. . . ." In the United States a similar trend has been observed. There are even some indications of growing numbers of females in professional jobs in some countries of the West. So far, however, this latter increase has manifested itself in terms of absolute numbers rather than in a rise of the female share in the growing professional labor force. Indeed, in the United States the share of women in high-level professional occupations—and in one or two occupations even the absolute number—has decreased during the last quarter of a century.[7]

Female labor force participation in the white-collar occupations is rising also in Japan, particularly among the lower grades of white-collar *shokuin*. In West Germany, between 1950 and 1960 the number of female workers in the white-collar group grew by 80 per cent, twice as fast as that of their male colleagues. Almost half of the white-collar workers are female.

Equally significant has been the growth, absolutely and relatively, of the professional and technical groups. In the United States its share in the labor force has risen from 4.3 per cent in 1900 to 10.8 per cent in 1960—thus by some 125 per cent. This growth rate is only exceeded by that of the clerical workers, who rose from 3 to 14.5 per cent of total employment, i.e., by almost 400 per cent. Current forecasts lead one to expect a slowdown in the rate of growth of the numbers of clerical workers, while there is no indication yet of a similar slowdown among the professionals. French statistics group together the supervisors, technicians, and professionals. Their number has risen by 31 per cent "in the span of six years." For England the average growth rate of professional groups since 1911 is indicated as 3 per cent per annum, with engineers and scientists showing a growth rate of 5 and 6 per cent, respectively. Technical employees are the fastest growing subgroup among the white-collar employees in Germany. In Japan the proportion of engineers, technicians, and clerical workers rose threefold in the quarter of a century ending in 1955. The share

[7] John B. Parrish, "Professional Womanpower as a National Resource," *Quarterly Review of Economics and Business*, Vol. I, No. 1 (1961), pp. 54-63.

of white-collar workers employed in education and in public employment appears to be growing everywhere in the West. In the United States, state and local government employment has risen steeply since the end of World War II.

There is thus little reason to doubt that a substantial change in the structure of the labor force has occurred. The demand for (and supply of) highly skilled manpower has risen substantially while other data indicate a decline of demand, at the other end of the scale, for unskilled labor. While these shifts are bound to level off at some stage, it is doubtful whether this moment is yet in sight in most of the industrial societies of the West. At the same time, some of the old white-collar jobs are being downgraded and the volume of demand is sometimes maintained at that lower level of job content. Conversely, other jobs which were in the past classified as lower or middle level white-collar jobs have now moved up to supervisory or technician's classifications. No simple statement can thus summarize the effect of technological change, change in the size of the firms, and changes in social conventions upon the job content and the status of the white-collar groups.[8]

The absence of a clear and simple trend is suggestive of the tremendous variety of occupations covered by the term "white-collar." They represent neither a closed nor a homogeneous class. Their jobs show a bewildering variety of degrees of difficulty, of social ambiance, of responsibility, of educational and training requirements, etc. No wonder, then, that these groups demonstrate very different responses to the phenomena of industrial development and technological change which affect them in very different ways. It is also not surprising that the attitudes toward enterprise, society, and union of this so heterogeneous group run the whole gamut of possible responses. Whatever they are, however, the impact of the changes in the structure of the labor force upon the social, political, and cultural life of the industrial nations in the West is bound to be tremendous and long-lasting.

[8] It should be observed that employment statistics do not simply indicate changes in the demand for different types of labor—as seems to be assumed in many statements—but the interaction of supply and demand as well as the effects of changes in the wage structure (and of changes in noneconomic factors affecting demand and supply of different types of labor). Moreover, in the Western countries, all these shifts occur around a trend of rising educational levels in the population. For the short and medium run, when noneconomic factors may be assumed to be reasonably constant, and supply is undergoing fairly determinable changes, alterations of the wage structure, together with changes in the volume of employment by category, are primary symptoms of changes in the structure of demand.

UNIONS AND WHITE-COLLAR WORKERS

One of the most immediate effects of this evolution can be seen in the trade-union movements of the West. Traditionally, the labor unions of the United States, Great Britain, Germany, and Sweden have been far more effective in organizing blue- than white-collar workers. In the United States, for instance, in 1960 only 2.2 million of the 17 million union members were in white-collar occupations. White-collar workers thus accounted for about 12 per cent of all union members—even though they represented some 35 per cent of the labor force. The degree of unionization of the white-collar employees is on the average one-third of that of the blue-collar workers.[9] The shift in the structure of the labor force in the direction of a larger white-collar population endangers the relative strength of the American labor movement. The danger confronting the movement is, of course, not its extinction, but rather the possibility that it may fail to grow with the growth of the labor force. Most important, organized labor may be kept out of the most dynamic sectors of the economy and thus lose some of its vitality. This threat is accentuated by some of the circumstances accompanying the shift in the proportion of white-collar workers, such as the growing participation of women in the labor force and the especially rapid growth of the number of engineers, scientists, and other professionals. All of these groups have tended to be less receptive to unionization in the United States than those categories which now represent a shrinking proportion of the labor force—male workers and manual labor.

To what extent do events in other industrial nations justify those fears held by many American trade unionists and observers?

With the possible exception of Japan, all industrial nations seem to share the American experience that white-collar workers are more difficult to organize into unions than blue-collar workers (and probably, though we made no special study of this, that women are less inclined to join unions than men). Even in as highly unionized a country as Sweden, the percentage of unionization among white-collar is estimated at about 70 per cent as compared with 80 per cent among

[9] These figures are lower than those in Solomon and Burns, *op. cit.*, who estimate white-collar union membership at 2.8 million in 1962, including unaffiliated local unions. The date of the estimate is inferred from the term "current" used by the authors. For 1960, their estimate is 2.7 million. E. Kassalow comments that these estimates are high. As for percentage figures, self-employed white-collar workers, who represent a sizable proportion, are not always fully excluded from the estimates of white-collar workers. As a result, the proportion of those organized in relation to those eligible for unionization may be underestimated in some cases.

blue-collar workers. In France, the well-organized civil service and teachers' unions tend to improve the relative standing of the white-collar unions; in the absence of reliable membership figures it is difficult, however, to be precise in evaluating the relative degrees of unionization of blue- and white-collar workers.[10] Yet it would appear that blue-collar workers are better organized. Union structure in Great Britain, Germany, and other countries makes impossible exact comparisons, since many unions organize both blue- and white-collar workers and most often do not count them separately. But whatever estimates are available indicate clearly that in general white-collar workers are less well organized than manual workers. Only for Japan is there a suggestion that the relationship may be reversed. Some 35 per cent of the union members are white-collar workers, a greater proportion than would correspond to their share in the labor force. In general, we are told, Japanese unions are strong where the white-collar workers are strongly represented in the labor force. White-collar workers played a key role in the entire development of the Japanese labor movement after World War II. This is undoubtedly an exceptional situation among the industrial nations, though parallels could be found in some of the newly rising labor movements of non-Western nations. In the great majority of cases, the unions in Western nations share the American experience that white-collar workers are more difficult to organize than blue-collar workers.

Yet, there are differences in the degree of white-collar resistance to unionism. Some of these differences emerge in a survey of the countries considered in this volume.

As a proposition of fairly universal validity, at least in the West, white-collar workers are organized best where unionism in general is strong. Sweden and Austria—countries with a high degree of unionization in general—have also succeeded in enrolling large proportions of their white-collar workers into unions. Great Britain with a somewhat lower degree of unionization—as measured by the ratio of union members to nonagricultural civilian labor force—has also a lower percentage of union members among the white-collar workers, followed by Japan, Germany, and the United States. To place France in this system offers, however, some special difficulties, given the problem of precisely defining union membership in that country.

International experience thus may suggest as a first conclusion that, if white-collar workers are to be organized on a larger scale in

[10] See the estimates in Val R. Lorwin, *The French Labor Movement* (Cambridge: Harvard University Press, 1954), p. 177.

the United States, a preliminary step might be to organize the blue-collar workers more extensively. Compared with the proportions of union membership in countries like Sweden, Austria, and Great Britain, American unions have still a very large membership potential among manual workers to recruit from.

While white-collar workers as a group are more difficult to organize than blue-collar workers, different white-collar groups show considerable variations in their receptiveness for unionism. Certain groups stand out as particularly apt to accept unionism; others are especially difficult to organize. Properly understood, this means that for some white-collar groups the proportion of union members is high relative to average unionization of white-collar workers in their society; for others the relationship is the opposite. Some white-collar groups are more readily available for unionization than even some of their blue-collar colleagues.

What do the reports in this volume indicate in this respect?

PUBLIC EMPLOYEES

In several countries civil servants and teachers are relatively well unionized.[11] Public employees frequently seem to organize more readily than private employees. The term "public employee" may include, in addition to the civil servants in the conventional sense of the word, employees performing ordinary industrial functions in enterprises owned by the state (or some subdivision of it). We are compelled to lump this group together since the dividing line between civil servants and other public employees is often fuzzy and varies from country to country.

In Japan and France, white-collar workers in public employment show a higher degree of organization than their colleagues in private enterprise. One-half of all white-collar unionists in Japan are employed by the government; government workers were the first to form unions after World War II. The teachers' union is the largest national union in the country. Similarly, civil service unions in France are well organized, and so is the teachers' union which is not affiliated with any confederation. As far as one can judge in the absence of reliable sta-

[11] In the United States, unionism among white-collar workers is strongest in the entertainment industry, in the railways and other transportation services, and in the postal services. Railways and postal service are in practically all Western nations government owned, except for the railways in the United States, which are in private hands though subject to government regulation. Unionism of civil servants in the United States is fast growing since the Kennedy administration smoothed the way for the unions.

tistics in these two countries, the level of organization in these occupations appears conspicuously high by comparison with the average degree of organization in the nonagricultural sectors of the economy, manual workers included. In Sweden, the unionization of the employees of the central government is very high by any standard (82 per cent) and that of the employees of the local governments not much lower. By comparison, the degree of organization of white-collar employees in private employment is less than 50 per cent. Austria's public employees are organized in about the same proportion as Swedish local government employees. In the United Kingdom, unionization of manual and white-collar workers in the nationalized industries is very high, e.g., 95 per cent in the coal mines, 85 per cent in the railroads, about 50 per cent higher than in private industries such as paper and printing, metal manufacturing, engineering, etc. Such high degrees of organization could hardly be achieved unless a substantial proportion of the white-collar workers were organized as well. These are public employees, but not civil servants in the proper sense of the word. As to the latter, Professor Routh informs us that "the numbers organized in national and local government and education are very much above the national average." In the United States, however, teachers are unionized to a far lesser extent than white-collar workers in general and even other professional workers, although one nonunion professional association of teachers has been behaving more and more as if it were a union and has even been invoking "sanctions" that are sometimes difficult to distinguish from strikes.[12]

Civil servant or government employee is, of course, a much wider concept than white-collar worker in public employment. Large numbers of manual workers are included among the civil servants. There is some evidence, particularly in the United States, that manual civil service workers have tended to join unions more readily than their white-collar colleagues. To some extent, therefore, statements about the relatively greater readiness of civil servants than other white-collar groups to join unions, will have to be properly interpreted to avoid misunderstandings. In the absence of separate statistics for manual and nonmanual civil servants and their respective union membership, we can only guess at the extent to which this factor affects our generalization. This writer's estimate nevertheless is that in most countries white-collar civil servants and employees of public enterprise join

[12] The National Education Association (NEA) has organized more than three-quarters of a million teachers. At the same time, the United States teachers' union has been gaining members, especially in some of the largest cities.

unions more readily than their colleagues in private employment. In the case of Germany where there is a special civil servant association limited (or almost) to white-collar workers, membership is exceedingly high. This, of course, is not the case in the United States, where only recently official encouragement—by way of Executive Order 10,988 of January 17, 1962—has opened the door for widespread unionization of civil servants. Everett Kassalow estimates that about two-fifths of the 1,070,000 government union members are from the white-collar ranks. This, of course, is a much larger proportion of union members than can be found in private employment. As to employees in education, union membership is nearly all white-collar in most countries.[13]

No obvious explanation is available for the tendency of public employees to unionize more readily than their colleagues in private business. Experience derived from other circumstances suggests several hypotheses: one relates to the size of the establishment, another to the onesidedness of the employment relationship; other hypotheses may refer to the nature of the power at the disposal of the employees.

Generally speaking, unionization tends to be more intensive in larger than in smaller enterprises. In several of the reports, particularly those on Austria and Japan, reference is made to the fact that the density of union membership increases with the size of the firm. Indeed, one of the basic problems of white-collar unionism results from the fact that potential union members are often spread in small numbers over a great many establishments; this applies particularly to trade and commerce. Organizing small groups of members or individual members in different establishments is difficult and costly.

[13] It should be understood that in many, if not most, Western nations the right to strike of civil servants and public employees is limited, but not abrogated. Thus there is no restriction on the right to strike of employees in the nationalized enterprises in France (except those very substantial ones that exist for all employees—manual or white-collar) and Great Britain. The principles of collective bargaining that operate in private employment are also applicable to the employees in the nationalized coal mines, electricity works, gas, etc., in the United Kingdom. For civil servants proper, restrictions exist, depending on the nature of their work rather than that of their employer. In England and France rules exist regarding arbitration of disputes and the avoidance of surprise strikes. (Jean Touscoz, "Le Droit de grève dans les services publics et la loi du 31 juillet 1963," *Droit Social,* Vol. XXVII, No. 1 [January 1964].) Restrictions apply in some countries to the right to strike of policemen or firemen because of the essential nature of their work rather than because "you cannot strike against the government." In Austria, however, no restrictions seem to apply at all, as a strike of policemen in 1964 would indicate. The availability of the strike weapon does of course have some effect upon the unionization of government employees.

The same is true, of course, for "servicing" union members after they have been organized. Public employment tends to be concentrated in large or even gigantic establishments making both organizing and "servicing" easier and less costly. It is perhaps no accident then that the degree of unionization of municipal employees, as the report on Sweden indicates, is less high than that of the white-collar employees of the central government. The average size of the establishment in the local government is most probably less than that of the central government, even though individual local establishments may be larger than many agencies of the central government.

In the second place, civil service employment is based in principle upon a set of rules unilaterally determined by the employer. Wages and working conditions are set down by regulations and decrees. The individual sees himself confronted by an overwhelming power. The protection of the union seems indispensable to him, if he is to influence his own fate at all.

Third, government employees appear to find unions a more effective device for the defense of their interests than white-collar employees in private employment. This might indicate that the kind of pressures which the union can bring to bear upon the government are held to be more powerful than the pressures ordinarily used against private enterprise. The weapons available to the union against the government—as distinguished from, or in addition to, those that can be used against private enterprise—are mainly the voting power of the union members and the censure of public opinion directed against a government unable to keep government services running satisfactorily. White-collar workers are usually described as less ready than manual workers to use the strike weapon; striking in public employment may be even less promising than in private enterprise. Yet, white-collar workers would hardly hesitate to employ their voting or lobbying power as a means of pressure. These methods may be effective against the government; they would have less influence upon private enterprise. It would follow that unionization is likely to be more appealing to white-collar workers in the civil service than in private employment.

A conspicuous feature of white-collar unionism in many countries in Western Europe is the organization of supervisory personnel. This may include not only foremen, but higher personnel, sometimes close to executive rank. Some of the organizations are independent from manual and other trade unions as in the case of the French Confédération Générale des Cadres (CGC), the General Confederation of

Higher Personnel. In Sweden these groups are organized either in TCO or SACO while the Austrian GAP organizes them within the general framework of the trade-union confederation (ÖGB).

The example of supervisors forming "their" union has frequently induced other white-collar workers to accept unionism in general. To belong to a union then may become the accepted way of life, a regular attribute of one's job, or even a mark of distinction.

SPECIAL WHITE-COLLAR UNIONS

Union structure has an important bearing upon the evolution of white-collar unions. In several countries this has been and continues to be a basic issue between white- and blue-collar workers and their organizations. The main issues are these: Are white-collar workers to be included in industrial unions together with their blue-collar colleagues? If so—what degree of autonomy are white-collar workers to have within the industrial union? If there are to be separate white-collar unions which may straddle industrial boundaries, are they to be affiliated with the same federation to which the unions of blue-collar workers belong? Is there to be a separate federation of white-collar unions and what ought to be its relationship with the blue-collar federation? Only some of these problems can be illuminated in the light of information contained in this volume.

First of all, are there to be separate white-collar unions? This raises no problem as far as sales employees or school teachers are concerned where occupation and industry nearly coincide so that the white-collar occupations represent almost the entire employment of the industry. For other white-collar occupations—e.g., office workers, engineers, and many other professionals—the issue is very real: are they to be organized in industrial unions together with the blue-collar employees of their industry, or should there be an occupational organization that may or may not cut across industry lines? The craft versus industrial union issue arises with at least the same intensity that it had in the history of the American labor movement.

Indeed, three main structural types of white-collar unionism may be distinguished:

a) vertical unionism of the industrial union type;
b) horizontal unions combining employees of the same occupational groups in several industries;
c) occupational unions limited to one industry or enterprise.

In several of the reports in this volume reference is made to these issues. The solutions found vary considerably among the countries studied. They range from the white-collar unions affiliated to the DAG in Germany and the Swedish TCO to the industrial unions of the United States and the enterprise unions of Japan. A related basic issue of union structure arises when separate white-collar unions exist, either for those occupations where occupation and industry are almost coterminous or when the craft principle has been adopted for white-collar workers, in part or altogether; in other words, unions of types (b) and (c) above. Are the white-collar organizations to be affiliated with the federation of the industrial unions and the craft unions of the manual workers? Or are they to be part of a special white-collar federation? If the latter, what is the relationship between the two federations? Once again, the reports show great differences in the solutions adopted by the movements of different countries. Moreover, they indicate a certain "messiness" of the solutions which may be the result of fortuitous historical events or, perhaps, indicate that for different white-collar groups different solutions appear appropriate. These are clearly problems whose solution may depend on the attitudes of different white-collar groups toward manual labor and traditional unionism in general, with whatever associations these concepts evoke in different nations and cultures, and—most probably—at different stages of the industrialization process.

Not all Western countries have special white-collar unions. Even when these exist, not all organized white-collar workers belong to them. Japanese unions—the "enterprise union"—combine both blue-collar and white-collar workers, with the latter more often than not providing some of the leadership of the common organization. Austria, at the other extreme, has special white-collar unions extending over the entire spectrum of the economy. In between are the other countries considered in this volume. Most of them have no clear distinction between blue- and white-collar organizations except insofar as a particular industry or craft consists overwhelmingly of workers of one or the other type, but maintain in addition special office workers' unions without clear demarcation lines. This is the case of the United States. Slightly different patterns are represented by Germany and Sweden where both industrial unions and special white-collar unions attempt to organize white-collar workers. In Germany this has resulted in a state of more or less open competition between the two kinds of unions; in Sweden cooperation appears to be stronger than rivalry. The relations between the Australian Council of Salaried and Professional Associations (ACSPA) and the Australian Council of

Trade Unions are similarly friendly. French unionism knows two kinds of competition for white-collar membership—competition among unions organized according to different structural principles as well as the rivalry of ideologically divided unions for the allegiance of all working class groups including the white-collar workers. Elements of ideological differentiation are not entirely missing in the case of organizational divisions in other countries.

Similarly varied are the connections between white-collar unions and the labor organizations of blue-collar workers or joint blue- and white-collar federations. This relationship seems to be delicate in almost all countries considered—the main exception being Japan where the existence of the enterprise union appears to have solved the problem for the time being. In some countries where separate white-collar unions exist, they form their own federation apart from those of the manual workers or the federations of mixed white- and blue-collar organizations. This applies to Germany where both DAG and the civil servant federation DBB keep apart from the DGB, the general trade-union federation, even though the DAG is closer to the DGB in philosophy and personal relations than is the DBB with its emphasis on the special status of the civil servant in German society.[14] The Swedish TCO and the other white-collar unions of the country have a separate existence from LO, the general federation of Swedish labor. In Great Britain a few of the smaller and most of the larger unions with preponderantly white-collar membership belong to the TUC, but the civil service union of professional workers and the National and Local Government Officers' Association (NALGO) do not.[15] In the United States independent white-collar unions are not infrequent, even though the bulk of the organized white-collar workers—not counting professional associations—probably belong to unions affiliated with the AFL-CIO. The Austrian white-collar unions are affiliated with the union federation, as are many of the French white-collar unions, although there exists a special federation of the "cadres" (upper personnel).

These facts do not allow for simple generalizations. Leaving aside the special case of Japan, one is tempted to conclude that, at least in several of the most advanced industrial nations, substantial white-collar groups prefer to be organized in separate organizations rather than in

[14] It should be noted, however, that DGB unions polled a majority of government officials' votes at the elections of personnel representatives in 1964. Perhaps the status consciousness of the civil servant is slowly giving way to the different structural concepts of a modern industrial society.

[15] NALGO recently (1964) voted affiliation.

joint blue- and white-collar industrial unions—if they are to be organized at all. In general: the wish for a separate organization seems to be the more intense the greater the social distance and, consequently, the difference in fate and interests which, in the view of the white-collar group, exists between it and the bulk of the manual workers. If, however, the wish for a separate white-collar organization is met by the organized labor movement, cooperation between at least some white- and blue-collar unions does not seem too difficult to establish. The examples of Austria and Sweden point in this direction. The issue is not the degree of aggressiveness with which the interests of the particular group are to be defended. Even though white-collar workers are less strike-prone than their manual colleagues, they are often no less effective in the defense of their group interests by different means. The German officials' union (DBB) is known to be very aggressive in representing both status and material interests of its members. What is at stake is rather whether manual workers recognize the peculiar character of the white-collar worker and his special needs and interests and are willing to make the required adjustments in union structure, policy, and leadership. These adjustments vary in character from one white-collar group to another. They are most clearly pronounced in the case of professional personnel with advanced education. Thus the kind of union that many white-collar groups—particularly the professionals—in Western industrial nations find most acceptable appears to be a mixture between professional association and union. Maintenance of professional standards seems the center of union activity. This is only partly a device to restrict entry into the profession in order to maintain or raise income levels. To a considerable extent, education, continued training, and retraining are sincerely intended to raise the standards of the profession. In addition, the organization may set minima of remuneration for various grades and even intervene in personal grievances. But its main activities and its style are quite distinct from those of a conventional blue-collar union.

Another problem that, according to the reports in this volume, tends often to arise between white- and blue-collar workers is the relationship of the trade unions to politics or sometimes to particular political parties. The diversity of the white-collar group manifests itself clearly in the variety of attitudes toward this problem. In both Sweden and Great Britain this is regarded by most observers as one of the main issues between at least some white-collar unions (their members perhaps even more than their leaders) and the central trade-union federation of their country. While LO is closely related by history, personnel, and organization to the Social Democratic Party, TCO is politically neutral. It does advocate social reforms, defends the principles of democracy, and does not hesitate to state its views on current issues, but refuses to accept any commitment to a political party. Many of its members are politically to the right of the Social Democratic Party although the latter counts many friends among TCO leaders. In Britain several of the main white-collar unions are affiliated with TUC and Labour Party, but others are not. The Post Office Workers Union is affiliated with the Party as is the Transport Salaried Staffs' Association, while the union of professional civil servants is not.

Since the unions in Austria, Germany, and the United States are not officially committed to any party, this issue is of less relevance in these countries. The generally pro-Socialist tone of the labor movement in Germany, however, may nevertheless contribute to the distance which the officials' organization (DBB) tends to keep from the DGB. White-collar workers in commerce, too, seem to find it easier to join the DAG rather than the big industrial unions of the DGB, partly because of the "proletarian" character of the latter and partly because the great majority of the industrial unions' leaders and members are social democrats. The ideological divisions of the French trade-union movement are reflected in the differing degree of attractiveness of the unions for white-collar workers. The Christian unions and Force Ouvrière have a relatively stronger following among white-collar workers than the communist-led CGT, although in absolute numbers the relationship may well be reversed. Japan presents once again a special case, but perhaps more in appearance than in essence: the white-collar workers have greatly contributed to the left-wing (political) character of the Japanese trade-union movement after World War II, but in a peculiar fashion they have also accentuated some of its (professionally) conservative traits. This case apart, white-collar workers and their unions are as a rule attracted by conservative or even right-wing parties far more than are manual workers. In Germany and Austria white-collar workers provided substantial support for Nazi and Pan-German movements during the first half of this century.

Government workers' unions, as mentioned above, may have a special relationship to politics different from that of both blue-collar and the mass of white-collar workers. For them the ballot may be part of their bargaining power, indeed often its main element. This often induces unions of government workers to enter into intimate relations with other unions including manual workers so as to associate their voting power with that of the civil servants. The resulting apparent identity of attitude on short-term issues may conceal considerable differences in political philosophy. The "concrete immediate objective" radicalism of civil servant unions in given situations should not necessarily be identified with radical ideologies.

INFERENCES

The first and most obvious inference that can be drawn from the comparisons among the countries examined in this volume is that there are some traits and trends common to all or most of them. While Japan, the newest, most rapidly evolving industrial nation, is still carrying along stronger elements of its precapitalistic past than the others and thus stands apart in some respects, it nevertheless shares with the other countries several common features, in addition to tremendous diversity in other respects. The North Atlantic nations demonstrate greater similarities although cultural differences, time lags, and other elements of diversity are ever present. With these and many other qualifications, we can attempt to suggest generalizations and hypotheses.

The trends in the evolution of the labor force and its structure in modern industrial societies seem to be fairly regular. Growth of the white-collar population, growing share of professionals, growing female participation in the labor force, growing employment in the service industries—these seem to occur in all industrial nations that we have examined. There is, moreover, no fact yet in sight that seems likely to reverse the main trends, even though it seems probable that the rate of progress of some of them is due for a decline.

A second basic group of facts relates to the diversity of the group that is classified as white-collar. There are some differences from country to country as to who belongs in the group as well as some changes over time.[16] But most important, there are so many and such basic differences within the group that few generalizations apply to all sectors of the white-collar group. To find constitutive characteristics that permit speaking of a white-collar group at all has been a problem challenging sociologists for a long time. The white-collar

[16] German law makes distinctions between white- and blue-collar workers. These distinctions are, however, not the same according to—say—labor legislation and social security legislation. The same employees may thus be treated as white-collar workers under one law, as blue-collar workers under another. Wolfgang Linke, *Die Stellung der Angestellten in der modernen Gesellschaft* (Cologne, 1962), p. 13.

workers represent today such a diversity of occupations and levels of responsibility within the enterprise that in the words of a German sociologist, "their attitude toward the enterprise and society runs a whole gamut and can hardly be brought onto a common denominator." There is indeed in many respects little that a top executive and a clerk in the office have in common. Yet, somehow they both belong to "white-collar."

WHAT CONSTITUTES WHITE-COLLAR?

It would seem that two or three quite different factors have a bearing upon the constitution of the white-collar group and its evolution. The first of these relates to status.

Modern industrial society evolved out of precapitalistic social forms in which manual work carried low status. Long after industrial capitalism has arrived on the scene, social disqualification for manual labor continues to exist. The prestige of different occupations reflects quite clearly and far into the modern industrial society feudal and other prejudices against manual labor. The strength of this tradition can be seen to this day, most distinctly in many of the newly industrializing nations, but also, though less and less clearly, in many of the industrialized societies of the West.

The progress of industrialization, however, gradually undermines the division of society that has been inherited from the past. The traditional class structure related to status does not fit the requirements of an industrial society. In the latter, people belong to a multitude of social groups many of which have overlapping memberships and borderlines that are fluid and often fuzzy. Social stratification is, in principle, based upon achievement (which does not necessarily require only desirable personal characteristics). The actual society is a combination of traditional and new structures. Some of the existing groupings still reflect, though to a decreasing extent, the precapitalistic traditions; others represent the new order and its group distinctions. The latter express the value system of the industrial society, a value system intimately related to achievement, market valuations, and the functions performed rather than to status. This evolving change in the social structure with increasing opportunities for participation in the race for achievement is in essence what is called the "process of democratization" characteristic of the rise of the industrial society.

Neither the traditional stratification principle nor that of the industrial society is thus applied fully or decisively in the contemporary societies. Instead, we are—as always—in a period of transition in which one principle of classification is declining but not yet eliminated, the other rising but not yet totally victorious. A good part of the fuzziness, and inconsistency, of the white-collar concept results from this mixture of tradition and present needs. Some occupations are classified in the white-collar group because this was their status in the past: many office workers and routine bookkeepers belong to this part of the white-collar category. Other groups have moved into the white-collar category as a result of a re-evaluation of their functions. Thus, the professional engineer has been accepted into the white-collar group because of his occupational situation in today's society.

This picture is greatly affected by the rapid change of technology. The nature of occupations, their status, their prospects are undergoing vast and frequent transformations. Expressions of these changes can be found in the job content of different white-collar occupations, in the wage structure, and in differences in the attitude toward unionism. We shall deal now with changes in job content, their relationship to status, and the impact of these on unionization. The issue of the wage structure will be taken up later.

One of the most significant characteristics of any job is the degree to which the job holder controls or influences the content of his job. The higher the ranking of the worker, the greater is the degree to which he has such control. Among the white-collar workers, this "freedom" is most limited for the modest clerical worker who files documents or types letters. Even here, there may be more "freedom of self-expression" than a worker has on the conveyor belt though less than the freedom available to a craftsman or a technician. In any case, there is little "freedom" in the job of the filing clerk as compared with that of the professional. At the highest levels there may be freedom resulting from the clash between professional competence and administrative authority, or there may be outright bargaining between the professional and his supervisor about the amount of time the professional is to devote to different activities, e.g., research.[17]

[17] See, for instance, the example given in James W. Kuhn's excellent paper, "Success and Failure in Organizing Professional Engineers," *Proceedings* of Industrial Relations Research Association (Boston, December 1963). Control over job content is one characteristic of white-collar jobs which registers clearly the impact of changing technology upon white-collar occupations. The peculiar relationships of the professor to his dean or of the patient to his doctor are further illustrations of the idea stated in the text. In a different way, Elliott Jaques's studies of the Glacier Metals Company in Great Britain have drawn attention to the significance of what he calls the "time-span of discretion"—the "longest period that the job-holder is acting on his own without direction from his supervisor." *Business Week* (November 7, 1964), pp. 166-70.

The hypothesis is suggested that the origin of the white-collar status of a group has a diminishing influence upon its attitudes toward unionism in general and traditional blue-collar unionism in particular and that, vice versa, with the progressive functionalization of society the present role of a group in the plant, and perhaps even more, its long-term prospects on the labor market play an increasing part in shaping its basic attitudes. Thus the elevated status of the German official "Beamte," derived from his role as representative of the King, is gradually being reduced by the progressive democratization of society to the level of the corresponding (in terms of function) white-collar groups. The stress upon separate organizations for academically trained white-collar workers—distinct even from other white-collar organizations—may appear less and less appropriate as the educational level of the population rises. A functional organization may, in due course, take its place.

A further hypothesis suggested by some of the reports and other material is that unionism may be an instrument by which discrepancies between traditional status and that based upon present functions are maintained for as long as possible. Thus white-collar groups whose status is primarily based upon tradition and whose position in the plant (and consequently in society) is declining are more susceptible to unionism than groups whose status is confirmed or enhanced by the new technology and labor market balance.[18] White-collar unions then are regarded by the first group as defensive organizations to maintain the threatened status quo. In particular, they may be used to resist the "proletarianization" of white-collar workers or their inclusion in a blue-collar bargaining unit. Unions of this type are of that "middle class" character—often of a highly aggressive nature—that many observers have pointed out. They resist the real or alleged "egalitarianism" of blue-collar workers and their unions. Such white-collar unionism emphasizes status symbols and aims particularly at maintaining or re-establishing income differentials toward blue-collar occupations.[19]

The opposite situation—functionally rising status contrasting with low status tradition—may also lead to unionization. For such groups

[18] George Strauss, "White Collar Unions Are Different," *Harvard Business Review* (September-October 1954).

[19] "I am not really an inveterate advocate of the class struggle," Rolf Spaehten, leader of DAG, the German white-collar union, is quoted, "but we must advance again to avoid egalitarianism." *Der Spiegel*, Vol. XVI, No. 26 (June 27, 1962), p. 24.

unionization serves primarily as a device to resolve the conflict between tradition and the present. Organizations then may be quite short-lived. They fulfill their mission to adjust status, wages, and working conditions to the new situation and then disappear. Some of the engineering unions may be of this nature.

Another hypothesis may be derived from the observation that as a rule white-collar occupations requiring lower skills and less education are better organized than the top skill groups. This may relate to the better market situation of the latter, but since the differential attitude toward organization is of long standing while the long-run trend of mass education has been upward, a different explanation may be more plausible. It might involve what appears to be a basic trait of many white-collar workers, namely, their belief that they have far greater possibilities of professional advancement as compared with the outlook of most blue-collar workers. The higher the probability of personal promotion is estimated to be, the lower is the readiness to unionize. Where the opportunities for personal advancement appear to be especially favorable, unionism holds little appeal.

By contrast, when such opportunities seem small or nonexisting, organization may appear desirable. Two different cases should be distinguished. In one situation, changes in function resulting from new technology or new systems of organization make for infrequent possibilities of personal advancement. Such a white-collar group will tend to rely on collective action to improve its situation. A different problem is presented by a situation in which institutional arrangements tend to block possibilities of promotion which might otherwise exist.

In this situation, concern with possibilities of promotion—keeping the channels of social mobility clear in an upward direction—appears to be a major feature of white-collar unions. To establish rules of promotion according to merit rather than favoritism may prove to be an effective union appeal, quite different from the standard seniority clauses in a blue-collar contract. In some part, therefore, white-collar workers can be paid in discounted future earning increments, if the chances of promotion appear reasonably favorable, and opening up such chances may be credited to the union as much as general wage increases. Quite possibly the union will be given even more credit for having defended professional standards of promotion than for a general wage improvement.

VARIETY OF ORGANIZATIONAL TYPES

Just as the white-collar group itself shows great diversity, the combination of market situations, traditional status levels, present functions, and individual promotion possibilities for different kinds of white-collar labor may result in a great variety of white-collar organizations. In the text above, we discussed their structure in relation to blue-collar unions. What we are considering now is the degree to which white-collar organizations may appear in the traditional trappings of unionism.

The conventional view of the union sees it as primarily or even essentially a collective bargaining agency: negotiating the terms of the labor contract and participating in its application to the individual worker. But this is a simplified view. There are many types of organizations of employees defending the interests of their members in different ways. There is, for instance, a whole range covering the span between a collective bargaining agency and a pure professional association engaged exclusively in maintaining or improving professional standards. Along this spectrum we may find organizations setting entrance requirements for the profession, thereby restricting the supply of a given type of skill. This, by implication, determines the incomes derived from this skill. Other types of organizations may set minimum standards for different levels of education or different types of experience, leaving it to their members to bargain individually about their incomes by using as a base the minima set by the organization. A great variety of other types of organizations exist or can be conceived of which correspond partly to the model of a professional association, partly to that of a union.

Stress upon the concern with individual promotion possibilities will tend to move the organization toward the professional end of the spectrum, away from conventional unionism. The "common rule" at which unions aim, according to the Webbs, is a device to reduce competitiveness. The greater the emphasis on the need to improve the situation of the group as a whole or to prevent its situation from deteriorating, the closer does the organization move along the spectrum towards the traditional union pattern. A professional association, however, may wish to maintain or allow competition, even though it may regulate it.

A favorable market situation will induce the organization to be concerned with professional standards rather than the immediate terms of employment. It will tend to be a professional association repudiating any thought of being a union. A long-term decline in the demand for the particular type of skill, however, may induce the same organization to aim at job protection, seniority rules, etc. The conventional arsenal of unionism will prove appropriate under the circumstances.

Similarly, status threatened by technological change may induce the white-collar workers to adopt the pattern of union action even while they affirm their fundamental hostility toward the unionism of manual labor. Improvements in function as contrasted with conventional status may have a similar, though perhaps temporary, effect.

White-collar organizations may thus be situated at different points on the spectrum. The professional emphasis may be greater, the admixture of conventional unionism less, according to a number of factors. The higher the skill, the heavier is the stress upon promotion possibilities, and thus the professional character of the organization. Categories favored by the market may find professionalism—and the attendant relative restriction of supply—more satisfactory than outright collective bargaining, perhaps after a short phase of aggressive unionism to establish the new status or relative income level of the group.[20]

Organizations do not necessarily stay in the same position. Changes in the factors that influenced their original strategy may shift their locus on the spectrum. Thus the National Education Association and the nurses in the United States have reluctantly moved toward a position in which conventional unionism is no longer excluded from their weaponry.

It follows that white-collar organizations are likely to show far greater diversity than most observers seem to have suspected. Trade-union leaders may have to show unusual imagination and tolerance if effective cooperation between the organizations of manual and white-collar workers is to be established and maintained. For many white-collar groups, moreover, organization may be attainable for a long time only in the form of a professional association sharply opposed to any apparent form of union action. Finally, as the example of the Belgian physicians' strike in 1964 indicated, white-collar union action may arouse bitter hostility among other unionists. Not every unionization must be of necessity to the advantage of the labor movement as a whole or be welcomed by it.[21]

A modest measure of verification of these propositions may be found in the behavior of the wage structures, although they have been subject to many influences beyond those implied in our hypotheses.

[20] Civil servants, for the reasons stated in an earlier section, may depart from this pattern.

[21] For an attempt at analyzing some of the professional societies in engineering, see George Strauss, "Professionalism and Occupational Associations," *Industrial Relations,* Vol. II, No. 3 (May 1963).

WAGE STRUCTURE

In our context the term "wage structure" refers to at least two sets of relationships: first, that among the various white-collar wages and, second, the relationship between them and the wages of blue-collar workers.

To begin with the latter, comparison is complicated by fringe benefits, income tax progression, or changes therein, and the difference in the stability of employment.

As to fringe benefits, since World War II they have tended to represent a growing portion of the income of the dependently employed in general. At the same time, benefits which used to be specifically reserved to white-collar workers have often spread to manual workers as well. Paid vacations offer one example. In other cases differentials in the application of fringe benefits have been reduced—as in the case of waiting periods under sickness insurance in Germany. Family allowances differentiated according to the number of children rather than income have tended to reduce income differentials in terms of percentages, though not of absolute amounts. The spreading of fringe benefits that occurred during the last two decades may on balance have reduced income differentials between middle-level white-collar workers and blue-collar workers, and possibly resulted in the reversal of some income relationships between low-grade white-collar workers and their blue-collar colleagues. Evidence is insufficient to hazard more than guesses.

Another factor to be taken into account is the impact of progressive income taxes. This, of course, varies from country to country as does the proportion between direct and indirect tax burdens.

A fuller comparison of wages would have to consider incomes during the entire working life. This involves the degree of regularity of employment as well as the fact that white-collar workers often can expect personal wage increases throughout their working lives far in excess of personal wage increases of blue-collar workers.[22] Even though general wage increases of the latter may be larger than those of many white-collar categories, personal wage increases may offset differentials in the general wage movements or exceed them. Part payment in prestige—though perhaps less and less accepted as a substitute for cash—and agreeable working conditions will also have to be considered.

[22] Female white-collar workers, many of whom withdraw from the labor market for long periods, present different problems from those of their male colleagues, as far as lifetime earnings are concerned.

A systematic comparison of white- and blue-collar wages and of their evolution—say since World War II—would thus be a large-scale enterprise.[23] Theoretically, we should expect that temporary factors such as the income adjustments to the postwar inflations would have tended to decrease income differentials as percentages if not in absolute terms. Rising educational levels on one hand and changes in the structure of demand for white-collar workers, on the other hand, might be regarded as long-term factors operating, to some extent, in opposite directions: better mass education would tend to reduce many white-blue income differentials; the changing structure of demand for white-collar services might perhaps polarize the skill requirements of the labor force—lowering requirements at one end, raising them at the other end. This would result in a spreading of the internal white-collar wage structure and—depending upon the respective weights to be assigned to the two tendencies of the polarization process—to a widening or narrowing of the blue-white differentials. One possibility thus is that we are heading for a situation in which the internal wage spread of the white- and blue-collar wage structures and the overlap between the two may be greater than the average white–blue-collar differential. Indeed, it may become meaningless to speak of an average blue- or white-collar income; incomes in each group may be polarized at the extremes rather than bunched together around a central tendency.

Factual information in this area is sadly lacking. While the long-run tendency toward higher educational levels in the population can hardly be questioned, we have little information in particular about the quantitative impact of technological change upon educational requirements and the structure of demand for various types of labor. Most assertions about automation "upgrading" or "downgrading" labor are based upon generalizations from insufficient empirical data, often from one or two case studies. Michel Crozier expresses the idea that automation may tend to routinize some of the white-collar occupations, particularly those of office workers, but raise standards for some of the other white-collar occupations such as engineering and other professional work. Although there is some evidence supporting this observation, not enough research has yet been done to be reasonably certain of these results, and even less to estimate the relative quanti-

[23] In the U.S. a narrowing of the differential right after World War II seems to have been followed by a rapid—absolute and relative—improvement of many white-collar salaries. Observers have expressed the view that American unionism missed a major opportunity for white-collar unionization during the first postwar years.

tative impact of each of these trends: higher levels of mass education, polarization of educational requirements.[24] If further empirical data were to refute the hypothesis of the "polarization" of skill requirements, a general narrowing of the wage structure could be expected.

Since white-collar unions represent the lower white-collar grades to a larger extent than they represent the upper grades, their members are more likely to be among those whose wage advantage compared with blue-collar workers has been shrinking. A hint of confirmation for this inference can perhaps be found in the fact that most white-collar unions have complained about the compression of the wage structure and the reduction of traditional differentials between blue- and white-collar workers.[25] One of the main objectives of the Australian white-collar unions has been to re-establish these differentials. The same applies to Austrian, French, and German white-collar unions and, probably, to many others. To what extent are these protests related to the temporary factors referred to above—e.g., equal or proportionate cost-of-living adjustments in inflationary periods, equal children's allowances—or to the operations of the progressive income tax? To what extent are we confronted with a long-term trend in the direction of a widening of the white-collar wage structure within a general trend that seems to make for a lessening of wage differentials in general? Beyond these theoretical speculations we have little em-

[24] Differently from past experience, spreading advanced specialization—one of the possible consequences of automation and technological advance in general—may tend nowadays to decrease supply elasticities of highly trained specialized labor. This may produce differential rents and reduce interest in collective bargaining. At the same time, the danger of obsolescence of knowledge and experience is increased. Some part of the income differential may thus be regarded as a compensation for the risk of obsolescence. Other challenging problems created by the pace of technological change are income differentials between newly trained and older men in the same job category in favor of the former, and high entering salaries in general.

[25] The London *Economist* (May 23 and 30, 1964), contains a study of the evolution of white-collar incomes in Great Britain, by comparison with the growth of blue-collar incomes and net national product. The comparison is rather sophisticated in taking into account various factors in addition to the cost of living and the growth of GNP. However, it does not take into account some other significant phenomena—such as changes in fringe benefits—mentioned above. The tentative conclusion of the *Economist* is that since the end of 1955 white-collar earnings have risen more rapidly than those of blue-collar workers. Mr. Kassalow's study shows a general narrowing of the white-blue wage differential—referring most probably to direct wages only—for the period from 1939 to 1950, but a widening for the period 1950 to 1962. Within the white-collar group the professionals have gained more than the clerical workers. The internal white-collar wage structure has thus widened. The data, rough as they are, correspond in some respects to what theoretical reasoning would lead one to expect, but differ in other respects.

pirical evidence. Can we expect a decline in the intensity of white-collar protests? Which groups would it concern? How would such a decline affect the prospects of white-collar unionization?

The general evolution of a mass-consumption society is another major factor in this context. Differences in living standards tend to become more and more distinctions of taste—not always in favor of the higher income—and of degree; they do not reflect the existence of two or more separate markets of consumer goods as they did thirty or forty years ago and in some Western countries even more recently. The once widespread conviction—based upon tradition as well as moral standards—that white-collar incomes must exceed those of blue-collar workers (which was never altogether true in fact) has given way to different sets of expectations. The incomes of well-organized craftsmen and technicians—a group that straddles the dividing line between blue- and white-collar—are greatly superior to those of many categories of office and sales personnel and this is more and more being accepted as justified by whatever standards society is using in judging the fairness of relative wages at any given moment. Legal distinctions between blue- and white-collar workers appear increasingly out of date and arouse more and more criticism and resistance. This is especially so because they are based not upon functional distinctions but upon traditional classifications. Increasing bitterness of the blue-collar workers has resulted from these obsolete distinctions.[26]

At the upper end of the scale white-collar workers with occupations of a professional nature find the market for their skills rapidly expanding. Opportunities seem limitless in most, though not all, industrial nations. The favorable market situation permits the individual to assert himself, even in a mass organization. Individual bargaining appears quite meaningful and effective in many cases. Automation and the rapidly changing professional requirements at that level of work often render skills obsolete, but even more often—since this is an expanding area of the labor market—make certain skills and experiences rare items for sale to eagerly bidding buyers.

The lower grades of white-collar workers are in a different situation as far as the balance on the labor market and the impact of technological change are concerned. They feel threatened by advancing technology, their skills may become obsolete, aggregate demand for the services of some groups, though increasing, may do so at a

[26] One of the longest strikes in German post–World War II history originated in an issue of this kind.

lower rate than the rate of increase of supply as a result of rising educational standards in the population. In some respects this group is most amenable to traditional union appeals, though not necessarily to the conventional forms of unionism.

CONCLUSIONS

Does the weight of the preceding evidence indicate that white-collar workers are unlikely to become unionized on a large scale? International experience as well as the facts in the United States themselves provide some assistance in answering this question.

International experience indicates that it is possible to organize white-collar workers on a large scale, even though they lend themselves less well to organization than most blue-collar workers. The white-collar group is, however, very heterogeneous. Its component parts respond in different ways to given appeals, in particular to the traditional appeals of unionism. These differences seem to depend on many factors, among them the impact of technological change upon the white-collar group, the origin and nature of its status in society and—last but not least—its long-term prospects on the labor market.

Experience thus leaves little doubt that many, if not most, white-collar groups can be effectively organized. Even the high skill professional groups are no exception to this statement. Indeed many of them are effectively organized—in professional societies located at one end of the spectrum, far distant from the area of routine collective bargaining. Yet they often exert decisive influence upon the material and other conditions of their members' worklife by any of the indirect methods described above.

It follows that white-collar organizations may show a great variety of forms and employ a variety of methods ranging from conventional unionism based upon collective bargaining to professional associations centered on the defense of professional standards.

The emergence of the white-collar workers as a large and rapidly growing group within the labor force will have a powerful impact upon the labor movement and all other elements in the industrial relations system. This is not surprising. Fundamental changes in the structure of the labor force have always led to basic readjustments of the structure and the policies of the labor movement.

Trade unionism in England, the Webbs tell us, had its origin in the emergence within the labor force of workers who "had ceased to be independent producers, themselves controlling the processes, and owning the materials and the product of their labor, and had passed into the condition of lifelong wage-earners, possessing neither the instruments of production nor the commodity in its finished state." [27] The rise of the machine and the substitution of the machine-tender for the skilled craftsman formed the basis for one of the most dramatic chapters in the history of labor and shaped the structure, the objectives, and the weapons of the labor movement for more than a generation.

With the emergence and rapid growth of the mass-production industries the semiskilled worker moved to the center of the stage. Industrial unionism with all its implications for labor ideology, leadership, strategy, and methods came to the fore. Prolonged internal conflicts arose within the labor movements. The division in American trade unionism was merely one of the extreme forms in which the transformation of Western labor resulting from a basic change in the structure of the labor force expressed itself.[28]

These examples may serve to suggest the kind of problem which the growth of the proportion of white-collar workers in general and of professionals in particular is bound to create in the different labor movements of the industrial world. The adjustments necessary to cope with these momentous developments are no less fundamental than those required by past major changes in the structure of the labor force. Indeed, it seems likely that at least in some countries the transformation to the new kind of movement which would correspond to the new structure of the labor force will be exceedingly difficult to achieve. Whether the labor movement in this country is willing to undergo such a transformation and is ready and capable of facilitating it, is a question that lies outside the scope of this study.

[27] Sidney and Beatrice Webb, *The History of Trade Unionism* (London: Longmans, Green and Co., 1902), p. 24. For the American counterpart, see e.g., Foster Rhea Dulles, *Labor in America, A History,* second revised edition (New York: Crowell, 1960), p. 53.

[28] Michel Collinet, *L'Ouvrier Français: Essai sur la Condition Ouvrière 1900-1950* (Paris, 1951); and *Esprit du Syndicalisme* (Paris, 1951), reflects upon the impact of the change in Parisian industry upon French syndicalism. The disappearance of the small craft shop and the emergence of heavy mass-production industries in the Paris area changed the character of the labor force and, in Collinet's view, that of the Parisian labor movement.

INDEX

70
71
72
74
75
76
77
79
81
83
85
88